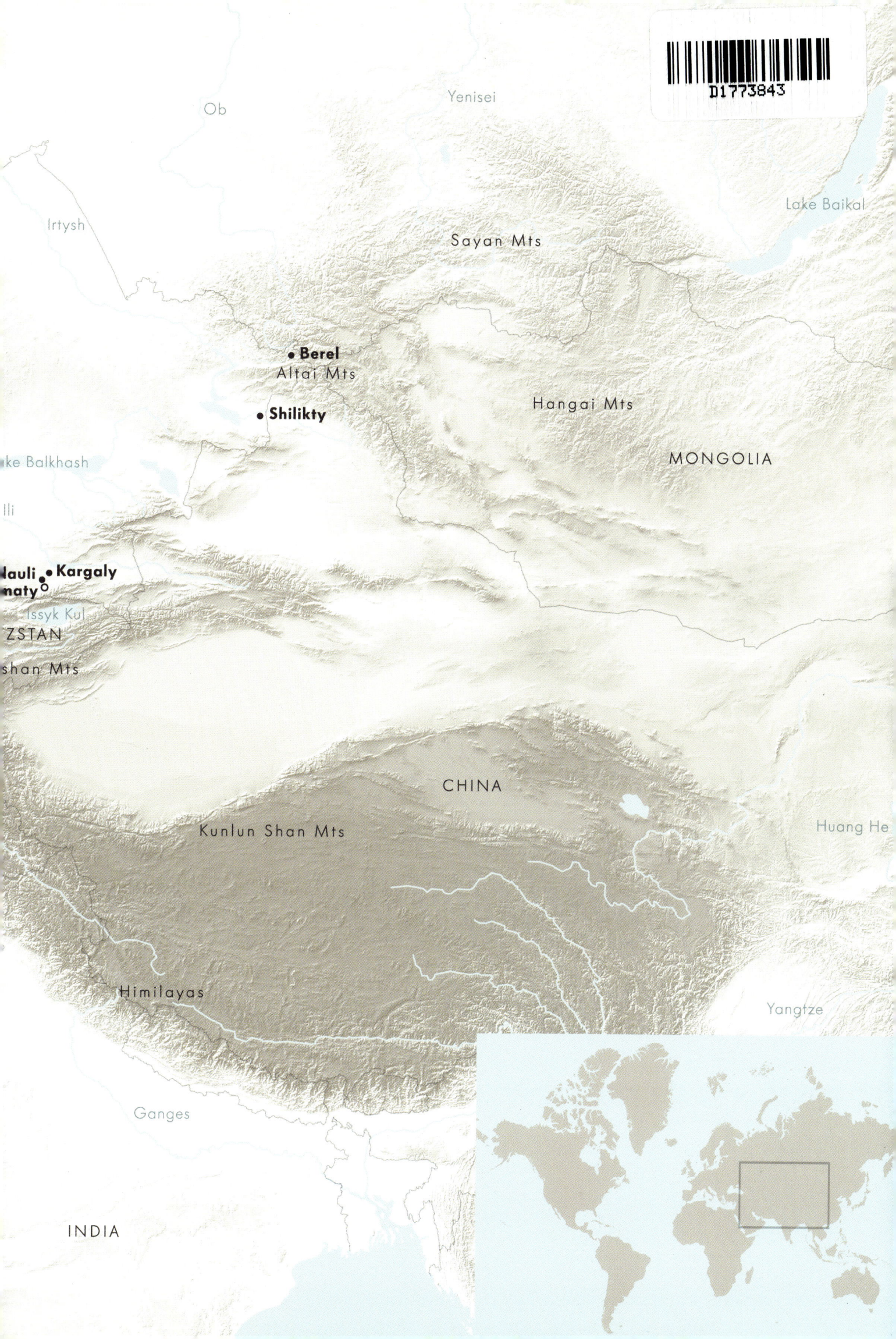

NOMADS AND NETWORKS

The Ancient Art and Culture of Kazakhstan

NOMADS AND NETWORKS

The Ancient Art and Culture of Kazakhstan

Edited by Sören Stark and Karen S. Rubinson with Zainolla S. Samashev and Jennifer Y. Chi

Including contributions by Nursan Alimbai, Nikolay A. Bokovenko,
Claudia Chang, Bryan K. Hanks, Sagynbay Myrgabayev, Karen S. Rubinson,
Zainolla S. Samashev, Sören Stark, and Abdesh T. Toleubaev

Institute for the Study of the Ancient World
at New York University

Princeton University Press
Princeton and Oxford

Published by the Institute for the Study of the Ancient World at New York University and
Princeton University Press on the occasion of the exhibition *Nomads and Networks: The Ancient Art and Culture of Kazakhstan*, March 7, 2012–June 3, 2012, and distributed by Princeton University Press.

Institute for the Study of the Ancient World
New York University
15 E. 84th Street, New York, NY 10028
isaw.nyu.edu

Princeton University Press
41 William Street, Princeton, NJ 08540
press.princeton.edu

The exhibition *Nomads and Networks: The Ancient Art and Culture of Kazakhstan* was organized by the Institute for the Study of the Ancient World at New York University in collaboration with:

The Embassy of the Republic of Kazakhstan to the United States

Ministry of Culture of the Republic of Kazakhstan
The Central State Museum of the Republic of Kazakhstan
The Presidential Center of Culture of the Republic of Kazakhstan

Ministry of Science and Education of the Republic of Kazakhstan
A. Kh. Margulan Institute of Archaeology of the Republic of Kazakhstan
Museum of Archaeology of the Republic of Kazakhstan

The exhibition and the accompanying catalogue were made possible through the support of the
Leon Levy Foundation.

Managing Editor: Julienne Kim

Copy Editor: Mary Cason
Designer: CoDe. New York Inc., Jenny 8 Del Corte Hirschfeld, Mischa Leiner,
Susanne Schaal, and David Stadel
Color Separations and Printing: Professional Graphics Inc., Rockford, IL

Copyright © 2012 by the Institute for the Study of the Ancient World at New York University
and Princeton University Press

All rights reserved. No part of this book may be reproduced in any form or by any electronic or mechanical means, including information storage and retrieval systems, without permission in writing from the Institute for the Study of the Ancient World and Princeton University Press except by a reviewer, who may quote brief passages in a review.

The book was typeset in Futura and Weiss,
and printed on Productolith Matte Text.

Library of Congress Control Number: 2011943869
ISBN: 978-0-691-15480-0

Printed and bound in the USA

10 9 8 7 6 5 4 3 2 1

CONTENTS

4 Letter from H. E. Erlan Idrissov
Ambassador Extraordinary and Plenipotentiary, Embassy of the Republic of Kazakhstan to the United States of America, and Honorary Chair

5 Letter from Roger S. Bagnall
Leon Levy Director, Institute for the Study of the Ancient World (ISAW), New York University

6 Foreword, Jennifer Y. Chi
Exhibitions Director and Chief Curator, Institute for the Study of the Ancient World (ISAW), New York University

9 Acknowledgments

12 Map of the Region

14 Introduction, Sören Stark, ISAW, and Karen S. Rubinson, ISAW

20 **1 THE ROOTS OF IRON AGE PASTORAL NOMADIC CULTURE**
Nikolay A. Bokovenko and Zainolla S. Samashev

30 **2 THE BEREL KURGANS: SOME RESULTS OF INVESTIGATION**
Zainolla S. Samashev

50 **3 RESULTS OF MULTIDISCIPLINARY STUDIES AND RECONSTRUCTIONS OF MATERIALS FROM THE BAIGETOBE KURGAN AT SHILIKTY**
Abdesh T. Toleubaev, Al-Farabi Kazakh National University

62 **4 SOME QUESTIONS REGARDING THE ROCK ART OF KAZAKHSTAN**
Sagynbay Myrgabayev

76 **5 BURIAL PRACTICES AND SOCIAL ROLES OF IRON AGE MOBILE PASTORALISTS**
Karen S. Rubinson, ISAW

92 **6 MOUNTED WARFARE AND ITS SOCIOPOLITICAL IMPLICATIONS**
Bryan K. Hanks, University of Pittsburgh

106 **7 NOMADS AND NETWORKS: ELITES AND THEIR CONNECTIONS TO THE OUTSIDE WORLD**
Sören Stark, ISAW

140 **8 CYCLES OF IRON AGE MOBILITY AND SEDENTISM: CLIMATE, LANDSCAPE, AND MATERIAL CULTURE IN SOUTHEASTERN KAZAKHSTAN**
Claudia Chang, Sweet Briar College

152 **9 SOCIETY AND CULTURE OF THE NOMADS OF CENTRAL ASIA THROUGH TIME**
Nursan Alimbai, Central State Museum of the Republic of Kazakhstan

164 Appendix A: Technological Analyses of the Horn Artifacts from Berel Kurgan 36

165 Appendix B: Elemental Analysis of the Gold Decorations from the Baigetobe Kurgan at Shilikty

167 Appendix C: Horse Tack Terminology as Shown on a Reconstruction of the Horse from Kurgan 36 at Berel

168 Exhibition Checklist

184 Bibliography

194 Photography and Drawing Credits

LETTER FROM H. E. ERLAN IDRISSOV

Ambassador Extraordinary and Plenipotentiary, Embassy of the Republic of Kazakhstan to the United States of America, and Honorary Chair

It is with great pleasure that I introduce *Nomads and Networks: The Ancient Art and Culture of Kazakhstan*, an exhibition on view at the Institute for the Study of the Ancient World (ISAW) at New York University from March 7 through June 3, 2012, organized by ISAW in collaboration with the Embassy of the Republic of Kazakhstan to the United States of America and four of Kazakhstan's national collections of ancient material.

Kazakhstan marked its twentieth year of independence in 2011. In this short span of time, it has achieved dynamic progress in nation building, ensuring economic prosperity for its citizens, promoting political stability, and highlighting its rich cultural heritage for audiences abroad. The exhibition at ISAW is one such cultural project, focusing on a specific time and region in our history and placing a lens on the nomadic cultures of the Iron Age (eighth–third centuries BCE) in the mountainous regions of the Tianshan and Altai. The objects selected represent an extraordinary range of material that forms part of our ancient identity—from elaborate bronze cult stands to golden works of personal adornment made for elite groups, to carved decorations in wood that constituted part of the elaborate regalia for horses. The nomads that used these objects also established networks with neighboring peoples, both East and West, indicating their receptiveness to cultural exchange.

Apart from considerations of the exhibition's narrative, the entire project serves as an excellent example of what can be produced through close cooperation between institutions in Kazakhstan and those in the United States. From the inception of this exhibition, individuals at ISAW worked directly with those at Kazakh institutions and collaborated on important aspects, including the selection of objects, crafting the exhibition narrative, and formulation of the catalogue. *Nomads and Networks* is a reflection of true partnership, and I am therefore extremely proud to serve as the Honorary Chair of this exhibition. Projects, such as this one, that fall under the banner of the twentieth anniversary of our independence, and of Kazakh-U.S. diplomatic relations, contribute to the further strengthening of direct ties between our countries.

LETTER FROM ROGER S. BAGNALL

Leon Levy Director, Institute for the Study of the Ancient World (ISAW), New York University

Nomads and Networks: The Ancient Art and Culture of Kazakhstan is the third international loan exhibition to be organized by the Exhibitions Department at the Institute for the Study of the Ancient World. With every exhibition our view of the ancient world is broadened, and now our sights have arrived in the heart of mountainous Central Asia. Brilliant examples of nomadic art are on display in our galleries at 15 East 84th Street in New York City. Some of the recently excavated and conserved gold and wood plaques are on view for the first time anywhere, while other objects are already world famous.

We are grateful to the Ministry of Culture and in particular Minister Mukhtar Kul-Muhammad for their support of this project. The Central State Museum in Almaty and its director, Dr. Nursan Alimbai, have been exceptionally generous in allowing us access to significant portions of several groups of objects, including the Zhalauli and Kargaly treasures and the gold finds excavated at Shilikty. The Presidential Center of Culture in Astana and its director, Dr. Myrzatay Zholdasbekov, have been especially open in making available to us the trove of finds excavated in the last few years at Berel in the Kazakh Altai, many of which have never been exhibited before.

Our gratitude is also extended to the Ministry of Science and Education and in particular to Minister Bahytzhan Zhumagulov. The A. Kh. Margulan Institute of Archaeology in Almaty and its general director, Dr. Bauyrzhan Baitanayev, granted loans of material recently excavated from kurgans 9, 10, and 36 at Berel, including a complete set of horn horse trappings. The fourth critical lender is the Museum of Archaeology in Almaty; the museum and its director, Ms. Roza Bektureyeva, were unstinting in their receptivity and generosity toward the project.

His Excellency Erlan Idrissov, Ambassador of the Republic of Kazakhstan to the United States, has provided ISAW with critical advice and support throughout the entirety of this project, which ensured its success. We thank all our partners who helped bring to completion this complex exhibition project, which offers our visitors a deep view into the lifeways of the ancient people of the Altai and Tianshan regions of Kazakhstan.

FOREWORD
JENNIFER Y. CHI

Exhibitions Director and Chief Curator, Institute for the Study of the Ancient World (ISAW), New York University

The popular image of nomads is one of wanderers roaming across vast grasslands or deserts, members of small groups that are organized at the most basic level and that rely for subsistence on warfare or raids of nearby settled cultures. *Nomads and Networks: The Ancient Art and Culture of Kazakhstan* is designed to dispel the misguided notion that nomadic societies were less developed than sedentary ones. It is the first comprehensive U.S. exhibition to look fully at the ancient nomadic heritage of the Tianshan and Altai regions of eastern and southern Kazakhstan during the Iron Age (eighth to third centuries BCE).

For thousands of years, nomadic peoples have been a defining factor in the overall cultural and historical makeup of the Eurasian steppes, their lives defined by seasonally determined patterns of movement. In the Altai and Tianshan regions, these patterns were vertical in nature, as nomadic groups and their herds moved in a regular cycle from lowland pastures in the winter to mountainous regions in the summer. The archaeological record indicates that specific activities, whether economic or ritual, were attached to particular geographic points along the annual route. *Nomads and Networks* illuminates this way of life by providing a sense of the sophisticated rituals practiced by these groups, illustrating the importance of environment and landscape in the overall formulation of a nomadic world order, and highlighting the networks of communication and cultural exchange between the nomads and their powerful foreign neighbors.

The exhibition is installed according to discrete but interrelated narrative themes, beginning with an exploration of Berel, in the Altai region, the most important Pazyryk site in Kazakhstan. Situated in a mountainous valley near the Bukhtarna River, Berel must have been a burial site for some of the culture's most elite members. Of the twenty-four kurgans, or burial mounds, that have been discovered there, the exhibition focuses on three of the most recently excavated Iron Age examples. Objects from these include a series of expertly carved appliqués in wood—once entirely overlaid in gold and tin—that formed part of a set of horse tack, and that illustrate the critical importance nomads placed on their relationships with horses as well as on all of the animal world. These nomads embraced the Scytho-Siberian style of animal imagery, characterized by the representation of animals, such as felines, horned sheep, and deer, that were frequently transformed into fantastic creatures in equally fantastic poses. The most dramatic and impressive objects in this section of the exhibition are two magnificent sets of wooden horns, which together with several wooden appliqués show the full decoration of a horse, a deliberate, transformative action that clearly had ritual purposes, although their exact meaning is still unknown. A beautifully embroidered saddle showing felines attacking elk, which is on public display here for the first time ever, illustrates the pervasiveness of the animal style throughout the material culture of the Pazyryk peoples. Ornaments from the horse buried in one kurgan indicate that, in addition to wood, the horn of Siberian red deer was a popular medium for the carving of horse decoration. Taken together, the images and materials from Berel illustrate the nomads' deep connection to the natural world.

The exhibition also provides an exploration of the importance of the landscape in the overall worldview of the ancient nomadic cultures of the Tianshan and Altai. Portions of petroglyphs, or images carved on rock face, that once embellished the nomadic landscape were most likely created to demarcate sacred places. The images themselves represent a wide variety of themes, from actual animals that the nomads would have encountered in their environment to such scenes as chariots drawn by horses, perhaps referring to mythic or cosmic beliefs. Other objects—including bone plaques in the form of fish and belt ornaments, also of bone, representing boars—illustrate the importance of both land and water animals to the nomads' visual formulation of the world around them.

While it is difficult to reconstruct the ritual and sacred life of nomads, who left no written records, a group of massive bronze cauldrons and a series of elaborately decorated bronze stands on view in the exhibition have been tentatively related to ritual activities. Most were found in the landscape without association to any architectural remains, and one interpretation suggests that these objects may have been placed outdoors at locations considered sacred. The usual function of the cauldrons as containers for cooked food, along with their large size, may indicate that nomads sometimes held ritual communal meals. The stands are more enigmatic, as their decoration is highly varied, ranging from processions of animals to a man holding a cup and seated in front of a horse. The scattered spots at which these objects were found suggest that the stands may have been placed at now unknown sacred locations in the outdoors, although such interpretations must remain tentative. These bronze works are complemented by stone trays on which materials could have been burned.

The nomads of the Tianshan and Altai were aware of and indeed connected with their foreign neighbors through networks of exchange. It was in the sedentary world that nomads were able to find and acquire valuable luxury goods that also became markers of prestige within their communities, helping to distinguish individuals with power from those without. As such goods circulated within their communities, they inevitably began to influence the artistic vocabularies that defined objects produced by and for nomadic groups. Two of the most spectacular examples of such cultural and aesthetic interaction are the Zhalauli treasure and the Wusun diadem. The first comprises golden objects clearly used as personal adornment, although the specific function of some individual pieces is unclear. Eight teardrop-shaped ornaments clearly came from a belt and in their overall composition and ornamentation show a fusion of both indigenous and foreign—perhaps Western—tastes. Likewise, the Wusun diadem—a spectacular openwork piece with both figural and landscape imagery, articulated through the inlay of semiprecious stones—shows a similar mixing of form and content. In this case, however, the imagery is drawn directly from Chinese celestial iconography, which nomadic groups would have encountered on Chinese-made objects. Items like the diadem indicate that the adornment of many of the nomadic elite must have been striking in its brilliance.

Together, the over two hundred and fifty objects on view in *Nomads and Networks: The Ancient Art and Culture of Kazakhstan* portray a world of nomadic groups that, far from being underdeveloped, fused distinct patterns of mobility with apparently sophisticated ritual practices expressive of a close connection to the natural world, to complex burial practices, and to established networks and contacts with the outside world.

ACKNOWLEDGMENTS

From its very early phases, *Nomads and Networks: The Ancient Art and Culture of Kazakhstan* has greatly benefited from the advice, interest, and expertise of many people. In the spring of 2010, Karol Wight, who was then Head of the Antiquities Department at the J. Paul Getty Museum, gave me the contact information of Steven-Charles Jaffe, Honorary Consul of Kazakhstan in Los Angeles. Steven had seen our exhibition *The Golden Graves of Ancient Vani* at the Getty Villa and was so impressed that he brought His Excellency Erlan Idrissov, Ambassador of the Republic of Kazakhstan to the United States, to view it during one of his trips to the West Coast. It was at the exhibition that they recognized a show of ancient Kazakh material on a similar scale could be as spectacular.

A subsequent visit by the Ambassador to the Institute for the Study of the Ancient World (ISAW) confirmed his commitment to such a project, and by the fall of 2010 ISAW's curatorial team had been granted research access to the four main collections of ancient nomadic art in Kazakhstan: the Presidential Center of Culture in Astana, and the Central State Museum, the A. Kh. Margulan Institute of Archaeology, and the Museum of Archaeology, all in Almaty. We are enormously grateful to Ambassador Idrissov, who throughout the entirety of the planning process provided ISAW with invaluable advice and support, and we are honored that he serves as the Honorary Chair for *Nomads and Networks*. Nurzhan Aitmakhanov, Assistant to the Ambassador, also provided ongoing logistical and practical support that helped greatly with the successful completion of the project. We are grateful as well to former Minister of Culture Muhktar Kul-Mukhammed, for his openness to our joint effort as well as to Dr. Ilias Kozybaev, Chairman of the Cultural Committee at the Ministry, and Mr. Bazarbai Altayev, Head of the Division of Culture Committee. Steven-Charles Jaffe and his partner at Helix Films, Gaukhar Noortas, both traveled with me on my initial trip to Kazakhstan, and were instrumental in facilitating early key meetings both with the Embassy and with institutions and individuals in Almaty and Astana. We thank them for their commitment to furthering cultural projects from Kazakhstan in the United States.

In Astana, the capital of the Republic of Kazakhstan, we worked with the Presidential Center of Culture. Dr. Myrzatai Djoldasbekov, Director of the Center, made available to us the entirety of the Center's Berel collection, including material in storage; we are extremely grateful for his generosity, as the loans from the Center greatly enhanced ISAW's Berel installation. Ms. Bibinur Sanakulova, Assistant Director for Museum Affairs, was our main contact, always ensuring that each of our requests was considered in a timely and efficient manner; in addition, she provided essential advice on the organizational requirements for an international loan exhibition.

Ms. Raushan Koskina, Chief Curator of the Center, made certain that our complicated object information requests were promptly fulfilled.

The Central State Museum, whose collection provides a comprehensive overview of Kazakh art and culture from the prehistoric period through modern times, provided ISAW with an unprecedented number of loans. Dr. Nursan Alimbai, Director, allowed us to borrow the majority of the Museum's gold collection, which as a group shows the networks that Iron Age nomads were able to create both East and West; we are grateful for his generosity. Dr. Alimbai also ensured continual curatorial and logistical support for ISAW's team. Dr. Beibitkali Kakabaev, First Deputy Director, was our primary contact at the Museum and ably dealt with our questions concerning a myriad of practical issues. Dr. Alisher Akishev, Researcher of Nomadic Material, provided curatorial advice during our selection process. Other valuable curatorial input came from Mukhambetkali Kipiyev, Chief Curator; Matsura Satybaldieva, Head of the Archaeology Department; and Dr. Babkumar Khinayat, Researcher. Additional logistical and administrative support was provided by Alya Gromova, Deputy Director of Finance; Luiza Alebekova, General Counsel; Alia Rakhmankulova, Specialist of Storage; Marzhan Zunnosova, Specialist of Storage; Olga Myakisheva, Specialist of Storage; and Elmira Zhanysbekova, Translator.

Dr. Bauyrzhan Baitanayev gave us unlimited access to the collection of the A. Kh. Margulan Institute of Archaeology, and we are grateful for his openness to the project. The Kazakh curator of *Nomads and Networks*, Dr. Zainolla Samashev, Head of the Astana Branch of the Institute of Archaeology, provided his expertise in the selection, description, and analysis of the Berel material in the Institute's collection. Throughout the entirety of the project, Dr. Samashev advised us on the narrative content of the exhibition and traveled extensively with the ISAW team during our many research trips. We are grateful for his role as the Kazakh curator of the exhibition.

At the Museum of Archaeology, Dr. Roza Bektureyeva was our key and constant contact; she worked tirelessly with us from the beginning, not only on selecting objects from her museum, but also aiding us in resolving questions concerning the general planning of the exhibition project. We are extremely grateful for her willingness to share her expertise. Her curatorial team, which was always extremely helpful during our research trips, consisted of Nurzhan Satybaldy, Bahytzhan Nisambekov, and Aliya Mahambetova.

We are also grateful to the conservation lab of Mr. Krym Altynbekov. Working on the new finds at Berel, Mr. Altynbekov assured us that our entire selection of material would be ready at the time of our scheduled installation—not an easy task given that a significant portion of the Berel material is from recent excavations at the site. His able team of conservators consisted of Ryskaly Akhmetkaliyev, Vladimir Alexandrov, Dana Altynbekova, Elina Altynbekova, Nurzhan Altynbekov, Vladimir Kruglov, Charlina Lyubov, Saida Pridanova, and Vera Yakovleva.

At ISAW our curatorial team included Peter de Staebler, Assistant Curator in the Exhibitions Department; Karen Rubinson, Research Associate; and Sören Stark, Assistant Professor of Central Asian Art and Archaeology. Each provided a nuanced contribution to the exhibition's narrative content. Peter's work focused largely on refining the checklist and grouping objects in a coherent manner; Karen's expertise shaped the exhibition didactics; and Sören took a lead as the catalogue's editor, formulating its structure in partnership with Karen. I am grateful for their devotion to the project. Julienne Kim, Managing Editor, created another beautiful publication. Irene Gelbord, Department Manager, ably handled all internal logistics, and Abby Lepold ensured that the exhibition arrived on time and was installed in an exquisite manner. Mischa Leiner and Susanne Schaal of CoDe. Communications and Design provided an inspiring aesthetic for the exhibition, graphic, and catalogue design. Maya Naunton was our translator, who always made herself available. Mary Cason was our trusted copy editor. As head of the Exhibitions Department, I remain amazed at the effortless manner in which my staff functions as a team—one of the main reasons why our exhibitions program has been so well received—and I am grateful to work with such a talented, energetic, and devoted group. Finally, this exhibition and catalogue would not have been made possible without the generous support of the Leon Levy Foundation.

Jennifer Y. Chi
Exhibitions Director and Chief Curator
Institute for the Study of the Ancient World, New York University

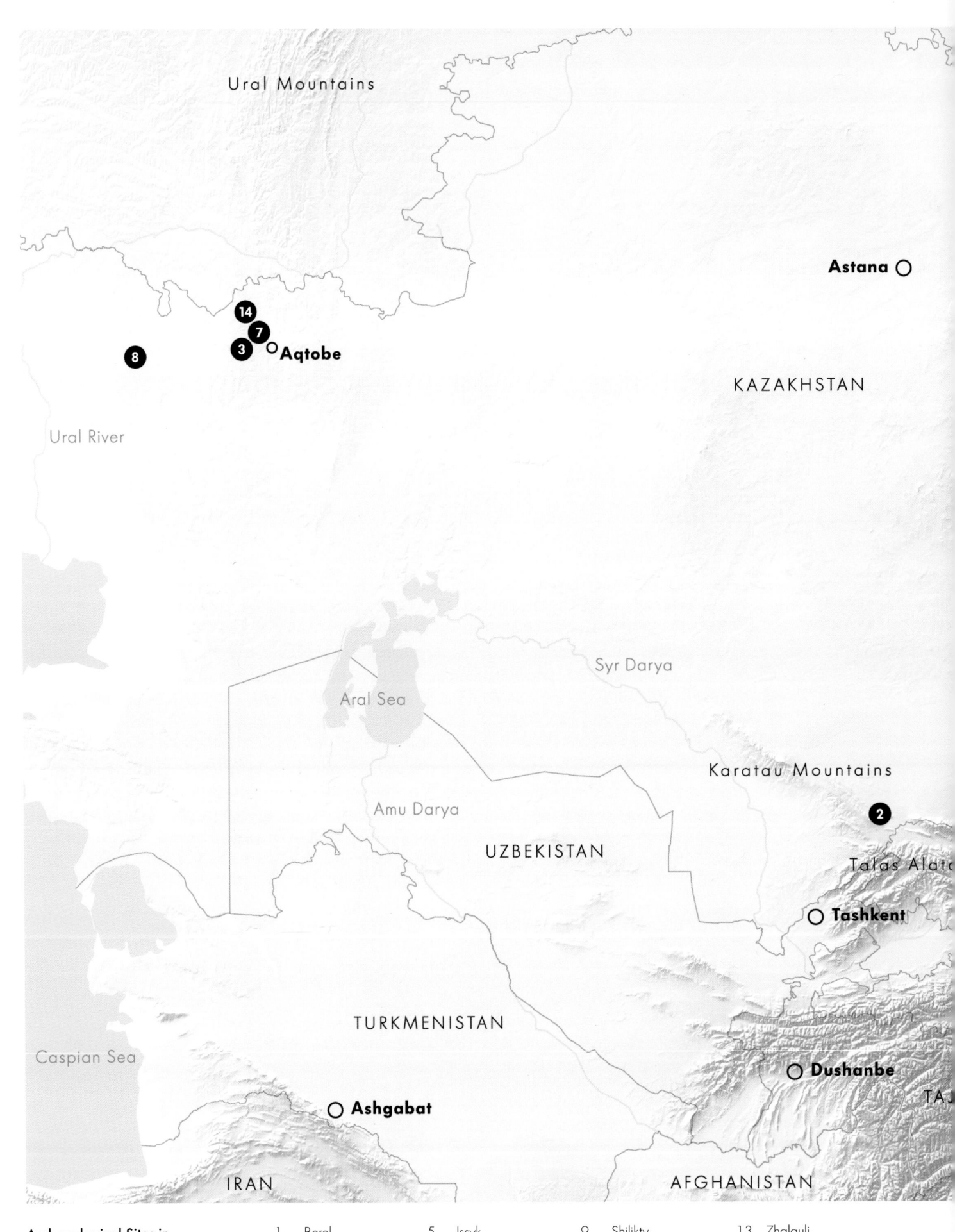

| Archaeological Sites in Kazakhstan for Objects Featured in the Exhibition | 1. Berel
2. Berkara
3. Besoba
4. Eshkiolmes | 5. Issyk
6. Kargaly
7. Kuraili
8. Lebedevka | 9. Shilikty
10. Tamgaly
11. Tasmola
12. Tenlik | 13. Zhalauli
14. Nagorinsk
15. Nurmanbet |

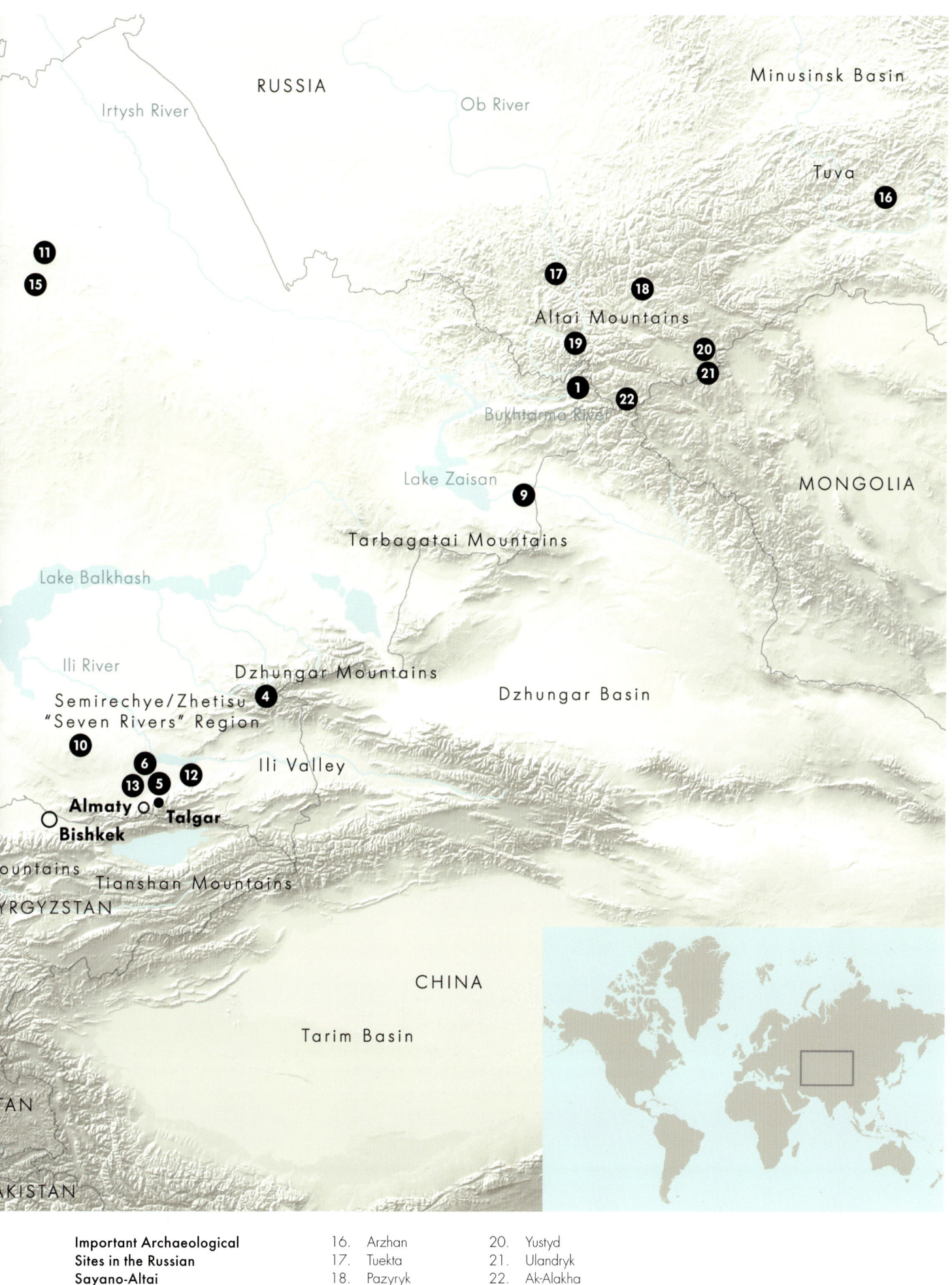

Important Archaeological Sites in the Russian Sayano-Altai	16. Arzhan 17. Tuekta 18. Pazyryk 19. Bashadar	20. Yustyd 21. Ulandryk 22. Ak-Alakha

INTRODUCTION

Sören Stark and Karen S. Rubinson

In 1975 "animal style" objects from frozen tombs of Early Iron Age nomads in the Altai mountains were first displayed in the United States.[1] Ever since, interest among a wider public in these fascinating materials from High Asia has never ceased. With the independence of the Republic of Kazakhstan in 1991, archaeological research in the region has intensified and yielded spectacular new results, in particular at the site of Berel. The systematic application of modern scientific methods in both excavation and conservation—now often carried out in international cooperation—has greatly contributed to an increased understanding of the culture and lifeways of the various nomadic peoples inhabiting the territory of present-day Kazakhstan in the first millennium BCE.

It is the aim of this exhibition to assemble and show a selection of these new results—primarily from southern and eastern Kazakhstan, and some presented to the public for the first time—in the context of materials already known for many decades. In this way both the exhibition and the accompanying catalogue explore the multitude of ecological and cultural aspects that determined the life of mobile pastoralists in this region of Central Asia during the period under consideration.

Nomads—from the Greek νομάς, "roaming about for pasture"—have, over the past three millennia at least, decidedly shaped the cultural landscape of the Eurasian steppes (and other parts of the so-called Old World Dry Belt, ranging from Northern Africa to Northern China). Their mobile way of life, relying predominantly (but not exclusively) on livestock production, was not a stage of development between hunter-gatherer societies and those of sedentary agriculturalists, as postulated in evolutionist models of the eighteenth and nineteenth centuries.[2] On the contrary, nomadism should be seen as a highly sophisticated subsistence strategy that coexisted as an alternative to the sedentary cultures of agricultural and urban societies.[3] As such it was perfectly adapted to specific ecological conditions in extensive but only seasonally productive grasslands. Following seasonally determined migratory routes in a year-round cycle, nomads made optimal use of rangeland resources by maintaining the grazing capacity of these grasslands. Using their herding animals as the medium, nomads "transmuted" the scant resources of otherwise often uninhabitable regions into meat, milk products, wool, hides, and other benefits that secured their survival. At the same time, mobility provided the strategic potential to react to unstable political conditions.

In southern and eastern Kazakhstan, these migratory routes frequently combined lowland-steppe pastures during the winter and alpine highlands during the summer into a single and sustainable system of land use (known as vertical nomadism), primarily for horses, sheep, goats, and camels—the latter mostly used as beasts of burden. The distances covered by these migratory cycles varied considerably from group to group, depending on local conditions and herd composition but also on cultural preferences.[4] In addition, this general rhythm structured the social life of communities: in summer pastures pastoralists dispersed into small herding units, comprising only a single household or just a few households. But during late autumn and winter, these small herding units tended to assemble in larger winter camps, and it was during this time of year that raiding took place and social rituals, including tribal hunts and sacral ceremonies, were performed, reviving communal identities at larger social and political levels. The altar-like stands shown in the exhibition are probably related to these rituals.

Thus, we see that nomadism in the Eurasian steppes (and beyond) was more than just an ecological adaptation: the specifics of mobile herding resulted in particular forms of social organization and material culture in mobile pastoral societies—through an "independent socioecological mode of culture."[5]

In the entirety of their social relationships, value systems, and material forms of expression, nomads were independent from evolutionary trends within the sedentary world, but they hardly ever did without close economic and cultural contacts with their sedentary neighbors, even in specific ecological niches. This was in part because mobile stockbreeders were more prone to crises than were sedentary societies, as the loss of economic resources (which included not only herds but also beasts of burden, means of transportation, and mobile housing) could directly endanger the nomads' traditional mobile lifestyle. As a strategy to cope with this danger, mobile pastoralists tended to diversify their potential resources—both within their regional communities and by entering into relations with other pastoral and nonpastoral populations.

The result was the development of complex networks complementing the economy of mobile pastoralists and generating large zones of economic interaction and integration throughout Eurasia. Farming played an important role, either in ecologically favorable niches (for Kazakhstan see the essay by Claudia Chang in this volume) or in areas adjacent to the steppes. Networks were often established to secure access to important resources, like the rich mineral deposits in the mountain systems of the Tianshan, the Tarbagatai, and the Altai. Already in prehistory the "adaptive variability" of pastoral systems was accompanied by far ranging networks fostering complex economic and sociopolitical interactions among regionally continuous "pastoralist landscapes" across vast reaches of Eurasia.[6] Such networks were particularly crucial for the formation and survival of social and political elites among pastoralists. The mobility and the military potential of these elites, based on mounted warfare, further increased sociopolitical interconnections across the steppes and far beyond, resulting in broader networks across the Eurasian continent.

Not surprisingly, many of these networks visually manifest themselves in objects of art, some of which are on display in the current exhibition (and more of which will be dealt with in various essays of the present catalogue). An important role in this context is played by artistic expressions created in a style often called the Scytho-Siberian animal style. They feature wild and domesticated animals as well as fantastic creatures on riding equipment, arms, objects of daily use, and tattoos, depicted in distinctive poses— for example, with their feet tucked under them, or curled into a circle. Clearly, the wide distribution of this artistic vocabulary not only reflects the roots of this artistic language in earlier Siberian art, but also points to a worldview frequently shared by the various nomadic groups inhabiting the vast steppelands in the heart of Eurasia.

The nine chapters of this catalogue aim to set the exhibition objects in the various and respective contexts of mobile pastoral lifeways during the first millennium BCE. The authors explore this topic from a variety of angles.

An early perspective is taken by Nikolay A. Bokovenko and Zainolla S. Samashev, who discuss "The Roots of Iron Age Pastoral Nomadic Culture," taking into account that while horse riding began earlier than the period covered by the exhibition, it became combined with social behaviors that caused both a rise in warfare and in rich elites early in the first millennium BCE. Central to their discussion are two of the earliest burial complexes, Arzhan 1 and Arzhan 2, which yielded remains of such behaviors and demonstrate characteristics that continue among the later groups discussed in other essays (including the burial of many horses, types of weaponry, and the nature of the horse tack itself). The sites of Arzhan 1 and Arzhan 2 are in Tuva, in what is today Russia, adjacent to Kazakhstan. It is probably only one of the areas where such practices arose.[7]

To date, the earliest nomadic elite burial from the territory of Kazakhstan is kurgan 82 at the cemetery of Shilikty 3. Although looted in antiquity (as were most of the other burials discussed in this catalogue), it nevertheless yielded spectacular finds that demonstrate how lavishly the early nomadic elite marked social (and perhaps political) status in funeral contexts. In "Results of Multidisciplinary Studies and Reconstructions of Materials from the Baigetobe Kurgan at Shilikty," Abdesh T.

Toleubaev, the recent excavator of Shilikty, presents the results of his work at this important site, with many details, some of them published here for the first time in English.

Equally important is the cemetery site of Berel in the Kazakh Altai, belonging to the so-called Pazyryk culture. It contained some burials that had been frozen for more than 2,000 years under permafrost, thus preserving organic materials often lost through time. The exhibition contains many objects from kurgan 11, a double burial that preserved large amounts of organic remains, including the bodies of thirteen horses. The wooden ornaments that decorated the horse tack illustrate the rich artistic vocabulary of the Pazyryk culture and offer a window into their belief system. Zainolla S. Samashev, the excavator, discusses the excavation and interpretation of that burial and others at the site in "The Berel Kurgans: Some Results of Investigation."

In addition to kurgan cemeteries, the "nomadic landscape" of the first millennium BCE in the foothills of the Tianshan and the Altai is shaped by rock engravings (petroglyphs). The actual meanings of these images remain difficult for us to understand, but their locations might be related to nearby camping sites or important hunting grounds, or they may point to the sacral significance of these spots to nomadic communities traversing the rocky areas with their flocks. In "Some Questions Regarding the Rock Art of Kazakhstan," Sagynbay Myrgabayev presents an overview of this important category of imagery "in the open," produced by mobile pastoralists in the first millennium BCE.

In "Burial Practices and Social Roles of Iron Age Mobile Pastoralists," Karen S. Rubinson discusses what we can learn from the burials at Berel about the roles they played in the life of the community, and the information they might convey about beliefs and social practices. Anthropological models indicate that the appearances of burials do not always literally reflect the ways of life of the individuals while they were alive, and that burial ceremonies and burials themselves actively construct memory and reconstruct society. From this perspective, Rubinson's essay explores some of the possible ways to understand the Berel burials.

As noted, the horse-riding militarism of first-millennium mobile pastoralists was emphasized in the texts of ancient historians such as Herodotus. Bryan R. Hanks looks at the actual practices as we know them from archaeology, and explores the social and environmental changes that probably led to the rise of this particular way of life. His essay, "Mounted Warfare and Its Sociopolitical Implications," contrasts the more nuanced picture we have today, as a result of scientific excavation, with the perception of a half-century ago.

Among the necessities of the political culture of these powerful and militant elites were exotic luxuries from outside the nomadic world, because their accumulation and redistribution enabled ambitious leaders to secure and increase their power. In his essay "Nomads and Networks: Elites and Their Connections to the Outside World," Sören Stark follows the strategies employed by the Sakā and Wusun aristocracies to acquire precious prestige goods from the Achaemenid Empire, India, and China. He also inquires into the impact of these imports on the local artistic vocabulary of the nomadic world of the Central Eurasian steppes.

The reputation of mobile pastoralists has been shaped by ancient texts and also by the fact that for centuries only the remains of warrior elites were known.[8] However, modern archaeological work has revealed information about the settlements of this period and the interrelationships between those who carried out agriculture and the elites, who were often buried with their horses. Claudia Chang, who has excavated settlement sites in eastern Kazakhstan, discusses the nature of settlement remains and models of interaction in "Cycles of Iron Age Mobility and Sedentism: Climate, Landscape, and Material Culture in Southeastern Kazakhstan." The varied physical landscapes of eastern Kazakhstan, with its alluvial fans and nearby high mountain pastures, have not noticeably changed since the first millennium BCE, so it is possible that mobility patterns observed today or in the recent past are quite similar to those present during the lifetimes of individuals whose burials and caches yielded objects in the exhibition.

Finally, the essay by Nursan Alimbai, "Society and Culture of the Nomads of Central Asia through Time," outlines the family, clan, and larger group structures of traditional Kazakh society. His discussion reminds us that "kinship" has been an important category to construct, express, and legitimate a variety of group relationships in traditional nomadic societies in the Eurasian steppe. Traditional social practices—even if they change through time—might provide valuable suggestions for the interpretation of remains of the past when direct evidence is largely "invisible" from archaeological contexts.

A final word seems necessary regarding the divergence of models based on archaeological data from narratives drawing on the testimony of ancient literary sources. One reason for this is that these sources were produced by authors outside the nomadic world who often held stereotyped and biased views of the unfamiliar lives of their nomadic neighbors. Recent anthropological models have, therefore, the uncontested merit of painting a more nuanced picture of the diversity and interconnectivity in Iron Age pastoral societies than can be gleaned from written sources alone. These models also shed much-needed light on non-elite segments of the societies they analyze. Another reason for the seeming contradiction between testimonies provided by some kinds of archaeological data and those provided by literary sources lies in the fact that social and political elites were more closely involved in interactions with their sedentary neighbors than then rest of the pastoral society (for a detailed exploration of this issue, see the essays by Sören Stark and by Bryan K. Hanks). Thus it is often the elites, leading a more mobile and war-like lifestyle, who figure in ancient texts.

Many of the objects shown in this exhibition clearly come from elite contexts, and consequently several of the essays take a perspective that is largely focused on the nomadic elite (Bokovenko and Samashev, Hanks, and Stark). Others, however, focus on such non-elite segments of pastoral society as settlement sites (Chang). Indeed, a nuanced and complete picture can only be drawn by integrating textual and anthropological perspectives, both of which ultimately complement each other. Karen S. Rubinson's chapter, in particular, demonstrates that texts can indeed assist interpretation of archaeological materials.

It is hoped that the essays assembled here will help the reader to more fully enjoy the exhibition, and to further explore the vivid picture painted by archaeological and art historical research of a long-lost world of ancient nomads in the heart of the Eurasian continent.

NOTES

1. The exhibition *From the Lands of the Scythians: Ancient Treasures from the Museums of the U.S.S.R., 3000 B.C.–100 B.C.*, organized in cooperation with the Ministry of Culture of the U.S.S.R, was on view in 1975 at the Metropolitan Museum of Art, New York, and the Los Angeles County Museum of Art; see Metropolitan Museum of Art 1975. Not long before, the first modern exhibition in the United States devoted to art decorated with animal-style ornament, *"Animal Style" Art from East to West*, originated at the Asia House Gallery, New York, and traveled to The University Museum, University of Pennsylvania, Philadelphia, and the M. H. de Young Memorial Museum, San Francisco; see Bunker, Chatwin, and Farkas 1970.
2. Although such views were rejected as early as the late-nineteenth century (see the pioneering work of Hahn 1891), they still enjoy some popularity.
3. Barfield 1993.
4. Khazanov 1984, 38.
5. Scholz 1995.
6. Frachetti 2008a; Frachetti et al. 2010, 623–24.
7. Wagner et al. 2011.
8. On the early history of research in the Eurasian steppe, see Вайнберг, Горбунова, и Мошкова 1992; Parzinger 2006, 31–40.

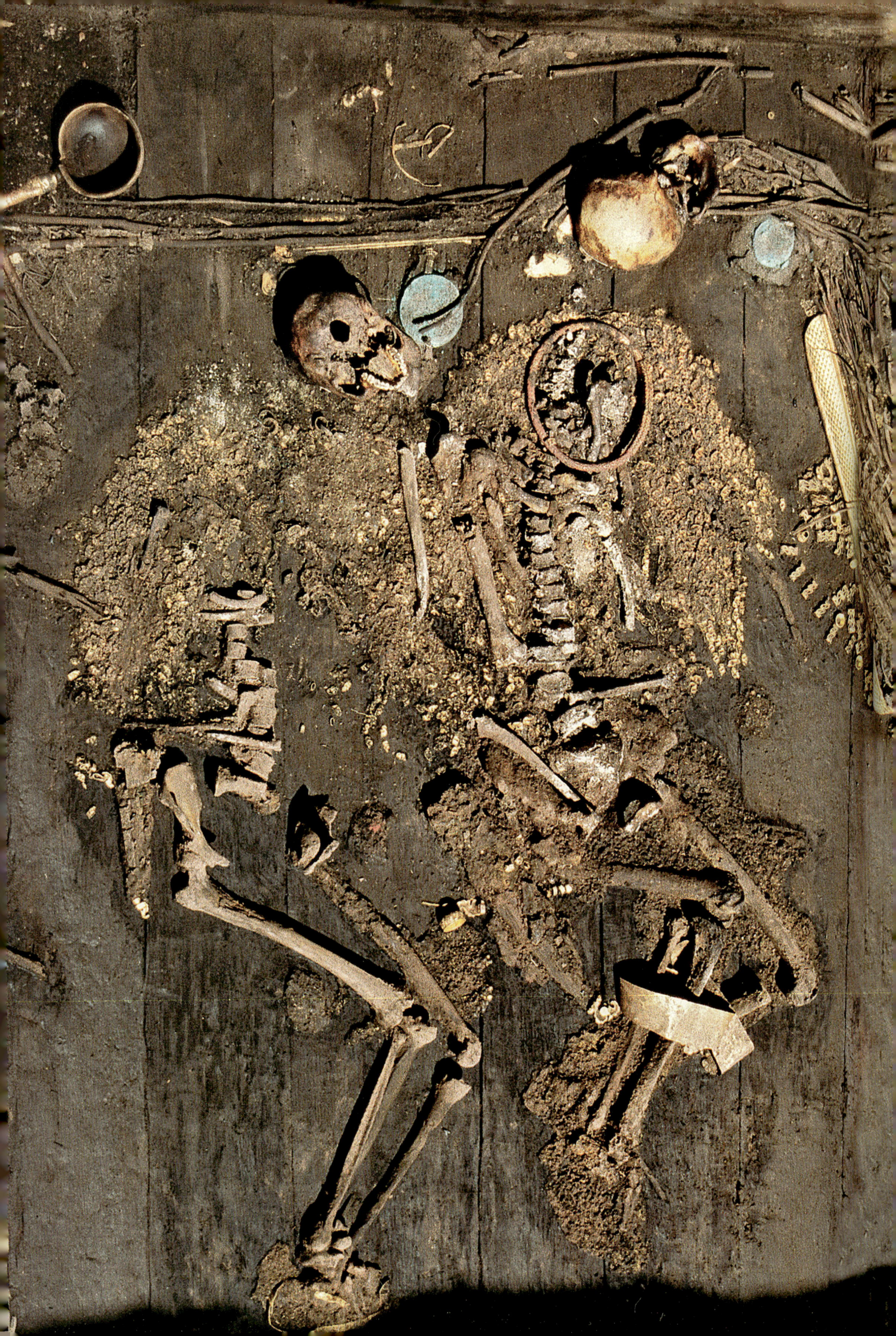

THE ROOTS OF IRON AGE PASTORAL NOMADIC CULTURE

Nikolay A. Bokovenko and Zainolla S. Samashev

During antiquity the Eurasian steppes formed a unique region that played an important role in the historical development of various peoples. In the north the steppes were bordered by taiga and large areas of forest, in the south by mountain ridges and deserts, and thus the population was generally able to move within this region in a longitudinal direction. The steppe region had unique flora and fauna, as well as stable systems for reproduction and adaptation, stimulating the emergence of the types of economies that were most suitable for ancient societies associated primarily with animal husbandry, which developed and improved depending on climatic changes.

Burial from Arzhan 2 during excavation.

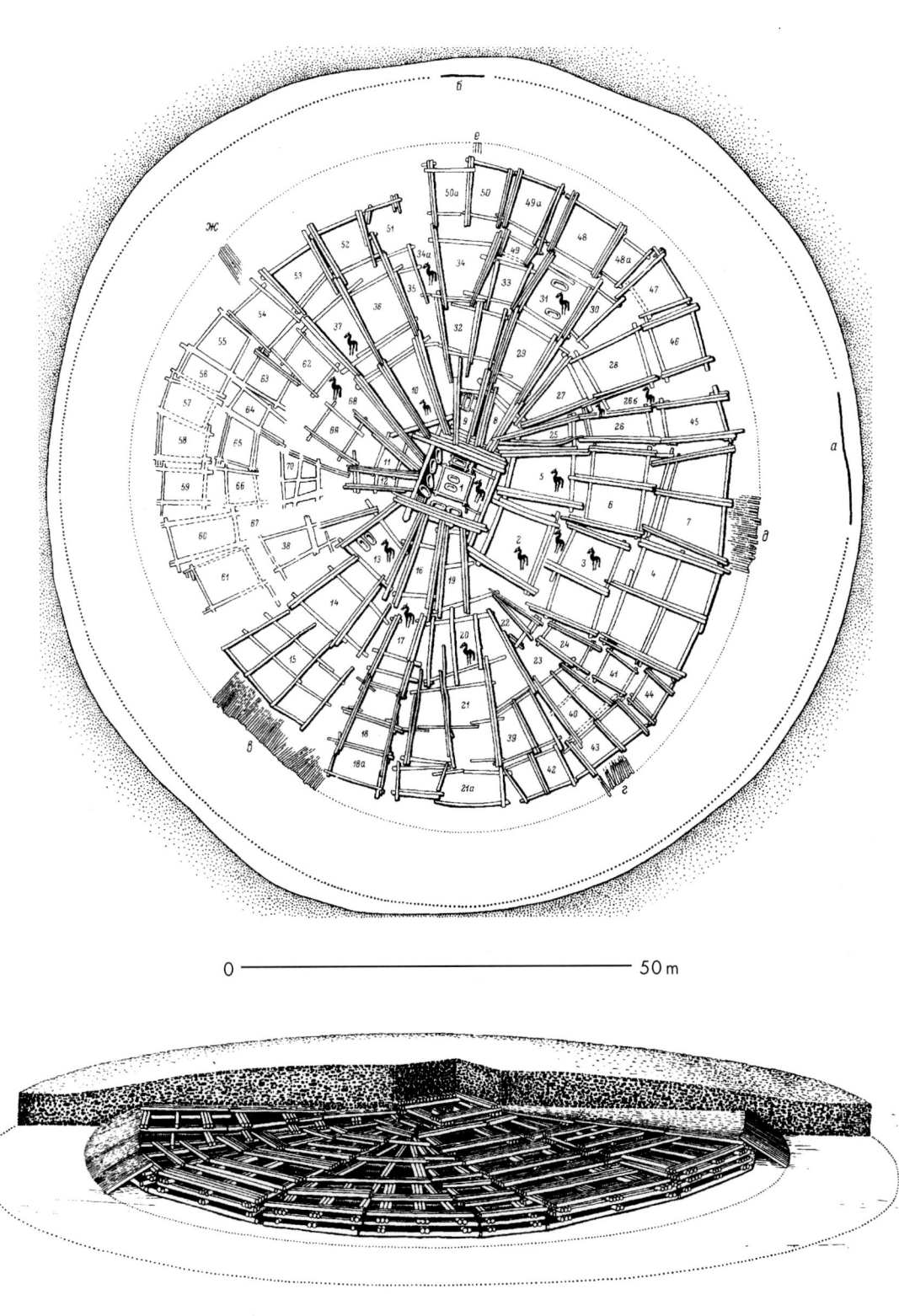

1-1　Plan and section of Arzhan 1 tomb complex.

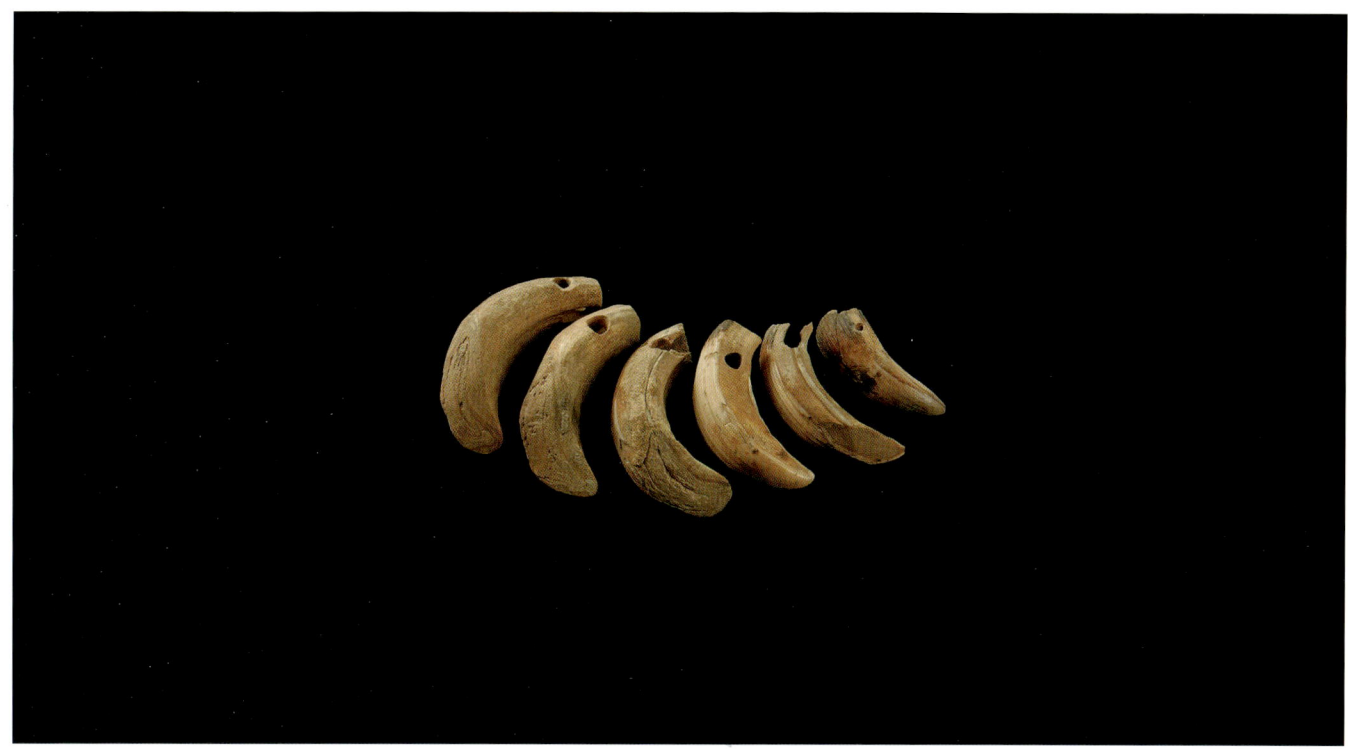

At the end of the second millennium BCE, Eurasian steppe peoples established an optimal economic system—nomadic pastoralism (with horizontal and vertical seasonal migrations), in which herds were formed mostly by horses, sheep, and goat, animals that do not require feed supplies stored for winter. The most favorable natural conditions for the development of a migrational form of animal husbandry (that is, year-round grazing) are in the area between the Ural Mountains and Mongolia.

The earliest known manifestations of horse-riding elites with great wealth and a military aspect characteristic of the Iron Age have been excavated in Tuva, a region in Southern Siberia that borders Western Mongolia, not far from the geographical center of Asia. Burial complexes from the initial stage (ninth–seventh centuries BCE) are represented by circular stone enclosing walls, inside which stone dome-like structures (cists) covering the deceased were constructed at the level of the ancient habitation layer. Cists with rectangular enclosing walls most likely appeared slightly later, along with pit burials.

The most spectacular kurgan of the early phase is known as Arzhan 1,[1] excavated by M. P. Gryaznov and M. Kh. Mannaî-ool in the Uiuk Mountain basin of Tuva. It was a gigantic stone structure of cylindrical shape, with a diameter of 120 meters and a preserved height of 4 meters, constructed at the level of the ancient habitation layer and reinforced at the bottom by a stone wall known as a *crepida*. Under the massive stone mound, there was a complex wooden structure that consisted of seventy large log chambers built out of large age-old larch trees (fig. 1-1).[2] The log chambers were arranged along radial axes, with a double log chamber in the center. The height of each chamber was about 2.5–3 meters, and the inside area measured 15–150 square meters. On all sides, the chambers were covered with an additional layer of wooden planks. According to Gryaznov, construction of this wooden structure would have required 1,500 people to work for seven or eight days. In the central chamber, a "king" and "queen," dressed in richly decorated fur clothes and wearing precious jewelry, were buried in smaller chambers within log sarcophagi, along with eight members of their retinue and six riding horses with harnesses. In other chambers there were seven male deceased of the same old age as the "king," all in rich clothes with jewelry and arms. Along with these or in separate chambers lay about 160 riding horses in full harness, including bronze bits and cheekpieces (*psalia*), gold and bronze plaques for bridle decoration, and boar-tusk pendants, similar to objects found at Berel (fig. 1-2).[3] Unfortunately, the Arzhan kurgan was looted

1-2 Pierced boar tusks (one decorated with relief carving). Boar tusks, Berel, kurgan 10(?), late 4th–early 3rd century BCE. A. Kh. Margulan Institute of Archaeology, Almaty. Checklist no. 93.

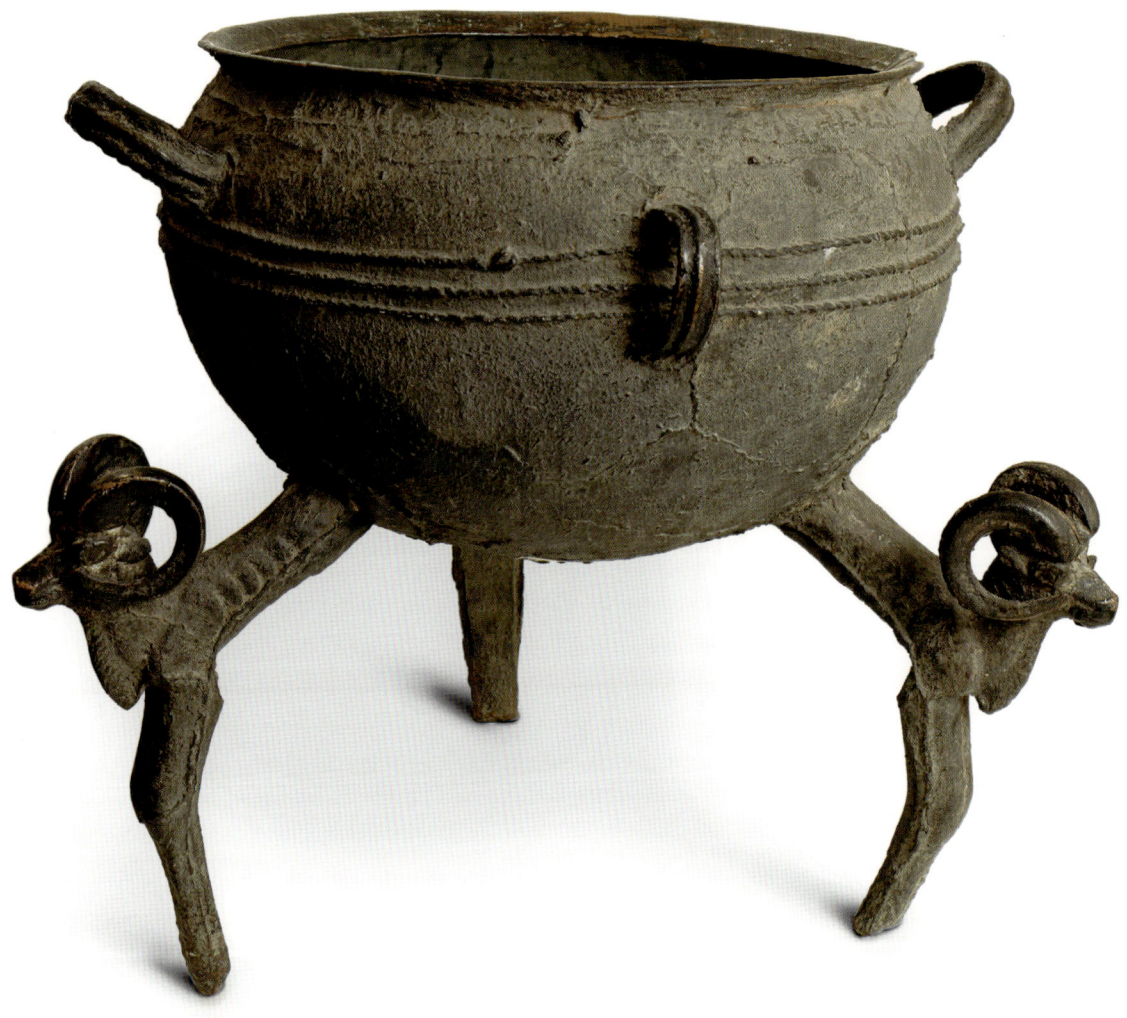

1-3 Tripod cauldron with legs in the form of horned sheep. Copper alloy, 5 km southwest of Almaty, chance find 1912, 5th–3rd century BCE. Central State Museum, Almaty: KP 2283. Checklist no. 135. Although this cauldron is dated later than Arzhan 1, and the Arzhan cauldrons cannot be reconstructed in detail, it conveys the enduring importance of these objects among mobile pastoralists for many centuries.

1-4 (opposite) Jointed bit and psalias. Cast bronze, Tasmola (Karaganda region), 7th–6th century BCE. Museum of Archaeology, Almaty: ЦКАЭ-61/62. Checklist no. 131. These objects are from a different and later context than the Arzhan 1 kurgan, but the bit ends with stirrup-shaped terminals are also seen at Arzhan 1.

1-5 (opposite) Bronze plaque with coiled feline from Arzhan 1. Aldan Maadyr National Museum, Republic of Tuva.

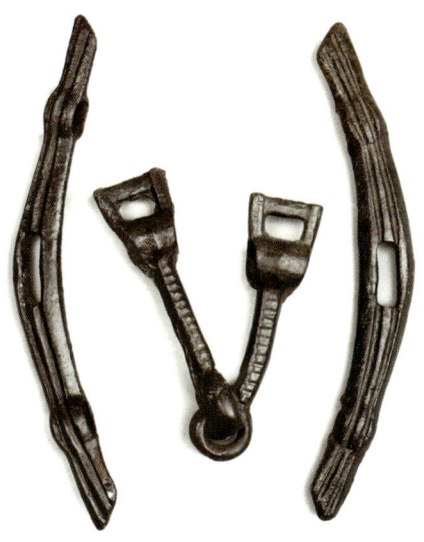
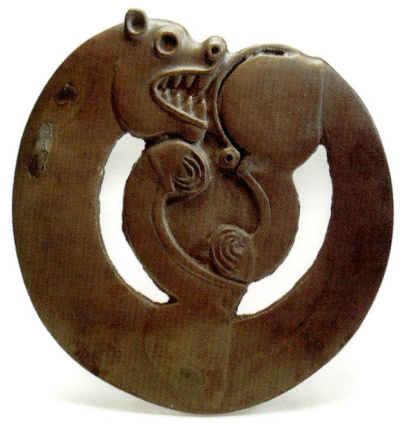

in antiquity, and many spectacular items that must have been in the burial of the "king" disappeared, but the preserved remains of clothes and the world's oldest preserved rugs, gold and silver jewelry, and beautiful cast-bronze objects in animal style all indicate that a very rich individual was buried here, possibly the chieftain of a tribal confederation. The arms include bronze daggers, axes (*chekans*), and arrowheads. Small pieces from several large bronze cauldrons, the shapes of which were not possible to determine, were found in chamber 1 of the Arzhan kurgan. This category of vessels was very popular in Asian steppes, as can be seen from examples in the exhibition that are dated later (fig. 1-3).

Numerous parts of horse harnesses were found in the Arzhan burial complexes, including bronze bits of twelve different types (with round, ellipse-like, and stirrup-shaped terminals; with an additional hole in the shaft; and so forth [fig. 1-4]); cheekpieces of six types (including psalia made out of leather and wood or bone, and three bronze rod-shaped examples with three openings in the shaft, a mushroom-shaped terminal on one end and a small conical head on the other); many plaques of various shapes (round and figure-eight shaped) made out of horn; and, as mentioned, boar-tusk pendants. Altogether, twenty-four different types of harnesses were in circulation at the same time.[4] Chest decorations for horses included both primitive appliqués made of horn and an impressive bronze disc-shaped plaque, 25 centimeters in diameter, with the image of a curled feline (a snow leopard) in bas-relief (fig. 1-5).

A broken piece of a "deer stone," round in section, was found in Arzhan 1; represented on the stone is a belt from which hang a whetstone, a dagger, and a bow, with a row of deer and boar figures underneath. According to Gryaznov, images of animals standing "on tiptoe" and rendered in this particular style are especially characteristic of the early stage of the development of Scythian-Siberian art.[5]

The cultural importance of Arzhan 1 is evident not only in the richness of the kurgan but also in the fact that typological analysis of the accompanying burial goods (horse harnesses, arms, art objects) allowed scholars to identify the specific geographical origins of the gifts for this powerful chieftain: the gifts found in the northern log chambers originated in eastern parts of Kazakhstan, the Altai, and the Minusinsk basin, while the gifts from the southern chambers arrived from Tuva and Mongolia.

Tuva continued to be an area where very rich burials of mobile pastoralists were found dating to subsequent periods. The funerary complex of Arzhan 2, from the middle of the seventh century BCE, was investigated in 2000–2004 by a Russian-German team. Like Arzhan 1, the complex clearly represents individuals who belonged to the upper stratum of the elite. The main burial, under a mound about 80 meters in diameter and more than 2 meters high, contained the bodies of two deceased (a male, forty to forty-five years old, and a female, thirty to thirty-five years old), whose high rank was indicated by their rich clothing, decorated with gold

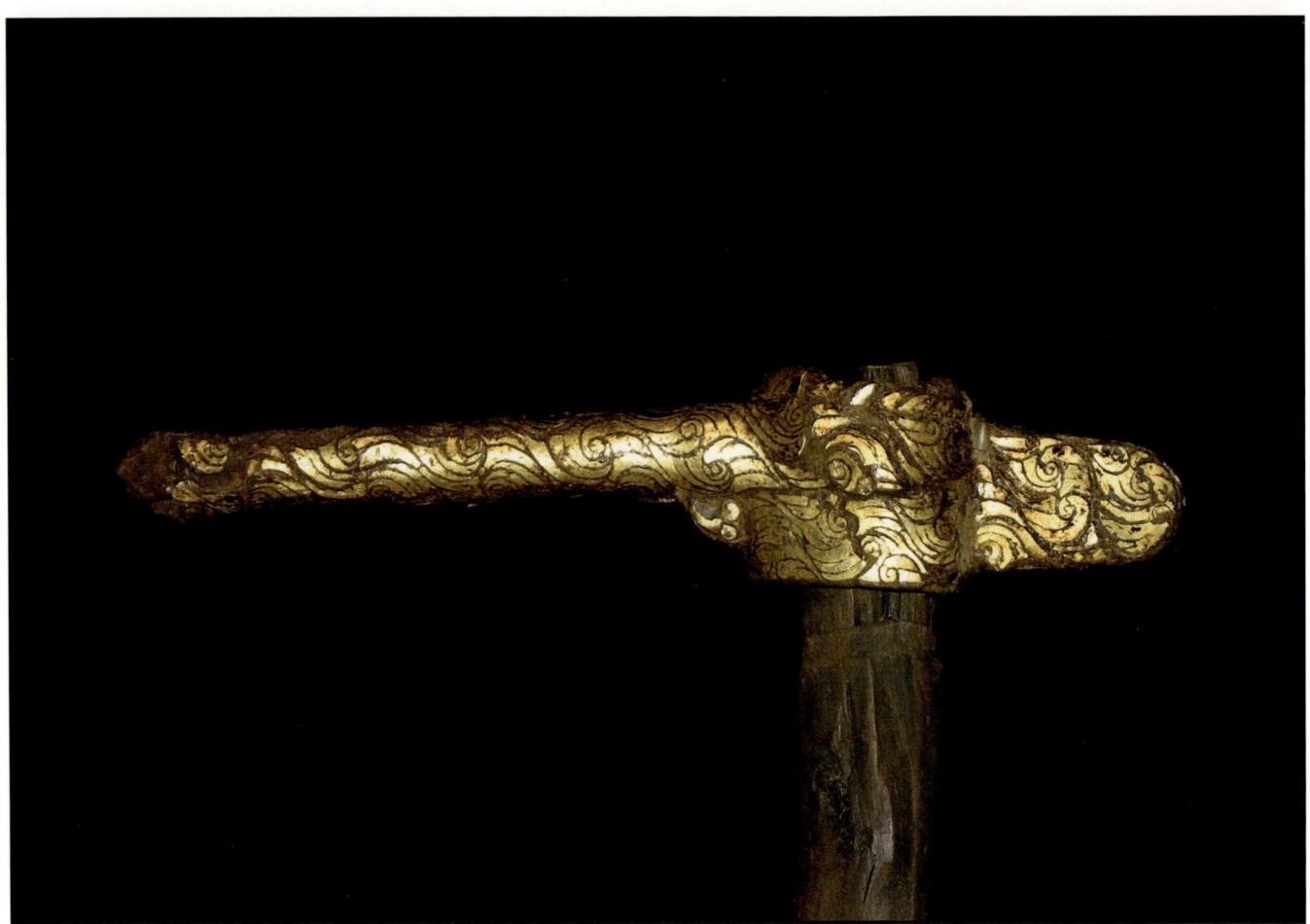

appliqués (see page 20). Other gold objects found in the burial included heavy gold jewelry (a torque, a pectoral, earrings, and other objects); a *gorytos* cover made from a thin sheet of gold; iron arms (an axe, or *chekan*, and arrowheads) with gold inlays (fig. 1-6); as well as bronze cauldrons. Near the mound were many stone circles that contained burned animal bones (sheep, goat, cattle, and horse), presumably burnt offerings made in connection with this principal burial mound.[6]

Southeast of the mound containing the rich human burial was a burial that contained fourteen horses with their legs folded beneath their bodies and their heads pointing to the west.[7] This burial contained the largest assemblage of horse tack. Each horse was bridled. The sets of bits and psalia were standard: thirteen bits with rectangular terminals and regular psalia. One horse had stirrup-shaped bits with an additional ring and psalia with three holes in the shaft.

Inside the wall enclosure, several bridle sets were placed between the vertical slabs of the facing of the stone circle (*kromlekh*). The largest set included forty-nine objects: bits, psalia, girth buckles, mounts, and other items.

The goldwork in the main burial was manufactured by a variety of techniques, including casting and hammering as well as sheet gold overlaying wood; some pieces were decorated with fine granulation. Stags, horses, boars, and other animals were presented in what is known as Scytho-Siberian animal style, already seen at Arzhan 1. Both the artistic style and the rich variation of precious-metal techniques became part of the self-representation of nomadic elites in southern and eastern Kazakhstan, as can be seen by the objects from the Zhalauli Treasure included in the exhibition (figs. 1-7–1-9).

1-6 Iron axe head with gold inlay from Arzhan 2. The State Hermitage Museum, St. Petersburg.

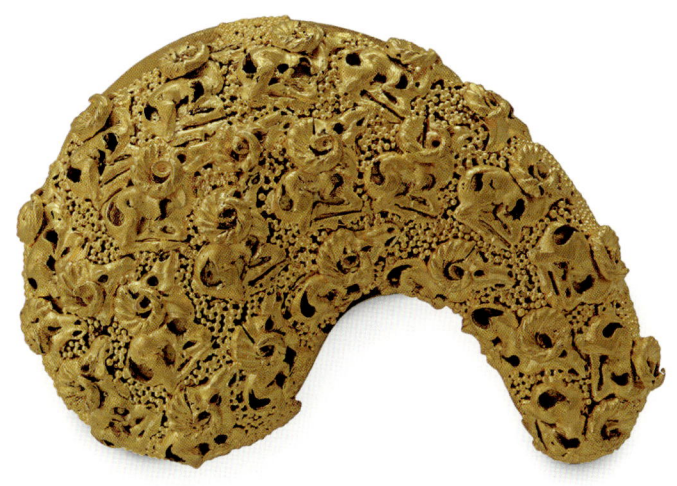

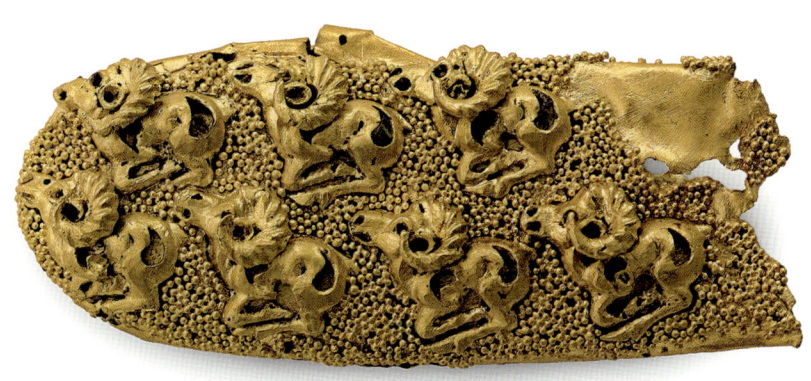

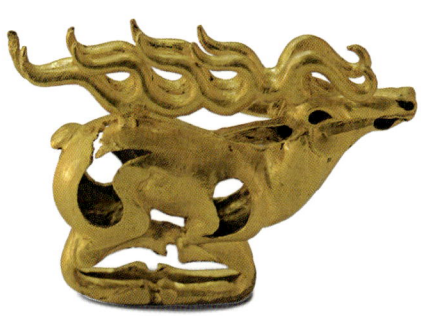

1-7 Teardrop-shaped plaque with granulation and argali decoration. Gold, Zhalauli (Kegen district, Almaty region), 7th–6th century BCE. Central State Museum, Almaty: KP 22030/1-8. Checklist no. 176.

1-8 Belt terminus with granulation and argali decoration. Gold, Zhalauli (Kegen district, Almaty region), 7th–6th century BCE. Central State Museum, Almaty: KP 22031/1. Checklist no. 177.

1-9 Horned deer with folded legs. Gold, Zhalauli Treasure, 7th–6th century BCE. Central State Museum, Almaty: KP 22030/10. Checklist no. 179.

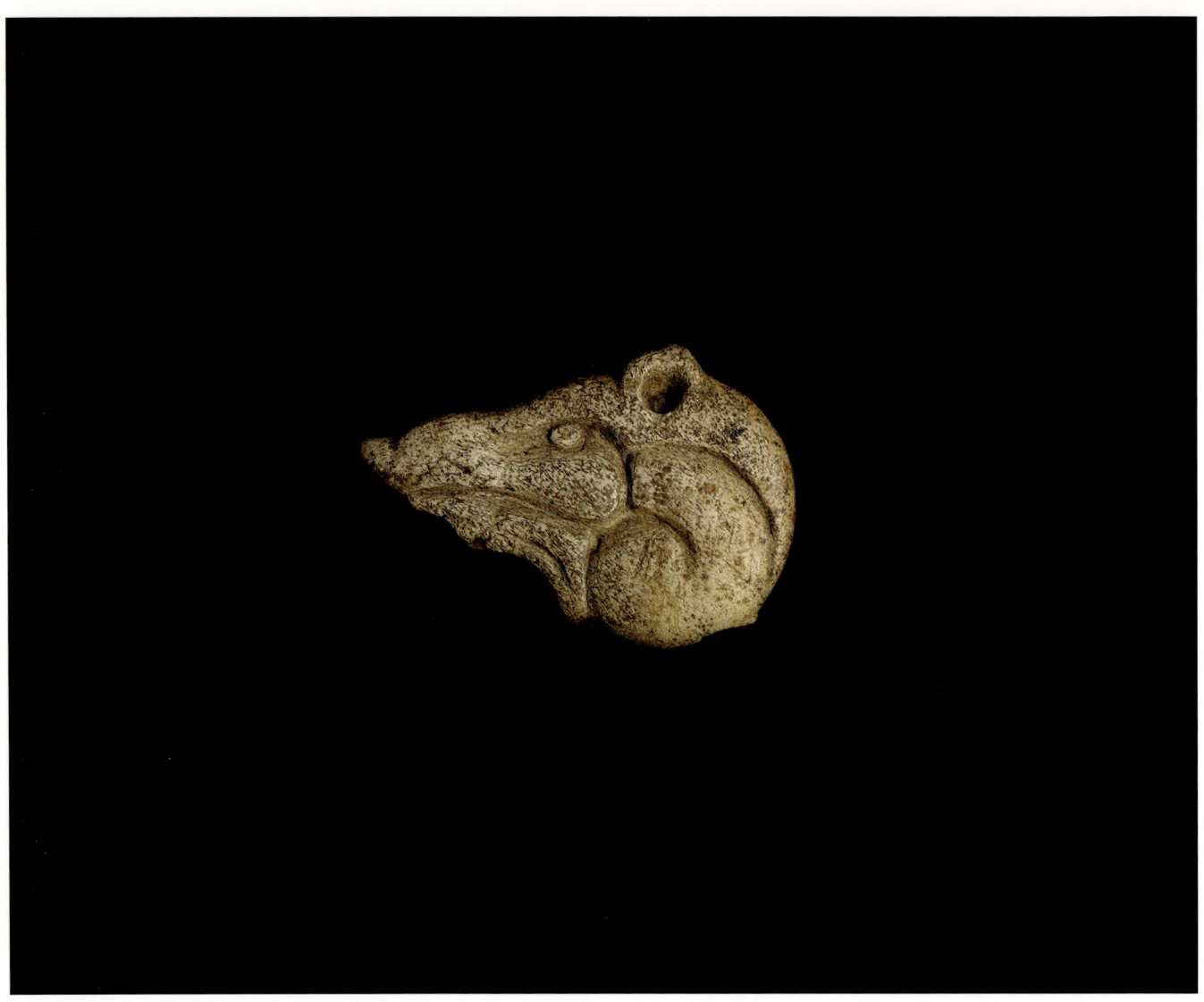

As can be seen in this brief description, the burial practices found at these earlier Arzhan sites share characteristics with those at Berel:[8] the deceased, buried under mounds, are accompanied both by rich grave goods and often by many horses, which are sometimes highly ornamented and show a range of bits and other tack elements. The burial traditions of the later first millennium BCE had deep roots in the past; presumably, other elements of belief and social life did as well (fig.1-10).

1-10 Harness ring in the form of a curled-up boar. Horn (maral, Siberian red deer), Nurmanbet 2, kurgan 3, 7th–6th century BCE. Museum of Archaeology, Almaty: MA 725. Checklist no. 115. This boar, dated somewhat later than Arzhan 1, illustrates that the curled-animal motif (such as that seen in the feline from Arzhan 1; fig. 1-5) continued to be part of the artistic vocabulary of the steppe pastoralists.

NOTES

1 Грязнов 1980; Grjaznov 1984; Bokovenko 1994, 48–49.
2 Although there are fewer details published for Shilikty, which is later than Arzhan 1, in both cases the burial was placed on the surface with a wooden superstructure under the mound. See Toleubaev this volume.
3 Грязнов 1980, 24, fig. 13.
4 Боковенко 1986a; Боковенко 1986b; Bokovenko 2000.
5 Грязнов 1980, 43, fig. 29/2.
6 Čugunov, Parzinger, and Nagler 2003; Čugunov, Parzinger, and Nagler 2006.
7 The horses in Berel kurgan 10 and kurgan 11 were in a similar position, with their legs folded, although their heads pointed toward the east.
8 See Samashev and Toleubaev this volume.

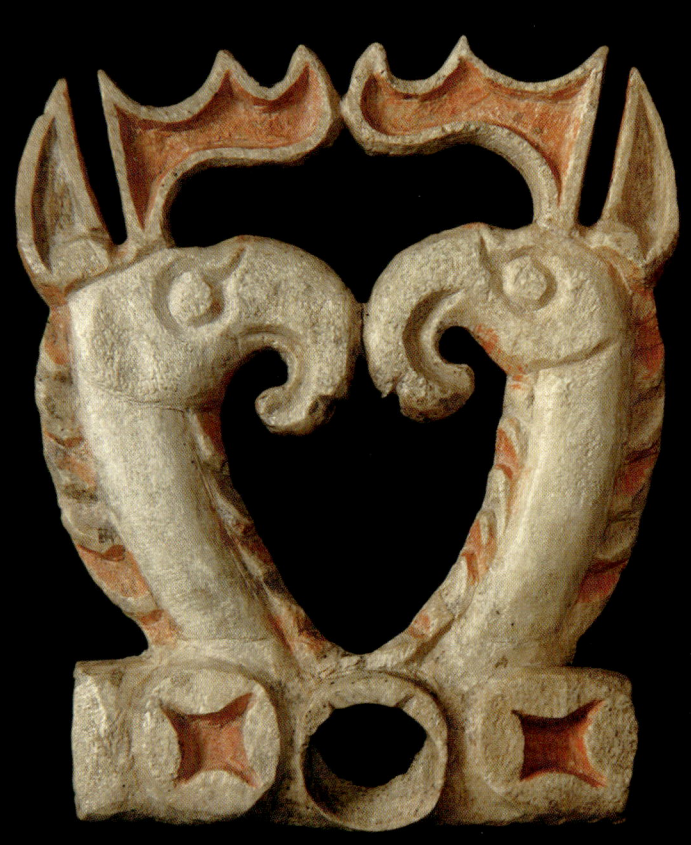

THE BEREL KURGANS: SOME RESULTS OF INVESTIGATION

Zainolla S. Samashev

INTRODUCTION
The kurgan cemetery of Berel is located in the Katonkargai district in eastern Kazakhstan, 7 kilometers southwest of the eponymous village, on the third terrace above the Bukhtarma River (fig. 2-1). The Berel necropolis was one of the first archaeological sites in the whole of Central Asia to be scientifically investigated, with excavations conducted by Wilhelm Radloff as early as 1865. But only recently have modern methods of excavating and the successful retrieval of organic materials allowed the kurgans at Berel to reveal their extraordinary wealth of objects and data. Systematic archaeological investigation of the site was initiated in 1998 and continues to this day.

Plaque of facing elk-griffin heads. Horn (Siberian red deer), Berel, kurgan 36, late 4th–early 3rd century BCE. A. Kh. Margulan Institute of Archaeology, Almaty: B36-21. Checklist no. 1.

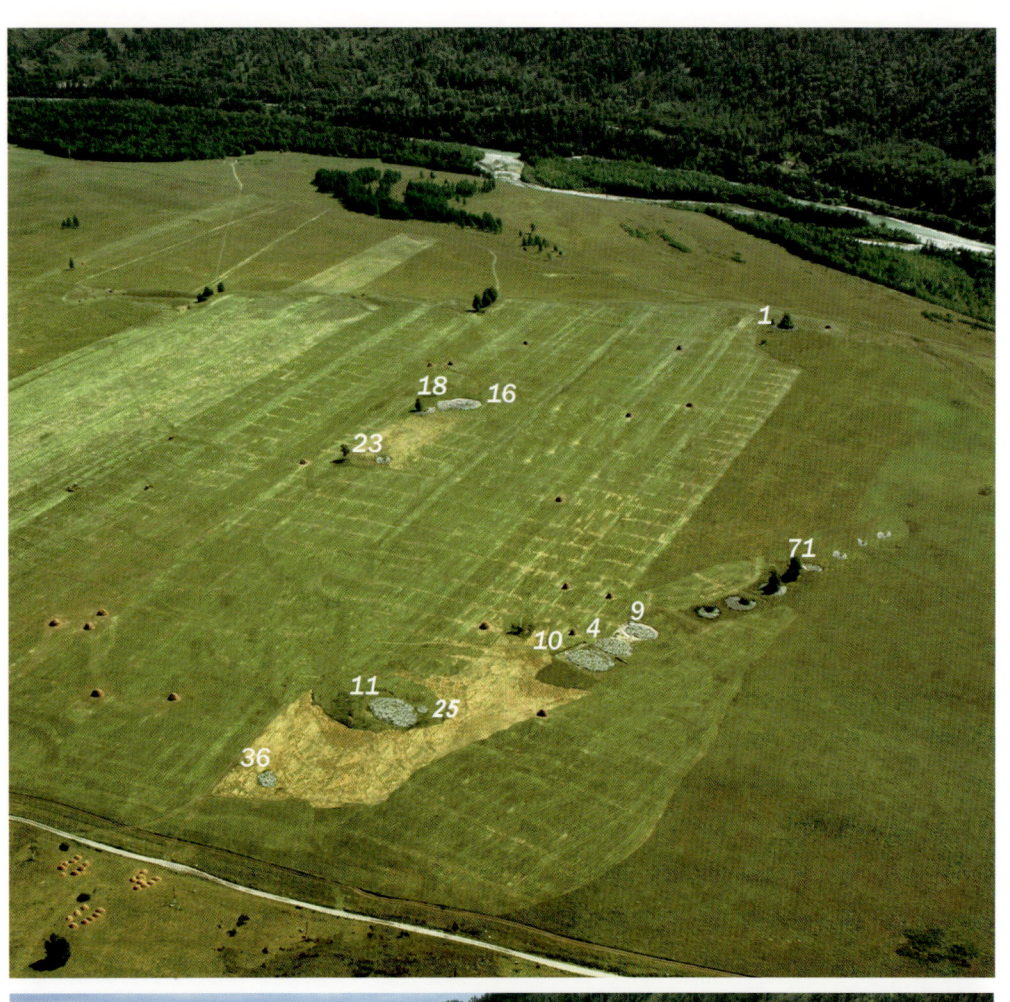

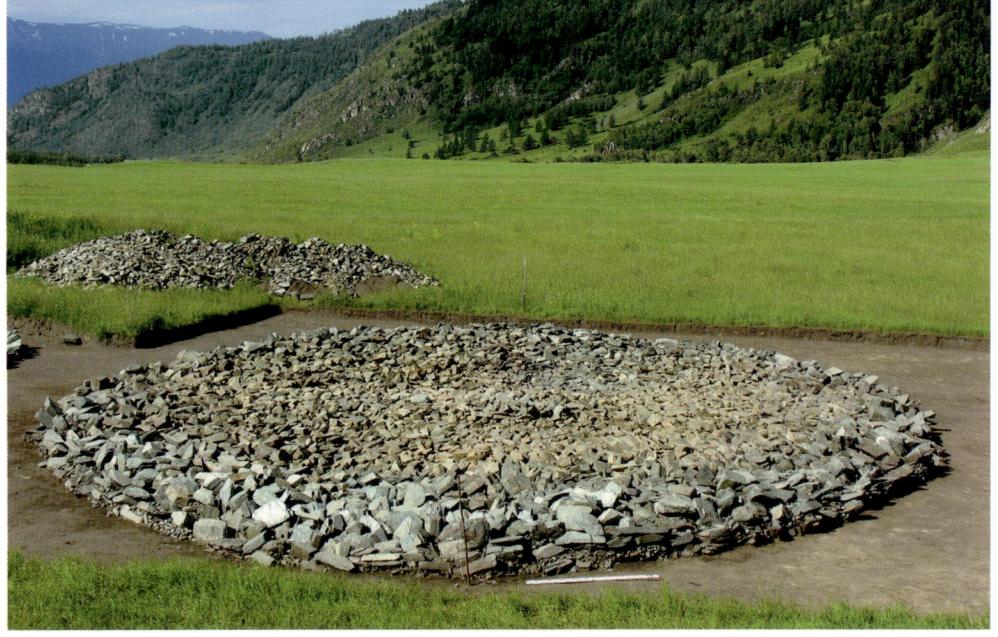

2-1 Aerial view of the kurgan necropolis at Berel.

2-2 General view of kurgan 10 during excavation.

As was already observed in the early excavations, specific microclimatic conditions caused by aspects of the construction of the burial mounds themselves led to the formation of localized permafrost ice lenses in the grave chambers. The size of the stones and the air between them created conditions to permanently freeze the ground below. Moisture in the ground would freeze, and the stones in the mound above, as well as the air between the stones, served as insulation, allowing the moisture to remain permanently frozen (fig. 2-2).[1] The existence of this phenomenon offered huge potential for the excellent preservation of organic materials. The recent excavations started with the largest unexcavated structure in the necropolis—Berel kurgan 11 (figs. 2-3a–c)—and indeed objects in organic materials, including items of costume decoration and horse-harness ornaments, were found there in excellent condition. They offer invaluable data for the reconstruction of the everyday life, burial rites, system of beliefs, and various aspects of the economic life of Iron Age nomads.

THE BURIALS OF KURGAN 11 AND KURGAN 36
Objects discovered during the excavation of kurgans 11 and 36 are highlights of the exhibition that this catalogue accompanies. The following discussion will help to contextualize these objects. To date, twenty-four kurgans have been excavated. With the exception of a few Early Medieval burials, all of the kurgans date to the later phase of the Iron Age and seem to belong to members of the nomadic elite. Significant variations regarding size and accompanying burial goods, however, suggest some degree of social differentiation within the elite itself.

The original construction of each burial began with a deep pit (fig. 2-3a). A chamber was built at the bottom of the pit, often a log cabin or a wooden framework with one to three horizontal rows of logs. The deceased was interred within the chamber, in most cases in a log sarcophagus (although on occasion the deceased was placed in a stone cist), with the head oriented to the east (fig. 2-3c). The accompanying burial goods included funerary food, weaponry, and household objects, and from one to seventeen horses. The log cabin with its log sarcophagus was usually located in the southern part of the burial, while the so-called horse section was located outside the constructed chamber in the northern part of the burial pit. When a large number of horses were interred, they could be buried in layers separated by sheets of birch bark (figs. 2-4a–c); in a simpler elite burial, a single horse is often found (fig. 2-5).

Kurgan 11 contained the burial of a male and a female, who were apparently not buried at the same time. The male died in his thirties or forties, while the female seems to have been somewhat older. Preliminary results of molecular genetic testing and anthropological examination of the human remains show that the deceased male was of a mixed anthropological type: both Caucasian and Mongoloid components are present. A fracture on the crown of the man's head and multiple healed rib and vertebral fractures indicate that he probably did not die of natural causes. A trepanation hole in the skull is clear evidence of posthumous manipulations of the body.

The burial of the man and woman was looted in antiquity, but the thirteen horses in full ceremonial regalia that accompanied them remained undisturbed. Palynological analysis performed on the stomach contents of some of the horses revealed fragments of tree needles, cereal stems, and bark fibers. According to the preliminary conclusions, the horses' last meal, and thus the burial ceremony, must have taken place in the beginning of summer.

Also of particularly interest is kurgan 36, located 81 meters to the northeast of kurgan 11, closer to the foot of the adjacent mountain. The superstructure of the kurgan revealed a complicated construction: the stone mound was surrounded by a ring of tightly spaced stone slabs, erected vertically or at a slight incline, which helped to reinforce the lower part of the mound. The burial pit was occupied by a multilayered stone structure with layers of soil between the stones; the pit itself was 1.70 meters deep, measured from the upper border of the pit. The inside of the burial chamber, in this case a cist, was faced with broad vertical stone slabs, the upper ends of which served to support cover blocks. A massive block covered the cist, and several other massive blocks of rounded or elongated shapes, each weighing 100–300 kilograms, were found covering the pit along its longer side.

Remains of a wooden framework made of three horizontal rows of logs were traced inside the stone cist; on the floor of the cist was a layer of pebbles covered with timbers and felt. Unfortunately, this

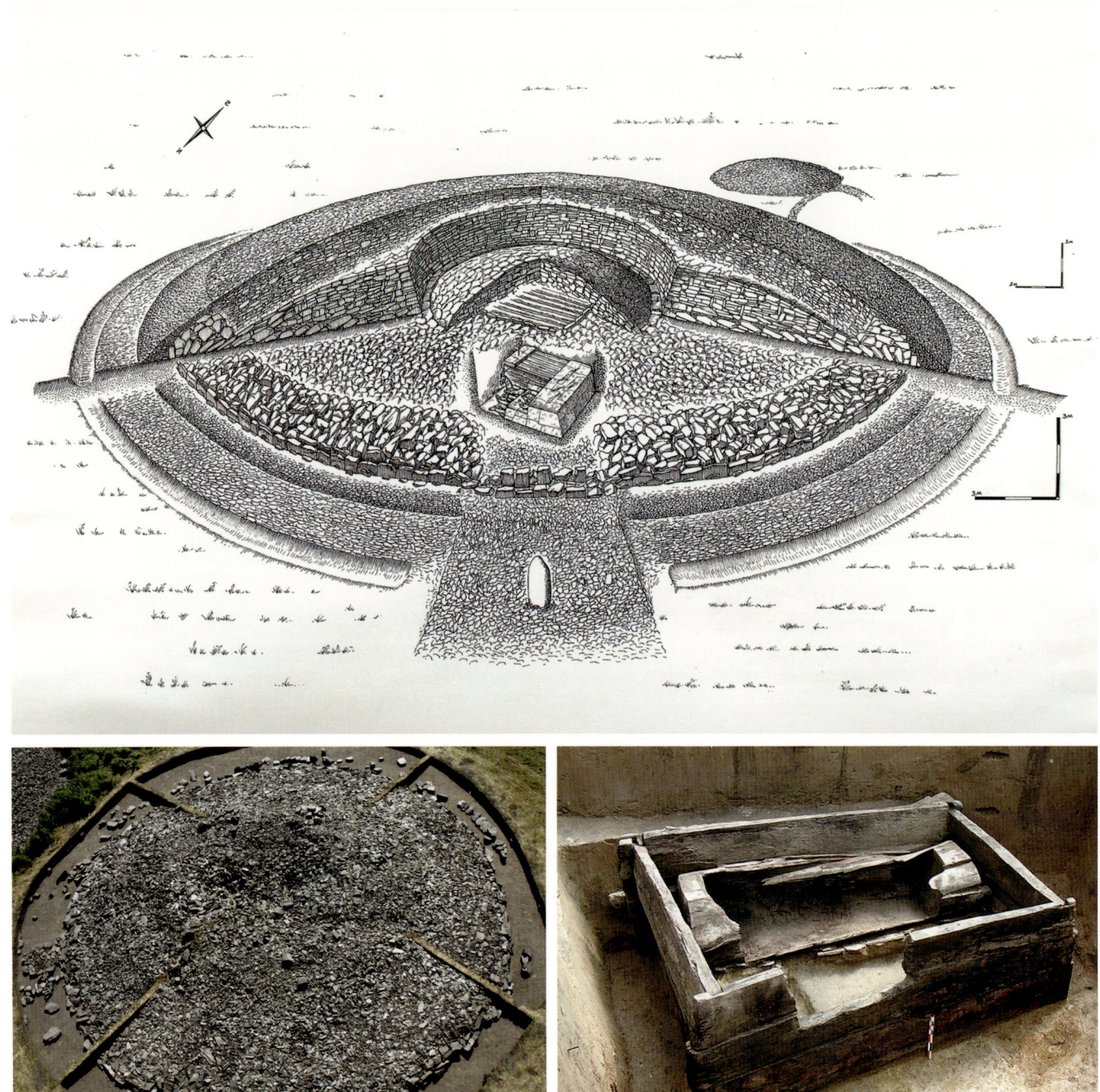

2-3a–c Kurgan 11: (a, top) Diagram showing construction. (b, bottom left) Aerial view during excavation. (c, bottom right) Wooden burial chamber and larch-log sarcophagus after excavation.

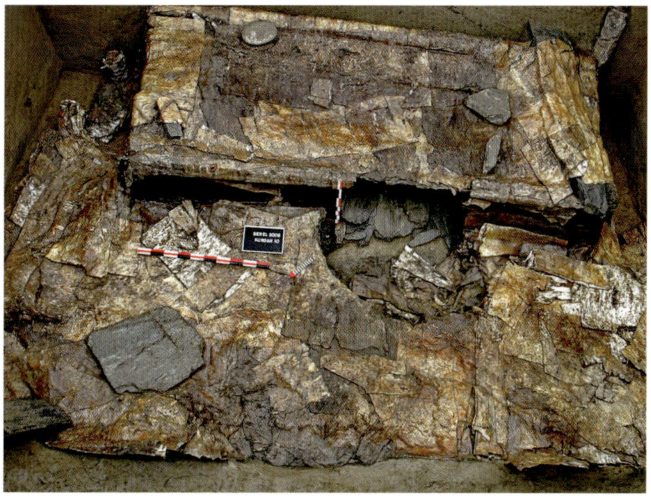

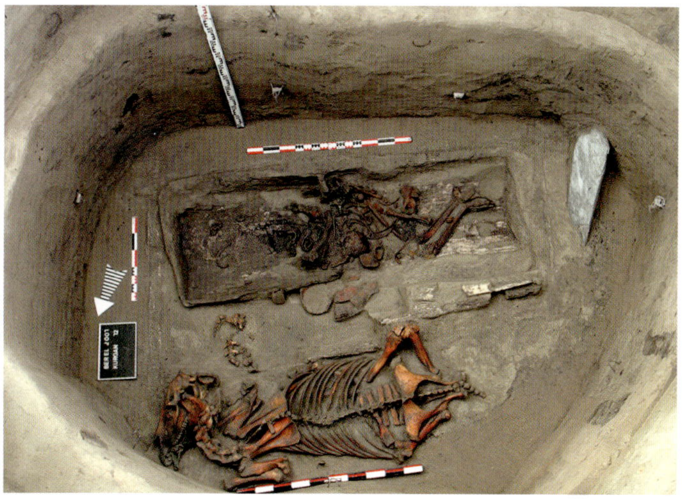

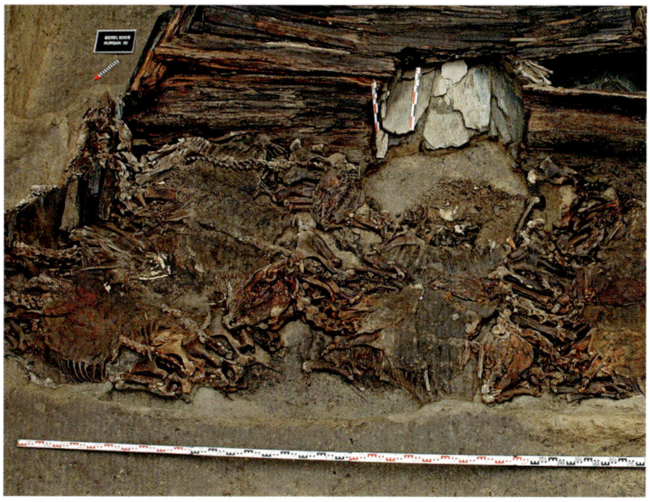

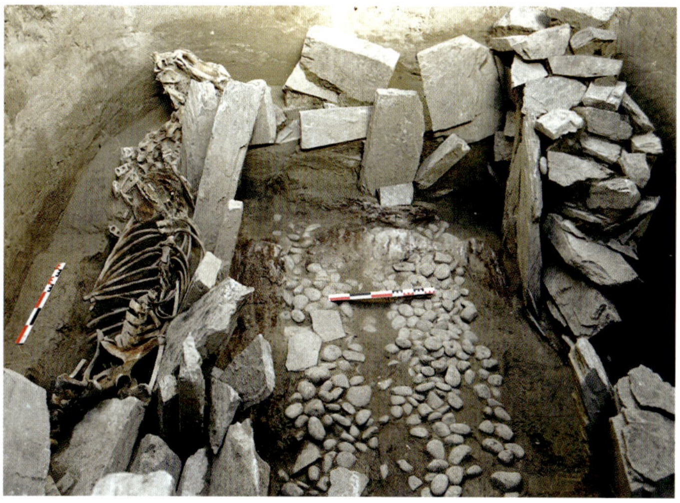

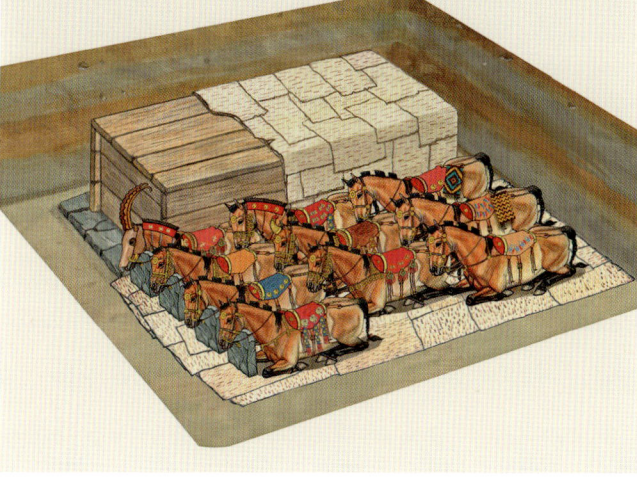

2-4a–c   Kurgan 10 during excavation: (a, top left) Before the pit was filled in, everything was covered with sheets of birch bark. At the center the hole left by ancient looters is visible. (b, center left) The log-cabin burial chamber is to the south and the "horse area" to the north. The human burial within the chamber was covered with slabs of stone. (c, bottom left) Reconstruction of the burial showing arrangement of ten horses.

2-5   (top right) Kurgan 72 during excavation.

2-6   (bottom right) Kurgan 36 during excavation: A pebble packing forms the floor of the burial chamber; the single-horse burial is arranged to the north.

burial was completely looted in antiquity; only individual bones of the deceased, fragments of gold leaf, and tubular beads made out of white paste were preserved. Judging from the remains of some decayed material with gold appliqués, the log cabin within the cist must have been decorated with a felt cover.

The burial in kurgan 36 was accompanied by an undisturbed single horse arranged in a distinctive way (fig. 2-6). A special bed for the animal was constructed behind the northern wall of the stone cist. The horse lay with its front legs tucked under its belly, its head and neck resting on a high step located on the eastern side. The body of the animal was completely covered with stone blocks, ensuring the preservation of the spectacularly decorated harness that it wore, which include sixty-six items carved from horn.

DATING

The good state of preservation of organic, in particular wooden, materials enabled the extraction of a number of radiocarbon and dendrochronological samples from the Berel kurgans.[2] In this way it was possible to establish an internal and relative chronology for kurgans 1 and 11, namely that kurgan 11 postdates kurgan 1 (excavated by Radloff) by sixty-six years. More difficult is absolute dating, as that involves a great number of variables. At present, dates suggested for kurgan 11 range from the last quarter of the fourth to the first quarter of the third century BCE.[3]

FINDS FROM BEREL: THE CONTENTS AND THEIR MEANING

The artifacts discovered at Berel can be divided into several categories, including cult objects, clothing, household items, objects of everyday life, and especially horse harnesses. Usually, the decoration of each horse harness focused on a single motif, found on all elements such as the bridle cheekpieces and psalias, and on plaques suspended from the saddle chest plate. The decorative repertoire on horse tack from kurgan 11 alone includes representations of real animals, such as elk (fig. 2-7), horned sheep (fig. 2-8), feline predators (fig. 2-9), and deer (fig. 2-10), as well as fantastic creatures, including horned tigers (fig. 2-11) and griffin protomes (fig. 2-12), and floral and vegetal patterns (figs. 2-13–2-15). In many cases animals are depicted in combat with each other, either as the motif of a set of horse trappings (fig. 2-16) or as the subject of an independent carving (fig. 2-17). In this respect, the iconographic spectrum found in Berel corresponds with that of the whole complex of Pazyryk decorative art: images of real animals from the Altai region (horned hoofed animals, such as deer, elk, argali, and various predators, as well as birds, fish, and others) appear alongside fantastic creatures that combine traits of several real-animal prototypes and even some anthropomorphic features.

Before taking a closer look at the most significant motifs on the objects from Berel, it is important to briefly consider their appearance on burial goods and the implications of this fact regarding the semantic value of the motifs. Burial goods, regardless of whether they were used previously in life, are always part of specific rituals, performed in accordance with the norms of religious ceremonies and rites existing in a given society. The objects are intended for preparation for the afterlife and the transition from the world of the living to the world of the dead. Obviously, those roles influence the semantics of visual images on burial goods, and in fact, these images can only be understood in the context of burial rites and funerary practices in a specific time and place. In Berel this context can best be exemplified by the decoration of the horse tack, which was clearly made with the intention to create a specific "iconographic program" for each horse. Each example thus seems to be decorated in a specific way to lend it the magical qualities necessary to its specific role in the afterlife.

IMAGERY AT BEREL

There are many fascinating motifs at Berel. Here we will focus on three: the griffin, the sphinx with horns, and the fish, all of which are featured prominently in the exhibition. The most prevalent motif in the decoration of the artifacts from Berel is the image of a griffin—as, for example, the type with outstretched wings from a set of horse trappings from kurgan 11 (fig. 2-18). The main morphological components are the beak and wings of a bird of prey, while the representation of the body as that of one or another animal changes, depending on the function of the object as well as on the mythical and ritual context. The image of a griffin in the mythology and art of Central Asian nomads probably took shape around the seventh to sixth centuries BCE. The peak of its development—that is, the period when multiple variations of its interpretation coexisted—dates to the fourth and third centuries BCE, based on data provided by both elite and ordinary kurgans from Pazyryk, Berel, and other sites in the Altai. Among the objects from Berel, one image of a griffin is distinctive in its form and placement. As the crowning element of a standard, the image serves as a symbol of power and as a sacral, even magical, device; it is the only truly three-dimensional representation of a griffin from this site, with curling horns made from leather (the leather wings are not preserved; fig. 2-19). Various animal elements were combined with bird elements to form griffins at Berel, and these images made of parts of powerful animals must have had significance to the population, although their meanings are lost to us. A specific variation, the "elk-griffin," is the most prominent motif in the decoration of the horse harness from kurgan 36 (see page 30). Here the syncretism is reinforced by introduction of the additional element of an elk's antlers. All these elements are partly colored red and selectively covered with tin- and gold-leaf overlay.

Another fantastic creature regularly met in the decoration of burial goods from Berel is the sphinx—a syncretic zoo-anthropomorphic creature with the body of a predator and a human head (figs. 2-20–2-21). One example is composed of two animal bodies joined as one, from which emerges a single, shared neck and a single head (fig. 2-20). Several individual figurines with the bodies turned either to the right or to the left allow us to assume that they were arranged in a linear fashion with a central focus.

Especially interesting are sphinxes on the appliqués decorating the felt covers of a saddle from kurgan 10—they remind us that our simple formula of a sphinx is not entirely adequate, at least in some cases. These images consist of the head of a bearded anthropomorphic figure in profile, but with the crescent-shaped horns and the ears of a mountain goat (figs.2-22a–b). The dual nature of this being is emphasized by the fact that the back part of its body is colored red, while the front is blue. This color juxtaposition is probably not coincidental. It can be assumed that the front part of the body, marked by a sky-blue color and the presence of elements associated with the sky and high altitude—a wing and a horn—symbolizes the most important, sacral sphere of beliefs, while the back part of the body, colored red, refers to the earthly sphere.

Somewhat surprising is the popularity of representations of fish in the animal art of Early Iron Age nomads throughout the Eurasian steppes. Naturally, the realm of water and its inhabitants evoked in the minds of ancient people various associations and mythological beliefs, which were then reflected in their religion and decorative arts. A saddle pendant in the shape of a fish with three pairs of fins on each side, made out of several pieces of very thin felt attached by neat stitches, was found in kurgan 11. If a horse could be transformed into a fantastic bird that was meant to deliver the soul of the deceased to the other world, then possibly a fish was thought to be able to help overcome obstacles created by water along the way, especially in view of the fact that rivers, particularly in mountain regions, were perceived in mythological consciousness as connecting routes among different spheres of the universe.

Overall, the spectacular objects of decorative art from kurgan 11, associated with a complex system of burial customs and funerary rites, demonstrate a high level of craftsmanship among ancient carvers and artists. They also reflect the mythical and poetic consciousness, religious views, and system of beliefs of ancient nomads of the Altai region of Kazakhstan.

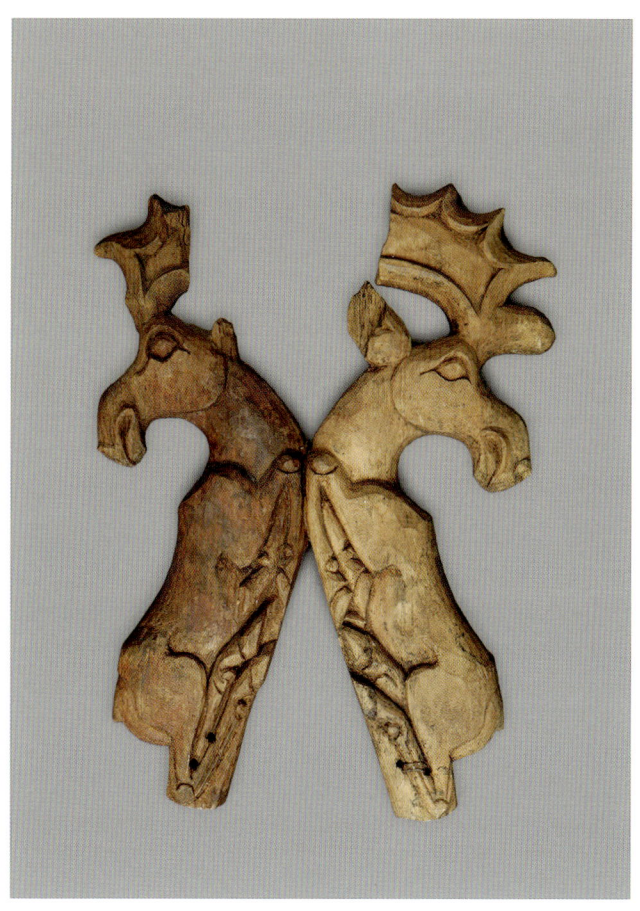

2-7 Bridle cheekpiece in the form of two elk from Berel, kurgan 11, late 4th–early 3rd century. Presidential Center of Culture, Astana.

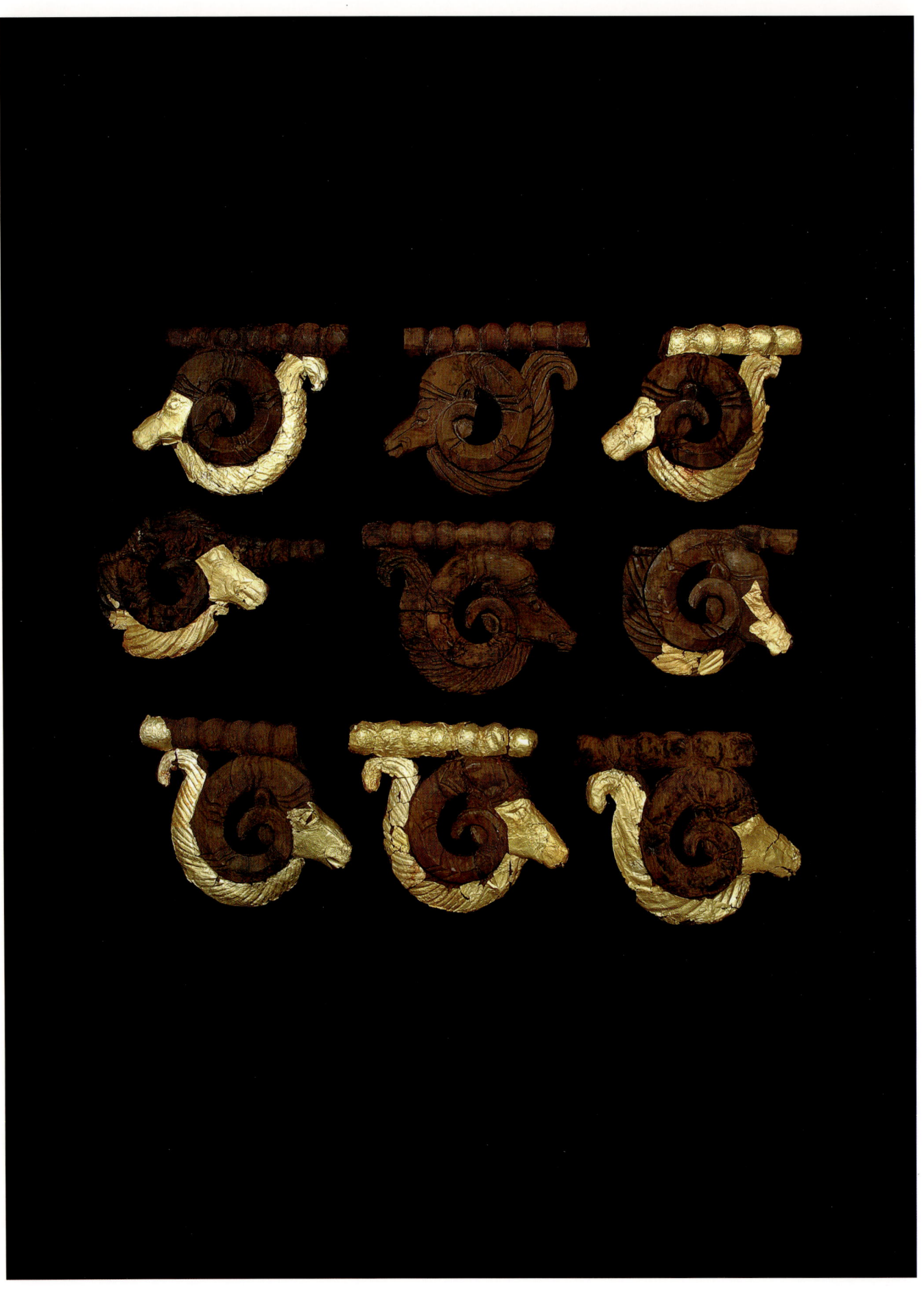

2-8   Plaques of argali heads suspended from ribbed bars, some covered in gold foil, from horse tack. Berel, kurgan 11, late 4th–early 3rd century BCE. Presidential Center of Culture, Astana. (See also checklist nos. 50–53.)

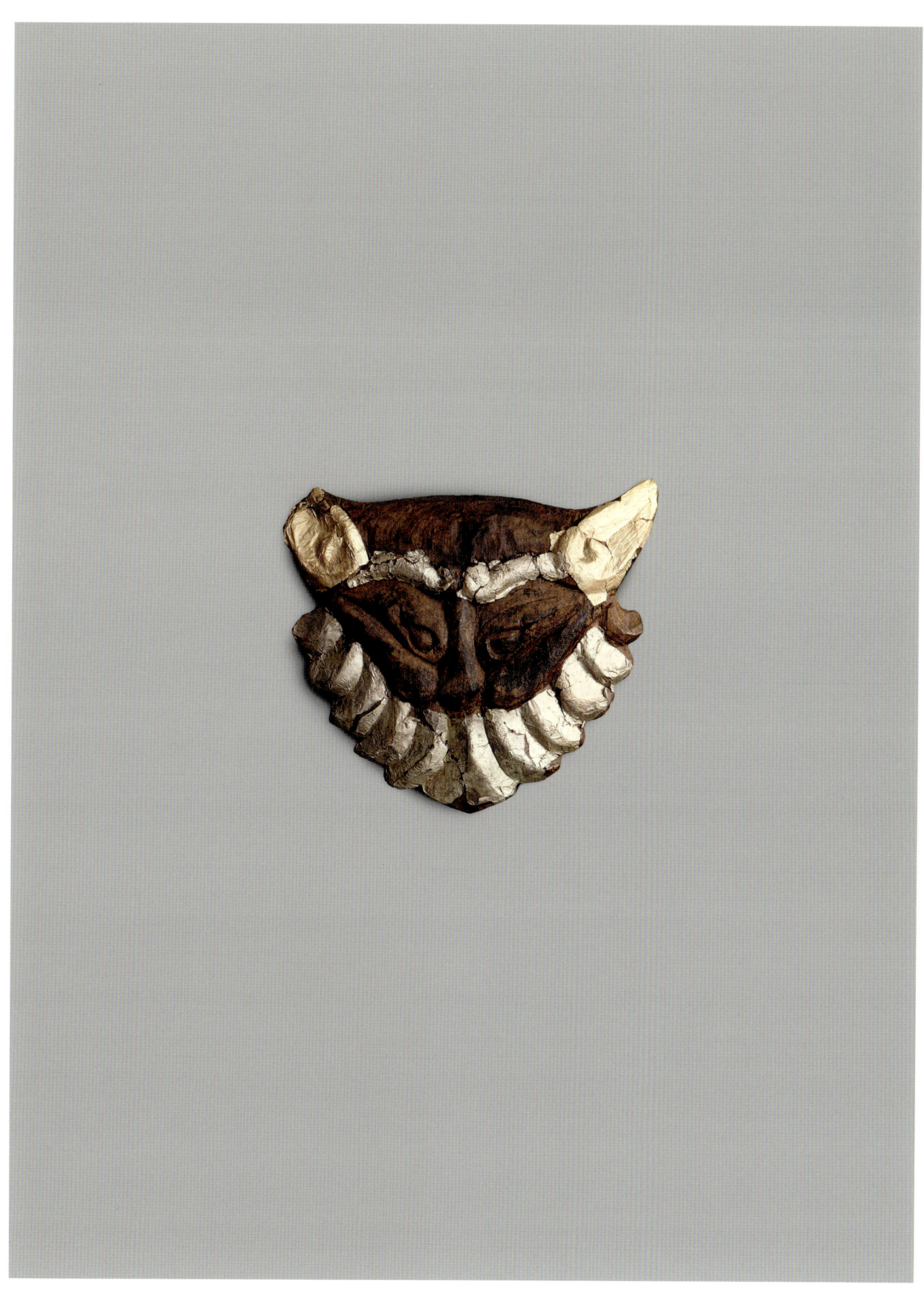

2-9   Feline face from horse tack. Wood and gold, Berel, kurgan 11, late 4th–early 3rd century BCE. Presidential Center of Culture, Astana: 4953. Checklist no. 46.

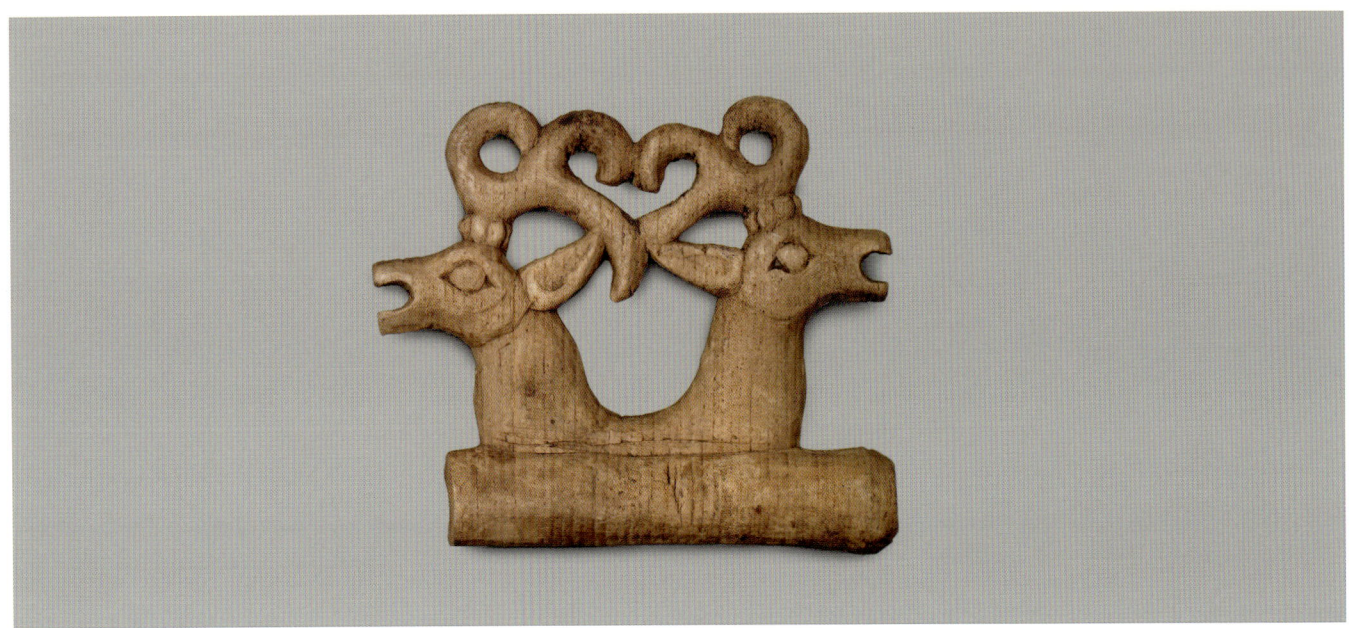

WOOD AND HORN CARVING

The kurgans of Berel, Pazyryk, and other sites in the Altai, preserved by permafrost, reveal to us a truly remarkable wealth of artistic traditions in wood and horn carving, otherwise almost completely unknown. While the wood-carving tradition has long been discussed, finds from Berel kurgan 36 notably further our understanding of techniques of horn carving (see page 30 and figs. 2-23–2-25).[4]

OBSERVATIONS ON ECONOMIC LIFE IN THE ALTAI IN THE LATER FIRST MILLENNIUM BCE

The climate and natural resources of the Altai provided a favorable environment, most importantly for the development of horse breeding as the main branch of animal husbandry among the people at Berel, prompted by the availability of pastures on a year-round basis. The kurgans of Berel yielded skeletal remains of over eighty horses. All the animals buried together with humans in the kurgans were stallions, following the ritual norm.

Short cool summers and an abundance of snow in the intermountain valleys in winter did not provide ideal conditions for sheep breeding, but judging by finds from the burials, enough sheep and goats were raised to produce plentiful meat and wool. The main component of the economic life of the people at Berel was extensive animal husbandry, with a clear dominance of horse breeding, as predetermined by specifics of the regional ecosystem. Animal husbandry was based on vertical seasonal migrations from winter pastures at lower altitudes of the mountain valleys to rather limited summer pastures high in the mountains. Thus, economic life and the natural ecosystem were tightly linked in this region.

While the image of the "pure" nomad is still persistent, it is somewhat misleading. This becomes clear when we take a closer look at Iron Age pastoralists in the Altai. Alongside their engagement in hunting, which supplied additional meat and fur and was a significant economic factor, there is evidence for the existence of semipermanent settlements. The development of seasonal settlements as well as elements of a more "sedentary" lifestyle—primarily in the harsh winter

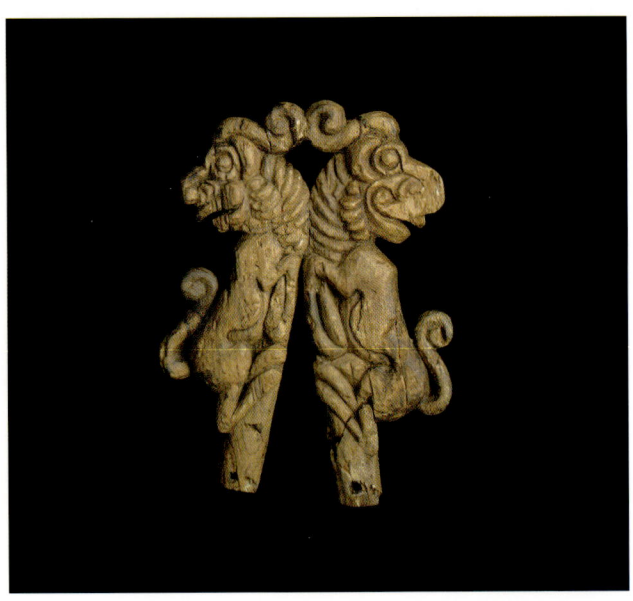

2-10 Plaque from horse tack of addorsed deer heads. Wood, Berel, kurgan 11, late 4th–early 3rd century BCE. Presidential Center of Culture, Astana: 8283. Checklist no. 57.

2-11 Bridle cheekpiece in the form of horned tigers from Berel, kurgan 11, late 4th–early 3rd century BCE. Presidential Center of Culture, Astana.

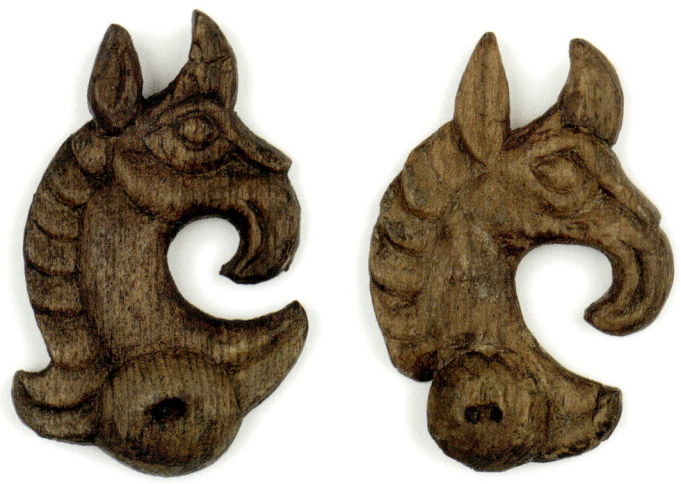

2-12 Plaques from horse tack of griffin heads. Wood, Berel, kurgan 11, late 4th–early 3rd century BCE. Presidential Center of Culture, Astana: 5576, 4961. Checklist no 60.

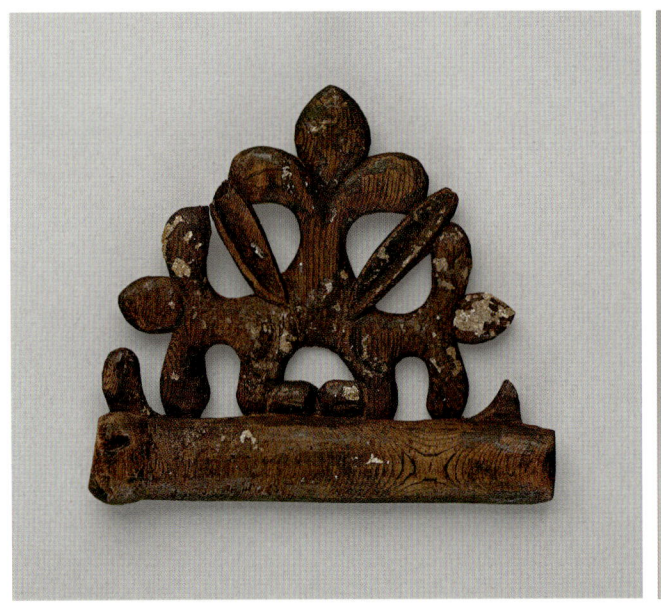
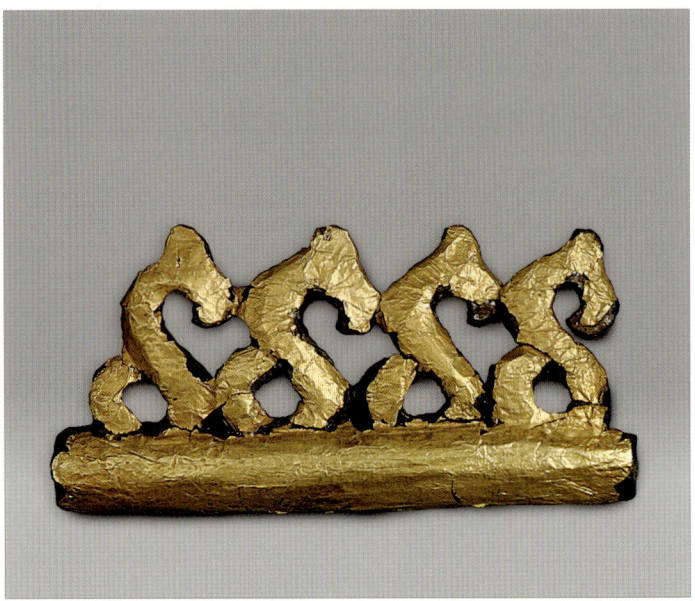
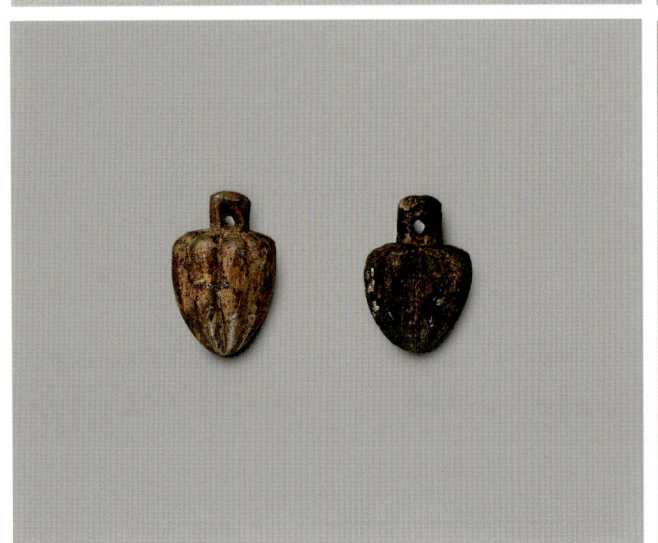
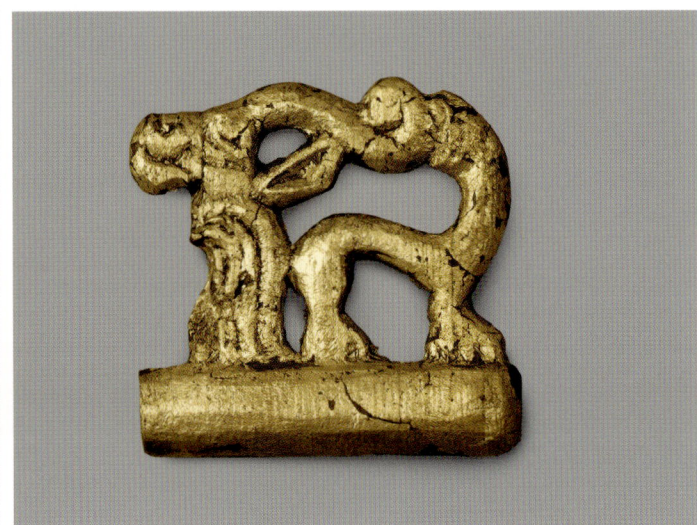

2-13 (top left) Plaque with vegetal and zoomorphic design from horse tack. Wood and tin foil, Berel, kurgan 11, late 4th–early 3rd century BCE. Presidential Center of Culture, Astana: 8802. Checklist no. 66.

2-14 (top right) Plaque with S-shaped ornament from horse tack. Wood and gold foil, Berel, kurgan 11, late 4th–early 3rd century BCE. Presidential Center of Culture, Astana: 4446. Checklist no. 69.

2-15 (bottom left) Ornaments from horse tack. Wood, Berel, kurgan 11, late 4th–early 3rd century BCE. Presidential Center of Culture, Astana: 6222, 6223. Checklist no. 72.

2-16 (bottom right) Plaque of feline attacking horned animal head from horse tack. Wood and gold foil, Berel, kurgan 11, late 4th–early 3rd century BCE. Presidential Center of Culture, Astana: 4932. Checklist no. 56.

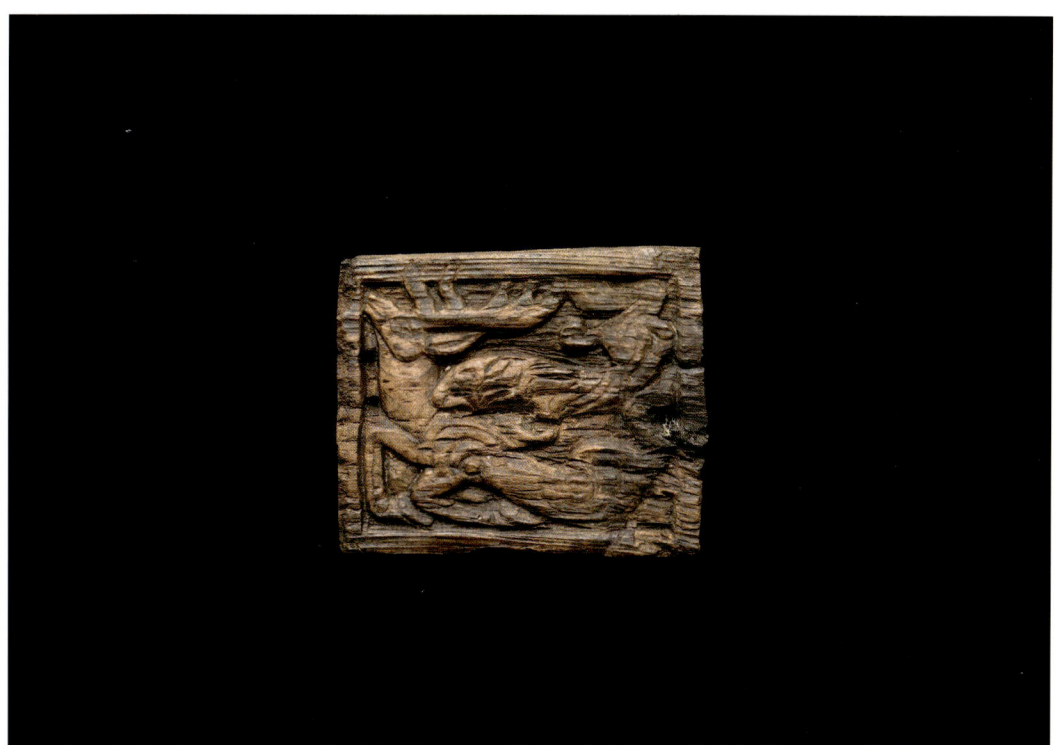

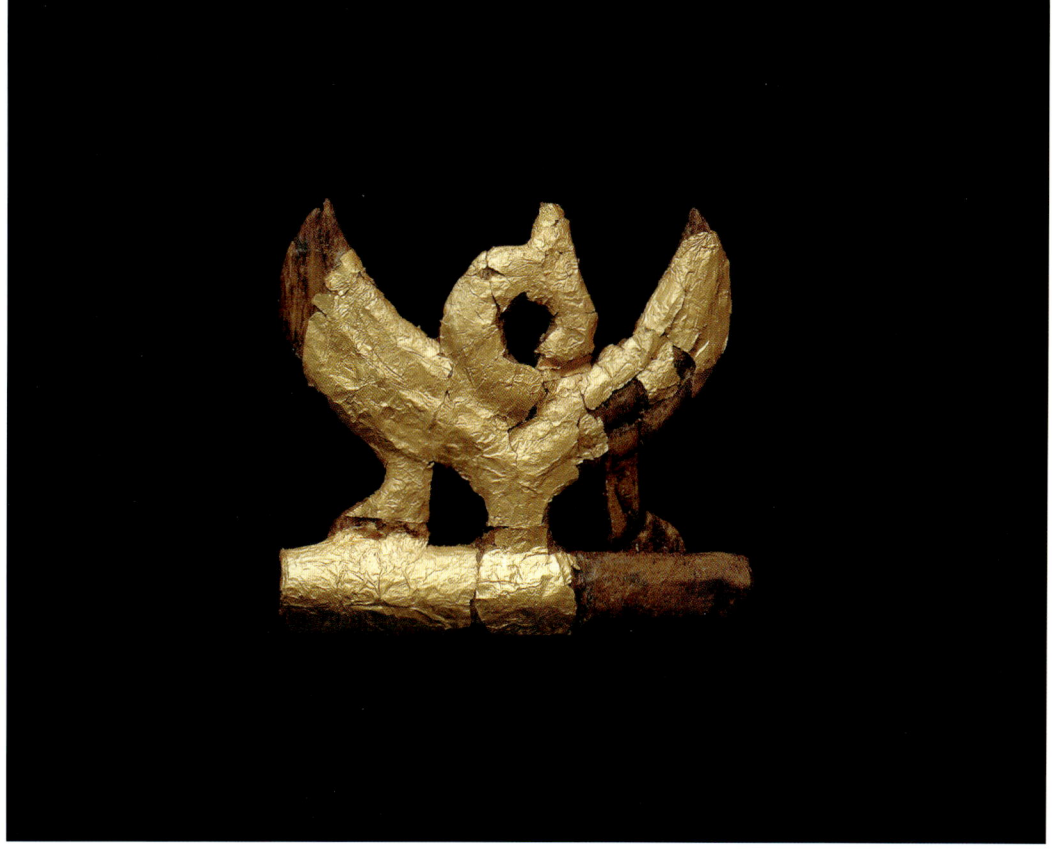

2-17 Plaque depicting tiger attacking an elk. Wood, Berel, kurgan 11, late 4th–early 3rd century BCE. Presidential Center of Culture, Astana: 4958. Checklist no. 70.

2-18 Plaque from horse tack of griffin with outstretched wings from Berel, kurgan 11, late 4th–early 3rd century BCE. Presidential Center of Culture, Astana. (See also checklist nos. 62–65.)

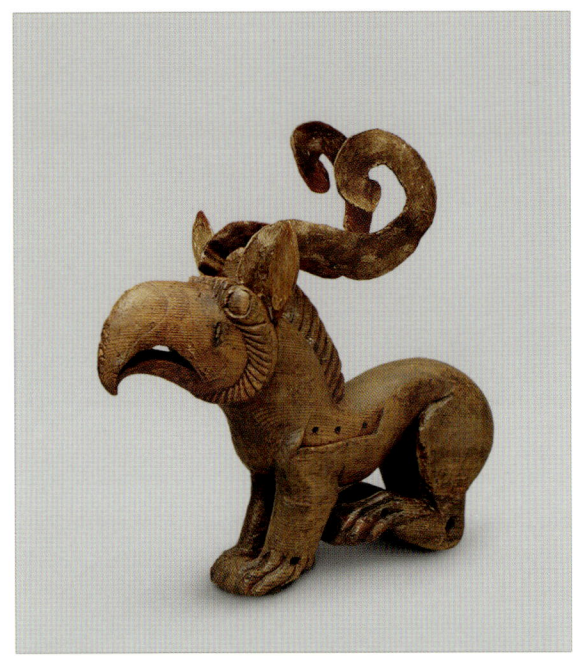

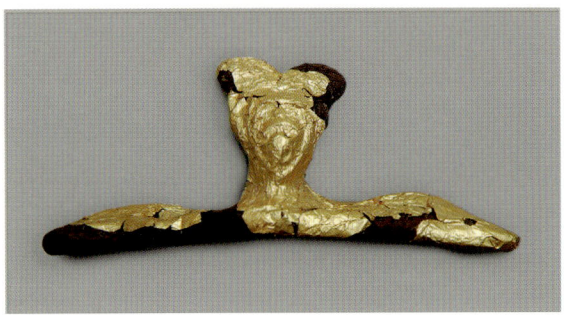

season—was favored by this specific type of vertically oriented, seasonal mobile pastoralism. Judging from tools found in these settlements, the inhabitants practiced a wide range of supplementary economic activities, such as textile industries, leather processing, bone and horn carving, and small-scale ceramic production. Of course, wool working and weaving, as well as the manufacture of felt items, were traditional occupations for the nomads. Analysis of the hair used in felt found at Berel, in particular from kurgan 11, confirmed that it was from sheep and goat. As no pigments were found in the composition of the hair, it can be concluded that most of the animals were white.

Judging from the presence of locally produced ceramic vessels among the funerary goods, the Berel kurgans also testify to some degree of local ceramic production among Iron Age nomads in the Altai. To date, however, no archaeological data from the foothills of the Altai region support the existence of complementary forms of agriculture among pastoral communities during the Iron Age in the Altai.[5]

Such semipermanent settlements might also have been the focal point for mining and metallurgy. Rich mineral resources of the region prompted the development of local metallurgy as early as the Bronze Age. The foothill zone of eastern Kazakhstan has well-known ore belts, including the Kalba-Narym gold-bearing zone, the iron-ore deposits in the lower reaches of the Bukhtarma River, a polymetallic belt that stretches from northwest to southeast across the region, and others.

The mining of gold, iron, tin, and copper ores and their transportation and processing require the mobilization of significant human resources from the population of the region, a high level of organization of labor, advanced technological processes, and last but not least the ability to defend mining and processing centers from potential outside attacks. Mining, metallurgy, and metalworking probably required the formation of a particular stratum in the population that possessed the necessary skills and knowledge, as well as the existence of sites with kilns, workshops, and other facilities for the production and storage of finished products. Therefore, it has been assumed that a specialized population of metalworkers existed in the Pazyryk society. Nevertheless, the activities of miners and metallurgists might have been to some degree integrated in the pastoral economic circle—for example, poor members of the nomadic community could be hired seasonally for mining work. To date, however, there is no direct archaeological evidence in the form of specialized settlement kilns and so forth from the Kazakh Altai.

The differentiated structure of Pazyryk society might be better characterized, in terms of the life of the entire community, by relations between the rich animal breeders, the poor ones, and the part of the social group engaged in work outside animal husbandry. The less-mobile part of the population probably included metalworkers, jewelers, potters, and textile makers.[6] The nomads of this region, similarly to other steppe nomads, undoubtedly had solid economic relations and contacts, both inside the nomadic world and with inhabitants of the adjacent territories, as well as with settlements and agricultural centers and with more distant ethnocultural zones.[7]

2-19 Griffin standard from Berel, kurgan 11, late 4th–early 3rd century BCE. Presidential Center of Culture, Astana.

2-20 Reclining double-bodied sphinx from Berel, kurgan 11, late 4th–early 3rd century BCE. Presidential Center of Culture, Astana.

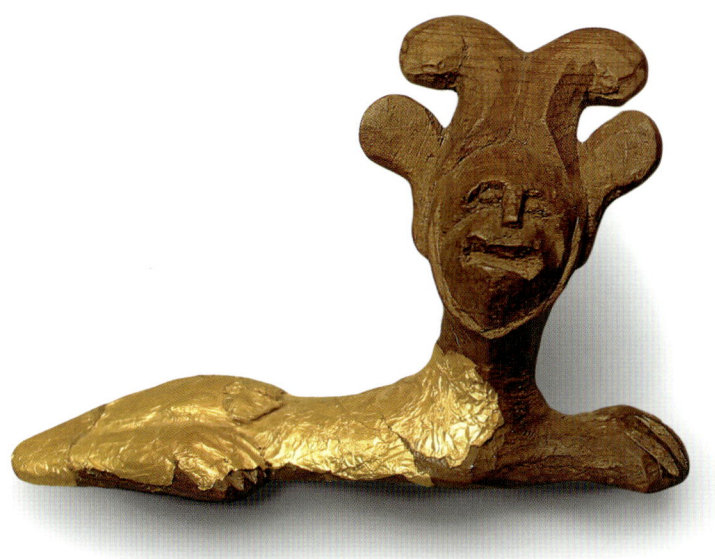

2-21 Horned sphinx from coffin shroud. Wood and gold foil, Berel, kurgan 11, late 4th–early 3rd century BCE. Presidential Center of Culture, Astana: 6212. Checklist no. 82.

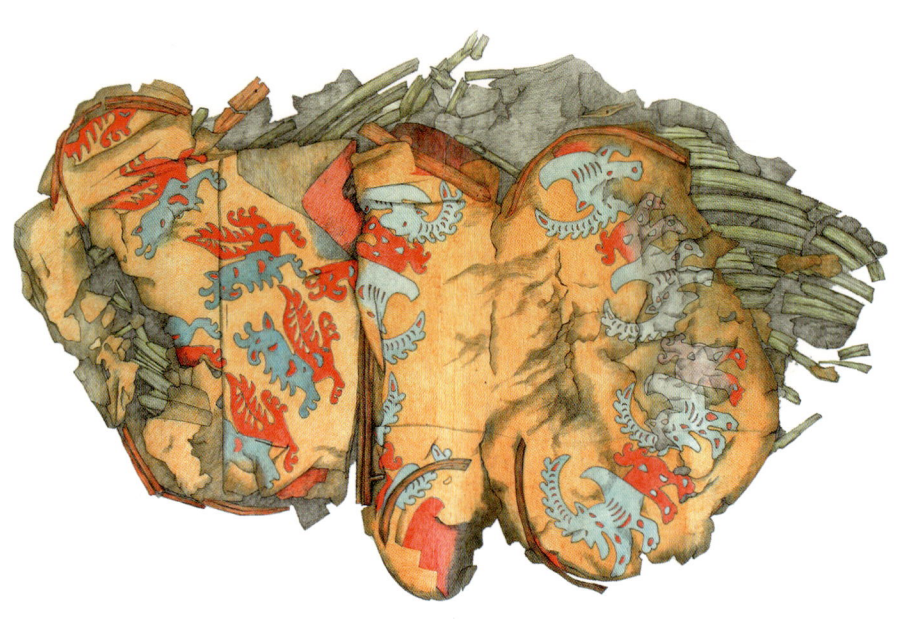
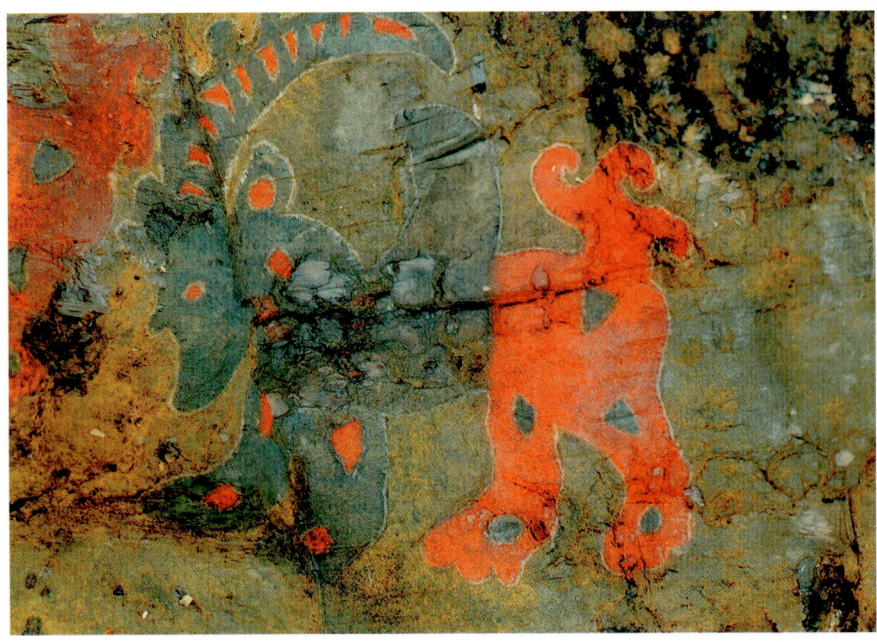

2-22a–b   Drawing and color-enhanced photograph of felt and wood saddle decorated with sphinxes from Berel, kurgan 10.

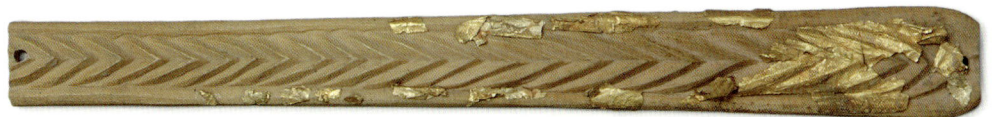

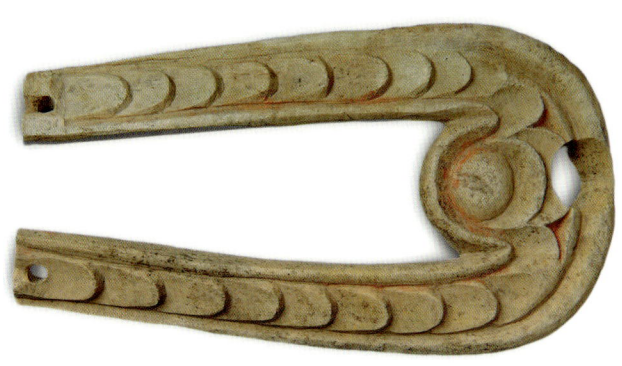

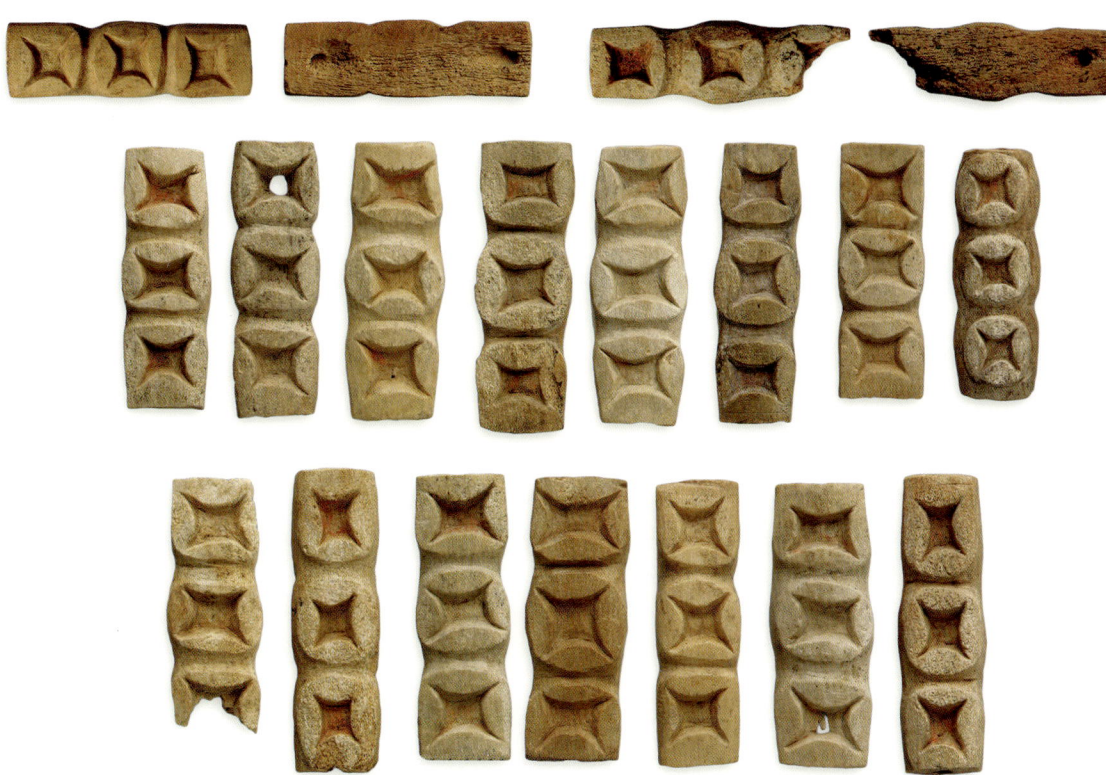

2-23 (top) Bar with chevron pattern from bridle faceplate. Horn (Siberian red deer) and gold foil, Berel, kurgan 36, late 4th–early 3rd century BCE. A. Kh. Margulan Institute of Archaeology, Almaty: B36-63. Checklist no. 19.

2-24 (center) U-shaped element with scale pattern from bridle throat latch. Horn (Siberian red deer) and gold foil, Berel, kurgan 36, late 4th–early 3rd century BCE. A. Kh. Margulan Institute of Archaeology, Almaty: B36-66. Checklist no. 22.

2-25 (bottom) Group of bars with cutout and painted ornament from horse tack. Horn (Siberian red deer), Berel, kurgan 36, late 4th–early 3rd century BCE. A. Kh. Margulan Institute of Archaeology, Almaty. (See also checklist no. 40.)

THE SOCIAL STRUCTURE OF THE PEOPLE OF ANCIENT BEREL

Finds from the Berel kurgans provide clear evidence that the ancient nomads in the region, who were part of the historical and cultural population group referred to as the Pazyryk culture, formed a heterogeneous society with very strong social differentiation based on property. This is clearly reflected in their burial complexes.

Two kurgans in the necropolis—kurgans 1 and 11—stand out among the monuments in the Altai area in terms of their large size, the richness of their contents, and the great numbers of horses accompanying the burials. These two kurgans therefore might well belong to chieftains of some supraregional power, while the other kurgans might belong to members of their clan.

As has been rightly pointed out by B. Genito, it is extremely difficult—based solely on archaeological data—to understand the complex nature of social and political relationships among nomads and to distinguish between tribal chieftainships and nomadic statehood.[8] But it has also been reasonably suggested that several distinct political centers must have existed across the entire area of the Altai, including Mongolia and Northwestern China, with Berel representing one of these centers.[9] At present, however, it is difficult to confirm the kind of polity these groups actually represented: confederate state formations with one political and administrative center; or separate autonomous (tribal) entities not well connected with each other but similar in terms of their culture, system of beliefs, lifestyle, and economic organization.

At this stage of the investigations, no firm conclusions can be made about the composition of Berel society in terms of the age and sex of its members. No burials of children have been found, and only a few female ones. The status of women, as seen in double burials in the elite kurgans 8, 9, 11, and others, appears to have been very high, judging by the burial context and the remains of grave goods. No single burials with a female deceased have been found at Berel, in contrast to other areas of the Pazyryk culture.[10] In the neighboring necropolis of Tarasu, where ordinary free members of the society were buried, only in one niche-grave has a female been discovered, a woman of twenty to twenty-five years of age.

CONCLUSION

Materials from the Berel kurgans investigated from 1998 to 2011[11] provide a remarkable wealth of new data regarding the social organization, economy, and worldview of those pastoral nomadic tribes who lived in the Altai during the fourth and early third centuries BCE.

The unique finds from the Berel kurgans demonstrate that, during the period in question, the population of the Altai region of Kazakhstan had a highly developed culture and art, as well as a complex system of beliefs. These finds also show that the culture of Early Iron Age nomads in eastern Kazakhstan developed a whole set of cultural features (mobile pastoralism, mounted warfare[12]) that remained essential for many centuries to come, and had considerable impact on the formation of the cultural complexes of many other peoples of Central Asia during the Middle Ages and subsequent periods. The visual art of Iron Age nomads provided a number of prototypes for the visual and decorative art of modern Turkic peoples, including the Kazakhs.

Translated by Valeriya Kozlovskaya

NOTES

1. Gorbunov, Samashev, and Severskii 2005, 13–29.
2. Samples from kurgans 11 and 18 were submitted for analysis to the laboratory of the Institute for the History of Material Culture at the Russian Academy of Science in St. Petersburg and to laboratories in Kiev and Berlin.
3. In a recent comprehensive study on scientific dating in the Eurasian steppes, the year 322 BCE is advocated as the absolute date for kurgan 11, Алексеев и др. 2005.
4. Бородовский 2005, 59. See details in Appendix A this volume.
5. See Chang this volume.
6. For a parallel situation in the Semirechye, see ibid.
7. See Stark this volume.
8. Genito 1994, 11–14.
9. Anufriev 1997, 110.
10. Linduff and Rubinson forthcoming.
11. Самашев, Фаизов и Базарбаева 2001; Самашев, Скрипникова и Верба 2001; Самашев и Мыльников 2004; Кашкинбаев и Самашев 2005; Кашкинбаев 2000b; Самашев и Косинцев 2004; Самашев и Бородовский 2004.
12. See Hanks this volume.

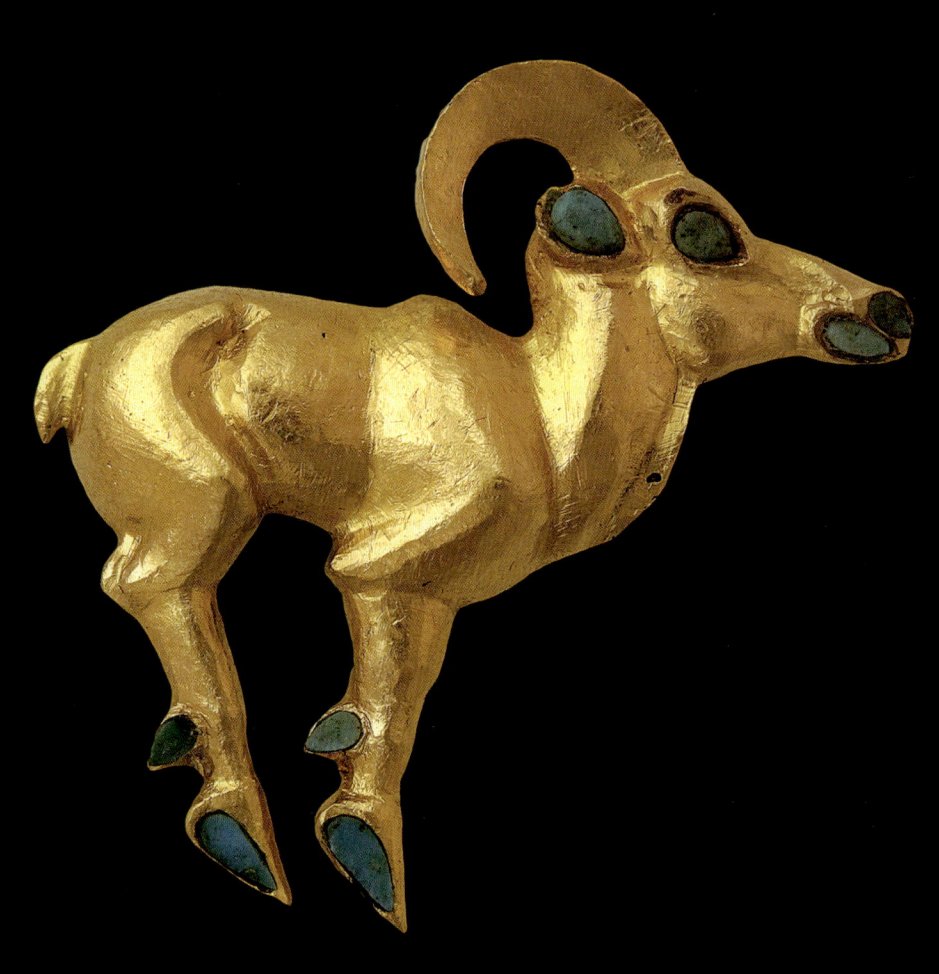

RESULTS OF MULTI-DISCIPLINARY STUDIES AND RECONSTRUCTIONS OF MATERIALS FROM THE BAIGETOBE KURGAN AT SHILIKTY

Abdesh T. Toleubaev

INTRODUCTION

Shilikty is located in a valley of the same name in the Zaisan area of the eastern Kazakh region (see map on pages 12–13). The valley, stretching to 80 kilometers in length and 30 kilometers in width, is surrounded on three sides by mountains: in the south and west by the main mountain range of Tarbagatai, in the east and north by its spurs, Sauyr and Manyrak. The valley is blessed by a mild climate: summers are cool, winters are warm and without snow. As a result, starting in the Bronze Age this area was densely populated by cattle breeders and early farming tribes. The site of Shilikty was first studied in the 1950s and 1960s by S. S. Chernikov. Altogether he excavated thirteen kurgans.[1]

Plaque of standing argali. Gold and turquoise, Shilikty 3, kurgan 82, 8th–7th century BCE. Central State Museum, Almaty: KP 26860. Checklist no. 166.

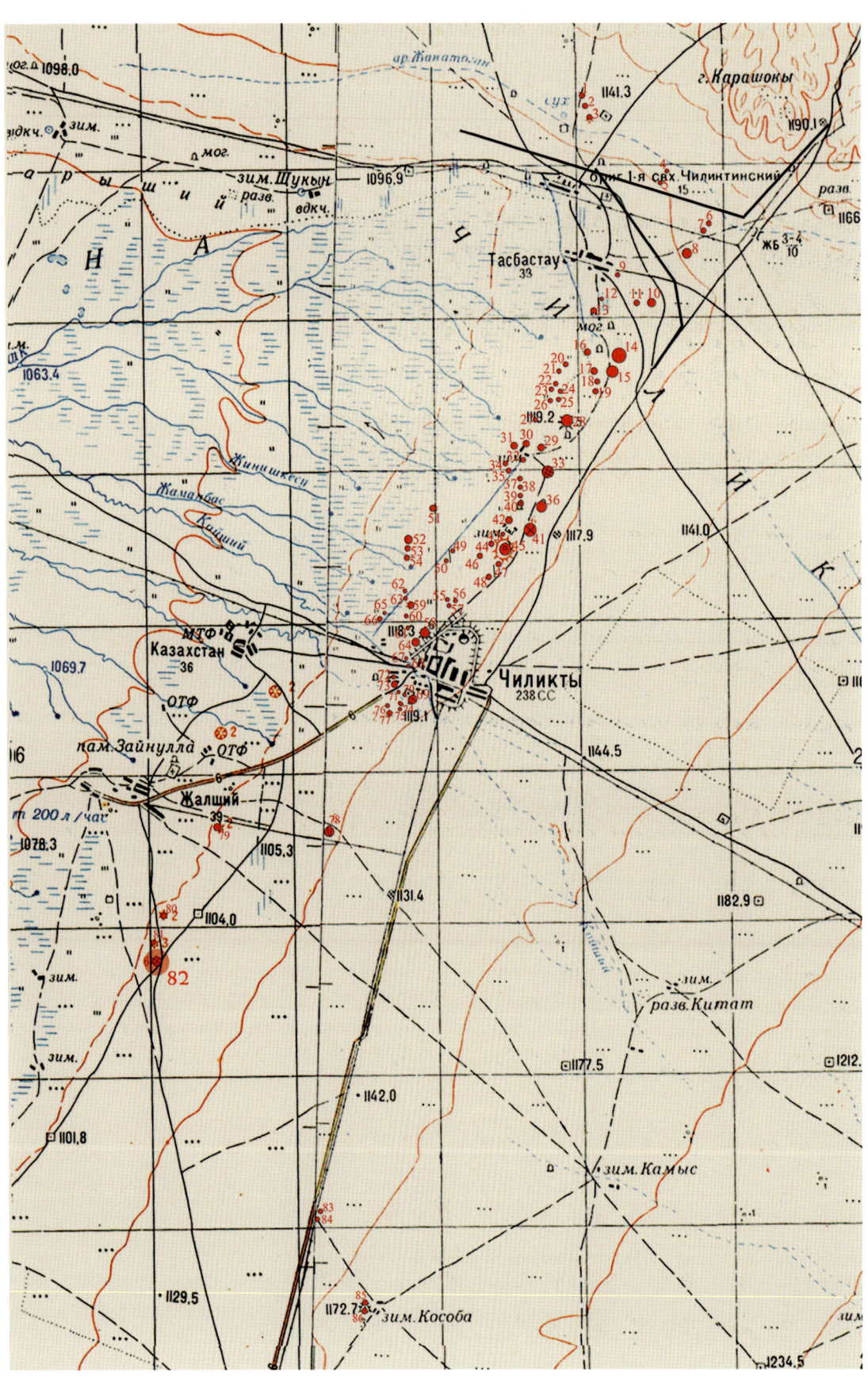

3-1   Map of Shilikty showing locations of kurgans, including kurgan 82 (Baigetobe).

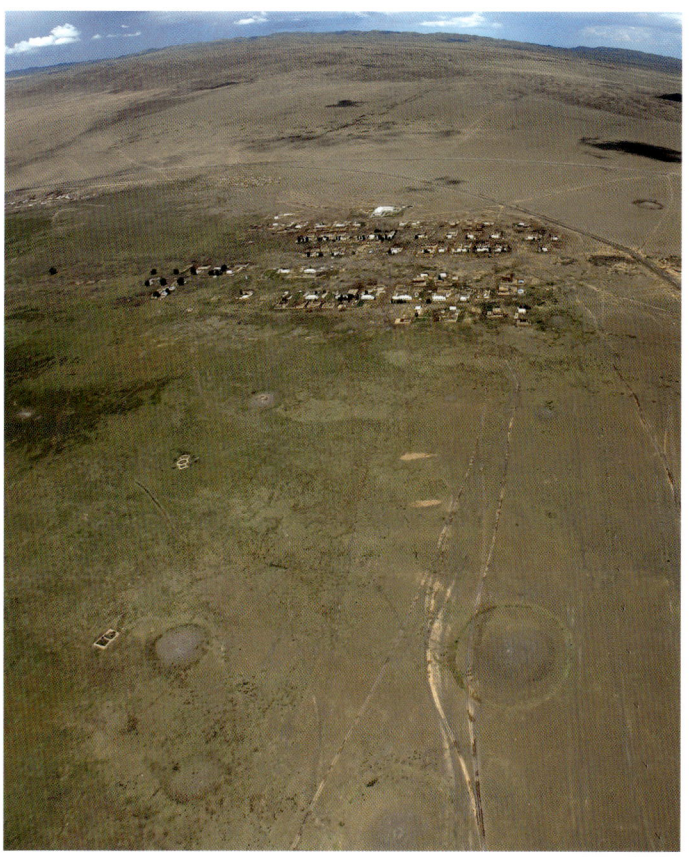

Investigations were resumed in 2003 by an expedition organized by Al-Farabi Kazakh National University in Almaty, headed by myself. During eight archaeological seasons, this group excavated and studied three large and more than fifteen small kurgans, and also surveyed and recorded sites in the Shilikty valley and its surroundings.[2] These investigations led to the discovery of hundreds of new sites in the valley and the surrounding foothills, among them settlements and burials of the Bronze and Iron ages as well as petroglyphs. More than 200 of these sites date to the Early Iron Age, approximately 120 of them being kurgans stretching over a territory of 6 kilometers.

THE ELITE BURIAL IN THE BAIGETOBE KURGAN AT SHILIKTY 3 (KURGAN 82)

The most spectacular material has been excavated in a kurgan called Baigetobe ("racing hill") by the local population, and which is part of the Shilikty 3 burial ground (fig. 3-1).

The Baigetobe kurgan 82 forms the beginning of a row of seven large kurgans (fig. 3-2). Structurally, the kurgan contains three elements (figs. 3-3a–b). The first level consists of a wooden burial chamber, built on the level of the ancient ground surface (fig. 3-4). The walls of the chamber are composed of overlapping logs arranged in two rows, with the open space between logs originally filled with stones (fig. 3-5). The chamber was covered with one layer of tightly fitted logs. The floor of the burial chamber has an area of approximately 20 square meters, and the height of the chamber is 3.7 meters. The second element of the kurgan consisted of a round stone mound (or perhaps a platform) built above the wood burial chamber (fig. 3-6). The mound was about 20 meters in diameter and 4.9 meters in height. At its center, an opening made by looters was clearly traceable.

The third element consisted of an earth mound over the burial chamber and stone mound. The preserved height of the outer mound was 7.9 meters, and the modern diameter of the kurgan, with a weathered surface, was approximately 90 meters (fig. 3-7).

In sum, the Baigetobe kurgan from the Shilikty 3 burial ground constitutes a complicated and grandiose architectural structure clearly pointing to the elite status of the person buried there.

DATING OF THE KURGAN

One of the central questions evolving from these observations is that of the dating of this extraordinary burial monument. Fortunately, the survival of logs in the burial chamber allowed for a dendrochronological study.[3] The results suggest a date of 810–750 BCE, making this kurgan one of the earliest known Iron Age kurgans so far discovered across the Eurasian steppe.[4]

THE ANTHROPOLOGICAL RECORD

As the burial was disturbed by looters, skeletal remains of the deceased were found thoughout the earth fill. However, a nearly complete skeleton could be reconstructed.[5] The results of study showed that all the bones found in the burial belonged to one person, a male of about thirty-five to forty years of age. The height of the buried person can be calculated at 178–80 centimeters.

The skull, the lower jaw, and most of the teeth were preserved. The brain case is rather high and somewhat long and narrow. Its facial features point to an individual belonging to a Caucasoid anthropological type with a slight Mongoloid admixture, thus corresponding with anthropological data from other Early Iron Age burials in Kazakhstan and Southern Siberia.

3-2   Aerial view of Shilikty 3 burial ground.

CONSTRUCTION STAGES OF THE KURGAN

I.

1 Alluvial I Layer
2 Pebble Layer
3 V Tier
4 IV Tier
5 III Tier
6 II Tier
7 I Tier

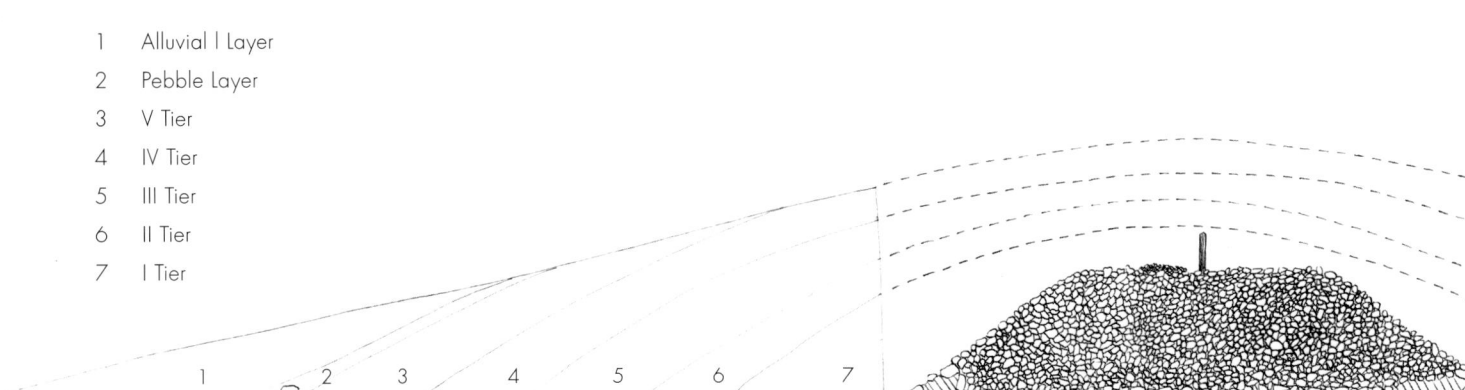

PROFILES OF THE STONE CONSTRUCTION

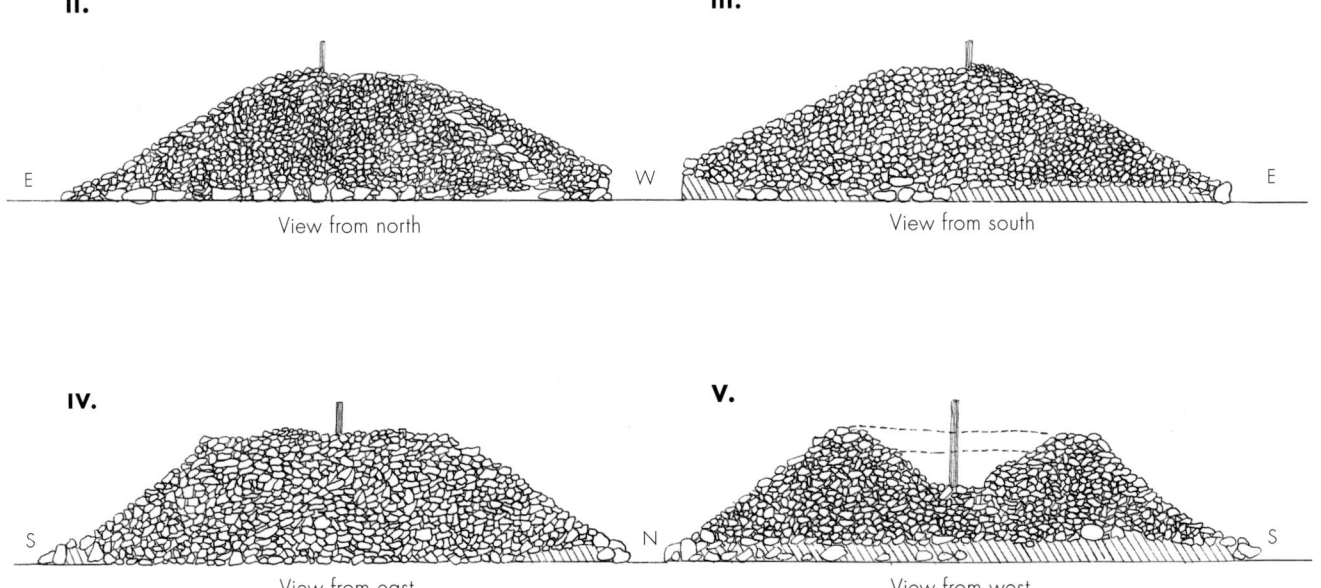

II. View from north

III. View from south

IV. View from east

V. View from west

3-3a–b   (top) Section through kurgan 82 showing stages of construction. (bottom) Views of stone construction.

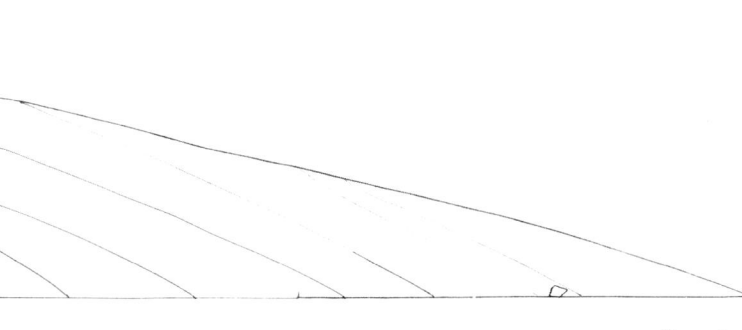

0 — 1m

An interesting detail is revealed by the fact that the bones of the hands and legs of the left side were slightly larger, indicating that the person was left-handed. Overall the osteological data point to good physical development, not only in terms of the bone structure but also in terms of the correspondingly high state of musculature development.

There were no major pathologies found in the bones of the skeleton. There was evidence of only moderate changes in the lower back, the lumbar, and the lower thoracic vertebrae, in the shape of small hollows and growths and a small deformation of the coccyx. In this case, such changes probably do not indicate disease or aging and are more likely related to increased stress put on this area of the body, suggesting a long-term sedentary position but one with high activity in the lower limbs in the area of the hips, most closely corresponding to horse riding as the significant activity of the deceased.

The premature fusion of the skull bones can be attributed to genetic factors as well as to individual peculiarities of mineral exchange (calcium, phosphorus, and others) in the organism, pointing to a diet predominantly consisting of meat and milk products as opposed to vegetal food.

The perfect condition of the bones, teeth, and teeth enamel, the absence of any noticeable pathology or developmental problems, and the absence of signs of sickness, trauma, and wounds indicate that the individual enjoyed health, a comfortable life, and a good diet.

INVENTORY OF THE BURIAL

As is the case for most of the other monumental kurgans, this burial was looted in antiquity. The looters dug a shaft in the middle of the kurgan to the depth of 4 meters and then, having broken through the wooden chamber, entered the burial chamber. Consequently, the inner part of the burial was completely filled with earth, which entered through the opening left by the looters. Despite the partial looting, the kurgan still contained a large number of objects. In addition, careful observations during excavation and thorough scientific analysis in the laboratory yielded further data regarding the original burial inventory,[6] including the presence of horse bones, textile fragments and pigments (see below), and ceramic fragments.

The following discussion concerns the three principal categories of objects found in the burial: toreutics, painting on wood, and textiles.

TOREUTICS

Altogether, 4,303 gold objects were found inside the Baigetobe kurgan of the Shilikty 3 burial.[7] Particularly interesting (apart from the sheer number) is that these gold objects were cast, in contrast to most other gold decorations of the Early Iron Age steppes. The objects provide invaluable new data regarding manufacturing methods and reveal a high standard of metalworking among Central Asian pastoralists at a very early date.[8]

The main types of plaques from Shilikty are as follows:

Plaque of standing argali (see page 50). The largest of all plaques discovered, this object was cast from pure gold, with the eyes, ears, nostrils, mouth, and hooves of the animal defined by turquoise inlay. The reverse of the plaque has a sharp negative relief, corresponding to the positive relief on the outside of the object. The plaque has two loops on the reverse side for sewing it to clothing.

The muscles of the neck, withers, lower jaw, and croup are well defined in crisp profile. This specific stylistic feature can be observed in many steppe ornaments from the beginning of the Iron Age and shows the influence of wood carving. With its hooves lifted to the front, the animal is depicted in a pose that suggests it is expecting danger and ready to leap.

Although only one representation of an argali was preserved in Shilikty, the animals are often encountered in the visual art of Early Iron Age pastoralists in Central Asia and Southern Siberia.[9]

Round plaque of five-pointed star (fig. 3-8). A single example of this type was found, and it is a unique piece, depicting a five-pointed star on a circular ground made of shell.[10] Lapis lazuli inlays form the points of the star, the edges of which are outlined with thin gold strips, while the center has a round convex shell inlay. The edges and the back of the plaque are wrapped in gold leaf. There is a gold loop on the reverse side of the object.

"Snow leopard mask" plaques (fig. 3-9). These objects are openwork concave-convex cast plaques. The eyes, nose, mouth, and ears of the animals are inlayed with turquoise. Indentations for the inlays were indicated on the models by means of thick ledges and ridges, and casts were prepared for the inlays by mechanically opening or embossing the walls of the sockets. Most of the inlays have fallen out of the sockets, but their original presence is indicated by the remains of glue preserved in the sockets as white coating. In addition, there are plaques with false sockets, which were not finished for inlays. Loops constructed from bent gold strips are soldered to the reverse sides of these plaques.

These objects are especially fascinating because of their sophisticated and deliberate play with visual ambiguity, since the images can be read in three different ways: as the frontal mask of a feline animal, as two profile heads of mountain goats facing each other, and as a bird with outspread wings seen from above.

Raptor plaques (fig. 3-10). Produced by casting, these objects show a predatory bird with its head turned to the right, its eyes large and round. The beak is strongly curved, and the ridge above it is emphasized. The depiction of the body is highly stylized.[11]

Cub plaques (fig. 3-11). These were also produced by casting. There are two loops on the reverse of each plaque. The decoration represents the cub of an undefined predator; it is difficult to determine exactly what animal the ancient craftsman wished to depict. Some details, especially the shape of the head and mouth, point to a newborn wolf cub, but the shape of the body, legs, and tail remind one of a bear cub. The head of each animal is lowered to the level of its feet, and is huge in relationship to its body—together with the neck the head constitutes about one-third of the figure. The eyes are big and round, the large ears are oval, and the jaws are clenched. The muscles of the forelegs are strongly defined, the tail is short, and the feet—with prominent, strong claws—are large. A very close parallel for this image can be found in a petroglyph from the Karatau range in southern Kazakhstan, discussed by Myrgabayev in this volume.

Deer plaques (fig. 3-12). These decorations are cast as well, and the eyes, mouth, nose, and ears of each animal are inlayed with turquoise. Each plaque depicts two deer, with the two heads looking away from each other and joined at the base of the neck. The necks and heads form the base of the plaque. The head of each deer looks slightly upward, with the result that both sets of antlers touch to form a single, fused composition. In the area where the necks of the deer touch, there is an oval depression with a pointed top, inlayed with turquoise. Each plaque has three loops on the back.

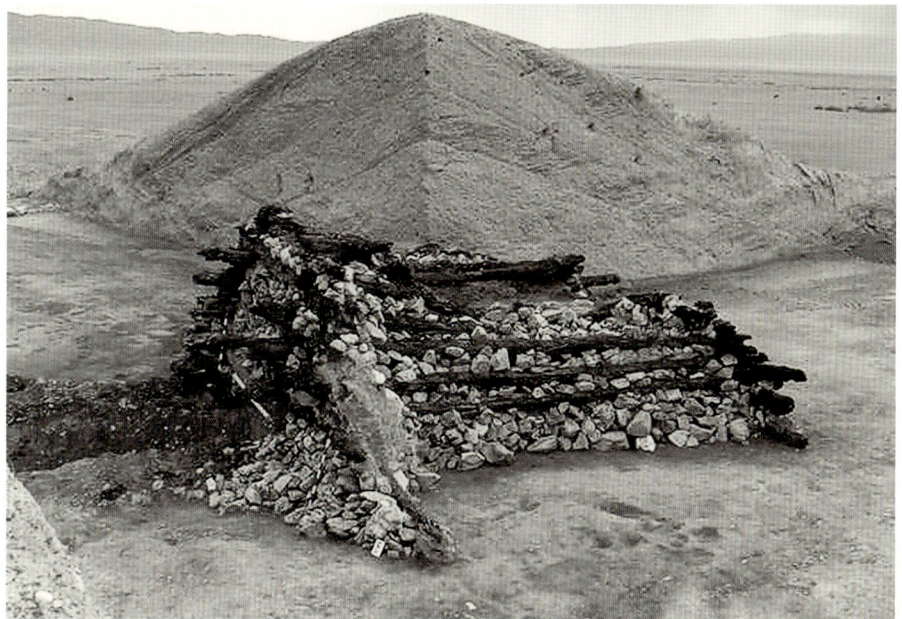
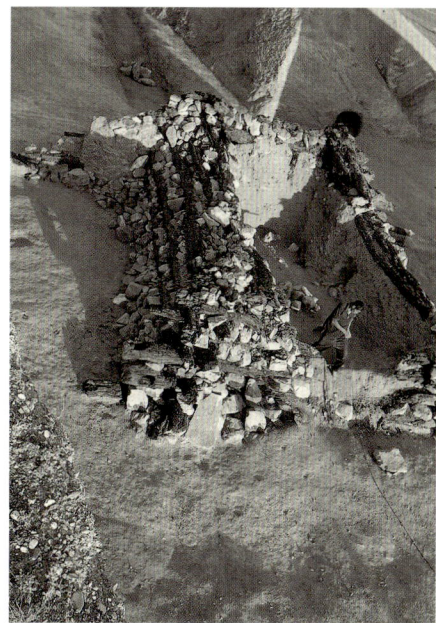
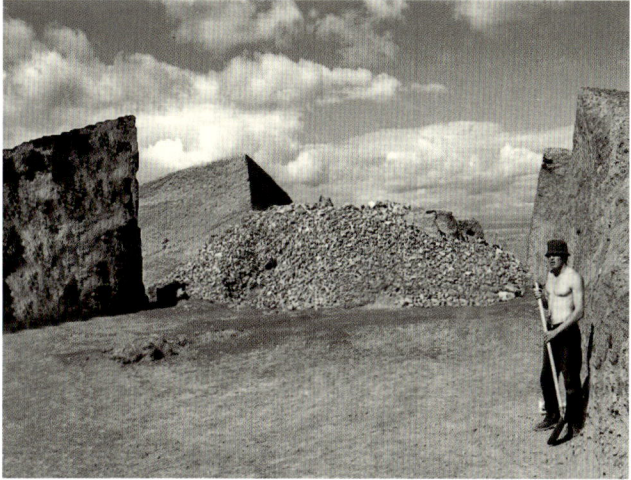
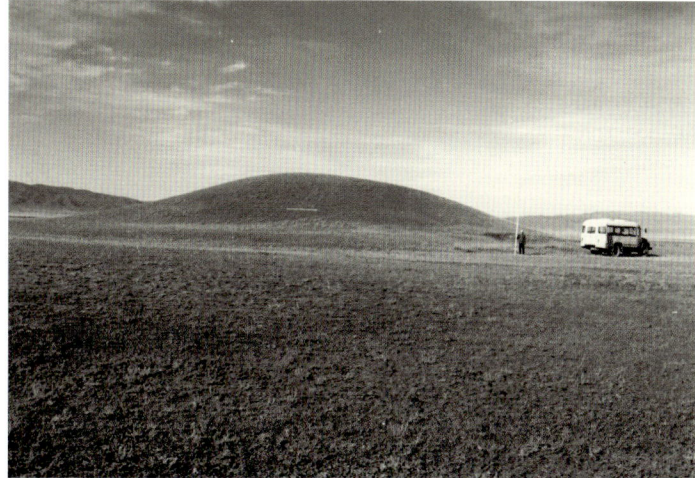

Analogous plaques have been found in Semirechye, in the Djalaulinskii hoard, although those plaques show the animals in their entirety.

OTHER GOLD OBJECTS

In addition to the cast plaques described above, the team's excavations found many small decorations made of sheet metal, such as metal wire and tubular beads, all of which were most probably used for clothing decoration. A number of small items, including miniature bells and half-sphere plaques, were soldered; for those made of gold a very sophisticated technique was employed.[12] Some of these miniature articles, which measure less than a millimeter in diameter, deserve special attention. Barely visible to the naked eye, these tiny objects have soldered loops for sewing them to clothing. The delicate procedure to create these miniature decorations—in particular, the soldering of their even smaller loops—would have been impossible without magnification and the knowledge of complex techniques of microsoldering.

THE ORIGIN OF THE GOLD

An important question is, of course, where the gold used in the Shilikty 3 objects was mined. As a first step toward answering this question, an elemental analysis of the gold decorations was performed (see Appendix B). The results show that the gold objects from the Baigetobe kurgan were manufactured from 22.4–23.28 karat gold. The other major elements in the gold were copper and silver.

3-4 (top left) View of wooden burial chamber built on ancient ground level.

3-5 (top right) Aerial view of wooden burial chamber.

3-6 (bottom left) View of stone mound that covers burial chamber, as illustrated in figs. 3a–b.

3-7 (bottom right) View of kurgan 82 before excavation.

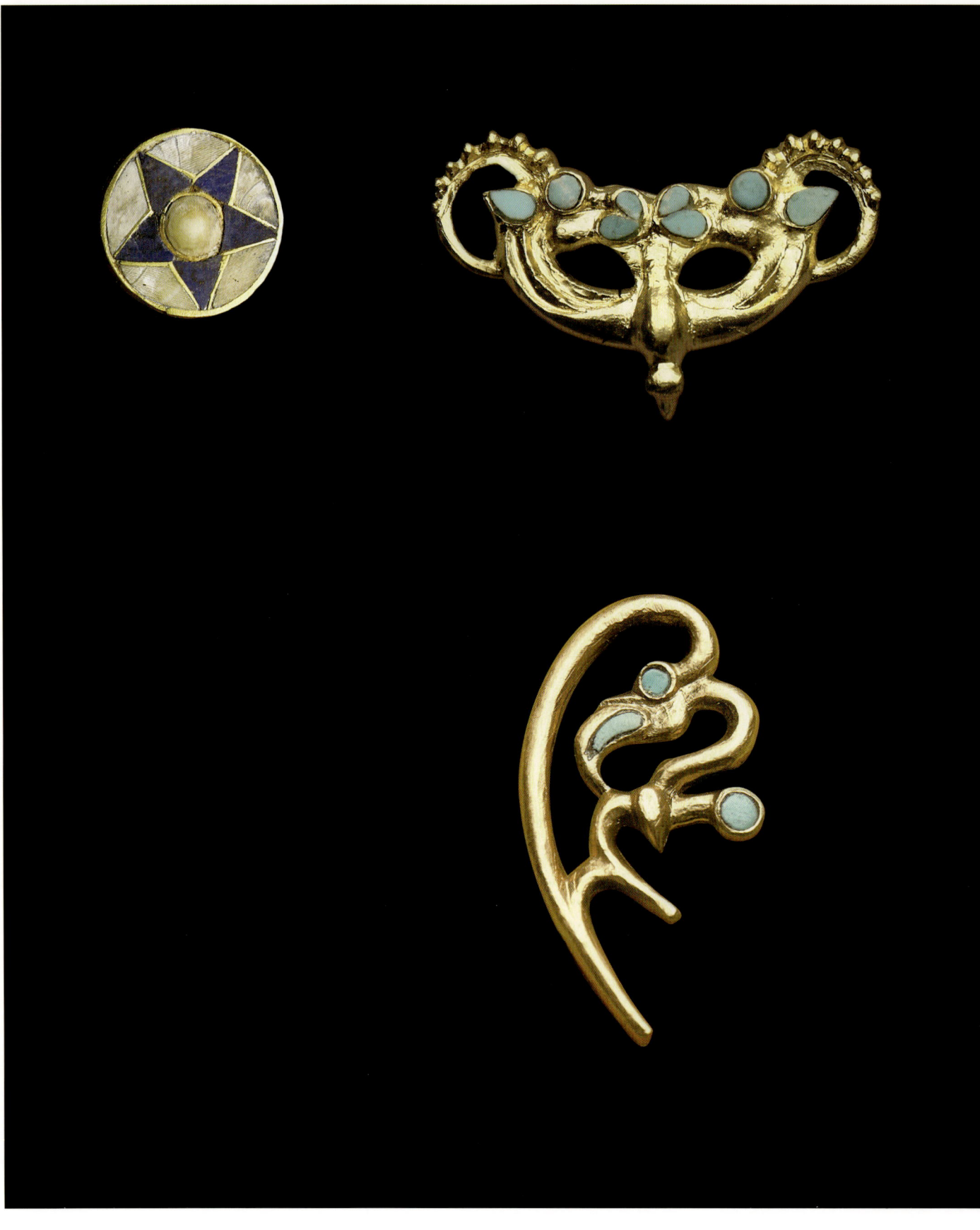

3-8 (top left) Round plaque of five-pointed star. Gold, lapis, and mother-of-pearl, Shilikty 3, kurgan 82, 8th–7th century BCE. Central State Museum, Almaty: KP 26861.

3-9 (top right) Plaque of "Snow Leopard Mask," consisting of two facing ibex heads and flying bird. Gold and turquoise, Shilikty 3, kurgan 82, 8th–7th century BCE. Central State Museum, Almaty: KP 26862. Checklist no. 167.

3-10 (bottom) Plaque of perched raptor (vulture?). Gold and turquoise, Shilikty 3, kurgan 82, 8th–7th century BCE. Central State Museum, Almaty: KP 26865/35. Checklist no. 169.

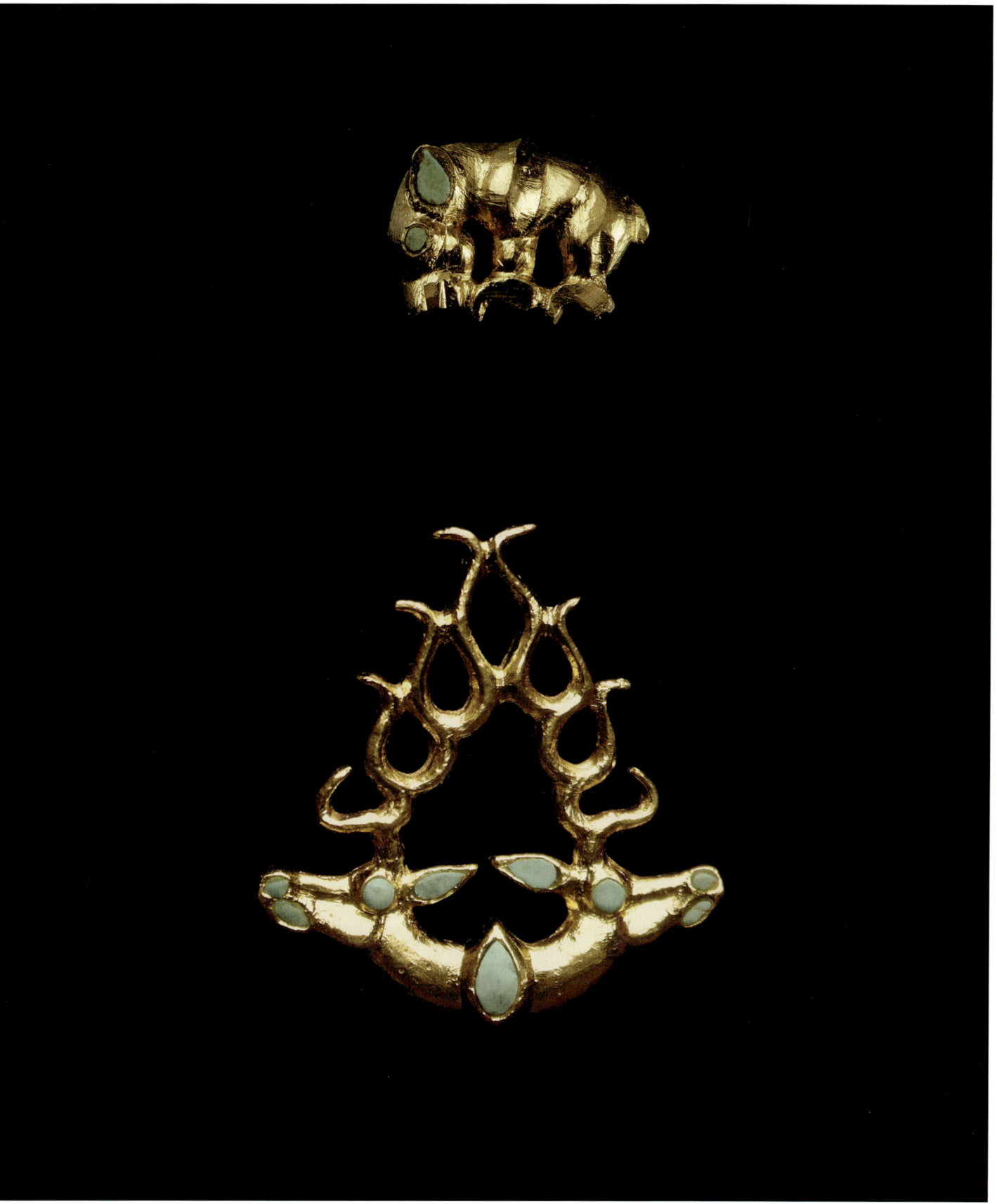

3-11 (top) Plaque of standing wolf or bear cub. Gold and turquoise, Shilikty 3, kurgan 82, 8th–7th century BCE. Central State Museum, Almaty: KP 26864. Checklist no. 171.

3-12 (bottom) Plaque of two addorsed deer heads. Gold and turquoise, Shilikty 3, kurgan 82, 8th–7th century BCE. Central State Museum, Almaty: 26866. Checklist no. 173.

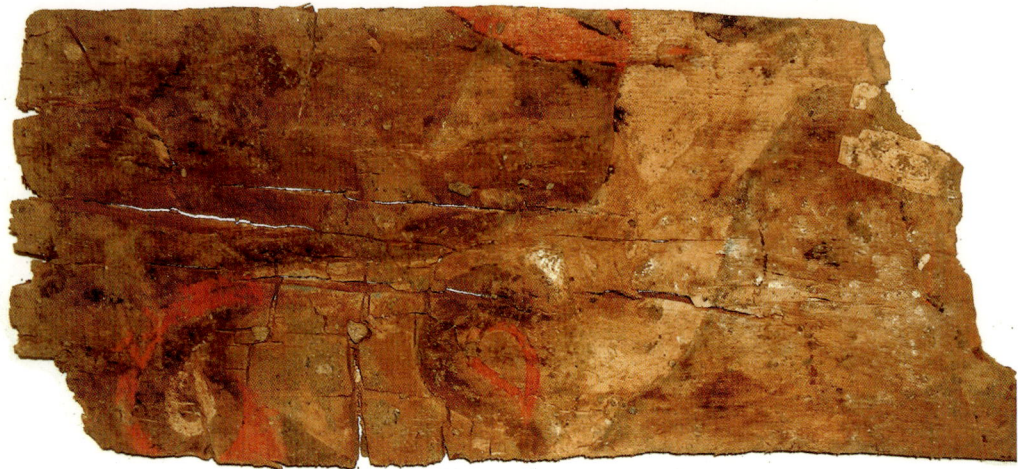

A geophysical survey was also conducted in the Shilikty territory to determine whether gold for these objects was mined and manufactured locally.[13] The preliminary conclusion was that the gold was mined in the Shilikty valley and that it was processed there as well.[14] This information corresponds well with late-nineteenth- and early-twentieth-century reports that mention a number of gold-mining operations in the region of Zaisan. According to statistical reports the purity of the gold mined and processed in that area corresponds exactly with those of the objects from Shilikty 3.

PAINTING ON WOOD

A truly exceptional find consists of two wooden panels, on one of which is the painted depiction of a deer; the second panel showed pigments, but the image could not be read. The object was found at the southeast corner of the kurgan, although this was probably not its original position. Its function cannot be determined. To date, there are no comparable artifacts known from the Early Iron Age in the Eurasian steppes. In fact, this object is the earliest known example of painting on wood in all of nomadic Central Asia (fig. 3-13).

TEXTILES

Due to the many factors that negatively affect the preservation of textiles, no visually detectable fragments of clothing were identified. Consequently, microstructural analysis was employed to identify textiles in the organic remains found in the soil within the burial chamber. Twenty-six samples, taken in various locations, were used for macro- and micro scopic analyses.[15] Fragments of a transparent brownish red substance with a fibrous structure were identified, and it is possible that they represent degraded bits of red silk in various stages of decomposition. Apart from this, samples 18 and 19 are of particular interest.

Sample 18 is a fragment (1.5 by 0.6 centimeters) of a two-color textile: one side is light to dark blue, the other of brownish red color. The shimmering appearance of this sample is substantially different from that of the other samples. Analyses confirmed the presence of silk. The sample is woven in simple tabby weave with single, thin yarns. The diameter of the yarns ranges from approximately 4.09 – 4.16 millimeters.

Sample 19 is a light-blue, somewhat compressed, and flat fragment that was found next to the south wall of the burial chamber. Color of this hue is sometimes the result of copper or bronze degradation.

The textile finds from Shilikty 3 are especially important as they seem to point to the use of silk textiles by nomadic elites from a very early period.

A STONE STELE

A well-preserved stone stele, 2.8 meters in length, was also found inside the burial. In all probability it entered the burial during the digging performed by the looters.

PERSPECTIVES ON FURTHER INVESTIGATIONS AT SHILIKTY

The results described above represent the culmination of multiyear, multidisciplinary studies by archaeologists and natural scientists. It is certain that such a multidisciplinary approach to the study of archaeological sites will yield additional valuable results in the future.

Translated by Maya Naunton

3-13   Fragment of ancient painting on wood from kurgan 82.

NOTES

1. Черников 1965.
2. The results have been presented in eight field reports totaling roughly seventy pages and in more than forty scientific publications.
3. The study was conducted by V. Skripkin and N. Kovalyuk (Kiev).
4. Editorial note: Other dates have been suggested in previous publications, e.g., Toleubaev 2006, 51: "8th century BCE," and Samašev 2007, 163: "Anfang des 7. Jahrhunderts."
5. The skeletal material was studied by Dr. A. O. Ismagulova. I would like to express my gratitude for her work. See Исмагулова 2008.
6. This research was carried out by Dr. K. Kashkinbaev. I would like to express my gratitude for this help. See Кашкинбаев 2000a.
7. This number includes: 153 plaques in the shape of a snow leopard's head, 36 plaques in the shape of a raptor, 20 plaques in the shape of a deer, 39 plaques in the shape of a wolf (or bear) cub, 1 plaque in the shape of the sculpted image of an argali, 1 plaque in the shape of the five-pointed star, 23 decorations shaped like small bells, 63 ridged-tube decorations, 17 gold-leaf strips, 7 gold-leaf wires, 141 miniature pendants shaped as half-spheres, 2,835 miniature pendants in the shape of a cup, 223 miniature tubular beads, 743 ring-shaped beads, and 1 miniature bracket.
8. Study of the technology and manufacturing methods of the gold decorations from Shilikty was undertaken by R. S. Minosyan, a renowned ancient-gold specialist from the State Hermitage Museum of the Russian Federation. See Миносян 2008, 18–32.
9. Руденко 1951, 139; Руденко 1958, 36; Киселёв 1951, 231, Табл. 20, Рис. 3,13; Табл. 22. Рис. 5, 6; Маргулан et al. 1966, 402, Рис. 66; Грязнов 1980, 39–40.
10. The only somewhat similar piece that comes to mind is a wooden plaque from a burial at the Uibat Chaatas at the Middle Yenisei. But this piece is dated much later (to the Tashtyk period; Киселёв 1951, 406).
11. S. S. Chernikov found nine examples of the raptor plaque in kurgan 5 of the Shilikty burial ground; see Черников 1965, 32–33. Despite some similarities, there are a number of differences between those nine examples and the ones found in Baigetobe. The raptors from kurgan 5 were constructed from sheet gold by beating the shallow relief over a matrix, and as a result they are not as well preserved as the plaques from Baigetobe. In addition, whereas the Baigetobe plaques have a snake head next to the foot of the raptor, in the plaques found by Chernikov this element is almost lost and there is instead a hole in that location. Moreover, the raptor from kurgan 5 has turquoise inlay in the eye socket with a small opening, the end of the beak is not attached to the bottom part, and the plaque does not have attachment loops on the reverse. While the heads of the raptors from Baigetobe are all turned to the right, the heads of some of the raptors from kurgan 5 are turned to the right and some to the left. Outside the Tarbagatai, a similar bronze plaque was found in Zyevskii cemetery on the Kama and dated by A. B. Zbrueva to the sixth century BCE. A distant echo of the Shilikty-style raptor is also found in the figures of raptors from the Minusinsk depression; see Збруева 1952; Черников С.С. Загадка золотого кургана.С.57.
12. This technique makes use of a very hot bit of coal on top, with the heat being raised by means of a small tube. In order for the plaque not to fly from the coal, the craftsman held it in place with a small needle inserted through a small loop, and as a result the opposite sides of these plaques often have indentations. My analyses show that the solder did not include any of the low-melting components (zinc, cadmium, etc.) but was composed only of copper-silver-gold alloy, with gold of a slightly lower carat. This soldering method was very secure but demanded high expertise from the jewelry maker.
13. The geological survey was performed during three seasons by a team under the leadership of Dr. T. M. Djautikov, head of the Department of Non-Ferrous Metals, K. I. Satpaev Institute of Geological Sciences, Almaty. During this survey samples were taken from the Shaganoba defile in the Altynkazgan area. The team also studied a furnace.
14. Жаутиков 2006.
15. This research was headed by Dr. K. Kashkinbaev, and I would like to express my gratitude for this help; see Кашкинбаев 2000a.

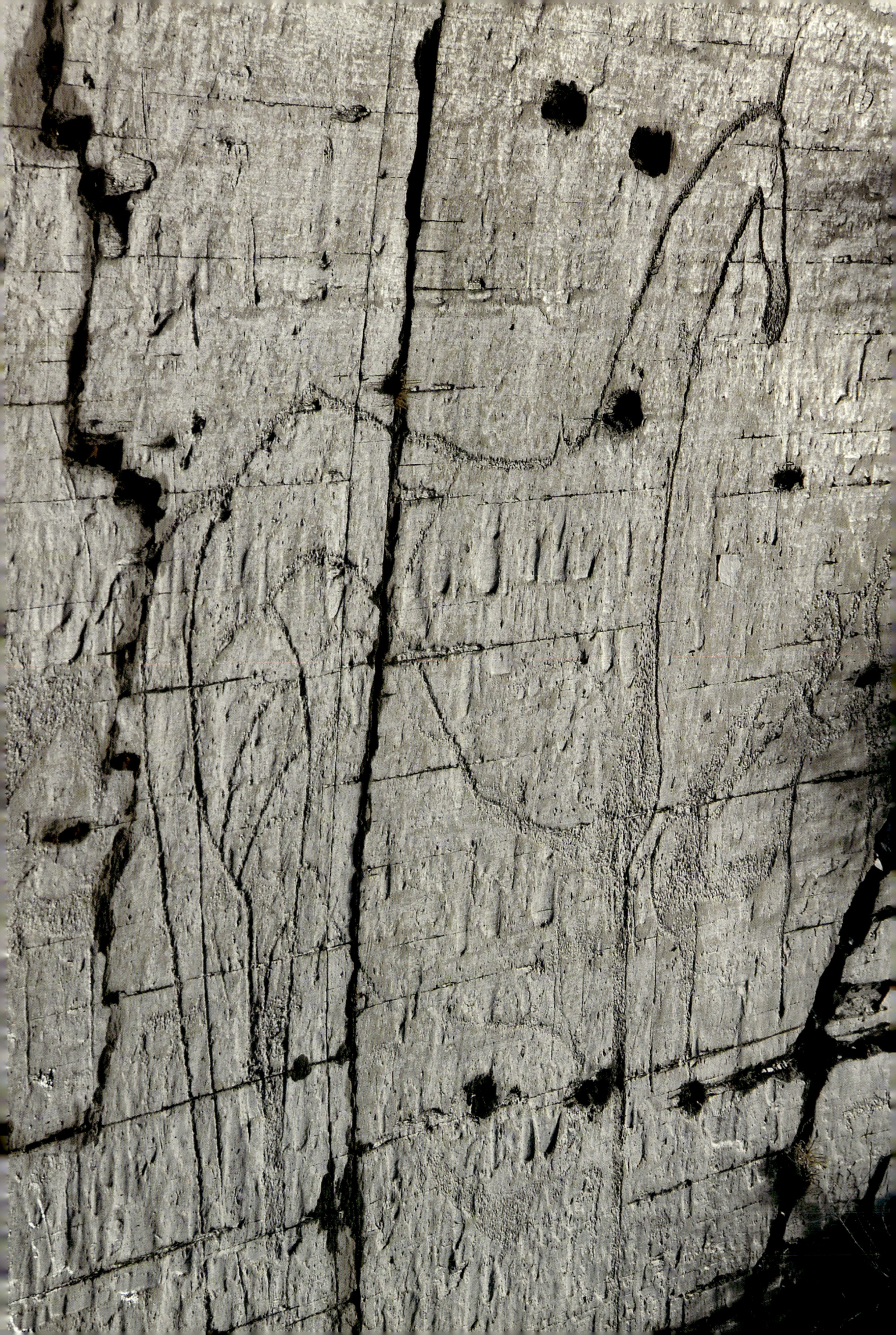

SOME QUESTIONS REGARDING THE ROCK ART OF KAZAKHSTAN

Sagynbay Myrgabayev

Carvings of images on rock in the landscape are an important visual source of information about the way of life and the worldview of Iron Age nomads in the high mountains of Central Asia. However, the interpretation of these rock art images is also a most challenging and difficult enterprise, with many questions still unanswered.

Sites with rock art are very widespread in the mountainous regions of Kazakhstan. They have not yet been studied comprehensively, but current systematic searches for new locations with rock art will surely expand the number of known sites and knowledge about them.

Among the great variety of images carved on rock, known as petroglyphs, those dated to the Early Iron Age and found in the Karatau mountain range are the focus of this essay. The Karatau ("Black Mountain" in Kazakh) Mountains are located in southern Kazakhstan just north of the Syr Darya River, known as the Iaxartes to the Greeks and Romans (see map on pages 12–13).

Petroglyph representing a "steppe racer" horse. Sauyskandyk, Karatau, Early Iron Age.

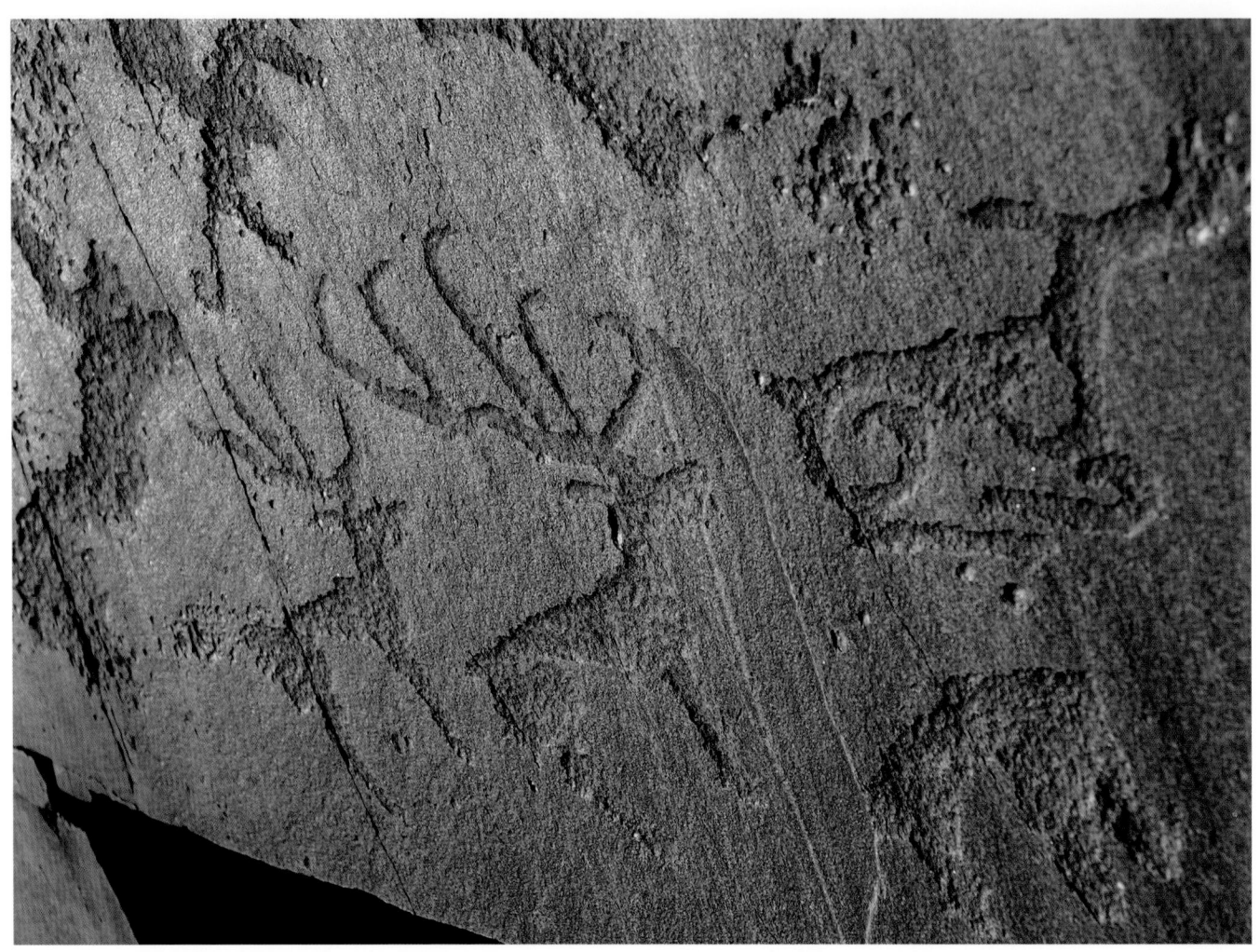

4-1 Petroglyph representing deer. Terys, Karatau, Early Iron Age.

4-2 (opposite) Drawing of a petroglyph representing deer in a variety of poses. Sauyskandyk, Karatau, Early Iron Age.

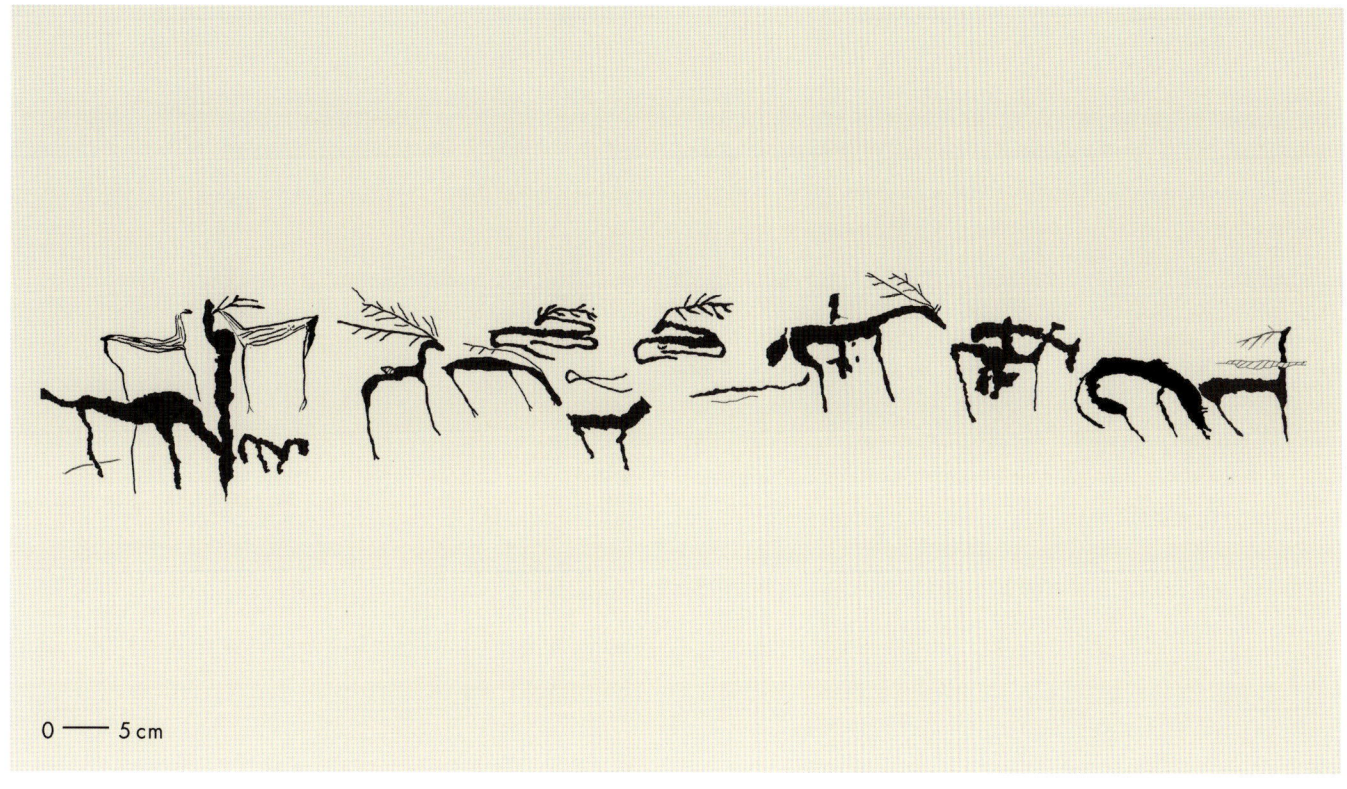

0 —— 5 cm

The visual art of Early Iron Age nomads is characterized by the domination of the so-called Scytho-Siberian animal style. Scholars have proposed a number of diverging hypotheses about the origin and spread of this phenomenon throughout the vast spaces of the Eurasian steppes and far beyond—from Northern China to Eastern Europe and the Near East.[1] The style derives its name from the fact that a large number of objects (weapons, clothing, household objects, horse trappings) were decorated using animal images in a distinctive style: the animals represented are feline predators or wolves curled into a circle, herbivores with legs folded under the bodies, hoofed animals standing "on tiptoe," and animals with twisted hindquarters. The style is also characterized by the emphasis and exaggeration of some parts of the body: ears, claws, eyes, faces, beaks, antlers, and so on. The main intent of this art was not purely as a decorative embellishment; rather, the specially chosen images of animals, arranged in a definite sequence, represent a sort of alphabet for conveying information. V. A. Korenyako, explaining the artistic essence of animalism among Early Iron Age nomads, calls the Scytho-Siberian animal style an "art of expressive deformation."[2] Obviously, the Scytho-Siberian animal style was tightly connected to the worldview of mounted warriors and hunters, to their religion, and to their conception of the world they lived in.

As mentioned above, a distinctive feature of the Scytho-Siberian animal style is its emphasis on specific parts of each animal, in particular those parts that are especially characteristic. In the case of predators, for example, claws and teeth are emphasized; in the case of deer, antlers; and so on. In addition, each animal is depicted in a characteristic pose: deer are shown with outstretched heads as in flight, while feline predators are curled into a circle.[3]

Petroglyphs of this period include a great number of deer images, and the rock art of Karatau is no exception (figs. 4-1, 4-2). Consequently, the rock art of Early Iron Age nomads is sometimes referred to as Deer Period petroglyphs. Some scholars explain the numerous deer images in the Early Iron Age by the arrival of new populations from Mongolia and the Altai Mountains, resulting in a more totemic worldview among the ancient people of Kazakhstan.[4] I completely agree with this opinion and would only like to point out that the visual style that developed in the southern Karatau under Eastern influence dates to the first half of the first millennium BCE. Clearly, the dominance of the deer image is related to the appearance of the so-called deer stones in Mongolia, Tuva, and the Altai by the late-ninth through the early-eighth centuries BCE (fig. 4-3). These stelae depict vaguely anthropomorphic figures with weapon belts and rows of deer images, the latter probably reflecting deer tattoos.[5]

In fact, the Karatau is the outermost southwestern appearance of images executed in the distinct style of the deer stones. Examples are found among the petroglyphs of Jingilshik (fig. 4-4), where the ancient artist followed the style of the deer stones but omitted antlers—the main component. Among images from the Talas Alatau mountain range and Semirechye, the number and their iconographic similarity to deer stones increases, confirming that during the Early Iron Age the main center of the dissemination of deer images was further east, in eastern Kazakhstan, Southern Siberia, and Mongolia.

As a whole, the animal style in Kazakhstan has its own distinctive features, including the common appearance of camels.[6] An expressive example of a camel image can be found in the petroglyphs of Arpauzen (fig. 4-5). In fact, it represents a fight between two male camels, a motif well-known throughout the Eurasian steppes. A close parallel can be found on a plaque discovered in the Besoba kurgan, dating to the sixth–fourth century BCE (fig. 4-6).[7] In addition to fighting scenes, Karatau petroglyphs include images of single camels as well as groups of camels following each other in a row (fig. 4-7). Recent research has shown that camel images already appear in rock art from the Karatau dating to the Bronze Age.[8] But Bronze Age camels are shown in a more static pose and sometimes depicted using complex ornament, with the bodies divided into irregular net patterns (fig. 4-8).

Bronze Age traditions clearly contributed to formation of the Scytho-Siberian animal style in the territory of present-day Kazakhstan.[9] At the same time components of Eastern visual traditions (from Southern Siberia, Mongolia) are clearly visible from the beginning of the first millennium BCE, resulting in the formation of a new visual canon in the southern regions of present-day Kazakhstan (including the Karatau). For example, the contoured image of a camel from group 1 in Sauyskandyk (fig. 4-9) is stylistically very close to examples from the ninth–eighth centuries BCE in the Altai and in Tuva, where, however, images of camels are rare.

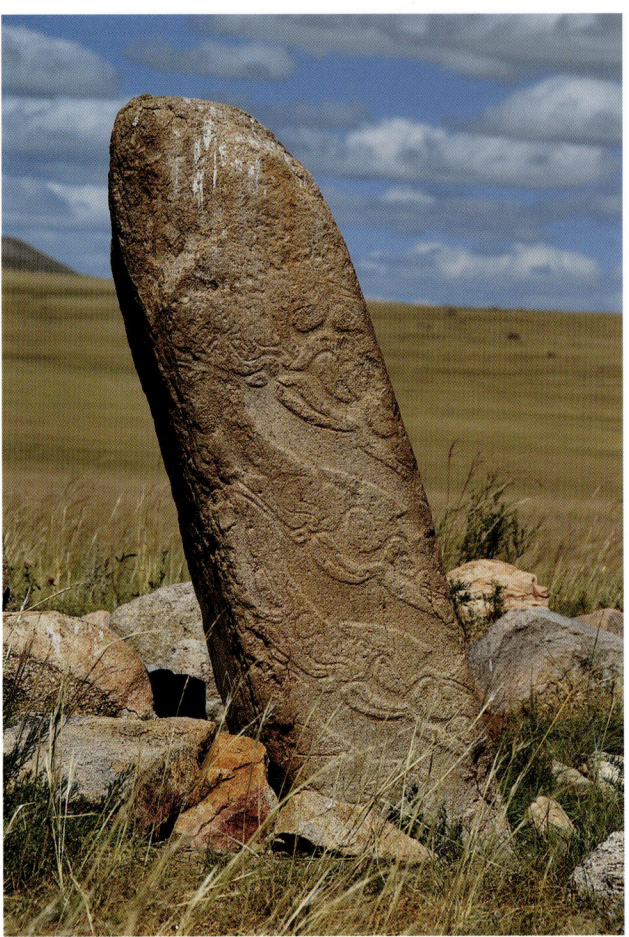

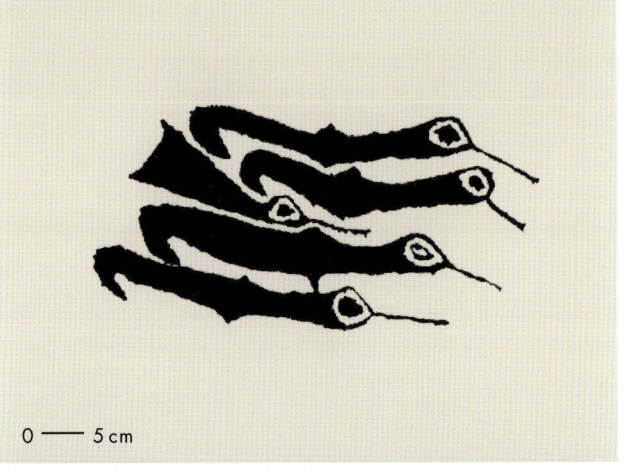

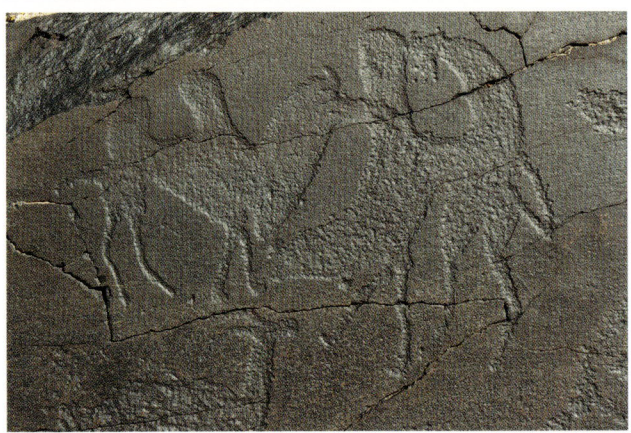

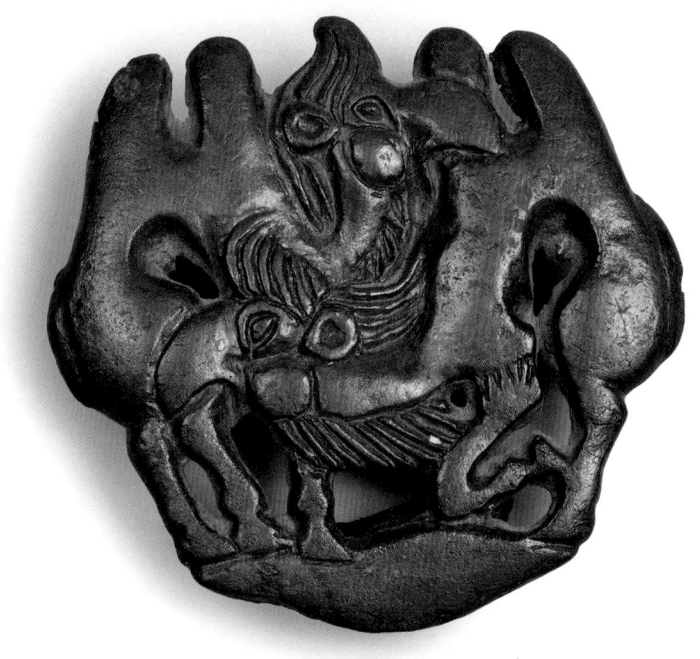

4-3 (opposite, top) "Deer Stone," Central Mongolia, 9th–8th century BCE.

4-4 (opposite, center) Drawing of a petroglyph representing deer without antlers. Jingilshik, Karatau, Early Iron Age.

4-5 (opposite, bottom) Petroglyph representing two fighting camels. Arpauzen, Karatau, Early Iron Age.

4-6 Plaque depicting fighting Bactrian camels. Bronze, Besoba (Aqtobe region), 6th–4th century BCE. Museum of Archaeology, Almaty: MA 76a. Checklist no. 111.

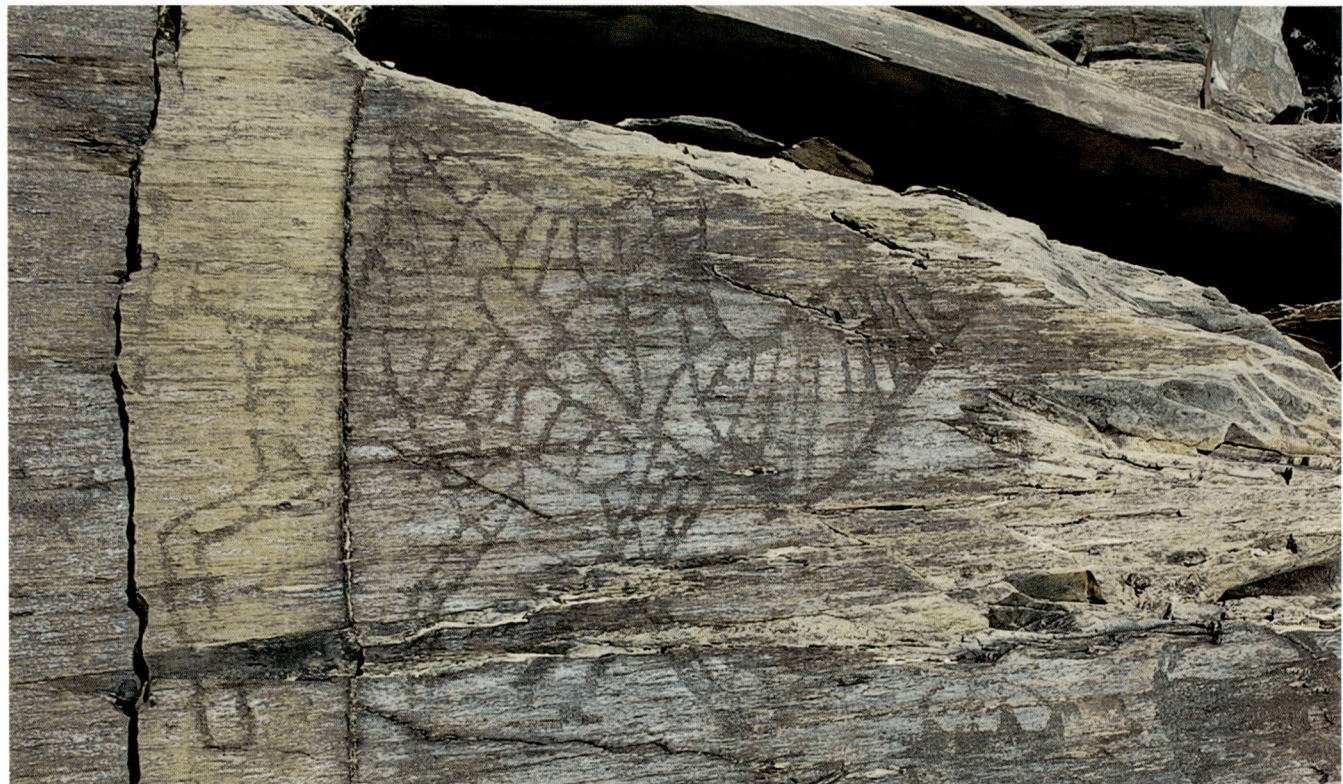

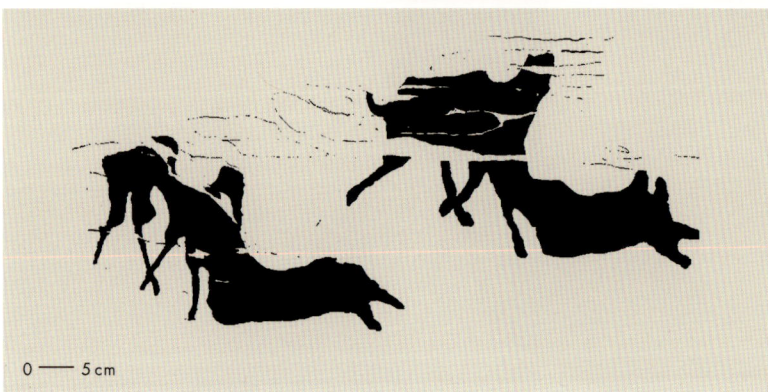

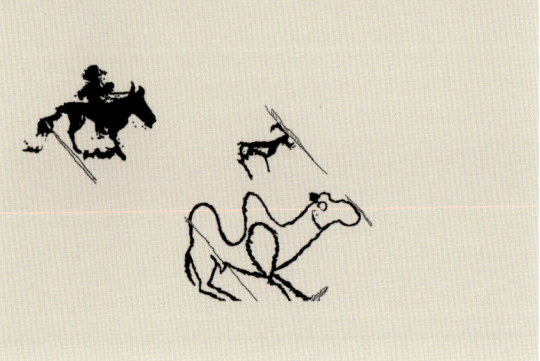

Other popular motifs in the corpus of Karatau petroglyphs from the ninth–eighth centuries BCE are images of mountain goats and wild boars (figs. 4-10–4-12). Typical depictions of mountain goats can be found in a composition from Sauyskandyk (figs. 4-13a–b)[10] that is distinguished by the pose of the animals "on tiptoe" and their teardrop-shaped mouths. Direct analogies can be found in the decorative arts of the Tasmola culture, from the sites of Uigarak and Tagisken at the Lower Syr Darya, in the finds of the Issyk kurgan, and on other decorative objects of the Sakā period.[11]

Images of boars seem to have been much more popular in the Early Iron Age than in the Bronze Age (figs. 4-10–4-12). Depictions of boars are executed in multiple ways. In some cases only the outline of the animal is chiseled out, while in others the entire rock surface is removed to depict a part of the animal's body (see fig. 4-15b). Especially interesting is the representation of three wild boars in Sauyskandyk (fig. 4-14): the animals are oriented in different directions, and one boar is larger than the others. The two smaller boars are distinguished by tusks that point upward. The lower teeth and jaws of the animals are depicted by curved lines,

4-7 (bottom left) Drawing of a petroglyph representing a line of camels. Karatau, Early Iron Age.

4-8 (top) Petroglyph representing a camel with the body divided into an irregular net pattern. Karatau, Bronze Age.

4-9 (bottom right) Drawing of a petroglyph representing a camel. Sauyskandyk, Karatau, Early Iron Age.

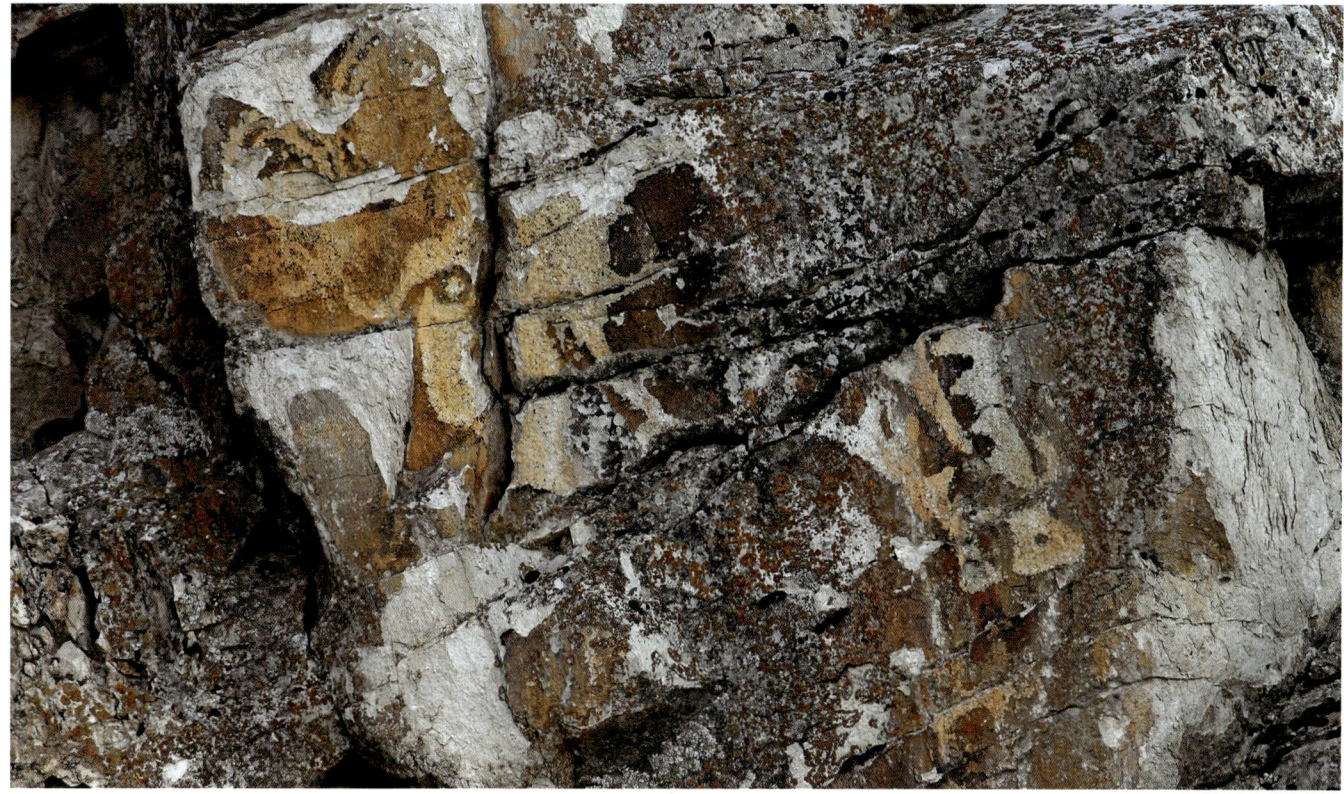

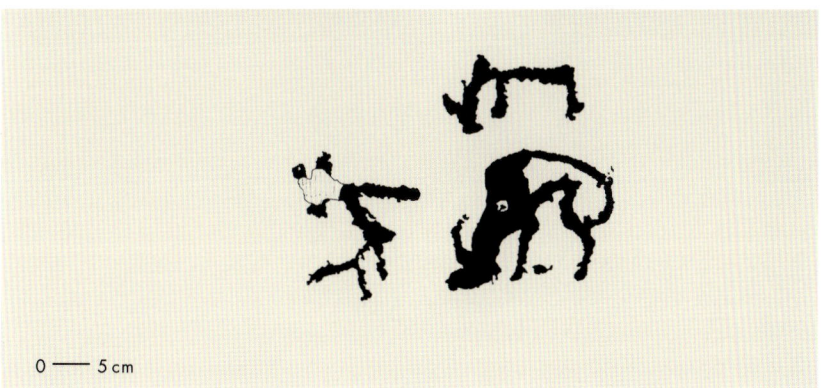

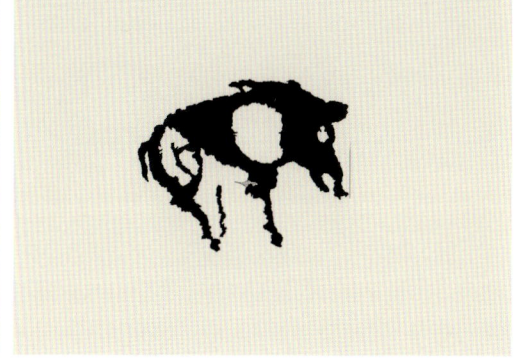

while their extremities are represented in the shape of "bird feet."[12] The images remind one not of boars commonly found in nature, but of a fantastic creature. A main feature for dating the Sauyskandyk boars to the Early Iron Age is the leaf-like shape of the shoulder blade, since a leaf, or teardrop, shape is a characteristic means for depicting parts of the animal body during the Early Iron Age.[13]

Wild boars also appear in another most interesting composition at Sauyskandyk (figs. 4-15a–d), in which three pairs of animals are depicted facing each other, on straight legs and "tiptoe." Below these pairs appear two deer with magnificent antlers, mirroring each other—almost heraldic in appearance. One of the three upper pairs consists of a feline and a boar (fig. 4-15b); another is of a boar and a bear (fig. 4-15c); and the third is of a feline and a bear (fig. 4-15d). The style of the animals is surprisingly close to that of animal images from the earliest phase of animal representations in the Early Iron Age. The composition, however, has no direct parallels from the Eurasian steppes.

4-10 (top) Petroglyph representing wild boar. Maidantal, Karatau, Early Iron Age.

4-11 (bottom left) Drawing of a petroglyph representing a wild boar. Boraldai, Karatau, Early Iron Age.

4-12 (bottom right) Drawing of a petroglyph representing a wild boar. Karamuryn, Karatau, Early Iron Age.

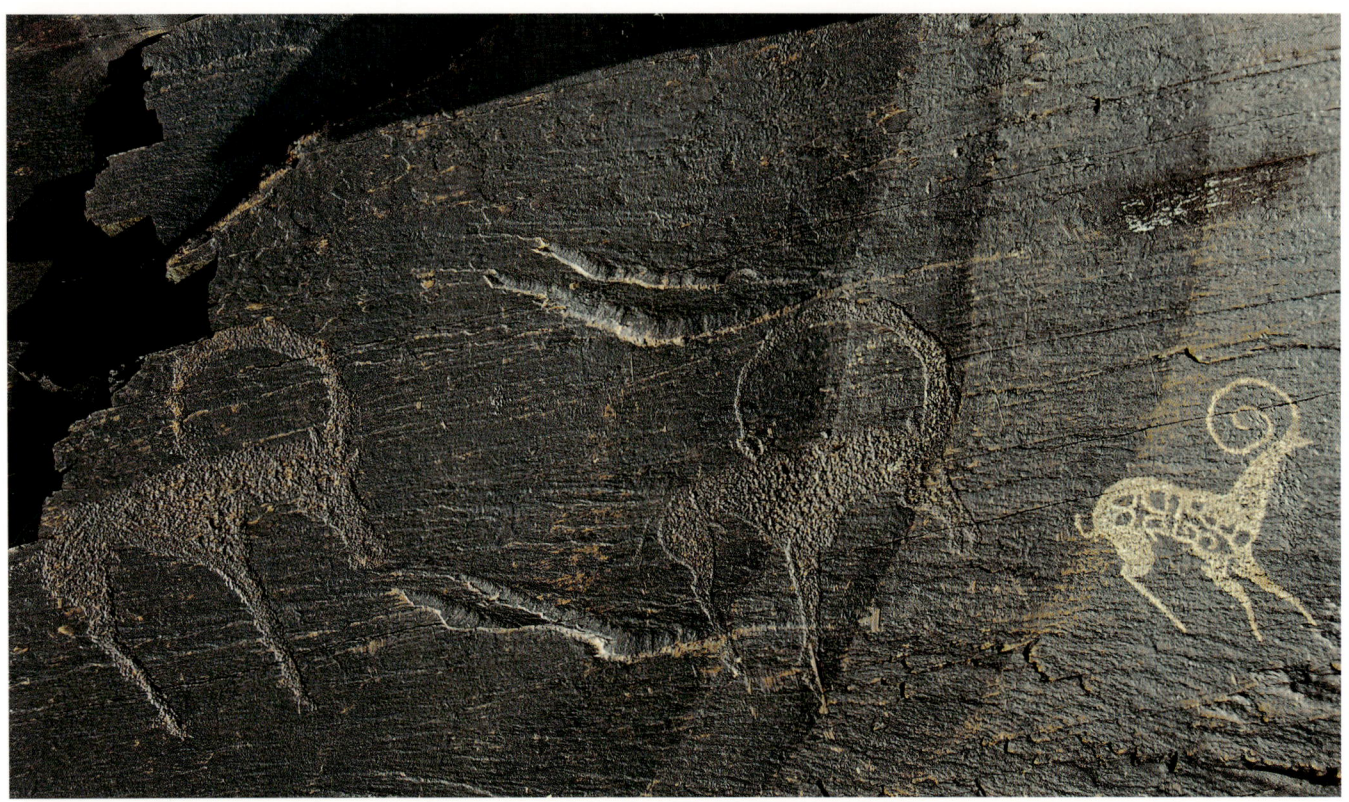
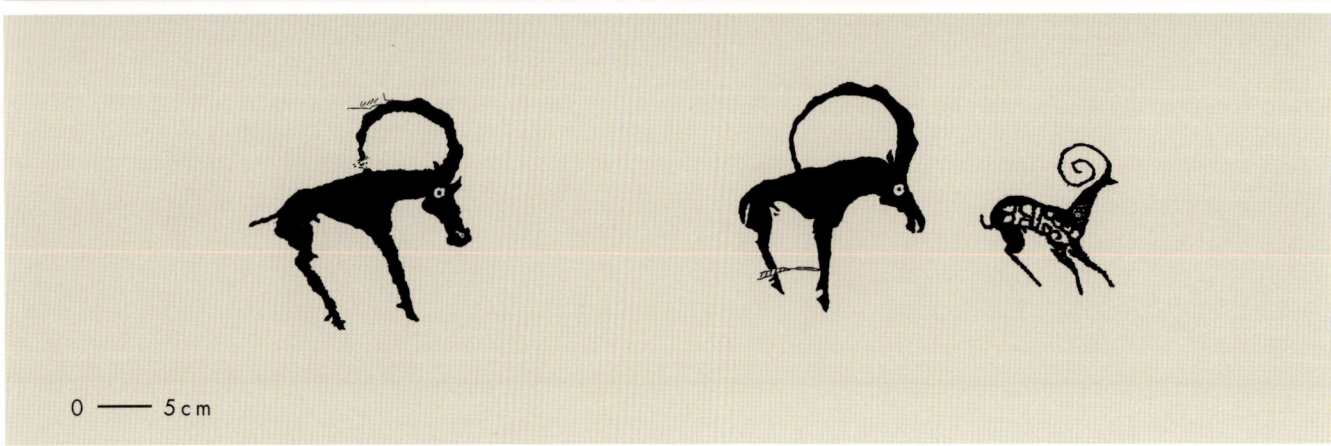
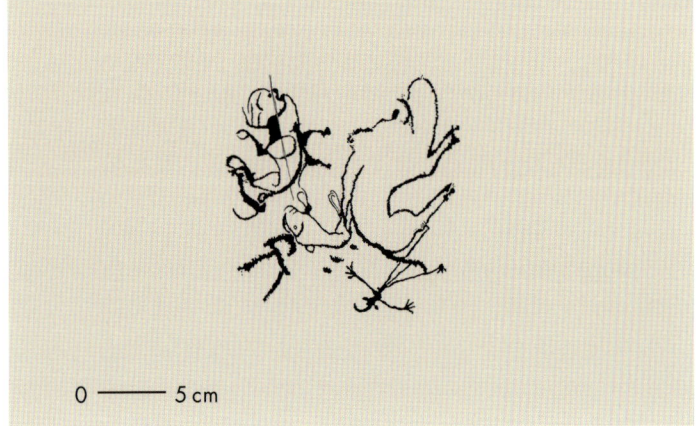

4-13a–b   (top and center) Petroglyph and drawing representing mountain goats "on tiptoe." Sauyskandyk, Karatau, Early Iron Age.

4-14   (bottom) Drawing of a petroglyph representing three wild boar. Sauyskandyk, Karatau, Early Iron Age.

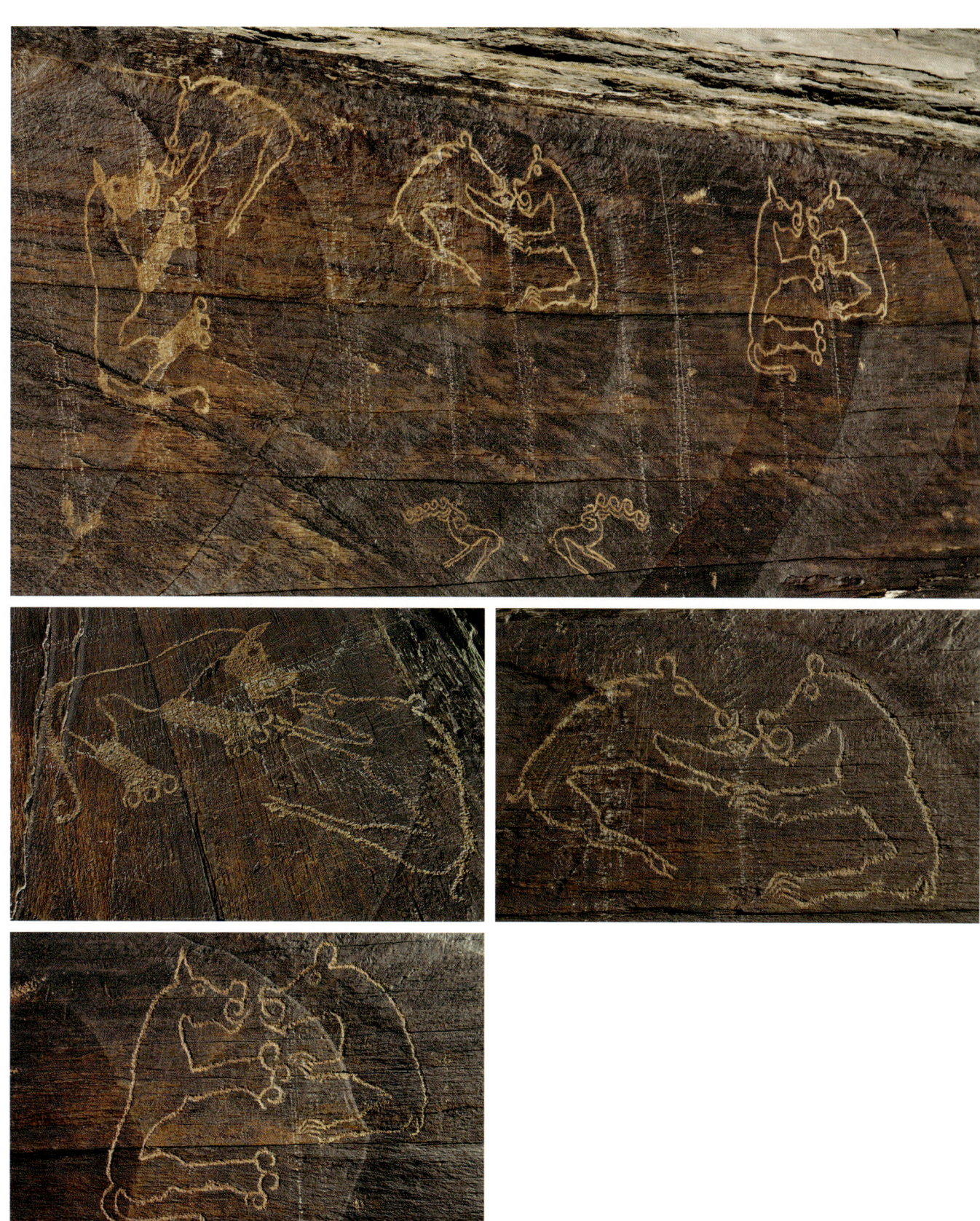

4-15a–d   (a, top) Petroglyph representing three pairs of animals with two horned deer below. Sauyskandyk, Karatau, Early Iron Age. (b, center left) Detail of feline and boar. (c, center right) Detail of boar and bear. (d, bottom) Detail of feline and bear.

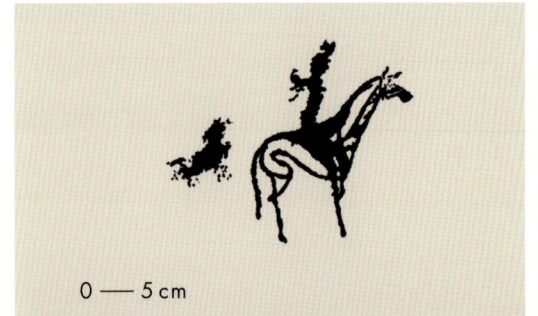
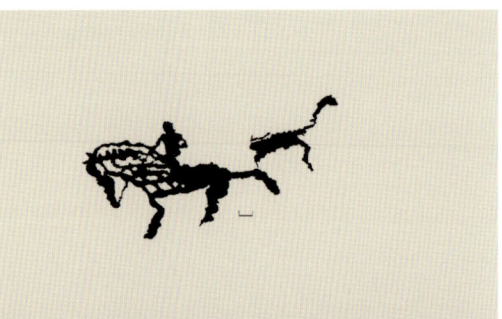

0 — 5 cm

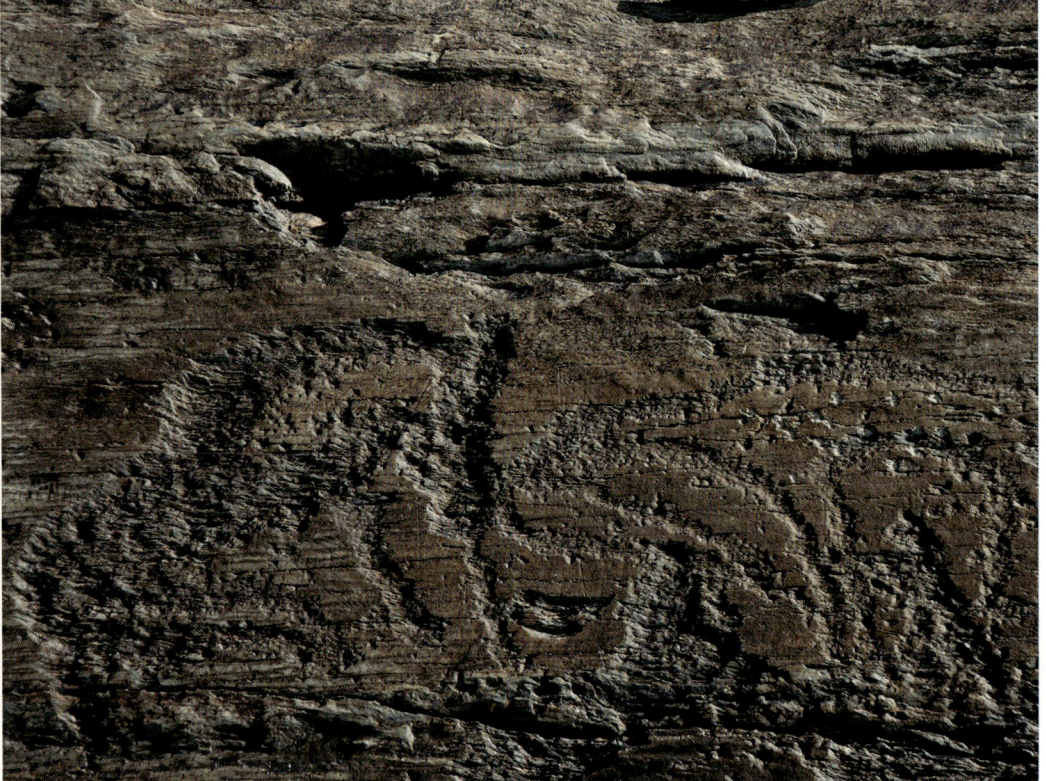

4-16 (top left) Drawing of a petroglyph representing a "steppe racer" horse and rider. Karatau, Early Iron Age.

4-17 (top right) Drawing of a petroglyph representing a horse and rider attacked by a feline predator. Karatau, Early Iron Age.

4-18 (bottom) Petroglyph representing two seated horses with folded legs. Sauyskandyk, Karatau, Early Iron Age.

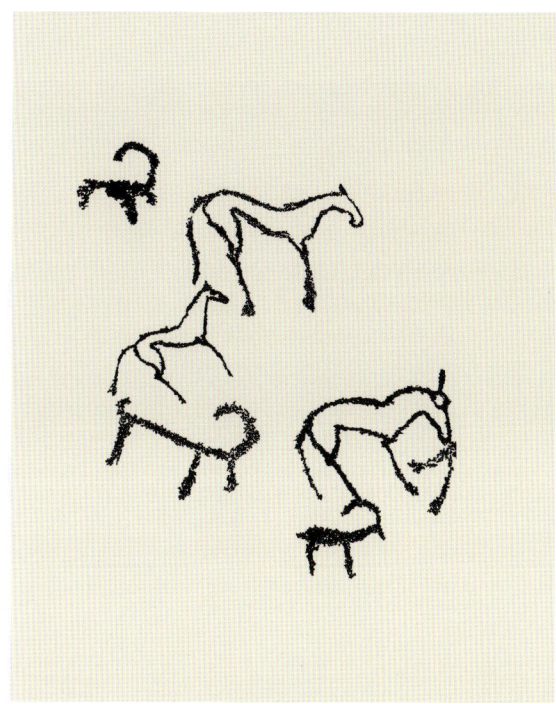
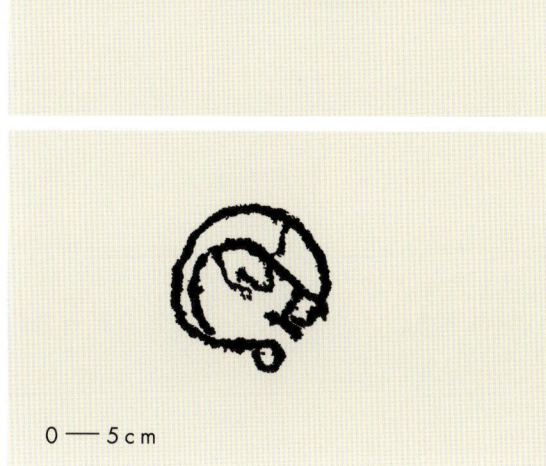
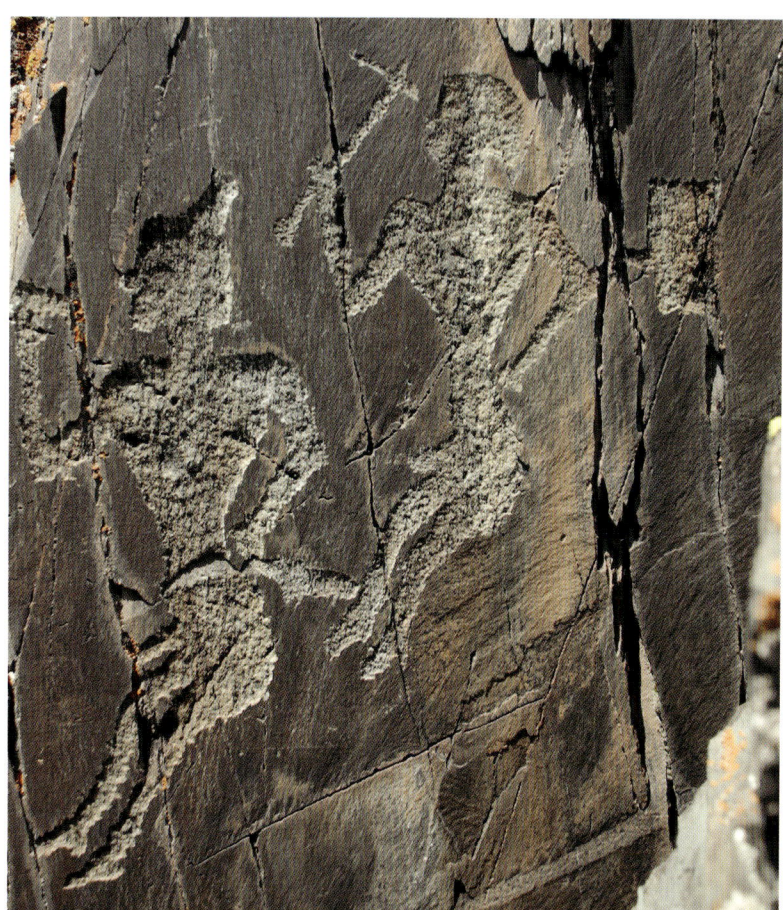
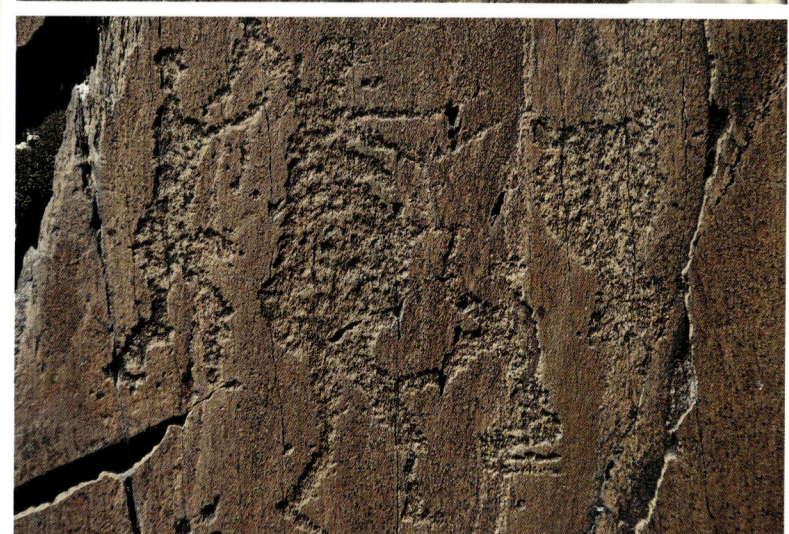

4-19 (top left) Drawing of a petroglyph representing three horses and other animals. Sauyskandyk, Karatau, Early Iron Age.

4-20 (bottom left) Drawing of a petroglyph representing a curled predator. Karaungur, Karatau. Early Iron Age.

4-21 (top right) Petroglyph representing two warriors with battle axes. Kuljabasy, Karatau, Bronze Age.

4-22 (bottom right) Petroglyph representing two figures and a cauldron. Kuljabasy, Karatau, Iron Age.

Among early nomadic-period petroglyphs, one occasionally finds images of horses wearing masks with the horns of a bull or mountain goat. Similar images are found in the petroglyphs of the Kyzylshin gorge. On the vertical surface of a cliff, above images from the Bronze Age, one composition depicts four engraved horses wearing masks with horns in the shape of a half-moon. Similar images are known among the petroglyphs of Tamgaly.[14] An interesting image of a horse with the long tail, claws, and horns of a mountain goat is found in group 2 of the Sauyskandyk ravine. The representation of a camel with horns is found among petroglyphs of Jingilshik. These images find vivid analogies among decorations on the headgear of the Issyk chief and direct parallels with the finds of the Berel kurgans of the Pazyryk culture.[15]

Horses hold a special place in nomadic society. Therefore, it is not an accident that one sees multiple kinds of horses and mounted riders in the petroglyphs of Karatau. Taking the place of Bronze Age horses—with their short bodies and straight drooping manes—are "steppe racers" (fig. 4-16 and page 62). The horses of this period have long legs, long and thin necks, and concave stomachs. Frequently, the hair of the horse's mane is cut or tied into multiple tufts. The tradition of decorating horses in this way is known from horse burials in Early Iron Age kurgans in eastern Kazakhstan. In one image a horse rider is depicted being attacked by a feline predator (see fig. 4-17). Particularly interesting is a composition from Sauyskandyk with two horses depicted as if "sitting" with their hind legs folded under them (fig. 4-18). In another composition from Sauyskandyk, that of three horses and other animals, one horse is depicted in the style of the ninth–eighth centuries BCE, with its round eye extending beyond the forehead (fig. 4-19). A recent new find also points to parallels with imagery from the ninth–eighth centuries in the East, namely the image of a curled predator found during a 2011 survey among the petroglyphs of Karaungur (fig. 4-20).

In my opinion, the two-meter representations of horses from the Sauyskandyk ravine should be attributed to the Early Iron Age (see page 62). Although some scholars attribute these large images to the Neolithic or Chalcolithic periods,[16] there are elements of the Scytho-Siberian animal style in the depiction of these grandiose horses, as their heads, eyes, and ears are depicted in the same way as the mountain goats described above.

Of course, one of the major problems when dealing with petroglyphs is their dating. Leaving aside stylistic considerations, scholars frequently rely on weapons and tools depicted on the petroglyphs, which provide evidence toward the dating of images. By using this method, it thus becomes clear that the depiction of two warriors with battle axes from Kuljabasy most probably dates to the Bronze Age rather than the Early Iron Age (fig. 4-21). However, also from the same site is a representation of a typical Iron Age cauldron, strongly suggesting that the warrior scene dates to the Early Iron Age (fig. 4-22).

Unfortunately, we cannot connect the rock art of the Early Iron Age in the Karatau with any other category of contemporary archaeological sites, such as Kurgan burials or settlements, because there are no sites known in the Karatau range dating to the first half of the first millennium BCE. This makes the Kazakhstan petroglyphs the only—and therefore an especially valuable—source on the culture and the worldview of those Early Iron Age pastoralists who used the Karatau as summer pastures and hunting grounds.

Translated by Maya Naunton

NOTES

1 Шер 1980; Idem 1998; Самашев 2007; Кореняко; Sher 1988; Francfort and Jacobson 2004; Jettmar 1967.
2 Кореняко 2002, 327.
3 Переводчикова 1994; Раевский 2001.
4 Кадырбаев and Марьяшев 1977, 187.
5 Самашев 1994.
6 Мургабаев 2008, 258–61; Мургабаев 2010, 58–64.
7 Самашев 2004.
8 The Bronze Age attribution of such images of camel fights is proven by the presence in one such scene of anthropomorphic bull-aurochs wearing masks.
9 Акишев 1973, 58. The precise Bronze Age origins are, however, a matter of discussion. See Пяткин and Миклашевич 1990; Шер 1980.
10 Other examples come from petroglyphs of the Shalabai ravine and Aktogay.
11 Самашев, Толеубаев, and Джумабекова 2004; Самашев et al. 2007.
12 A similar treatment of hooves can be found among the petroglyphs of Eshkiolmes and Arpauzen.
13 Шер 1998, 218–30.
14 Максимова, Ермолаев, and Марьяшев 1985, 63.
15 Самашев, Толеубаев, and Джумабекова 2004.
16 Сала and Деом 2005, 150.

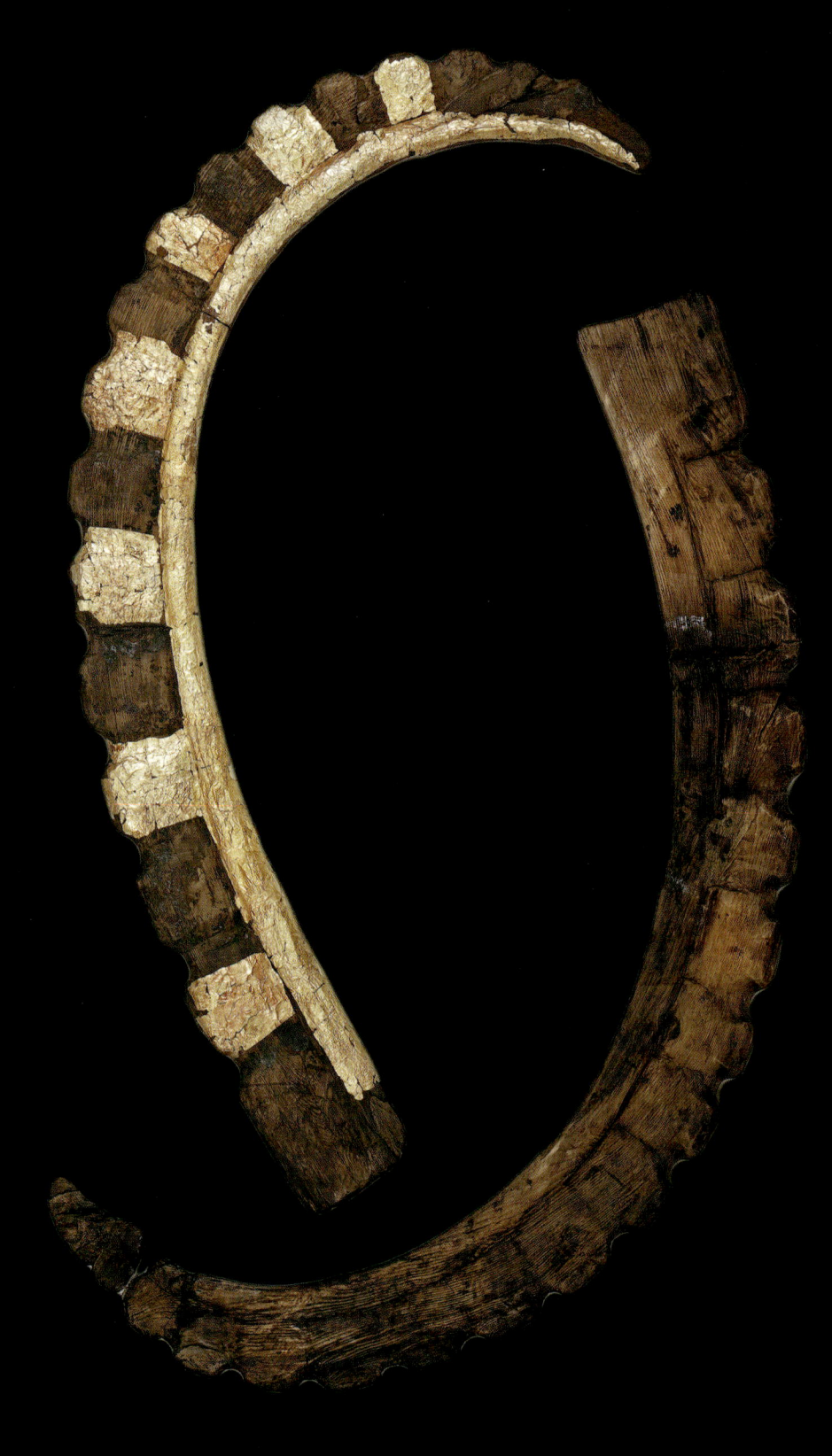

BURIAL PRACTICES AND SOCIAL ROLES OF IRON AGE MOBILE PASTORALISTS

Karen S. Rubinson

Most of the objects in the exhibition that accompanies this catalogue were excavated from burials of elite members of the mobile pastoral groups who lived in eastern Kazakhstan during the first millennium BCE. The burials were looted in ancient times, so it is not always possible to determine exactly how and where the objects were placed at the time of burial. However, at least in the case of Berel, many related burials from nearby areas of Russia and Mongolia can provide corroborative information. This essay addresses what can be learned about the appearance of the Berel tombs at the time of burial; the rituals associated with death and burial; the meanings of these burials for those who created them and for the deceased; as well as what we might and might not be able to reconstruct, based on the grave goods, regarding the ways these people lived.[1] In sum, the discussion below will endeavor to look at the humans behind the material remains.

Since the peoples whose belongings are featured in the exhibition did not write, all of these questions are challenges. As has been noted elsewhere in this catalogue, texts by Greek and Chinese historians—most especially Herodotus (ca. 484 BCE–ca. 425 BCE) in *The History of the Persian War*[2] and Sima Qian (ca. 145/135 BCE–86 BCE) in *Records of the Grand Historian* (史記)—mention these peoples or others who shared their lifeways.[3] While both Herodotus and Sima Qian wrote about lifeways and

Sculpted ibex horns from a ceremonial horse headdress. Wood and gold, Berel, kurgan 11, late 4th–early 3rd century BCE. A. Kh. Margulan Institute of Archaeology, Almaty. Checklist no. 48.

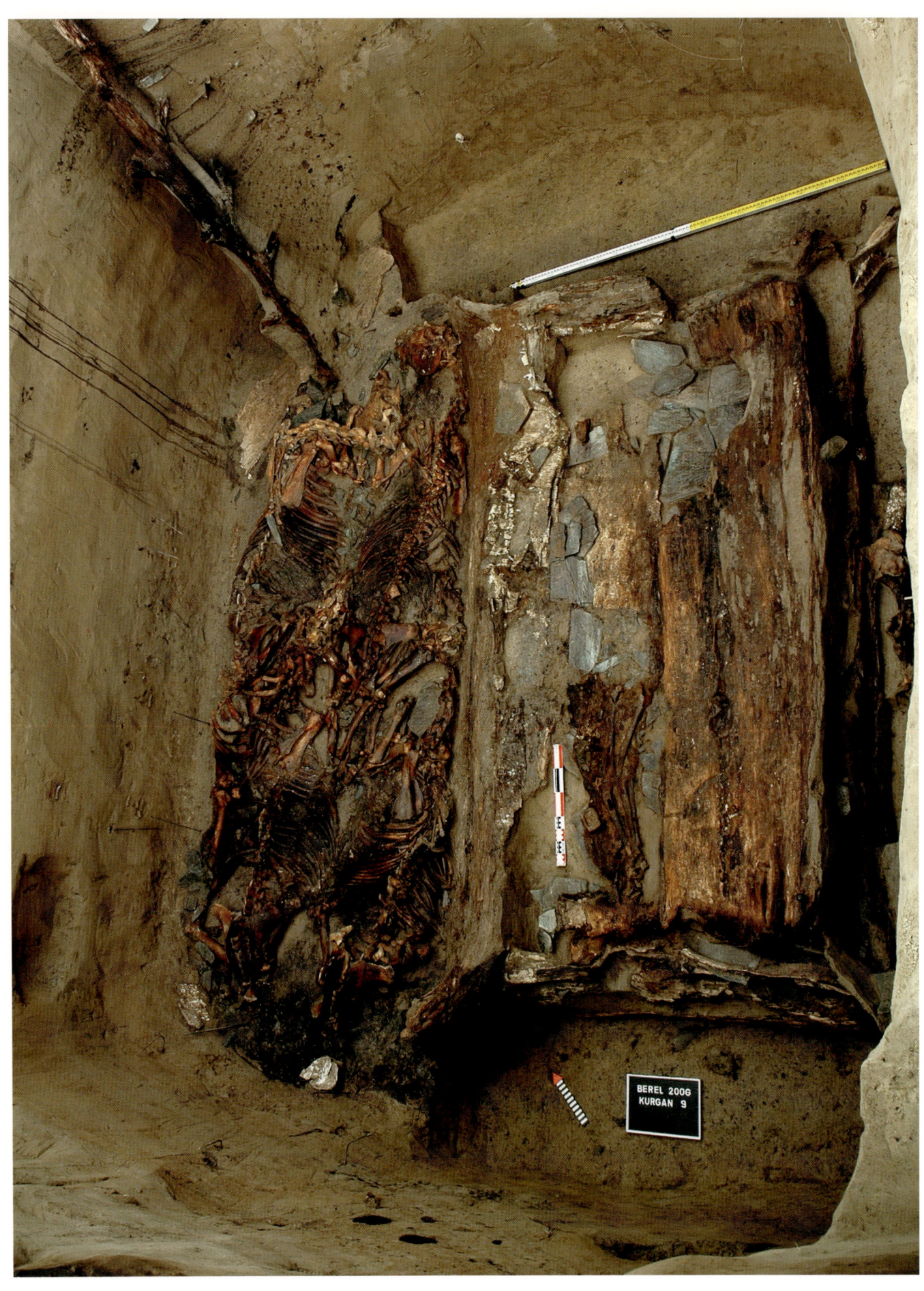

5-1 Berel kurgan 9 during excavation. This burial chamber resembles the arrangement of kurgan 11, which because of permafrost was not photographed in this manner. Note the horses lying outside the burial chamber.

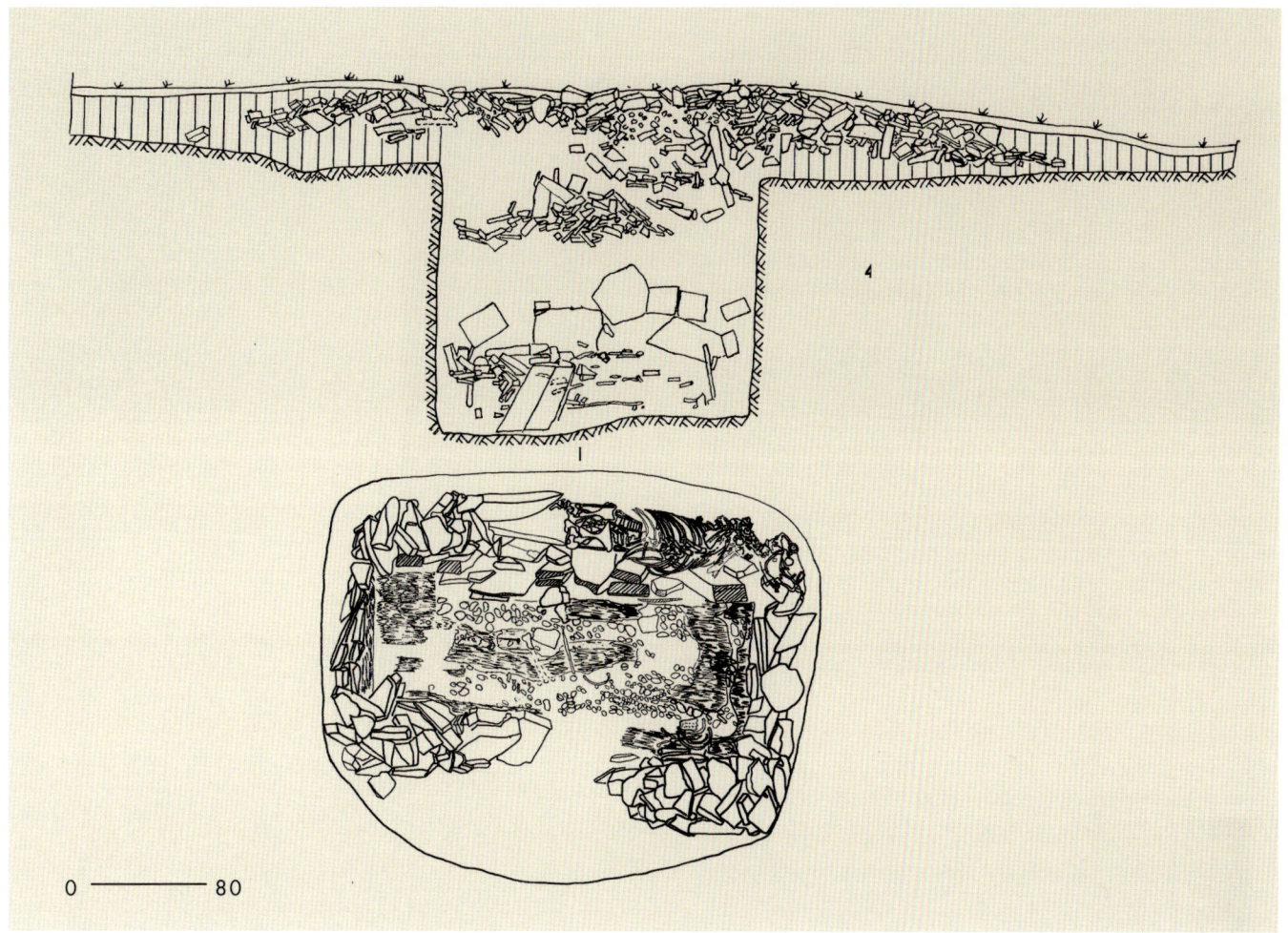

burial rituals, the Chinese historian's discussion of Xiongnu burial practices is less pertinent to the burials examined here.[4] However, Herodotus's reports provide a guide to some possible interpretations of what archaeologists have found through excavation. While the burials at Berel lie well beyond the areas with which Herodotus was directly familiar, his text does shed light on some practices observed in the Pazyryk culture of the Altai, to which Berel belongs. For example, he describes the elaborate treatment of the bodies of deceased elites, including first the evisceration and then the stuffing of the bodies with organic materials to preserve them. In Book 4.71 Herodotus records that "they take the king's corpse, and, having opened the belly, and cleaned out the inside, fill the cavity with a preparation of chopped cypress, frankincense, parsley-seed, and anise-seed, after which they sew up the opening, [and] enclose the body in wax. . . ."[5] Evidence for such treatment is clear among the remains of the Pazyryk culture, including, for example, in a burial on the Ukok plateau of an elite woman whose organs had been removed and whose body was subsequently stuffed with earth, dry grasses, and horsehair.[6] Some bodies of the Pazyryk culture also show remains of a resin on the skin.[7]

In the same chapter of *The History of the Persian War*, Herodotus notes that after a leader's body was preserved, it was taken through the lands he had overseen before burial. Although the explanation of the hiatus between death and burial may be different for the Pazyryk culture, studies show that the woman buried at Ak-Alakha 3 on the Ukok plateau had died in March or April, but that the burial did not take place until June, based on the grasses in the horses' stomachs.[8] That the male in Berel kurgan 11 predeceased his horses, and that the horses were killed just before burial, is also suggested.[9] Moreover, the contents of the stomachs of the horses in Berel kurgan 11 indicate that they were killed during June or July, when they could have eaten the pollen that was identified.[10] These Pazyryk-culture burials were located in areas that were frozen

5-2   Plan and section of Berel kurgan 36.

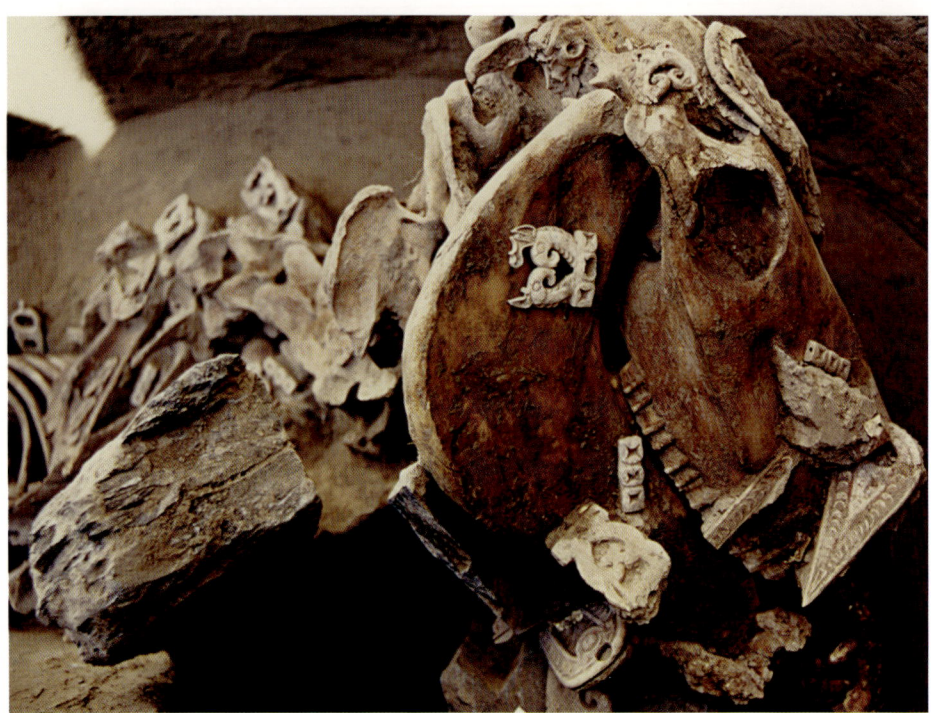

most of the year, allowing burial only for a short time in the summer, suggesting another reason for the preservation of the bodies: perhaps for cultural reasons a body that was visually lifelike was necessary for burial.[11]

The discussions of lifeways in these and other ancient texts can provide some alternatives to consider in an attempt to understand the patterns of life that may be indicated from the contents of the burials, including people and animals. In addition, ethnographic studies of living peoples can also supply patterns and practices both tangible and intangible that may suggest how to interpret what archaeologists find.[12] In fact, the earliest archaeological discoveries in the general region and the study of local traditional populations went hand in hand as Peter the Great extended Russian authority into the steppe during the early eighteenth century and asked that scientific materials be returned to him in St. Petersburg for study.[13]

INTERPRETING THE BURIALS

Archaeological excavation is a systematic process that traces and records a site while much of the actual site is physically deconstructed and destroyed by the excavation itself. In the case of these burials, how the kurgan, or mound, was constructed, how the burial and body were prepared, and how and with what the burial was filled are some of the data that archaeologists carefully log. Just like excavation itself, the interpretation of burials is the uncovering of multiple layers, but instead of material remains, they are layers of understanding and elucidation (figs. 5-2, 5-3a–b).

Burials are studied as burials, that is, in terms of death and its attendant elements, and also as indicators of the life of the deceased and his or her community.[14] This short essay considers only briefly a few examples of what burials may tell us. One way to investigate burials is to undertake an understanding of how the deceased and those who buried them viewed death and the role of the deceased in death. For example, the mound over Berel kurgan 11 was 33.5 by 22.8 meters, and it was preserved to a height of more than 2.5 meters.[15] The weight of the stones of the mound alone is estimated to be about 150 tons.[16] Production of a burial on this scale clearly was extremely labor intensive, so it must have been important to the members of the community to participate in its creation.[17] The very act of digging a burial pit, much less constructing a burial chamber and mound above, likely involved not only the elite person's relations but others over whom he exercised some kind of political, social, or economic power—making it worthwhile for the community to contribute its labor.[18] The very act of this participation would have reiteratively shaped the community's perceptions of social roles and the role of the deceased in society.[19] The large mounds, visible from afar, would have reinforced the memory of those roles and the participation of

5-3a Photograph of horse head, with bone harness elements, from Berel kurgan 36 during excavation.

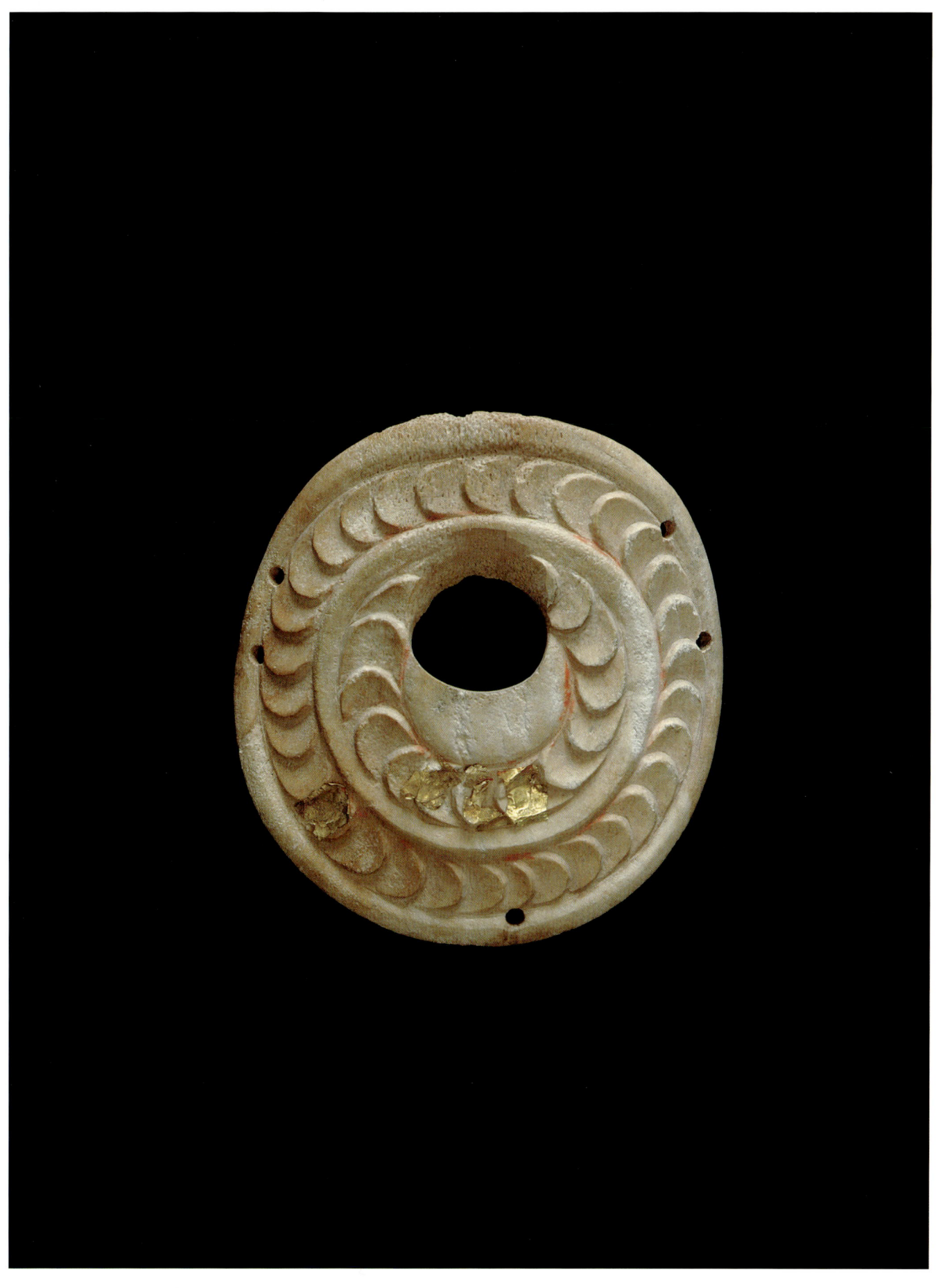

5-3b   Roundel that was located in the center of the horse's forehead, after conservation. Round element with scale pattern from bridle brow band. Horn (Siberian red deer) and gold foil, Berel, kurgan 36, late 4th–early 3rd century BCE. A. Kh. Margulan Institute of Archaeology, Almaty: B36-33. Checklist no. 18.

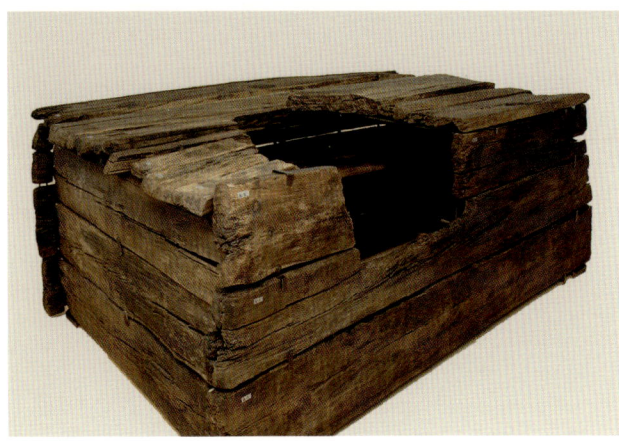

the community, however defined, in the rituals that surrounded the event of the death and burial. Although it is impossible to reconstruct the ceremony, it must have been an elaborate spectacle, accompanied by many rituals that together functioned as a group social event. In fact, there were constructions near kurgan 11 that may have had a ritual purpose.[20]

THE DECEASED

Materials from two burial kurgans, 11 and 36, at Berel compose many of the items in the exhibition.[21] Both mounds yielded much information and fascinating contents, even though they had both been looted (fig. 5-4). Study of the male and female in kurgan 11, who were not buried at the same time, demonstrates some of the tools that archaeologists use in the analysis of the deceased. One group of tools have been in use for a long time, including determining the sex and age of skeletons, and the bodies in kurgan 11 were not-well preserved. The male in kurgan 11, buried first, was around forty years old. His body was moved aside when the woman was buried; she was older than the man, between sixty and seventy. It is estimated that the two burials occurred between five and forty-five years apart.[22] Newer tools, including DNA analysis, were used to investigate the relationship of these two individuals, and some evidence suggests that they were blood relatives.[23]

Berel kurgan 11 is not the only burial of the Pazyryk culture that contained both a male and a female. At Pazyryk itself kurgans 2, 4, and 5 contained both an adult male and an adult female.[24] In kurgan 1 of Ak-Alakha 1 on the Ukok plateau, a male forty-five to fifty years old and a female about seventeen years of age were buried.[25] In the case of the latter tomb, there was no indication that the two individuals were buried at different times, and there was no mention of such a practice by S. Rudenko, the excavator of the Pazyryk kurgans. In fact, he assumed that the women were buried at the same time as the men with whom they were found, and he suggested that since, in general, women were treated well in Pazyryk society, based on ethnographic parallels of mobile pastoralists, those killed and buried must have been junior wives or concubines.[26] Other interpretations of the burials at Pazyryk suggest a higher status for the women in these graves.[27] The Ak-Alakha kurgan 1 double burial appears to be an exceptional case, since the man was riddled with arthritis and the woman was dressed and equipped like a man, which was a unique occurrence.[28] The excavator N. Polosmak suggests that there was a specific social and/or economic reason that the young woman had acquired this social role,[29] if indeed she was dressed in death as she had been in life, which cannot be certain. Perhaps, as in known ethnographic cases, this woman had been assigned a male role in lieu of an appropriate familial male.[30] What the meaning of any of these burials of a male and a female together indicates remains an open question, and there probably was more than one reason why such pairs were buried in the same tomb.[31]

Burials containing both men and women were not restricted to the elite graves of the above-mentioned sites but have also been found in burials of the Pazyryk culture excavated in the Russian Altai, which belonged to more-common people. These burials were sometimes accompanied by one or two horses and contained wooden ornaments with animal decorations, ceramic jars, and bronze weapons such as daggers in wooden scabbards. In some cases, a wooden carving was substituted for a dagger or a knife.[32] In contrast to the more elite sites, burials in these poorer and less elaborate graves contained many children. Of forty-four kurgans of Yustyd in the Altai containing a total of seventy-one burials, 37 percent were children, 33 percent were male, and 30 percent were female in various groupings.[33] At the site of Ulandryk, forty kurgans contained sixty individuals, of which 65 percent were women and children and 35 percent were males.[34] Unlike many of the larger, more elite burials, these were never found in frozen condition, so bodies have not been preserved.

Other modern scientific studies of the deceased individuals at Berel determined that both the male and

5-4 Burial chamber of Berel kurgan 11 after conservation. The hole was made by looters in antiquity.

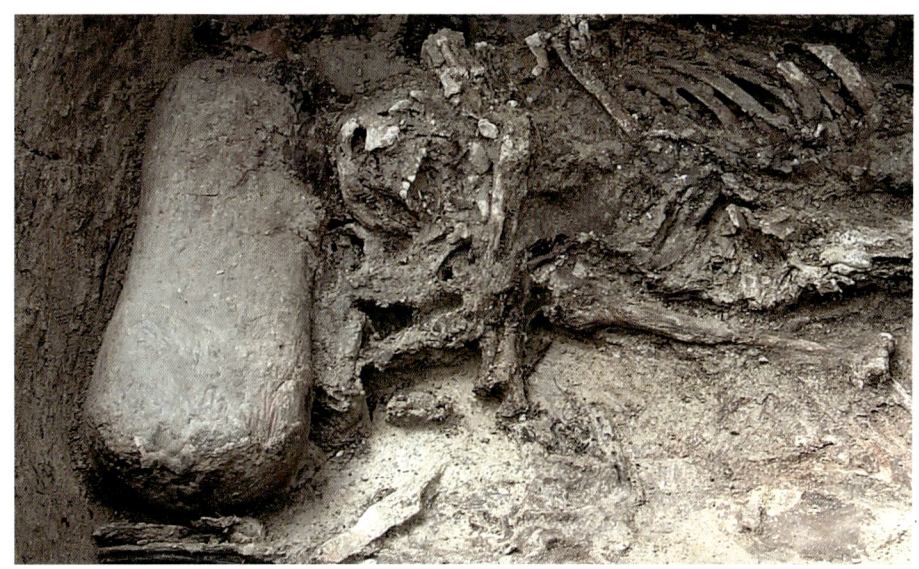

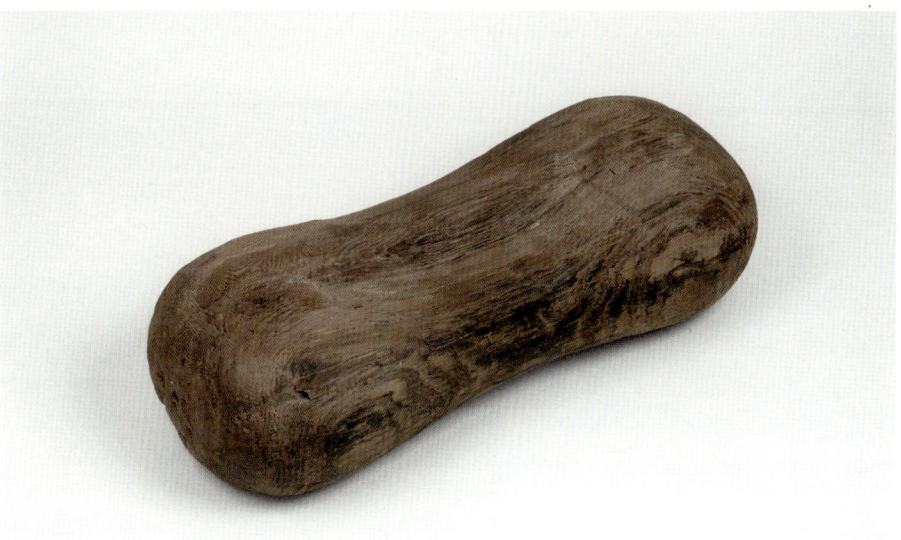

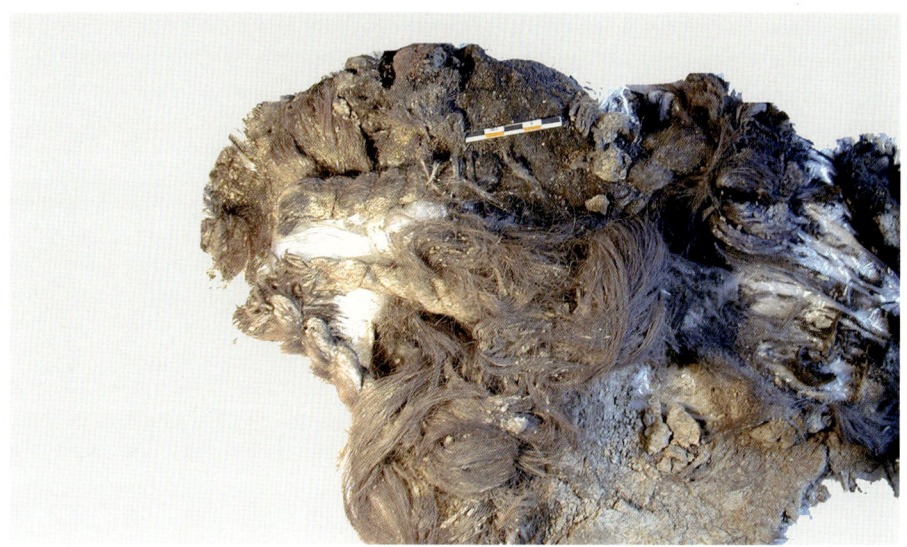

5-5   View of male in situ, Berel kurgan 11.

5-6   Headrest. Wood, Berel, kurgan 11, late 4th–early 3rd century BCE. A. Kh. Margulan Institute of Archaeology, Almaty. Checklist no. 84.

5-7   Wig of male buried in Berel kurgan 11.

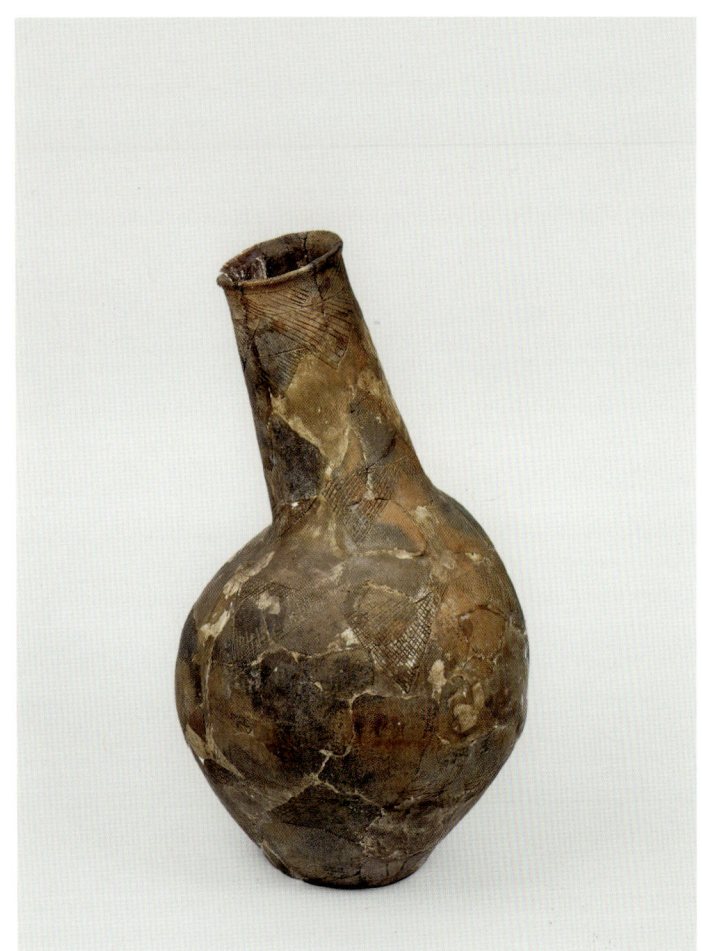
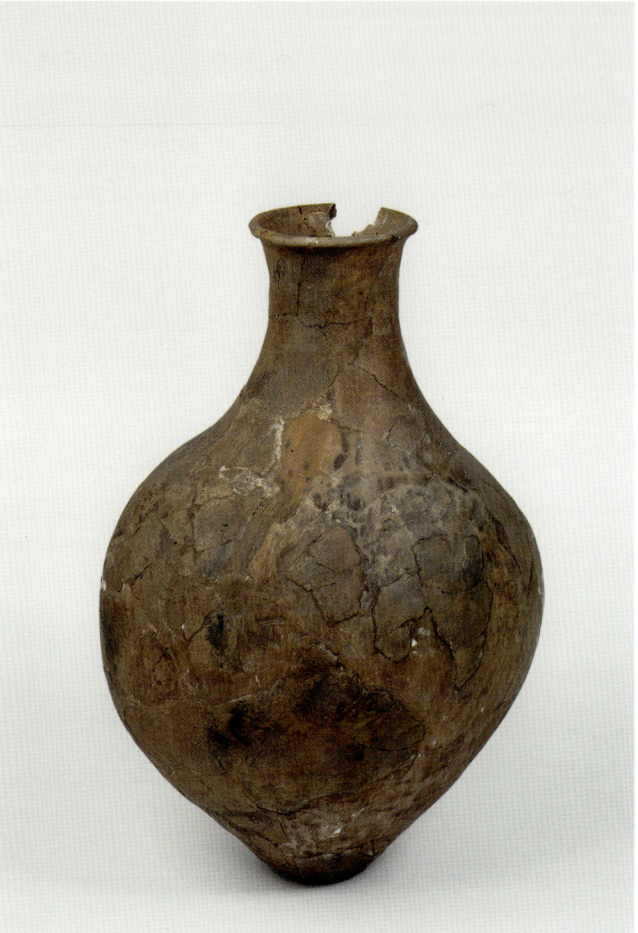

female from kurgan 11 were infested by the *Ankylostomias* (hookworm) parasite, native to warm climates. It is possible that individuals themselves had traveled far outside of the Altai, as has been suggested,[35] but since contact with more southerly areas was demonstratively part of the Pazyryk culture,[36] there may have been other means by which the infestations were acquired. This contact with not only southerly areas such as Central Asia, but with West Asia and China as well, is clearly shown through imported objects, such as Chinese mirrors, found in some burials and in the artistic references of the imagery on horse tack and other grave goods, including, for example, griffins. Much of this artistic evidence is explored and explained in the essay by Stark in this volume.

BURIAL CONTENTS AND DAILY LIFE

Some of the burial finds may have been far removed from daily life. One, or possibly two, examples can be seen in figure 5-5, which shows the remains of the kurgan 11 male at the time of excavation. At his head is a wooden pillow (fig. 5-6). Such pillows have been found in other Pazyryk-culture burials and seem to be associated with males, although this has not been systematically studied.[37] Whether such wooden pillows were also used in life cannot be determined—although Chinese ceramic pillows share the shape of some wooden Pazyryk-culture examples—and it cannot be said for certain that these objects were exclusively associated with burial. However, the wig that the man wore was likely part of his dress in death (fig. 5-7).[38] His head had been shaved and there was an effort at trepanation of the skull, whether to extract the brain at death and/or to try to save him after an axe-blow to the head.[39] Based on the evidence in Berel kurgan 11, this headdress, apparently attached by mastic, was at least part of the burial performance for this individual.[40]

5-8   (left) Jug with asymmetrical neck. Clay, Berel, kurgan 11/18(?), late 4th–early 3rd century BCE. A. Kh. Margulan Institute of Archaeology, Almaty. Checklist no. 96.

5-9   (right) Jug with lentoid body. Clay, Berel, kurgan 8, late 4th–early 3rd century BCE. A. Kh. Margulan Institute of Archaeology, Almaty. Checklist no. 95.

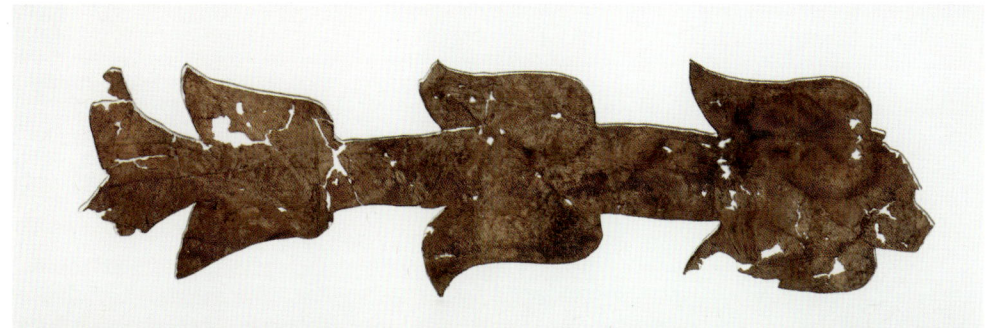

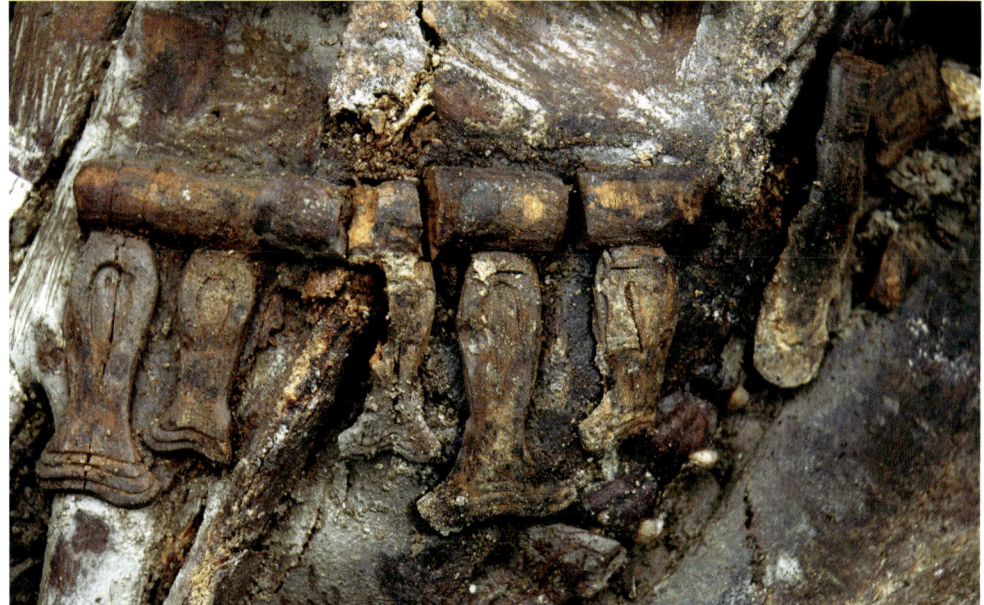

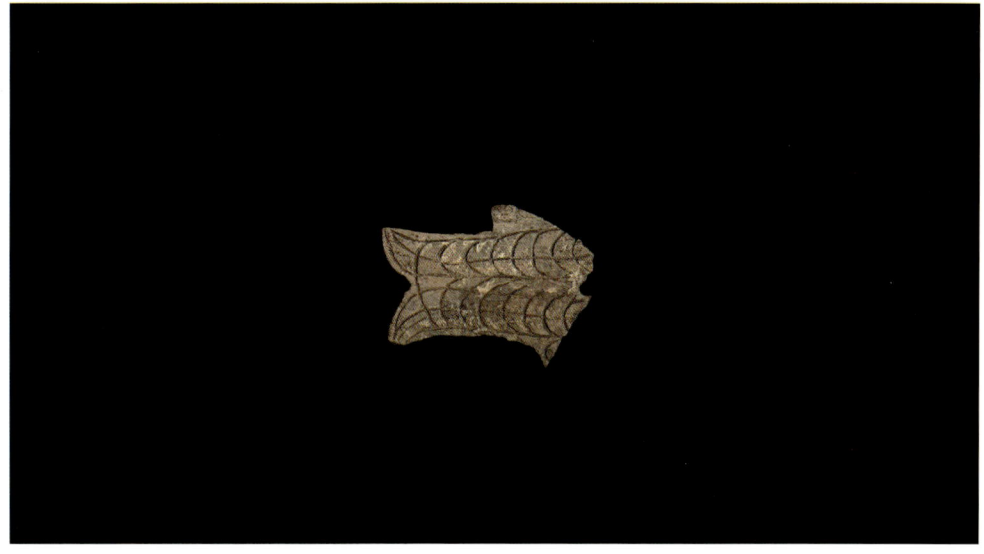

5-10　　Saddle-cloth element with fish ornament. Felt, Berel, kurgan 11, late 4th–early 3rd century BCE. A. Kh. Margulan Institute of Archaeology.

5-11　　Detail of excavation of Berel kurgan 10 showing part of a horse harness decorated with images of fish, in situ. (See also checklist no. 90.)

5-12　　Plaque in the form of a fish. Horn, 1st millennium BCE. Museum of Archaeology, Almaty. Checklist no. 116.

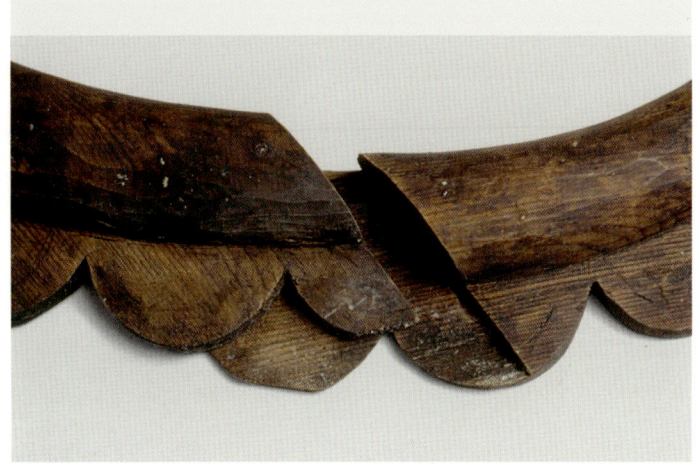

Other categories of grave goods undoubtedly were not used only for burial rituals. Based on their shapes, the ceramic vessels (figs. 5-8, 5-9) in the burial chambers once contained liquid, perhaps fermented mares' milk; the small wooden trays with removable legs held animal bones from a feast.[41] Whether these items were intended for the deceased in the next world, or were part of a funeral feast, or both, cannot be ascertained directly, but they could have been part of a ritual, communal meal.[42] The single shape of jars in the burials contrasts with the range of vessel shapes that are found in the settlement sites of Semirechye, including bowls, storage vessels, jars, and fragments of ceramic kettles.[43] Although no evidence of settlements has been found in the Kazakh Altai for this period, the same range of ceramic types in daily life is likely. Thus, in the case of the vessels from Berel kurgan 11, evidence of daily life is incomplete since the ceramics found do not represent all the types that might have been in daily use. Instead, the vessels represent a ritual requirement. Clearly, information from burials is selective.

Through the eyes of ancient historians and many who have followed their lead, Iron Age horseriders were seen as not having settlements of any kind. But among the burials at Berel and elsewhere in the Pazyryk culture, one sees substantial wooden structures—often log cabins roofed with timbers, bark, and felt—placed in the burial chambers. Rudenko long ago noted that these structures surely reflected houses of the living as well as the dead, and at Berel at least one timber of kurgan 11 may have originally been part of a dwelling.[44] At Ak-Alakha 1, timbers from a house were also used to construct a burial.[45] Based on this burial evidence, it is possible to infer something otherwise unknown about the way these people lived. Further support for the supposition that the tombs mirrored earthly dwellings can be found by applying information gained from the ethnographic study of similar mobile groups. Although current groups do not live exactly as peoples did in the past, scholars can judiciously compare archaeological and modern data.[46] For example, wooden structures are seen today on the Ukok plateau in the Altai in areas where Kazakhs live in the winter.[47]

More challenging is why such substantial structures resembling dwellings were used in many of the burials of the Pazyryk culture.[48] The people were placed in sarcophagi of single enormous larch logs that were then placed inside the wooden constructions; horses buried with the humans were placed outside the structure to the north. Were the humans, together with food and drink, meant to be presented as sleeping at home with their horses just outside the house, and thus viewed as remaining, in some figurative way, in the world of those who buried them? Was the world of the dead viewed as a replica of the world of the living? Since there is evidence that the bodies were preserved after death through elaborate processes (although there is little direct evidence from Berel),[49] and often bedecked with false headdresses, there was transformation of the deceased individuals between death and burial.[50] However, as M. Parker Pearson notes, "The dead may still be active members of society."[51] The situation of these burials in summer pastures, in structures that possibly reflect winter life, presents a conceptual representation of the annual cycle of these mobile pastoralists. Was it intentional?

A more prosaic hint of daily life can be seen in the imagery found on some of the burial goods. An ornament that hung from one of the saddle horses in Berel kurgan 11 represents a fish (fig. 5-10); in kurgan 10 at Berel, wooden fish decorated a horse bridle (fig. 5-11). Depictions of fish are also found in the art of mobile pastoralists in other media, for example, in bone plaques (fig. 5-12). At Pazyryk itself there are also saddle pendants with fish, and a similar fish with three sets of fins on the sides is tattooed on the male from Pazyryk kurgan 2. Rudenko identifies the fish as a burbot, a type that lives in fresh water and thrives in cold.[52] It can be inferred that because fish are applied both as a tattoo and as an ornament to elaborate horse decorations, there was some ritual or social significance in their artistic representations.[53] However,

5-13   Detail of construction of a sculpted ibex horn from a ceremonial horse headdress. Checklist no. 49.

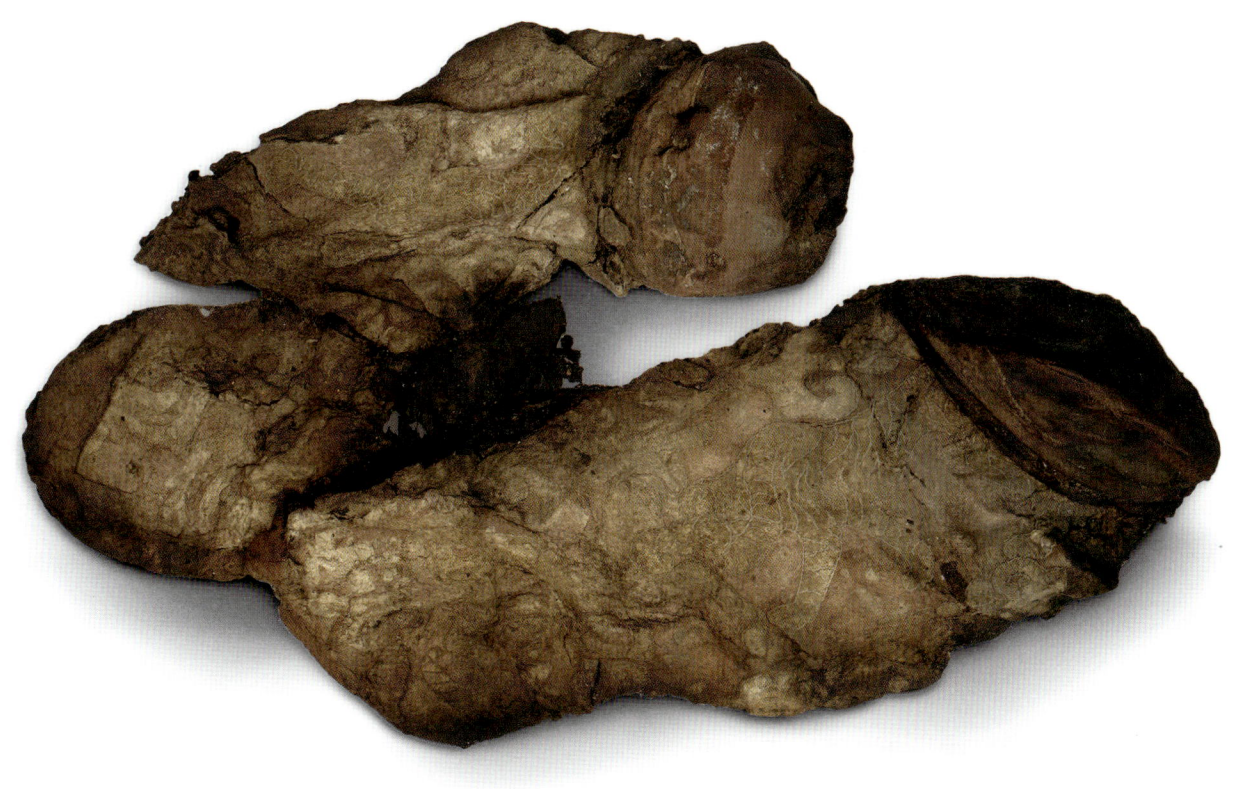

5-14　　Saddle decorated with tigers attacking elk, with border of horned, winged sphinxes. Felt and wood, Berel, kurgan 11, late 4th–early 3rd century BCE. A. Kh. Margulan Institute of Archaeology, Almaty. Checklist no. 79.

their appearance also implies that fish were part of the daily life of these individuals, providing food and perhaps other products as well.[53]

ART AND MEANING

According to Parker Pearson, "Material culture can ... be seen as a form of non-verbal communication through the representation of ideas."[54] It is this world of ideas that is most difficult to retrieve from burial remains, particularly from a culture without its own written texts to test interpretations. The elaborate trappings on horses buried in the Pazyryk graves provide a rich source of material culture. Many different approaches have been brought to bear in analyzing the decorations, and a summary will demonstrate how the varied points of view among scholars can broaden interpretation of data and deepen understanding of past peoples. In the exhibition the horse tack is displayed to reflect its original placement in kurgan 36, although organic remains, including the saddle, were not preserved. In addition, many elements of the horse trappings from kurgan 11 at Berel have been studied, although conservation is not yet complete (page 76, figs. 5-13, 5-14).

The broadest context for the outfitting of horses in Pazyryk culture requires discussion of both Pazyryk itself and Berel. Rudenko described the suites on the horses at Pazyryk in great detail,[55] noting that the adornment was probably for ceremonial use and not just for burial.[56] E. Jacobson, in contrast, argues that the horse tack was meant for burial and represents a fundamental and long-lived element of Siberian and steppe art: "the themes of predation and transformation ... organized around an implicit central vertical axis," represented by the head and body of the horses.[57] For example, Jacobson analyzes one of the horses from Pazyryk kurgan 1, with the mask of a feline with blue fur, and suggests that the panoply transformed the horse into a means to retell the mythic opposition of feline and winged/horned/antlered animal, thus embodying the concept of predation.[58] G. Argent approaches the material from the perspective of the horses' roles and their relationships to the human companions with whom the animals were buried.[59] She sees each suite as reflecting the age, training, and real-life role of the horse,[60] noting that the horse with the blue-fur feline mask is the oldest in Pazyryk kurgan 1. Its trappings were worn and mended in part, although they were not practical for daily use and therefore were probably ceremonial. Argent further suggests that the trappings could have represented a real event, the carrying of its human partner through a successful confrontation with a large wild feline, earning the horse high status among its horse and human community.[61] Parker Pearson sees the horses as "symbolically close to humans though they were treated not as equals but as companions to the dead," a relationship somewhat different than the one Argent envisions. He notes that the predator/prey motif is prevalent on Pazyryk saddle covers—the contact area between horse and rider—and implies a protective function for the decoration.[62]

In a study of the Berel horse ornaments, H.-P. Francfort, G. Ligabue, and Z. Samashev note that each animal was decorated with a consistent set of images representing a specific geographical region: the Near East, Sino-Mongolia, and local Siberia. They propose that allies of the male person buried in kurgan 11 brought their horses to be sacrificed at his funeral.[63]

This brief summary of varied suggestions about how to read the costumes of Pazyryk-culture horses, from the broadly political to the life history of an individual horse, from the perspective of the deep history of myth in Siberia to the role of image as apotropaic, samples the varied ways that archaeologists analyze data from burials to reach an understanding of the ways of thought of peoples of the past. The rich possibilities for finding the lives of the mind in the exceptional remains of Berel and other sites of the Pazyryk culture enrich our understanding of the worldview of Iron Age mobile pastoralists.

CONCLUSION

This essay has touched only briefly on what archaeologists can learn from the excavation and study of mortuary remains. Berel and other sites of the Pazyryk culture present an unusual opportunity to learn about the people who were buried at these sites. Although they did not leave us written records, the frozen organic materials that are so often lost through time provide the opportunity to learn much about the way of death of these people. Through modern scientific analysis and judicious use of ancient texts, anthropological approaches such as ethnographic analogy and landscape archaeology, and art historical analysis of the rich imagery, it is possible to reconstruct to some degree their way of life as well.

NOTES

1. See Samashev this volume for discussion of the excavations at Berel, and Toleubaev this volume for discussion of the excavation at Shilikty. Note that because of the exceptional preservation condition of Berel kurgan 11 (the contents were still frozen in the permafrost ice), much of the excavation was carried out in the laboratory to which the frozen contents were removed (Francfort, Ligabue, and Samashev 2006, 15–16). Effectively, the excavation still continues in the conservation laboratory, and a final report has not been published; many of the objects in the exhibition have been only recently conserved. Among the other publications of Berel are Francfort 1999; Samashev et al. 2000a; Samashev et al. 2000b; Samashev, Bazarbaeva, and Zhumabekova 2002; Samashev and Borodovsky 2004; Samashev and Mylnikov 2004; Gorbunov, Samašev, and Severskii 2005; Samashev 2006; Samashev 2007. The Shilikty burial was very disturbed due to ancient looting and will not be discussed in this essay.
2. One need only look at the index in the English translation of Rudenko's detailed discussion of the burials at Pazyryk in the Russian Altai to see how Herodotus's text has informed the interpretation of remains similar to those at Berel (Rudenko 1970, 336). For a recent discussion of Herodotus's approach and intent in his extensive information about various steppe pastoral groups, see Hind 2011. Finally, note the title of one of the articles about Berel in this context: "Die 'goldhütenden Greife' des Herodot und die archäologische Kultur der frühen Nomaden im kazachischen Altai (Samashev, Bazarbaeva, and Zhumabekova 2002). See also Stark this volume.
3. Although Sima Qian was discussing the Xiongnu—mobile pastoralists who lived northeast of eastern Kazakhstan and somewhat later than the burials at Berel—the lifeways of both peoples were similar. See Di Cosmo 2002, 267–90, for a summary of the way of life described for them.
4. Di Cosmo 2002, 273–74.
5. *The History of Herodotus*, trans. George Rawlinson, www.greektexts.com/library/Herodotus/Melpomene/eng/print/102.html.
6. For preburial preservation of bodies in the Pazyryk culture of the Altai, see Rudenko 1970, 279–83; Polosmak 1999, 156–57; Parker Pearson 2000, 61–64. For a discussion of burials geographically closer to Herodotus's home in the Black Sea region, where his reports are broadly confirmed by archaeological excavation, see Ivantchik 2011.
7. Polosmak 1999, 157, 159.
8. Ibid., 160. On the plateau where the Berel kurgans were located, the ground is frozen for half the year and it is only in the summer that excavation of the grave would have been possible (Gorbunov, Samashev, and Severskii 2005, 13, 16).
9. Gorbunov, Samashev, and Severskii 2005, 29. It is an assumption that the horses belonged to the male, but there is no evidence they were deposited later than the original burial, as the woman was.
10. Samashev 2006, 43.
11. Parker Pearson, 2000 ,63.
12. Barnard and Wendrich 2008a, 14; Frachetti 2008b, 368–72; and see Alimbai this volume.
13. Jacobson 1987, 2–7; Basilov 1989, 7–8; Hanks 2001, 39; Bokovenko 2006, 860.
14. Overviews of approaches to the archaeological study of burials include Jensen and Nielsen 1997; McHugh 1999; Parker Pearson 2000. For a summary of history and approaches to steppe burials in an adjacent region, see Hanks 2000. See Honeychurch, Wright, and Amartuvshin 2009, 344–45, for a model of how to interpret burial construction data. See Hanks 2002b for a discussion of the interaction of society and mortuary ritual.
15. Samashev et al. 2000b, 8.
16. Gorbunov, Samashev, and Severskii 2005, 31.
17. Parker Pearson 2000, 84.
18. See Chang 2008 for a discussion of reasons why the local community might participate.
19. Härke 1997, 23.
20. Gorbunov, Samashev, and Severskii 2005, 31.
21. See Samashev this volume for a discussion of the burials.
22. Samashev et al. 2000b, 11; Samashev, Bazarbaeva, and Zhumabekova 2002, 252; Frankfort, Ligabue, and Samashev 2006, 117.
23. Samashev et al. 2000b, 11. However, the same evidence has also been interpreted to demonstrate that they were not closely related (Francfort, Ligabue, and Samashev 2006, 118). For another interpretation of the evidence for the timing of the burials, see Samashev 2006, 40.
24. Rudenko 1970, 315, 323, 324.
25. Polosmak 1991; Polosmak 1994.

26 Rudenko 1970, 211–12.
27 Linduff and Rubinson forthcoming.
28 Polosmak 1991; Polosmak 1994; Полосьмак 2001.
29 Полосьмак 2001, 276.
30 Taylor 2010, 146.
31 Linduff and Rubinson forthcoming. See also Francfort, Ligabue, and Samashev 2006, 118–19.
32 Кубарев 1987, 59.
33 Кубарев 1991, 3
34 Кубарев 1987, 23.
35 Francfort, Ligabue, and Samashev 2006, 118. Tests yielded other parasites as well (Samashev 2006, 41).
36 See Stark this volume.
37 Rudenko 1970, 69. Rudenko thought that they might be stools rather than pillows. Due to the placement at the head and the shapes of some that are similar to Chinese ceramic examples, these objects are now considered pillows.
38 Some other Pazyryk deceased, both male and female, wore wigs. See ibid., 104–5.
39 Samashev et al. 2000b, 11.
40 Some Pazyryk-culture women also wore wigs in their graves and perhaps in life (Polosmak 1999, 147–48). Hair seems to have had a further ritual significance in the society (Polosmak and Trunova 2004).
41 Rudenko 1970, 65–68.
42 See Rudenko 1970, 60–61, 65–68; Samashev, Bazarbaeva, and Zhumabekova 2002, fig. 27.
43 For example, the ceramics at Tsenganka 8 (Chang et al. 2003, 304). See also Chang this volume.
44 Rudenko 1970, 62–64; Samashev et al. 2000a, 20; Samashev and Mylnikov 2004, 50.
45 Koryakova and Epimakhov 2007, 218.
46 See Frachetti 2008a, 107–17, for a comprehensive discussion of the theory.
47 See Полосьмак 2001, 20 and fig. 7, for a contemporary ethnographic example on the Ukok Plateau.
48 Other burials contained stone cists, as in kurgan 36, material from which is also featured in the exhibition.
49 Francfort, Ligabue, and Samashev 2006, 117.
50 Parker Pearson 1982, 61–64.
51 Parker Pearson 2000, 141.
52 Rudenko 1970, 247.
53 See Chang this volume.
54 Parker Pearson 1982, 100.
55 Rudenko 1970, 117–86, 229–39.
56 Ibid., 185–86.
57 Jacobson 1993, 57.
58 Ibid., 67.
59 Argent 2010.
60 Ibid., 164, notes that the horses at Pazyryk ranged in age from nine to twenty years. The horses from Berel kurgan 11 ranged from thirteen to eighteen or nineteen years, and from Berel kurgan 18 from ten to twelve years (Samashev 2006, 43).
61 Argent, 2010, 164, 165, 168–69.
62 Parker Pearson 2000, 67.
63 Francfort, Ligabue, and Samashev 2006, 122–23. They note that this suggestion was also made for the Arzhan 1 kurgan in Tuva (see essays this volume by Bokovenko and Samashev and by Hanks).

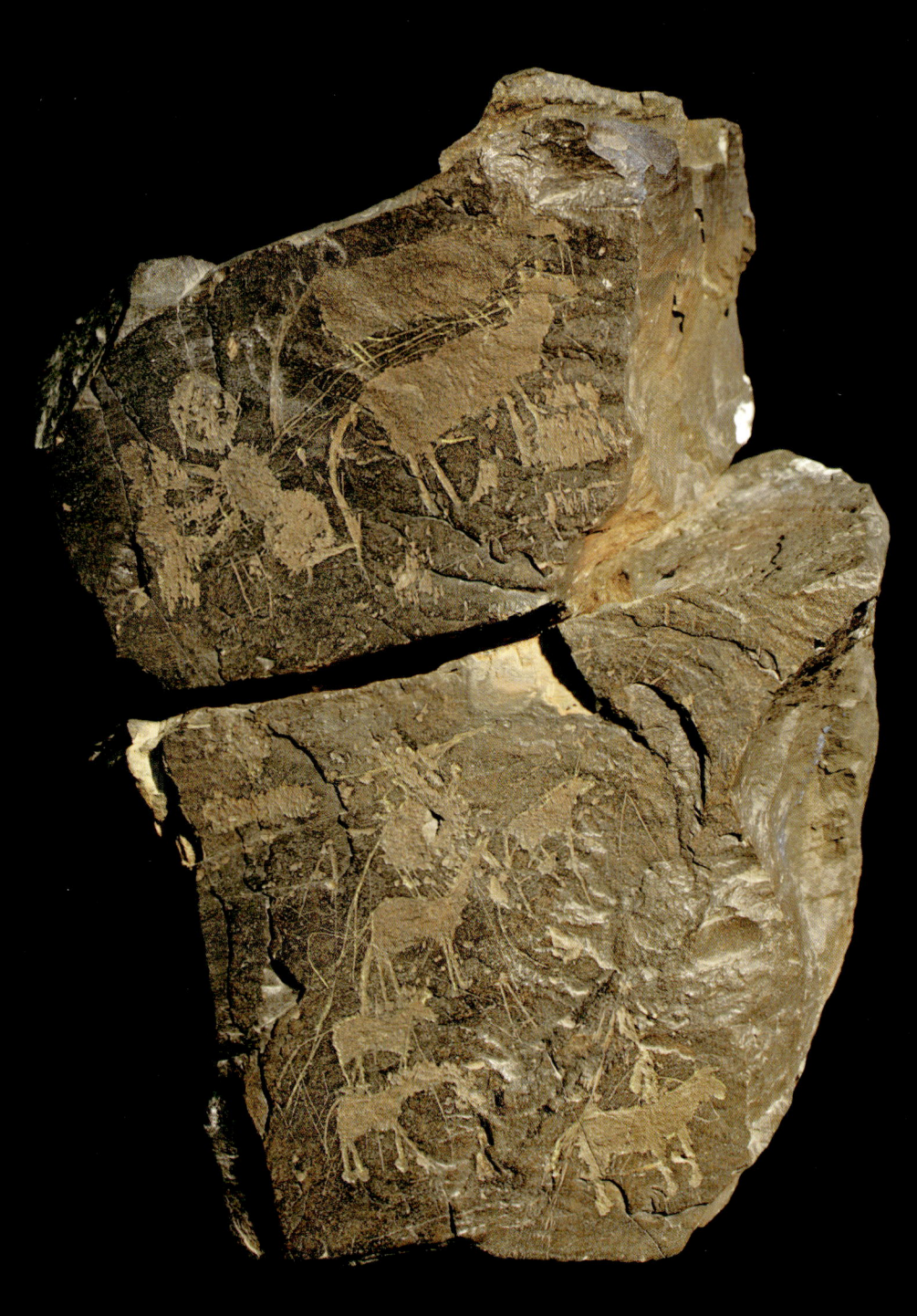

MOUNTED WARFARE AND ITS SOCIOPOLITICAL IMPLICATIONS

Bryan K. Hanks

After five centuries of migration between their winter settlements and their summer pastures the steppe peoples of the Late Bronze Age were ready for the change to a completely nomadic way of life. They were skilled horsemen, they had long been accustomed to using wheeled transport (carts drawn by a pair of oxen), and in some areas may already have been moving about from place to place during the summer. Then in the 8th century BC some particular tribe, or perhaps a number of tribes in different parts of the steppe zone, abandoned their settled way of life and took to nomadism, moving constantly in search of fresh grazing for their herds.

The nomads could carry out swift surprise raids on the settlements of the sedentary tribes and make off with their booty before the enemy was able to collect their forces; and they could carry out these raids without upsetting the normal processes of the nomadic economy. Thus the nomads with their elusive forces of armed horsemen became the scourge of the settled population of the region. In order to protect themselves against raiding and plunder by the nomads, and to be in a position to carry out similar raids themselves, the sedentary tribes were in turn compelled to change to a nomadic way of life and take up nomadic herding wherever local conditions made this possible.[1]

Petroglyph of two horses pulling a cart (above) and two horsemen and four horses (below). Stone, Eshkiolmes, Semirechye/Zhetisu (Dzhungar Mountains), 1st millennium BCE. Central State Museum, Almaty: KP 25866/1-2. Checklist no. 103.

INTRODUCTION

The excerpt above, from Mikhail Gryaznov's book *The Ancient Civilization of Southern Siberia*, vividly portrays the emergence of mounted warfare and pastoral nomadism in the first millennium BCE. Extraordinary archaeological discoveries, such as the frozen tombs from Berel in Kazakhstan, and other Early Iron Age tombs in the Altai-Sayan mountain system of Russia and Mongolia, provide unique windows through time by which to view the important connection between mounted warfare and new forms of sociopolitical power (see map, pages 12–13). The building of large tomb complexes through organized communal effort, the sacrifice and deposit of horses and riding gear, and the placement of valuable personal possessions with the deceased all contributed to underscore the power and wealth of early elites within these societies. Moreover, the visibility of these tombs and clusters of tombs within the landscape inscribed such relationships in the memory of the living and in the numerous descendant generations that would occupy these territories. There can be no doubt that such monuments played a crucial role in connecting constructed political territories with more traditionally understood and inhabited natural worlds.

This essay examines these important processes within the development of sociopolitical power in the Eurasian steppe region during the first millennium BCE. Such an examination requires that these developments be situated within a broader chronological scale—stretching from important monumental constructions and horse sacrifice in the Late Bronze Age to the rise of the earliest steppe confederations and empires in the Iron Age. In so doing, it is possible to better understand the unique trajectories and important horizons of development connected with mounted warfare that have become accepted as such an important element in the history of the Eurasian steppes.[2]

RECENT VIEWS ON THE EMERGENCE OF HORSE RIDING AND MOUNTED WARFARE

Much archaeological research has transpired since Gryaznov published his volume on ancient Siberia in 1969. New archaeological surveys and excavations in the Altai-Sayan Mountains and neighboring territories have brought to light new funerary tomb complexes and, increasingly, information on patterns of settlement and the social and environmental factors that led to the emergence of more-mobile forms of pastoralism.[3] Yet one of the most persistent questions connected with the prehistoric Eurasian steppe is, when did the horse first become domesticated and ridden? Recent research in northern Kazakhstan, focusing on the Eneolithic Botai culture (ca. 3500 BCE), is helping to shed light on this long-standing question. Excavations at Botai-period settlements have produced large amounts of horse bones that often make up 99 percent of the faunal remains recovered from these sites.[4] Analysis of these materials has suggested that many of these horses were hunted for food. Recent studies, however, have indicated that early forms of taming and domestication also took place. Detailed analysis of pottery as well as teeth and bones from ancient horse remains at Botai sites indicate that mares were milked and some horses were ridden. Evidence for this has been found through horse-milk residue in pottery vessels, bit wear[5] on the lower premolars, and morphological changes to the lower limb bones of horses.[6] Recent studies on the DNA of modern horses within Eurasia[7] also indicate that horse domestication and breeding were a multiregional phenomenon, and that evidence such as that found at Botai should be sought in other regions of Eurasia as well.

The evidence from Botai is important as it raises a number of additional questions about human–horse relationships and the process of domestication, horse riding, and the development of mounted warfare. Many scholars remain unconvinced that mounted warfare was a significant force in the Eurasian steppe until the late second to early first millennium BCE.[8] If horses were being domesticated and ridden by 3500 BCE, why are more-widespread forms of mounted warfare not visible until the first millennium BCE? It appears that one important stage of technological development connected with the use of horses in warfare was the light, spoke-wheeled chariot.

As R. Drews has suggested, the "evolution of horsemanship from display and recreation to war was accomplished *with the chariot* [original emphasis]."[9] Indeed, archaeological research in the southern Ural Mountains of Russia and in northwestern Kazakhstan has shown that chariot warfare emerged in these areas by the beginning of the second millennium BCE. Certainly the ability to ride horses must have spread throughout Eurasia in the fourth and third millennia BCE, and using horses for small-scale raiding between social groups would have naturally developed. Yet the more institutionalized and formal mode of cavalry warfare was much slower to develop and only evolved

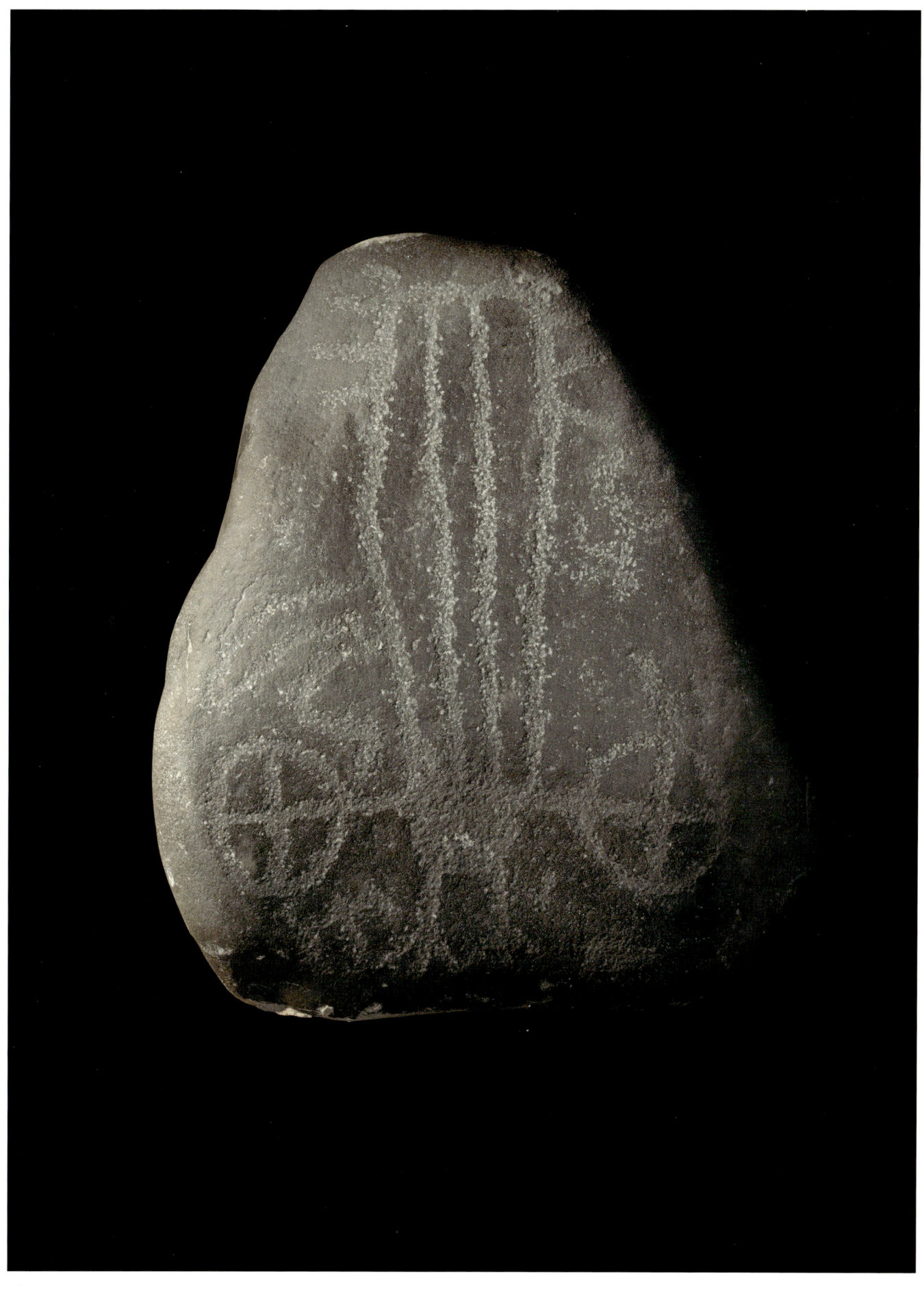

6-1 Petroglyph of a spoke-wheeled chariot. Stone, Tamgaly, Semirechye/Zhetisu (Almaty region), 2nd–1st millennium BCE. Museum of Archaeology, Almaty. Checklist no. 105.

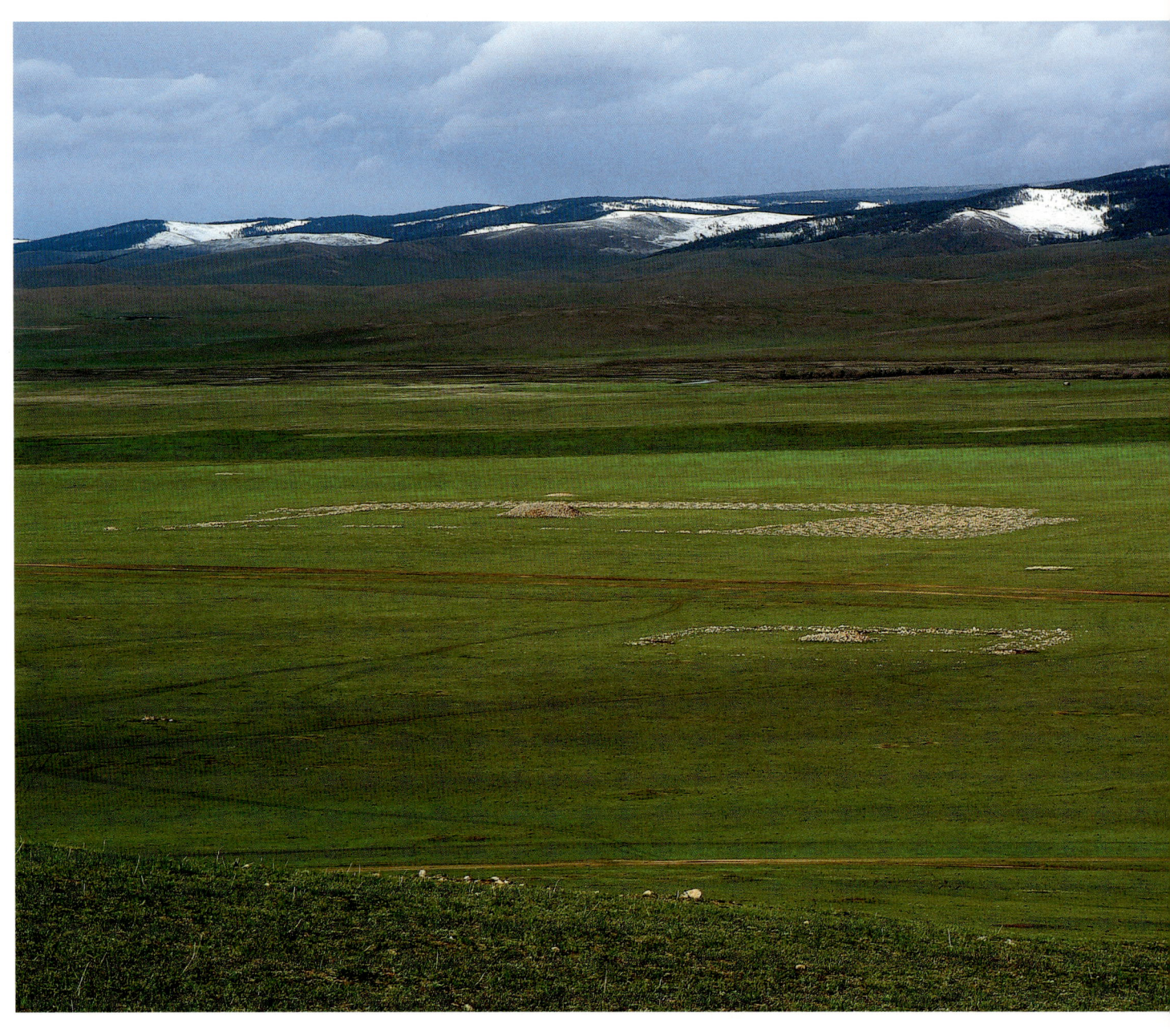

6-2a View of two khirigsuur monuments in the Khanuy Valley, at Urt Bulagyn, Mongolia.

6-2b (opposite) Archaeological plan of the key ritual features of the Urt Bulagyn khirigsuur.

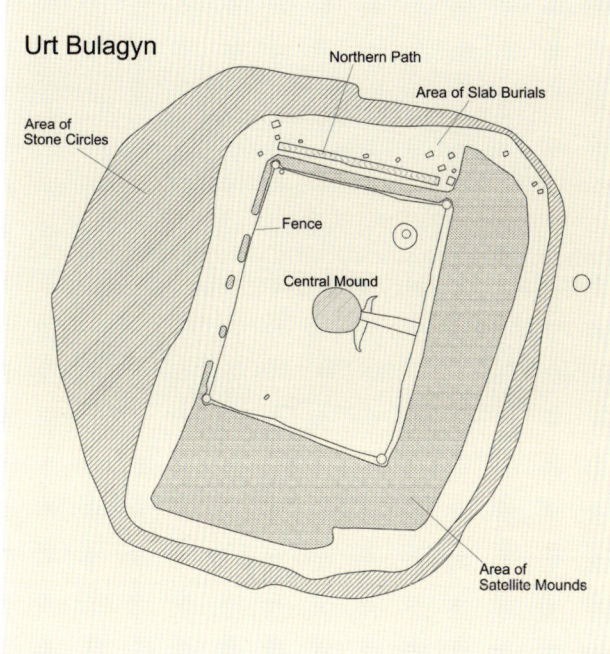

after the technology of chariots pulled by horses diffused throughout much of Eurasia. Thus far, the earliest dated archaeological evidence for chariot technology comes from burial deposits at the Bronze Age sites of Sintashta and Krivoe Ozero in Russia, which have been dated to around 2100 cal. BCE.[10]

Available archaeological evidence, therefore, suggests that the use of horses for pulling chariots appeared at least two or three centuries before the technology was used in the Near East, and that chariot warfare in the steppe preceded widespread mounted warfare by at least a millennium (fig. 6-1). The question of why the development of mounted warfare took so long to emerge, as it is so clearly expressed at sites such as Berel and Pazyryk, remains to be more fully answered. But such an answer must depend on a nuanced understanding of evolving sociopolitical practices in Bronze Age Eurasia and of how the nature of warfare and its related technologies were controlled. One important line of evidence for resolving the question is the appearance of large-scale monuments with horse sacrifice in the Late Bronze Age. Although such sites were well-known to Soviet-period scholars in the latter half of the twentieth century in Western Siberia and the Altai-Sayan Mountains, more-recent field research in Mongolia has produced important evidence dating to around 1200–800 BCE. Numerous complex stone monuments, known as *khirigsuurs* in Mongolian, have been identified, recorded, and in some cases excavated. This research has brought to light an important new class of monument with substantial evidence of horse sacrifice and the communal construction of complex ritual monuments.

EARLY MONUMENT BUILDING AND HORSE SACRIFICE

Soviet-period scholars produced an important record of archaeological sites and late prehistoric monuments throughout Western Siberia, the Altai-Sayan Mountains, and Central Mongolia.[11] In recent years the survey, excavation, and dating of archaeological remains from khirigsuur monuments in Mongolia has added importantly to this earlier work and generated a new perspective on the relationships among monument constructions, ritual activities, and the role of horse sacrifice. An excellent example of this research can be found at the site of Urt Bulagyn in the Khanuy Valley, Central Mongolia. Urt Bulagyn is one of the two largest khirigsuur sites in the Khanuy Valley, and work there has documented the construction of a large stone complex measuring nearly 400 by 400 meters with a 5-meter-high central mound that is 26 meters in diameter (figs. 6-2a–b). The complex also contains over 1,700 smaller "satellite" mounds around the periphery of the central "fence" and "central mound" area. Excavation of several of these satellite mounds has indicated that each contains an east-facing horse skull and/or vertebrae or lower leg bones.[12] A further 1,100 stone circles have been identified at Urt Bulagyn, and these have been found to contain cremated animal-bone remains of various species. The central mounds of khirigsuur monuments, which in almost all cases have been disturbed through looting, frequently contain human remains. Archaeological excavation and radiocarbon dating have suggested that smaller khirigsuur constructions may have been built by one to two centuries before larger monuments like Urt Bulagyn. This has led some scholars to suggest that the construction of these features in the landscape, combined with the burial of certain deceased members of the society, may have led steadily toward the rise of more powerful members of these societies. The sacrifice of horses as part of these ritual activities, in some cases on the very large scale seen at Urt Bulagyn, also suggests an emphasis on the horse and its important role in sociopolitical power within the region.

Another class of monument found either alone or in association with khirigsuur complexes is the "deer stone" (fig. 6-3). Deer stones are widespread throughout

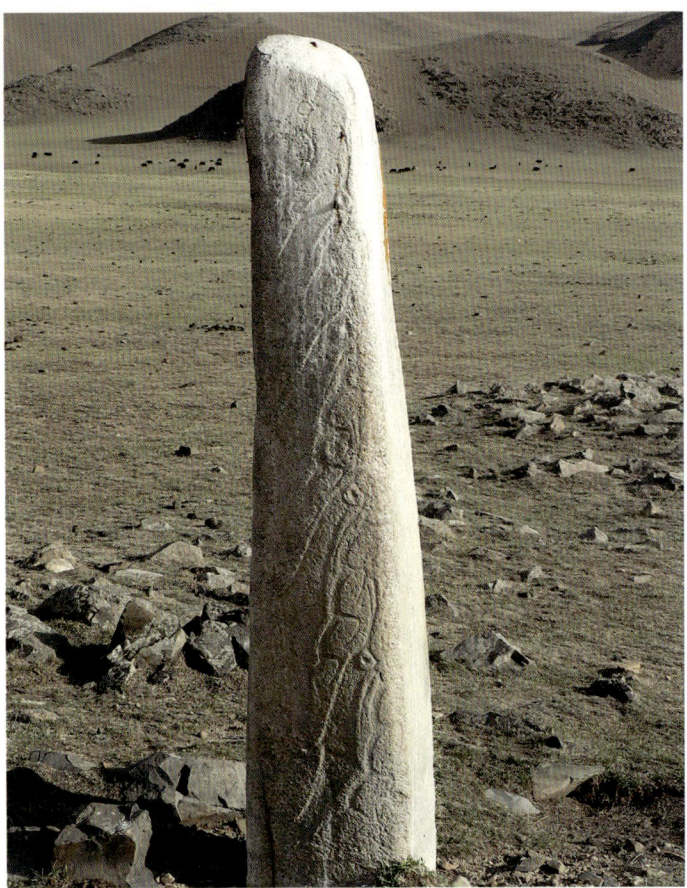

shared across these sites indicate ritual activities that emphasize animal-style imagery, horses and horse sacrifice, and warriors with associated weaponry. These elements of material expression, and their connection to martial themes, were soon to become prominently displayed throughout numerous Iron Age tombs within the Eurasian steppe region in the first centuries of the first millennium BCE.

This transition, which gave rise to the Early Iron Age phase in the Eurasian steppes, has conventionally been understood as a vibrant period of social, economic, political, and technological change.[17] The widespread diffusion of mobile pastoralism, a cavalry form of warfare, and similar forms of material culture known as the "Scythian Triad"[18] have been connected with processes of large-scale migration and groups known from early historians (Herodotus, Strabo, and so forth) as, for example, the Scythians and the Sakā. In recent years scholars have focused on identifying new evidence for the multiregional appearance of Early Iron Age groups. This has resulted in important new data on both mortuary and settlement patterning and a deeper understanding of the complex social and environmental processes that led to a more widespread pattern of mobile pastoralism and greater regional and interregional political and economic integration.[19]

Mongolia, Russia, and Central Asia but in form can vary substantially from region to region. Deer stones were intensively studied by Soviet-period scholars, and the iconography of these significant monuments were understood as being connected importantly to the Pre-Scythian period. Many deer stones portray cervids[13] with hybrid elements such as bird beaks, and it has been suggested that this imagery has a strong connection to ancient spiritual and cosmological belief systems of early Eurasian populations.[14]

Some deer stones show clear anthropomorphic characteristics and include belt lines with weaponry hanging from them. Soviet scholars were the first to suggest that these stylized stelae represent cenotaphs for deceased warriors of the Late Bronze and Early Iron ages.[15] Recent surveys in Mongolia by researchers from the Smithsonian Institution in Washington, D.C., have documented more than 1,000 deer stone monuments in Mongolia alone. Recent large-scale surveys and radiocarbon dating have indicated that deer stones, khirigsuurs, and rock art within Mongolia are all part of a distinct ceremonial complex of activities that emerged in the Late Bronze Age.[16] Elements commonly

EARLY IRON AGE TRIBES AND SUPRALOCAL SCALES OF SOCIOPOLITICAL POWER

In his numerous writings, field surveys, and excavations, the renowned Soviet archaeologist Mikhail Gryaznov contributed substantially to our understanding of the Eurasian Early Iron Age and to what has been termed the Scythian, or Scytho-Siberian, epoch. His exploration in the 1970s of important tombs such as Arzhan 1 in Tuva, which dates to the boundary of the eighth–ninth centuries BCE,[20] brought to light some of the earliest archaeological evidence for the appearance of an Iron Age mounted-warrior complex.[21] Even though the Arzhan 1 tomb had been looted substantially in antiquity, recovered artifacts from the site included metal horse bits, weaponry, and animal-style art imagery. In addition to the elite couple buried in the center of the tomb, and additional servants placed in surrounding chambers, nearly 160 sacrificed horses with riding gear were deposited throughout the monument (see Bokovenko and Samashev this volume, fig. 1-1). The tomb itself, a complex, radial mass of larch logs covered with stones, was 120 meters in diameter and 4 meters high.

6-3 Deer stone monument in the Khanuy Valley, Mongolia, dating to the late 2nd–early 1st millennium BCE.

The sociopolitical and economic significance of this massive monumental construction cannot be overstated. N. Bokovenko, a Russian archaeologist who specializes in the Iron Age, has suggested that it likely represents the entombment of a powerful chieftain who may have controlled a large-scale, pantribal confederation in the Altai-Sayan region at this time.[22] Arzhan 1 represents a very important "horizon marker" in the evolution of sociopolitical power in the northern Eurasian region and should be understood in the context of regional developments that preceded it in the Late Bronze Age.

The continual development of sociopolitical power in the region has been further documented through recent collaborative excavations by a Russian-German team in Tuva. The unlooted burial complex of Arzhan 2, which was discovered at the beginning of the present century and dates to the middle to the end of the seventh century BCE, has produced a wealth of fine artifacts, including over 5,600 golden objects (fig. 6-4). The discovery of this unlooted tomb has provided important new details concerning ritual activities connected with the burial of the elite couple, including sacrificial horses and numerous objects fashioned in the animal style. Both the Arzhan 1 and 2 tombs are set amid hundreds of additional kurgan complexes along the banks of the Uyuk River in the Tuva region—representing a landscape of wealth and power memorialized through numerous lineages.

The Arzhan 1 and 2 tombs predate many of the Early Iron Age tombs known from Mongolia, Russia, and Kazakhstan. Importantly, many of these later tombs, dating from the fourth–third centuries BCE, have yielded frozen remains preserved through permafrost conditions in these regions. The well-known excavations of S. Rudenko[23] at Pazyryk produced some of the finest preserved organic materials from the Early Iron Age. Excavations at other sites, including Berel, have yielded extraordinarily well-preserved artifacts, including metal horse bits, bronze axes, arrowheads, and wooden shields (figs. 6-5–6-8).[24] Animal-style imagery continued to be a significant and vibrant form of artistic representation, especially in connection with horse tack, including fanciful saddlery, masks, and headdresses (figs. 6-9, 6-10). Such artifacts clearly indicate the increasing importance placed on the horse and its role in warfare, as well as on the social and political performance of warriors and warrior elites.[25]

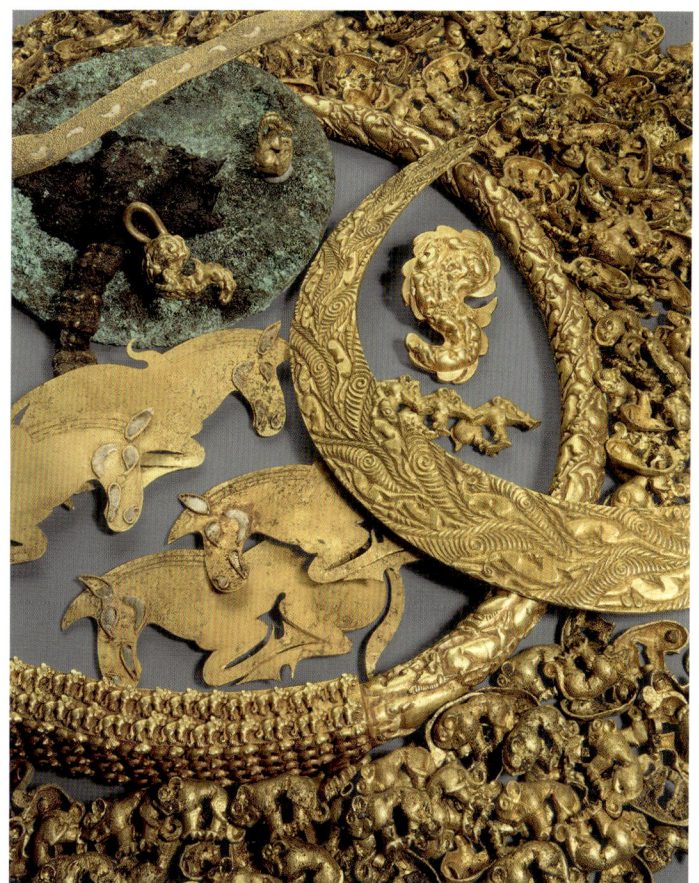

CONCLUSION

This chapter has reviewed several important archaeological sites in Kazakhstan, Russia, and Mongolia in order to highlight key developments connected with the early emergence of mounted warfare and the evolution of sociopolitical power. Important material elements connected with these transitions include the construction of large-scale monuments, the increasing significance of the horse as an effective technological and symbolic element for warfare, and the materialization of sociopolitical status and power by means of animal-style imagery and commemoration through death and burial (fig. 6-11).

One of the most fascinating aspects of this long trajectory of development is the changing relationship between humans and horses. Detailed evidence has now emerged for the use of horses as an important food source and for early forms of domestication by at least 3500 BCE in the steppes of Kazakhstan. Horse riding also likely evolved at this time, but the control and further elaboration of horses in warfare seemingly developed more in the direction of their use as traction animals for chariot warfare. The earliest evidence for this development has been found in the steppes of

6-4 Gold artifacts from Arzhan 2. Aldan Maadyr National Museum, Republic of Tuva, and The State Hermitage Museum, St. Petersburg.

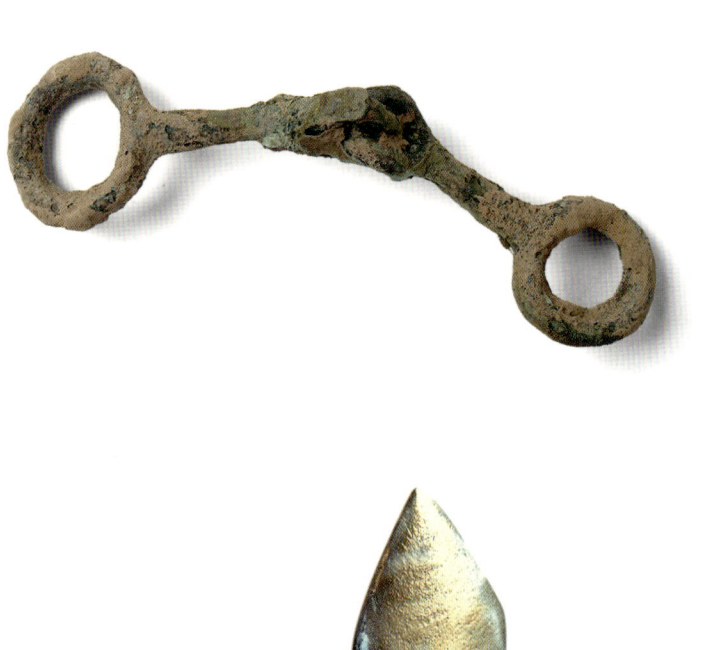

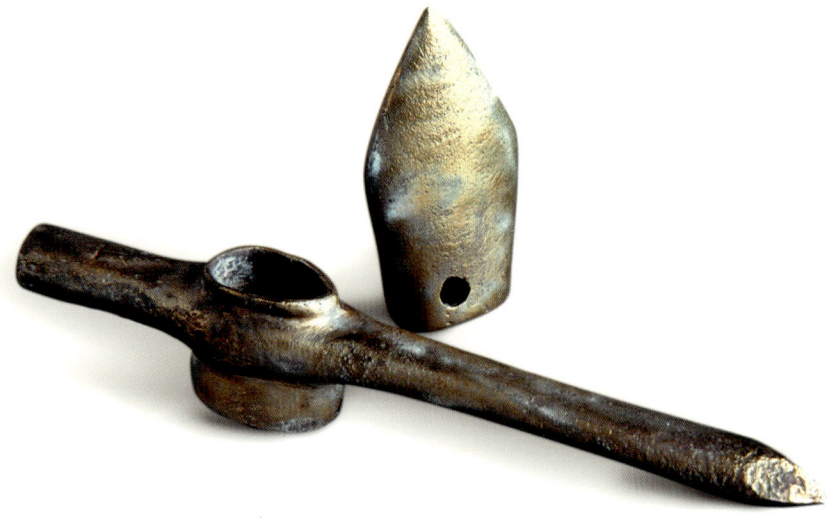

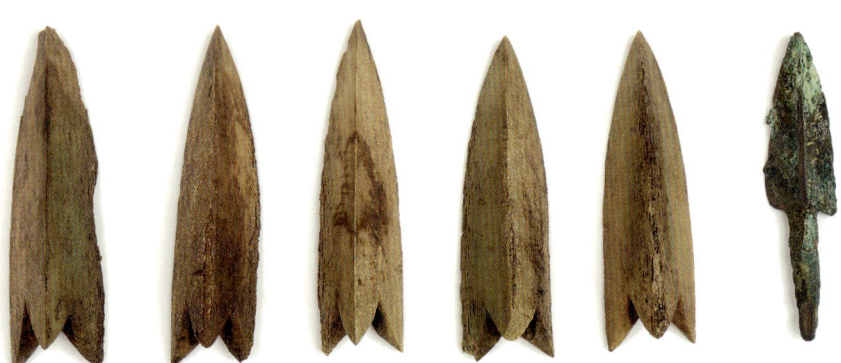

6-5 Jointed bit. Cast bronze, Berel, kurgan 72, late 4th–early 3rd century BCE. A. Kh. Margulan Institute of Archaeology, Almaty. Checklist no. 101.

6-6 Axe head. Bronze, 5th–4th century BCE. Museum of Archaeology, Almaty.

6-7 Arrowheads. Bone (5), bronze (1), Berel, kurgan 9, late 4th–early 3rd century BCE. A. Kh. Margulan Institute of Archaeology, Almaty: K9-N13. Checklist no. 98.

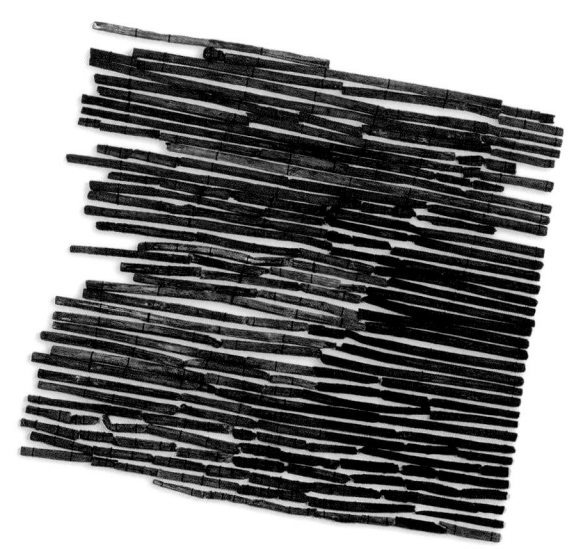

central Russia and northern Kazakhstan and dates to at least 2000 BCE. Importantly, another millennium passes before clear evidence of a mounted-warrior complex emerges at sites such as the burial complex of Arzhan 1 in Tuva, Russia. This site, constructed on the boundary of the eighth–ninth centuries BCE, provides unequivocal evidence for sacrificed horses with metal bits and other riding gear, weaponry, and the animal-style imagery that would come to signify the Scytho-Siberian epoch in Eurasia.

In the second half of the first millennium BCE, important burial sites such as Berel, Ak-Alakha, and Pazyryk, which date to the fourth–third centuries BCE, reflect the continuing development of mounted warfare and its relationship to wealth and power within these early societies. Mounted warfare was by then commonplace across Eurasia, and the overwhelming superiority of horse combined with bow and lance became the predominant force in many regions (fig. 6-12a–b). This trajectory ultimately led to the emergence of large-scale confederations known historically to us as the Xiongnu[26] in the eastern steppe zone and as the Scythians in the far western reaches of the steppe.[27] Of course, the ultimate extension of this powerful force would not be felt until the medieval period and the emergence of Chinggis Khan in 1200 CE and the materialization of his vast empire, which reached halfway around the world.[28] Yet perhaps what is most remarkable about the evolution of mounted warfare, and its catalyst for new forms of sociopolitical power, is the long trajectory of its development and some of the key elements by which it first materialized. These included a clear connection to the construction of ritual monuments set within natural landscapes that were no doubt highly charged with social memory and ancestral meanings. The appropriation of these sites, and the communal labor required for their erection and maintenance, provided a foundation for the emergence of new forms of ritual and social and political power. The appropriation and manipulation of ancestral symbolism and meaning associated with the animal world also appear to have been strongly connected to the emergence of warriors and horse cults, which now seem well represented by archaeological sites dating to the Bronze Age in Mongolia. Our understanding of these important developments has perhaps become more nuanced in recent years, and additional archaeological research and dating is helping to produce a clearer picture for the multiregional development of mounted warfare. While Gryaznov's vivid account in 1969 for the emergence of the Early Iron Age and mounted warfare still rings very true today, there is much work left to do and, thankfully, a few mysteries left to unravel.

6-8   War shield made of reeds with twine, recovered from Berel, kurgan 11, late 4th–early 3rd century BCE. A. Kh. Margulan Institute of Archaeology, Almaty.

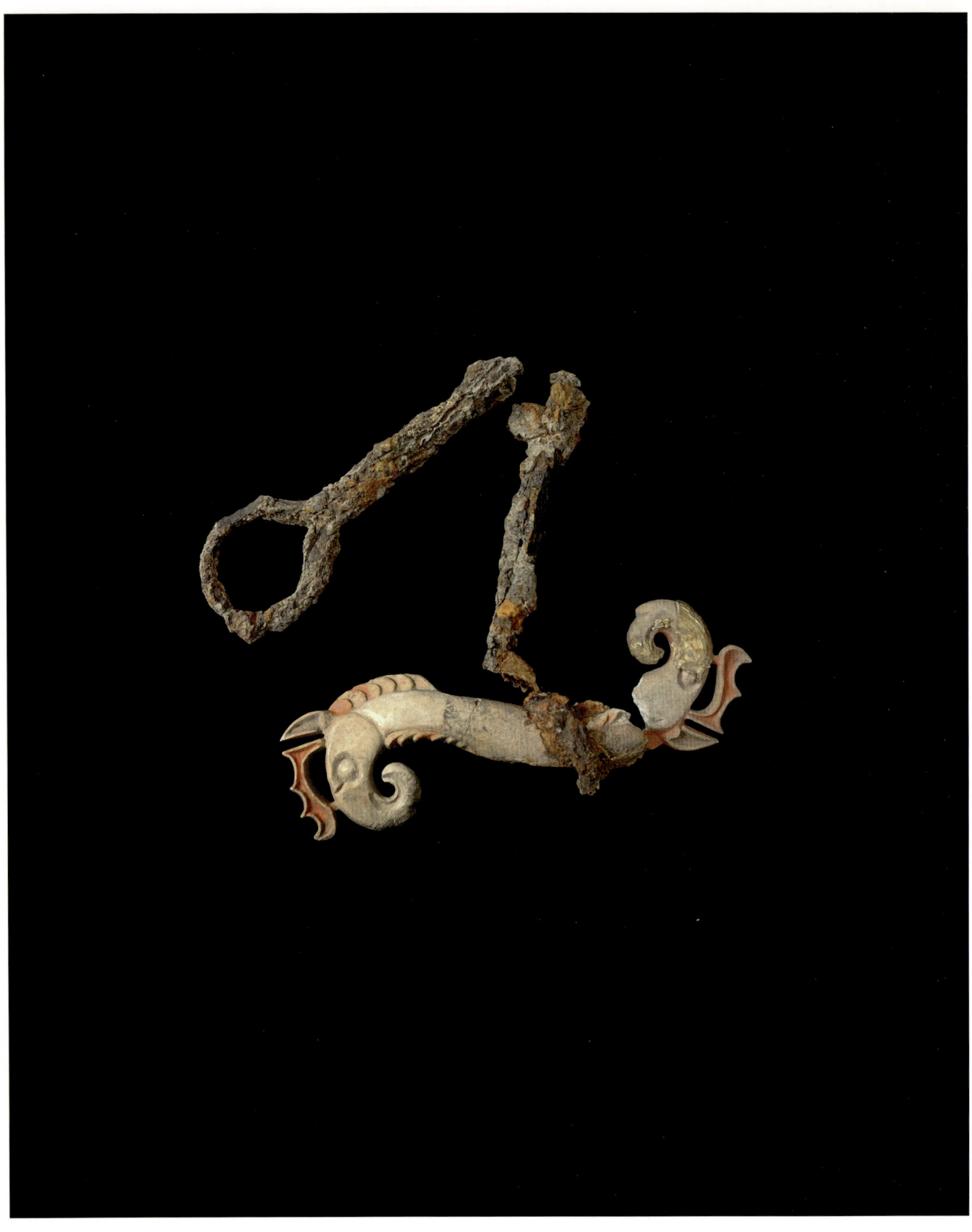

6-9 Psalia with elk-griffin head terminals and jointed bit. Horn (Siberian red deer), gold foil, and iron, Berel, kurgan 36, late 4th–early 3rd century BCE. A. Kh. Margulan Institute of Archaeology, Almaty: B36-56 and B36-03a,b. Checklist nos. 16 and 17.

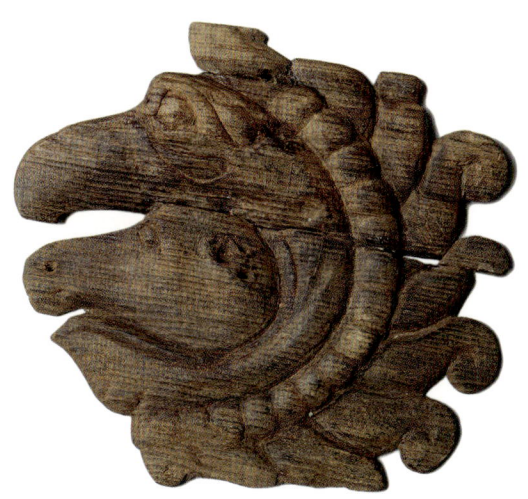

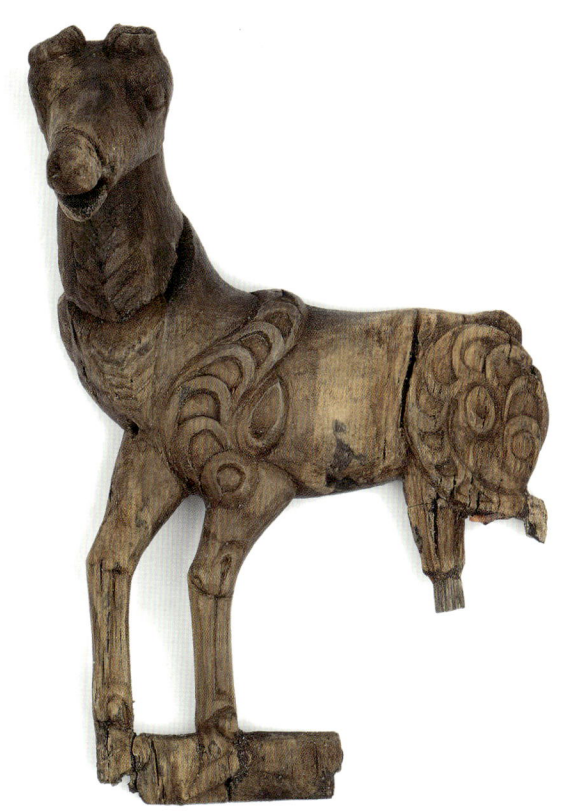

6-10 Plaque from horse tack of lion-griffin head with ungulate head in mouth. Wood, Berel, kurgan 11, late 4th–early 3rd century BCE. Presidential Center of Culture, Astana: 6203. Checklist no. 47.

6-11 Ornament from a human headdress depicting a horse with ibex and argali decoration. Wood, Berel, kurgan 10, late 4th–early 3rd century BCE. A. Kh. Margulan Institute of Archaeology, Almaty. Checklist no. 85.

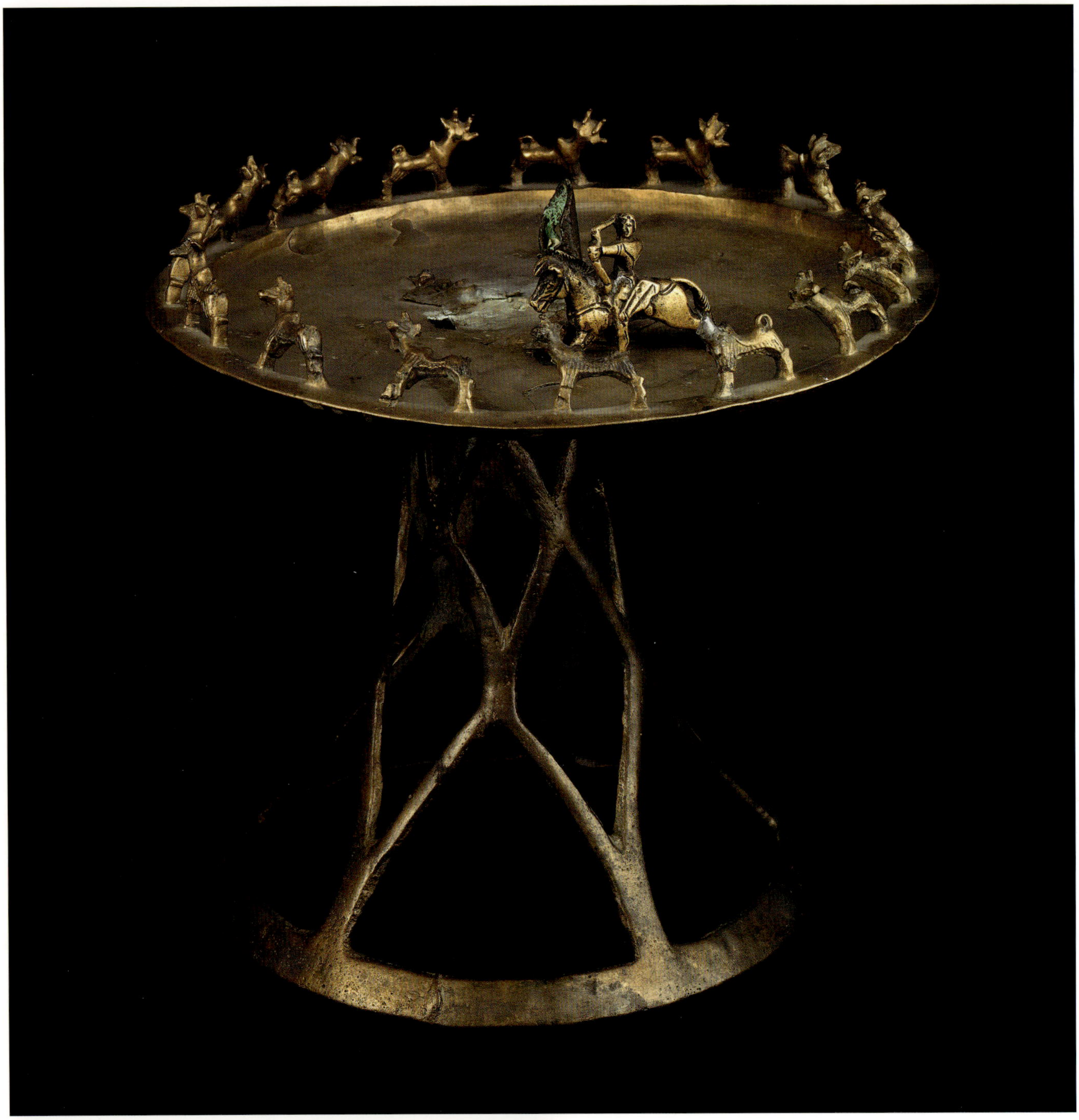

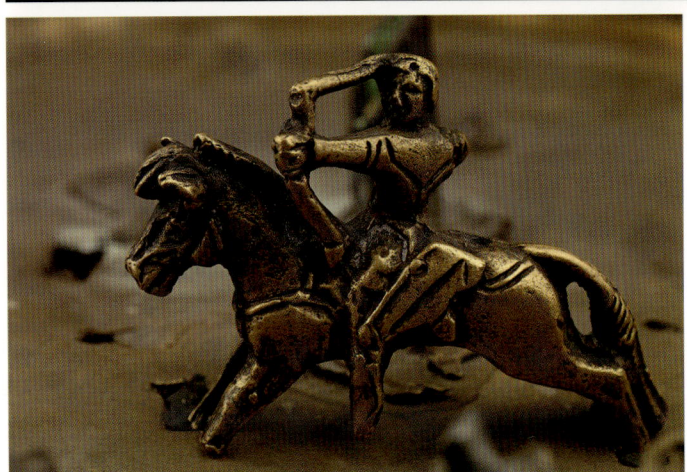

6-12a   Tray on conical stand with mounted archer in center and horned animals (15) around rim. Copper alloy, Semirechye/Zhetisu (Almaty region), 4th–2nd century BCE. Museum of Archaeology, Almaty: MA AA-1. Checklist no. 145.

6-12b   Detail of central figure on tray from fig. 6-12a.

NOTES

1. Gryaznov 1969, 131–32.
2. Hanks 2002a.
3. Chang et al. 2003; Frachetti 2008a; Wagner et al. 2011.
4. Olsen 2003.
5. Horse bits at this time were likely made of twisted rope or cordage, as bronze and iron metal bits are unknown until the first centuries of the first millennium BCE.
6. Outram et al. 2009.
7. McGaherrn et al. 2006.
8. Renfrew 2002; Drews 2004.
9. Drews 2004, 68.
10. Anthony 2007.
11. Волков 1981; Новгородова 1989.
12. Allard and Erdenebaatar 2005; Houle 2009.
13. Believed to be the elk or maral (*Cervus elaphus sibiricus*); see Fitzhugh 2009, 388, for discussion.
14. Jacobson 1993; Fitzhugh 2009.
15. Волков 1981; Новгородова 1989.
16. Fitzhugh 2009.
17. Hanks 2002a; Koryakova and Epimakhov 2007.
18. For further discussion, see Stark this volume and Yablonsky 2001.
19. Chang et al. 2003; Scott, Alekseev, and Zaitseva 2004; Chang 2008; Wagner et al. 2011.
20. See Zaitseva et al. 2007 for recent dating of Arzhan 1 and Arzhan 2 barrows.
21. Грач 1980; Grjaznov 1984.
22. Bokovenko 2000; Bokovenko 2006.
23. Rudenko 1970.
24. See essays this volume by Rubinson and by Bokovenko and Samashev.
25. See Rubinson this volume on the interpretation of horse–human relationships based on mortuary materials.
26. Di Cosmo 2002.
27. Kradin 2002.
28. Honeychurch and Amartuvshin 2008.

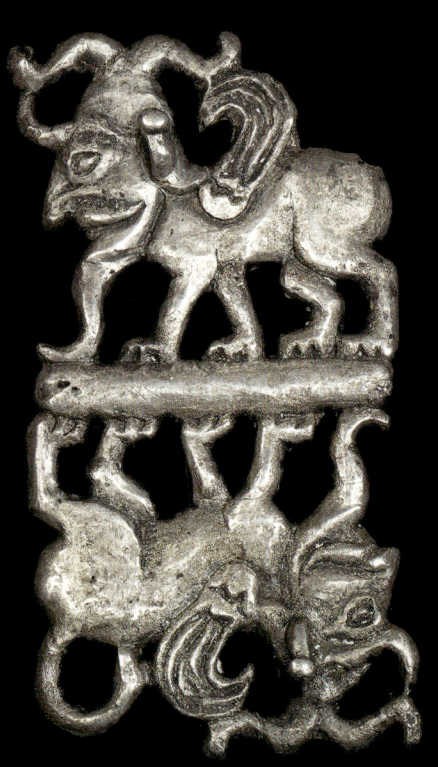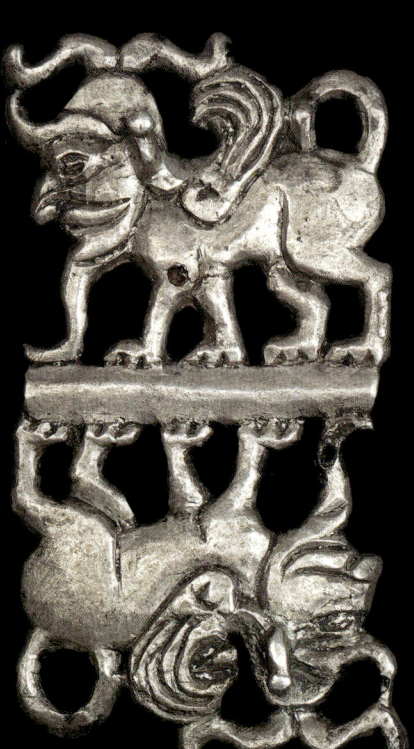

NOMADS AND NETWORKS: ELITES AND THEIR CONNECTIONS TO THE OUTSIDE WORLD

Sören Stark

Powerful elites—cultivating a military lifestyle, displaying social status via large-scale horse sacrifices, and expressing their worldview in a distinctive artistic language (the so-called Scytho-Siberian animal style)[1]—emerged in the Eastern Eurasian steppes as early as the Late Bronze Age.[2] Beginning with the transition to the Iron Age, these elites were shaped both by complex mobile pastoralism and by mounted warfare,[3] resulting in the appearance of a characteristic Early Iron Age mounted-warrior complex. The monumental kurgan burial of Arzhan 1 in Tuva, dating to around the turn of the ninth to the eighth century BCE, constitutes impressive early evidence for this phenomenon.[4]

Merely a hundred and fifty years later, potent nomadic elites, embracing key elements of the same "cultural code,"[5] appeared almost everywhere in the Eurasian steppes— from Tuva (Arzhan 2)[6] through eastern Kazakhstan (Shilikty 3)[7] and to the Black Sea littoral in the far west (Kelermes).[8] Soon after, they also surfaced just north of the Yellow River in what is now Northern China (Maoqingguo).[9] (See map, fig. 7-1.)

Plaques of double-horned winged sphinxes (2). Silver, Issyk, Semirechye/Zhetisu (Almaty region), 5th–4th century BCE. Museum of Archaeology, Almaty: MA 35 a, b. Checklist no. 155.

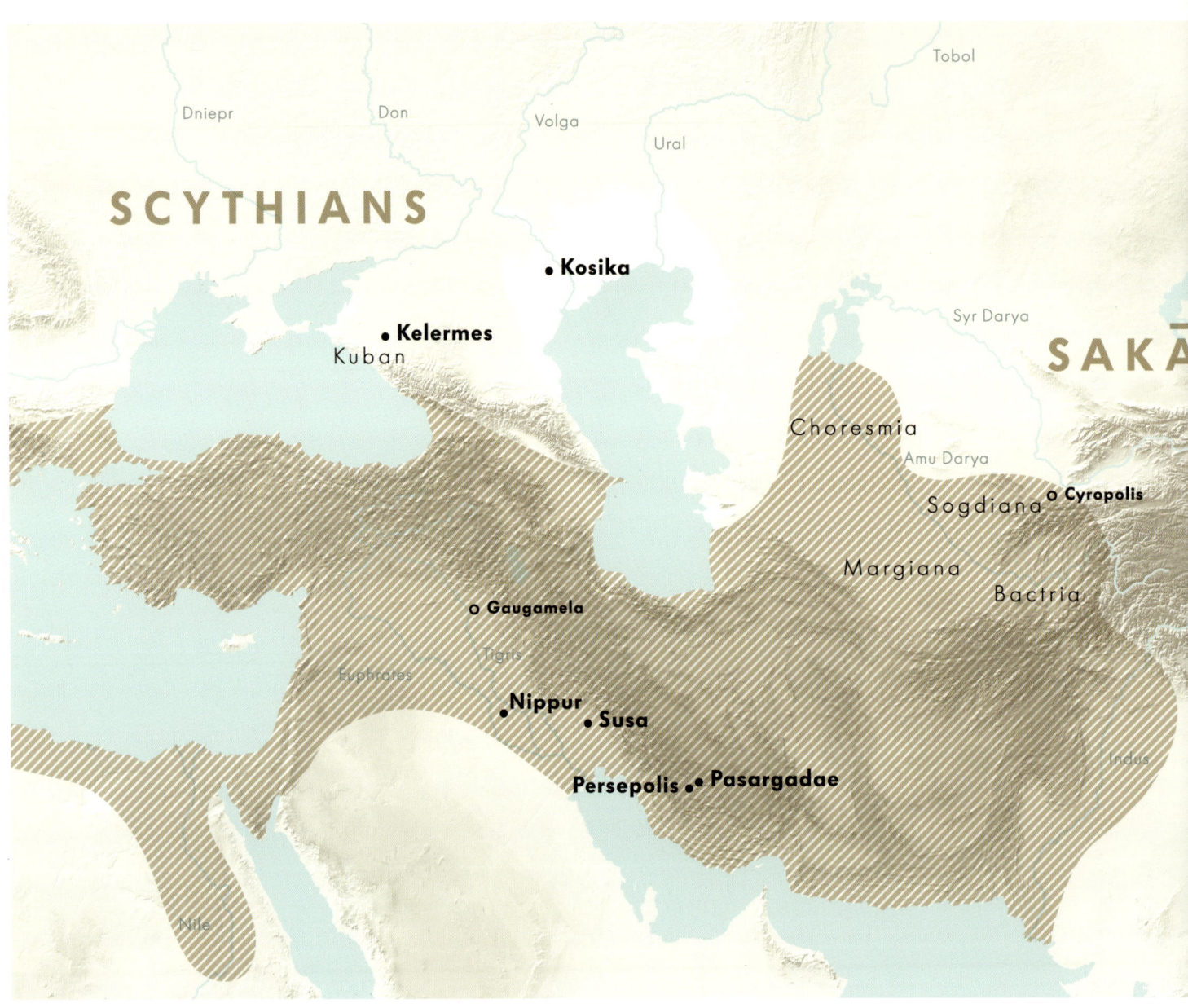

Achaemenid Empire around 500 BCE

The war-like nomadic nobility came into direct contact with the states and cultures of the sedentary sphere at both the western and the eastern ends of the steppe belt: from 714 they are mentioned in Assyrian documents—first as *Gimirrāya* (later known from Greek authors as *Kimmerioi*), slightly later also as *Iškuzāya*, that is, as Scythians.[10] At about the same time, some mounted-elite war-bands from the steppes might have operated in the wars between the *Zhou* (朝) and several *Di* (狄) and *Rong* (戎) peoples mentioned by Chinese written sources.[11]

These rich and diversified sedentary societies attracted nomads from the Eurasian steppes for a number of reasons. Although the economy of pastoral societies in the steppes was in fact much more diversified than the simplifying label "pastoral nomads" suggests,[12] mobile pastoralists would still have been eager to further complement their subsistence base by entering into exchanges with settled populations.[13] Thus, ordinary tribesmen sought to procure all kinds of agricultural products and also basic handicraft items for daily use, such as textiles, ceramics, or even utensils for their mobile camps, many of which, in fact, were produced by nonmobile specialists. These items were usually traded at frontier markets for the products of animal husbandry.

However, more importantly, the sedentary world was also the place where members of the nomadic

7-1 Eurasian steppes and the Achaemenid Empire down to the 3rd century BCE (with sites mentioned in this chapter).

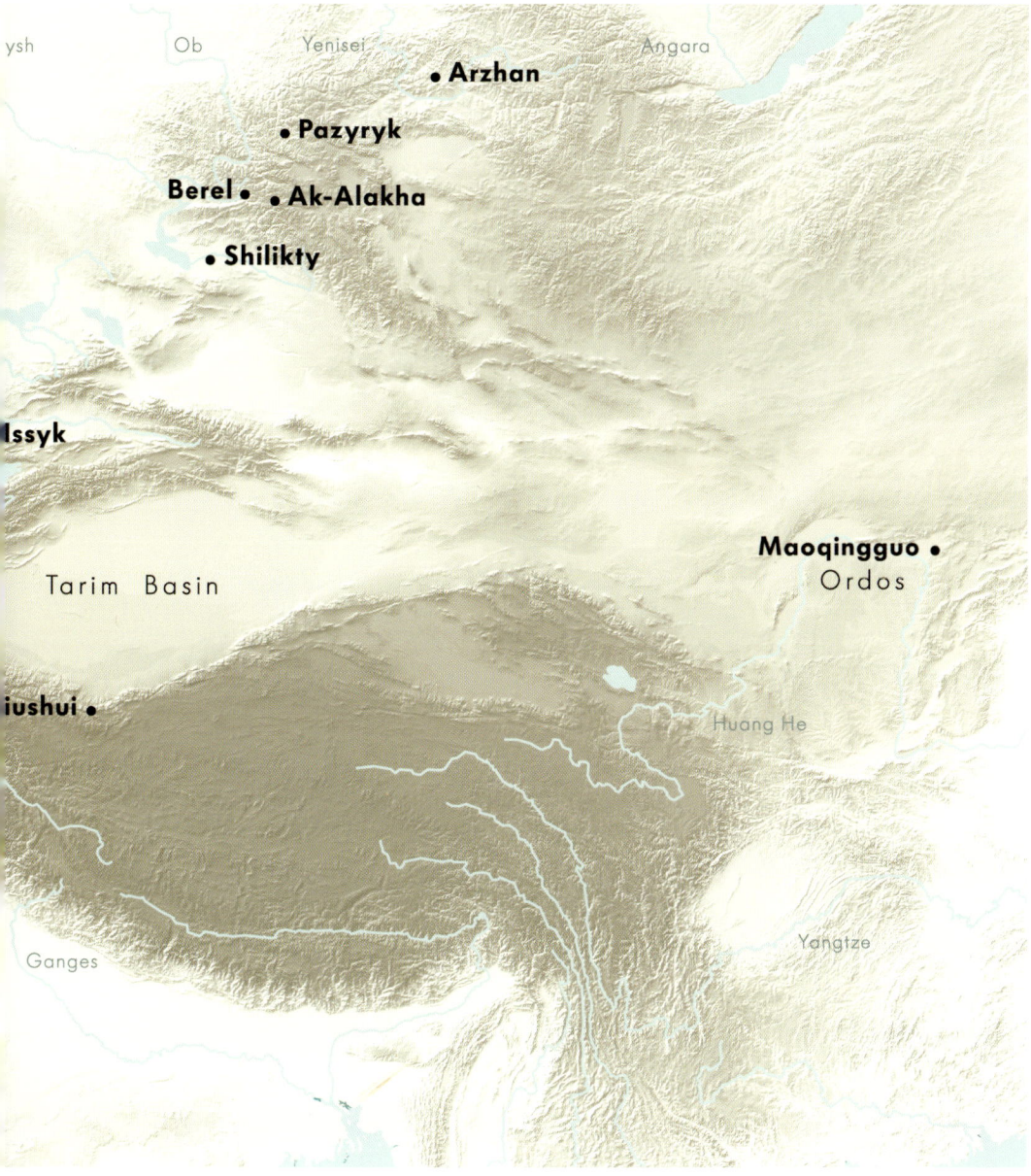

elite could hope to gain valuable luxury goods, which enjoyed a particular prestige within the pastoral nomadic society. Throughout the millennia the redistribution of prestige goods was one of the major strategies to create and secure firm relationships between aristocratic leaders and their followers.[14] These relationships, in turn, were of primary importance for the initiation of processes that could finally result in the establishment of "nomadic states."[15] Such processes were bound not to a tribal society, but to the milieu of elite war-bands and retinues with which everywhere in the Eurasian steppes ambitious aristocrats tended to surround themselves.[16] These war-bands and retinues formed personal guards, always at the chief's disposition. Membership was not predefined by membership in a certain tribe or clan. Instead, it was based on personal bonds between each member and the "leader." These bonds resulted in mutual obligations between the leader and his followers: in principle, loyal services were compensated by material gifts and, consequently, social prestige.

Exotic luxuries were, therefore, necessities in the political culture of the nomadic elite, forcing ambitious aristocratic leaders to gain and secure access to foreign prestige goods. The result was a complex network of communication throughout and beyond the Eurasian steppes. This basic constellation can also be observed among the elites of those Early Iron Age nomads who lived in the Western Central Asian steppes and who were generally labeled by their neighbors in the Achaemenid

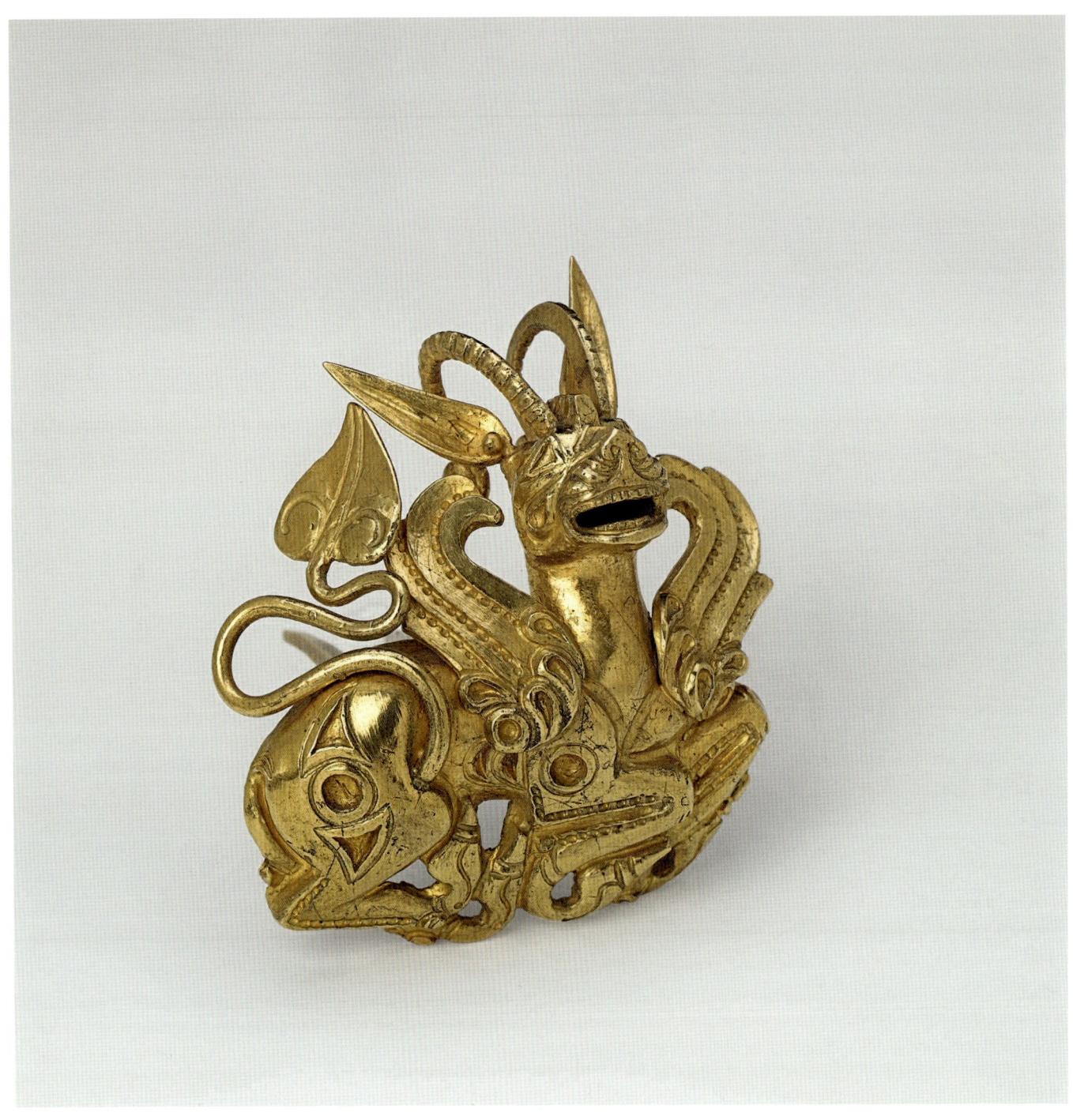

7-2 Gold plaque in the form of a lion-griffin, with body and horns of an ibex. Oxus treasure (probably from Takht-i Kuvad, Tajikistan). British Museum: ME 123924.

7-3 (opposite, left) Delegation of the so-called Persian Royal Hero, the Sakā Tigraxaudā. From the Eastern Staircase of the Apadāna in Persepolis. (After Walser 1966, pl. 18.)

7-4 (opposite, right) Chalcedony cylinder seal with battle scene showing the so-called Persian Royal Hero, the Sakā Tigraxaudā, and a captive. Provenance unknown. The British Museum, London: ANE 132505.

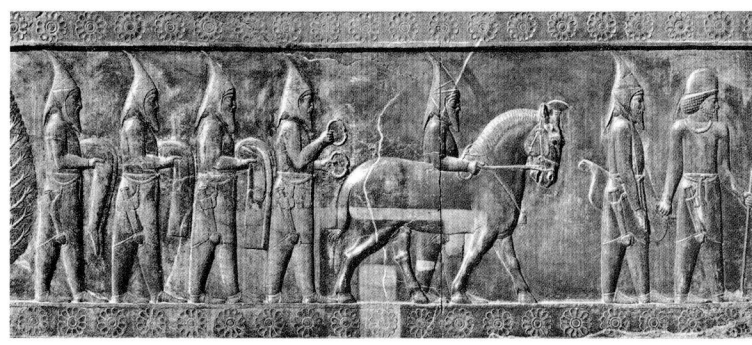
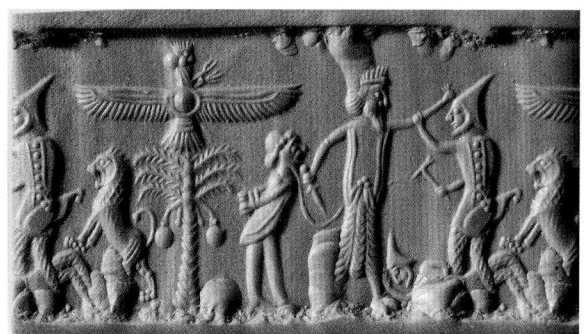

Empire as Sakā.[17] In the following discussion, I will first inquire into the main strategies adopted by the elites of these groups to supply themselves with coveted prestige items from the sedentary sphere by entering into direct contact with settled populations. Then, I will consider some consequences these contacts left in the material culture and, above all, in the visual art of the nomads themselves.

TRADE, FRONTIER MARKETS, AND SPECIALIZED PRODUCTION FOR NOMADIC ELITES

I have already mentioned the importance of frontier markets for ordinary tribesmen. Major frontier markets for the Sakā were doubtlessly the urban trading centers in the oases regions of Western Central Asia: Sogdiana, Choresmia, Margiana, and Bactria.[18] Along the Middle Syr Darya, the Achaemenid administration sought to establish a frontier toward the open steppe by founding several garrison towns, among them the famous Cyropolis, supposedly founded by Cyrus the Great (Strab. 11.11.4). But this was hardly an impregnable borderline, because it is known that some Sakā groups (Dahā) of this region lived "on this side of the border," that is, in Achaemenid territories (Arr. 3.28.8). Rather, the Persian administration aimed at regulation, control, and taxation by installing a military frontier zone where garrison towns could also flourish as trading posts, operating between the world of the steppes and the oases within the Achaemenid empire.[19]

Admittedly, very little is known about the trading activities of nomadic elites during this period. But there are interesting hints: for instance, some precious objects of the famous Oxus treasure show features typical of contemporary art in the steppes (fig. 7-2).[20] It is quite possible that these items were manufactured in the cities of Bactria or Sogdiana in jeweler's workshops that specialized in producing for nomadic elites beyond the oases by aiming at their taste—as workshops in Greek cities in the Northern Black Sea area did for Scythian elites.[21] The same has been assumed for the eighth and seventh centuries BCE with regard to Urartaean, Anatolian, and Iranian workshops employed by Scythian customers in the Kuban area,[22] as well as Chinese workshops that specialized in supplying nomadic elites in the Eastern steppe.[23]

DIPLOMACY AND GIFT EXCHANGE

One of the delegations depicted in the famous reliefs from the eastern staircase of the Apadāna in Persepolis, dating to the reign of Darius I (r. 522–486 BCE), is clearly arriving from the Sakā Tigraxaudā (literally, "the Sakā with pointed hats"), easily recognizable by their riding costume and characteristic pointed headgear (fig. 7-3). They bring a horse, torques, cloaks, and rider leggings—quite typical gifts from the hands of nomads.[24] What would they have received in return?

In fact, there is clear knowledge about the items used for gift exchange at the Achaemenid court: the "archetypal royal gifts,"[25] frequently mentioned in written sources, were precious robes, fine arms, horse decorations, and jewelry. According to the third-century CE Greek author Aelianus (whose text is based on older sources), ambassadors to the Persian king could expect to receive (in addition to one Babylonian talent of silver coins) "two silver cups weighing a talent each, . . . bracelets, an akinakes, and a necklace" (Ael. VH 1.22). Clearly, such embassies were a profitable method for the steppe aristocracy to extract luxury goods from foreign courts.

A substantial increase and more permanent flow of such items could be achieved by concluding marriage alliances. The promise of spectacular dowries must have been an enormous incentive for nomadic elites.

And indeed, again and again proposals of marriage figure in the sources—in fact, the earliest mention of Scythians in the Near East relates to exactly such a proposal, submitted in 674 by a certain Bartatua, "king of the land Iškuza," to the Assyrian king Esarhaddon.[26] The same motive might have inspired the "king of the European Scythians" to offer a marriage proposal to Alexander after the latter had taken over most of the former Achaemenid realm (Arr. An. 4.14.1).

MILITARY SERVICES
The search for luxuries from the sedentary world surely prompted many leaders of Sakā elite war-bands to enter the military service of the Achaemenid Great Kings (or their satraps). Indeed, in return for their military services, loyal and successful officers could expect to be lavishly rewarded (Xen. Oec. 4.7). In particular cases, allies of the Achaemenid Great Kings were even "recorded as benefactors of the king," qualifying them to receive especially magnificent gifts from the royal household.[27] Land allotments to soldiers (so-called bow estates) in Babylonia were another source of income for Sakā in Achaemenid military services, as can be learned from cuneiform documents from the archive of a business house at Nippur in Babylonia.[28]

It seems that, generally, Sakā war-bands in Achaemenid service operated under the direct command of their leaders, because Sakā contingents are regularly mentioned as *symmachoi* ("allies") within the Persian host (Arr. An. 3.8.3, 3.19.3, 3.25.3). This is most explicitly stated by Arrianus when he refers to a Sakā contingent fighting for Persians at Gaugamela (Arr. An. 3.8.3):

> They were followed by the Sakā (Σάκαι), a Scythian tribe belonging to the Scythians who dwell in Asia. These were *not subject* (οὐχ ὑπήκοοι) to Bessus [that is, the Achaemenid satrap of Bactria and Sogdiana], but were *in alliance* (κατὰ συμμαχίαν) with Darius. They were commanded by Mauakes, and were horse-bowmen (italics added).

Obviously, Sakā contingents were highly valued by the Persians as they are omnipresent in the Achaemenid army: they appear as "allies" as early as in the reign of Cyrus the Great[29] and were deployed by the Persians in regions as distant as Greece, where they excelled, for instance, as the best fighters on horseback at Plataea (Hdt. 9.71).[30] And this appreciation of nomadic warriors survived Achaemenid rule in Eastern Iran: a recently published Greek parchment from Bactria indicates that under Greek rule "Scythian" detachments were still employed, perhaps as mercenaries, in Bactria.[31]

RAZZIAS
The reader might have expected this "strategy" to be considered at an earlier point in this essay, because *razzias*, or raids, figure in ancient sources and modern conceptions as an almost "classical" activity of the "mounted nomad warrior." And the Sakā, "a nation fond of war and accustomed to live by plunder" (Curt. 4.6.3), were no exception.

But the phenomenon of "raiding" is much more complex. In fact, in many cases it is not easy to distinguish between "raiders" and "allies": a mercenary on the search for additional booty could easily turn into a raider, and the war-bands described above certainly took their chances along their way, as the following discussion will demonstrate. Sakā raids on territories of the Achaemenid Empire reached their zenith in a very particular historical situation, one that requires more detailed inquiry than the previous aspects of interaction.

Of course, relations between the Persian Empire and Central Asian nomads were, often enough, far from peaceful. The founder of the empire, Cyrus the Great, even met his death facing them in battle (Htd. 1.214), and visual evidence for military conflicts between Persians and Sakā is ample (fig. 7-4).[32] While in some cases, such as the wars of Cyrus the Great and Darius I, the initiative might have been on the side of the Persians,[33] the menace of "freebooters" from among the Sakā was certainly a widespread phenomenon. It was even recognized by the nomads themselves, as can be learned from the excuse expressed by an anonymous Sakā "king" to Alexander regarding nomad attacks from across the Syr Darya/Iaxartes (Arrian 4.5.1):

> Soon after this, arrived envoys from the king of the Scythians [that is, Sakā], who were sent to apologize for what had been done, and to state that it was not the act of the Scythian State, but of certain men *who set out for plunder in the way of freebooters* (καθ' ἁρπαγὴν λῃστρικῷ τρόπῳ σταλέντων) (italics added).

Clearly, chaos during the downfall of the Achaemenid empire, and especially the two years of constant warfare conducted by Alexander in Sogdiana and Bactria (329–328 BCE), must have been particularly favorable for the activity of such "freebooters," and there is ample evidence for their activity during these troublesome years. But did they all set out as raiders from the steppe? As noted earlier, Sakā contingents were highly valued as auxiliaries in the Persian army. And, indeed, Sakā contingents were recruited by Achaemenid officials for the Great King's war against Alexander. We should remember the case of the Sakā leader Mauakes, mentioned earlier: a nomad commander and his troops "allied" with Darius. Quintus Curtius Rufus tells us that, following the disaster of Issus in 333 BCE, Darius III "ordered . . . Bessus, the governor of the Bactrians, *to muster the largest army possible (quam maximo posset exercitu coacto)* and to come down to him" (Curt. 4.6.2; italics added). To this end, Bessus also probably sent messengers beyond the border at the Syr Darya to induce various Sakā leaders to join the army as "allies." That is obviously the reason why Bessus could later, during his own fight against Alexander, boast before his followers of his connections to "the Scythians dwelling beyond the river Tanais [that is, the Syr Darya]" (*ultra Tanain amnem colente Scythas*), whom he hoped to attract as "powerful allies" (*valida auxilia*) (Curt. 7.4.6).

But these "invited" Sakā contingents proved to be uneasy and unpredictable allies: already in the battle of Gaugamela (331 BCE), their main objective was the enemy's baggage train (Curt. 4.15.5, 4.5.12–18). In the ensuing chaos after Gaugamela, Sakā war-bands were able to roam more or less freely through the eastern half of the collapsing empire on the search for further booty. It was probably the same war-bands that the Bactrian noble Spitamenes could win slightly later as "allies" in his guerilla war against Alexander.[34] By the promise of booty they were "easy to convince to enter one war after the other" (Arr. An. 4.17.5). And the nomads took their chance—on every side: in the winter of 328/327, the prospect of plunder induced 3,000 Sakā[35] horsemen to join the Bactrian and Sogdian rebel forces on their raid against Alexander, who was wintering in Sogdia. But facing defeat at the hands of Alexander's forces, they quickly changed sides, plundered the baggage train of their Bactrian and Sogdian allies, and disappeared in the steppe (Arr. An. 4.17.7). Consequently, it does not come as a surprise that some Sakā contingents finally even enlisted in Alexander's army, which set off with him for India in the spring of 327 BCE (Curt. 8.14.5).

It is clear that during the numerous battles and skirmishes in the years that saw the downfall of the Achaemenid empire, substantial Sakā contingents joined practically all war parties, with the objective to take away as much booty as possible. As a result, an enormous number of luxuries, originating predominantly from the Eastern provinces of the trembling Achaemenid realm, must have flowed into the Central Asian steppes.

IMPORTED PRESTIGE GOODS FROM THE ACHAEMENID TERRITORIES

The range of prestige items brought into the steppes from the Achaemenid territories—either by trade, as gifts, or as booty—must have been very wide. From what has been said, we should expect all kinds of metalware, jewelry, and fine arms, but also precious textiles and a variety of small objects. Even foreign furniture, at least in later periods, was popular among nomadic elites.[36]

Indeed, a wide range of objects originating from the Achaemenid empire has been found in the Eurasian steppes. Excavations in Early Sarmatian (fourth–third century BCE) elite burials in the Southern Urals have yielded a surprising quantity of such items: Achaemenid and Achaemenid-style silver, silver-gilt, and gold vessels (including rhyta, double-handled jugs, cups, and phialae), jewelry, and arms, but also a small alabaster vessel with an Achaemenid royal inscription from Egypt.[37] Similar kinds of items (gold and silver vessels, fine arms, jewelry) of the so-called Achaemenid international style[38] are known from Scythian burials in the Northern Black Sea area.[39] In addition, a number of "Achaemenid" cylinder or stamp seals have been found in the Northern Pontic steppe.[40]

But objects originating from the Achaemenid realm are also known from the steppes further east, inhabited by or close to Sakā tribes. For many of them the exact provenance is unknown—for example, in the cases of an Achaemenid-style silver rhyton in the form of an ibex protome and most of the objects of Achaemenid origin from the Siberian collection of Peter the Great.[41] But fortunately a number of "Achaemenid" imports has come to light during excavations at Pazyryk: the most spectacular are certainly the famous pile carpet (figs. 7-5a–b) and a woolen saddle cloth (figs. 7-6a–b)

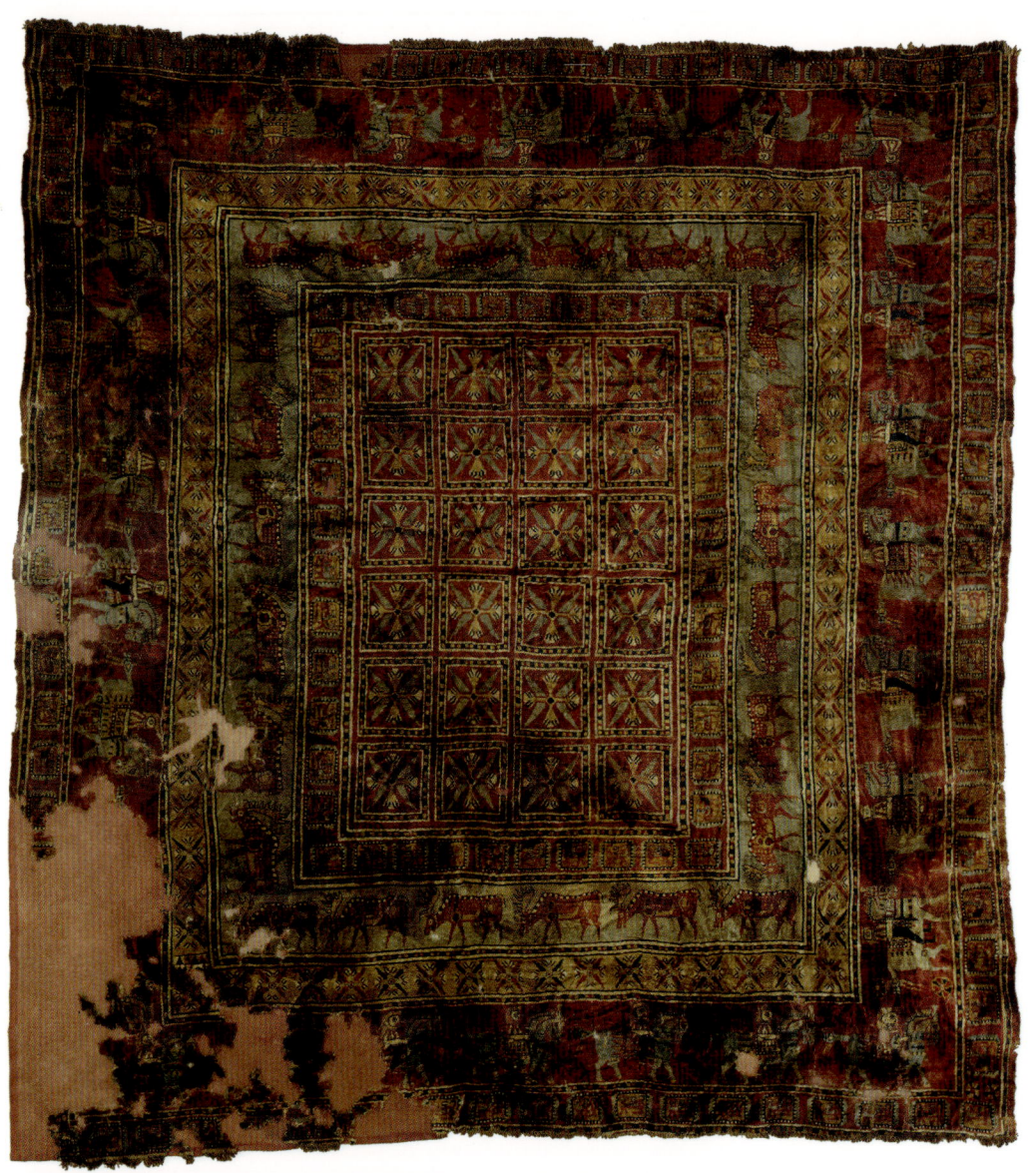

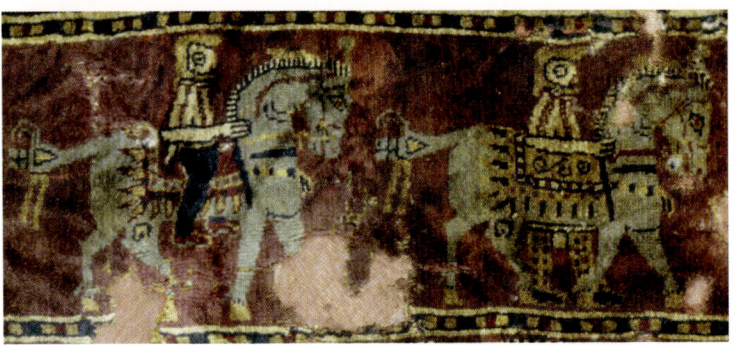

7-5a   Pile carpet dating to the 5th–4th century BCE. Wool, knot technique, 183 x 200 cm, Pazyryk barrow no. 5, 4th–3rd century BCE. The State Hermitage Museum, St. Petersburg: 1687/93.

7-5b   Detail of pile carpet from fig. 7.5a, showing a rider and a groom leading a horse.

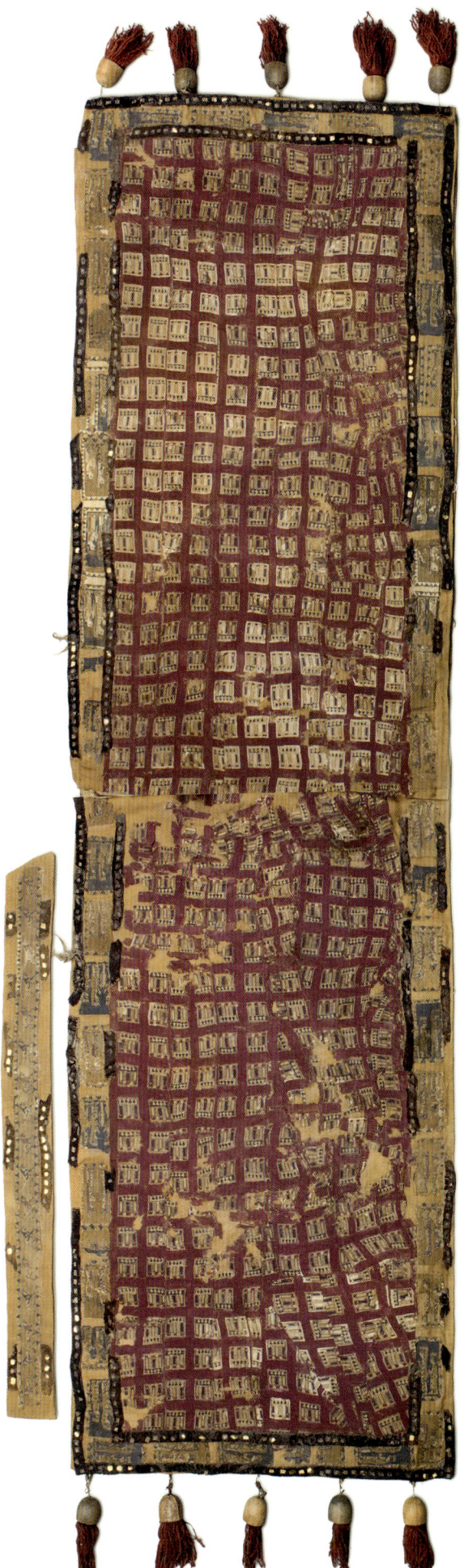
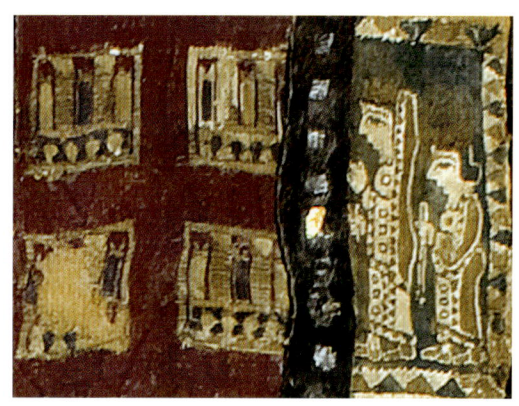

7-6a Saddlecloth (*shabraque*). Iranian wool and local felt, leather, and foil, Pazyryk barrow no. 5, 4th–3rd century BCE. The State Hermitage Museum, St. Petersburg: 1687/100.

7-6b Detail of saddlecloth from fig. 7-6a.

from kurgan 5, both of which have been shown to be imports from the Eastern satrapies of the Achaemenid realm, most probably from Bactria or Sogdiana.[42] In kurgan 2, a pair of cast-silver belt plates is probably of Near Eastern origin (fig. 7-7).[43] More difficult to establish is the exact origin of a woman's gold earring, also from kurgan 2. It is executed in the typical polychrome cloisonné style (with blue and red paste), which seems to have had its origin in Egypt but became fashionable throughout the Achaemenid empire.[44] Comparative examples are known from Susa, Pasargadae, and—most likely—Bactria. An interesting parallel is offered by a necklace now in the Metropolitan Museum of Art, New York (fig. 7-8).[45] It is not only executed in the same polychrome style of cloisonné work, but it also repeats the motif of horses being led by horsemen in riding gear that appears (alternating with riders on horses) on the pile carpet from Pazyryk kurgan 5 (fig. 7-5b).

Such an "Achaemenid" connection can also be traced for Berel, although no original imports have been found during excavations. But Achaemenid metalwork must have reached this microregion, as confirmed by an exquisite, partly gilded silver handle in the form of a fallow deer, now in the State Hermitage Museum, St. Petersburg (fig. 7-9). It was collected by Russian soldiers before or in 1735 in a "kurgan" in the Bukhtarma valley, where the kurgan cemetery of Berel is situated.[46]

There are good reasons to suppose that many of these "Achaemenid" imports actually came from workshops located in the eastern provinces of the Persian realm, namely in Bactria or Sogdiana. For some of the textiles from Pazyryk, this has been convincingly demonstrated by J. Lerner.[47] It might also be suggested, for example, for the magnificent torque with winged and horned lion finials from the Siberian collection of Peter the Great (fig. 7-10): this piece combines stylistic, iconographic, and technical features typical of Achaemenid court art—for example, the goblet-like ends of the horns and the polychrome cloisonné technique. But other features of the torque are instead typical of contemporary steppe art—for instance, a particular stylization of the "dot-and-comma" ornament[48] and abundant use of "teardrop" body ornaments (see Bokovenko and Samashev, this volume figs. 1-7–1-9). Similar adaptations to the taste of nomadic steppe elites are, as mentioned, clearly perceivable in some pieces from the Oxus treasure. It is, therefore, most probable that the torque in St. Petersburg was also produced by a Bactrian or Sogdian workshop in the late Achaemenid or early post-Achaemenid period, specifically for a high-ranking customer from the steppes.

In fact, such close ties between the steppe elites and the settled population in Bactria and Sogdia were much older than Achaemenid rule in these areas.[49] The findings of lapis lazuli in the inventory of kurgan 82 in Shilikty 3, dating probably to the late eighth or seventh century BCE, point to earlier imports from Badakhshān in Eastern Bactria (see Toleubaev, this volume fig. 3-8).[50] The same might be true for the silk also found in that burial.[51] And not only precious textiles or metalwork were imported and consumed by the nomadic elites: among the imports in Pazyryk kurgan 5 are seeds of cultivated coriander (*Coriandrum sativum*), which is not native to the Altai and must have been brought from the former Achaemenid territories.[52]

Finally, we should also not discount the possibility that seemingly "foreign" prestige goods might have been, in fact, produced locally but by foreign masters. There are many examples of foreign craftsmen who worked at nomadic residences and met the demand by nomadic elites for exotic prestige items. Best known are Chinese, Persian, and even European craftsmen living and working for the Mongol elite in Karakorum.[53] But the same has been assumed for the early Scythian complexes in the Kuban area with regard to craftsmen from the Near East.[54] And one wonders who actually produced the

7-7. Belt plaque with animal combat scene. Silver, cast and chased, 5.7 cm × 4.3 cm, Pazyryk barrow no. 2, 6th–4th century BCE. The State Hermitage Museum, St. Petersburg: 1684/231.

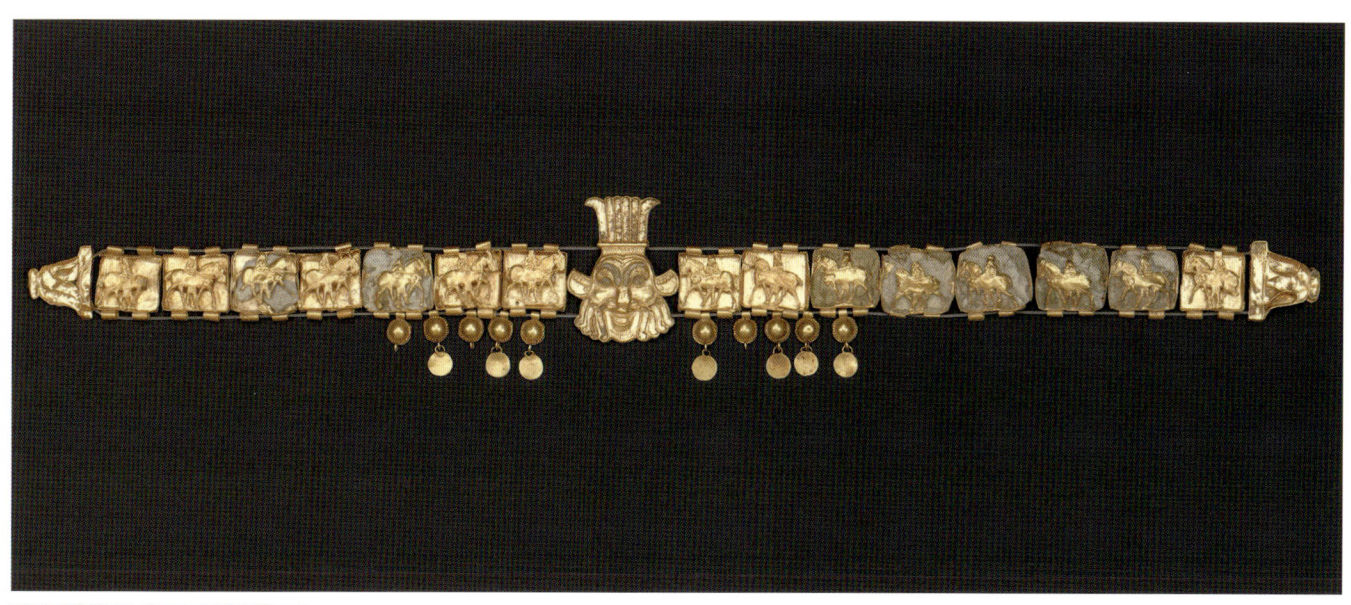

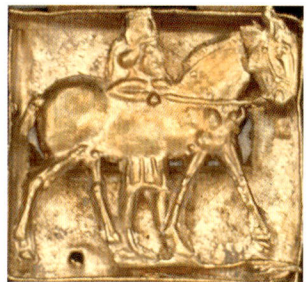

7-8a Necklace with the head of the Egyptian god Bes, a lotus, and male figures leading horses. Gold, L. 85.9 cm., Achaemenid, ca. 6th–4th century BCE. The Metropolitan Museum of Art, New York, Dodge Fund, 1965: 65.169.

7-8b Detail of necklace from 7-8a.

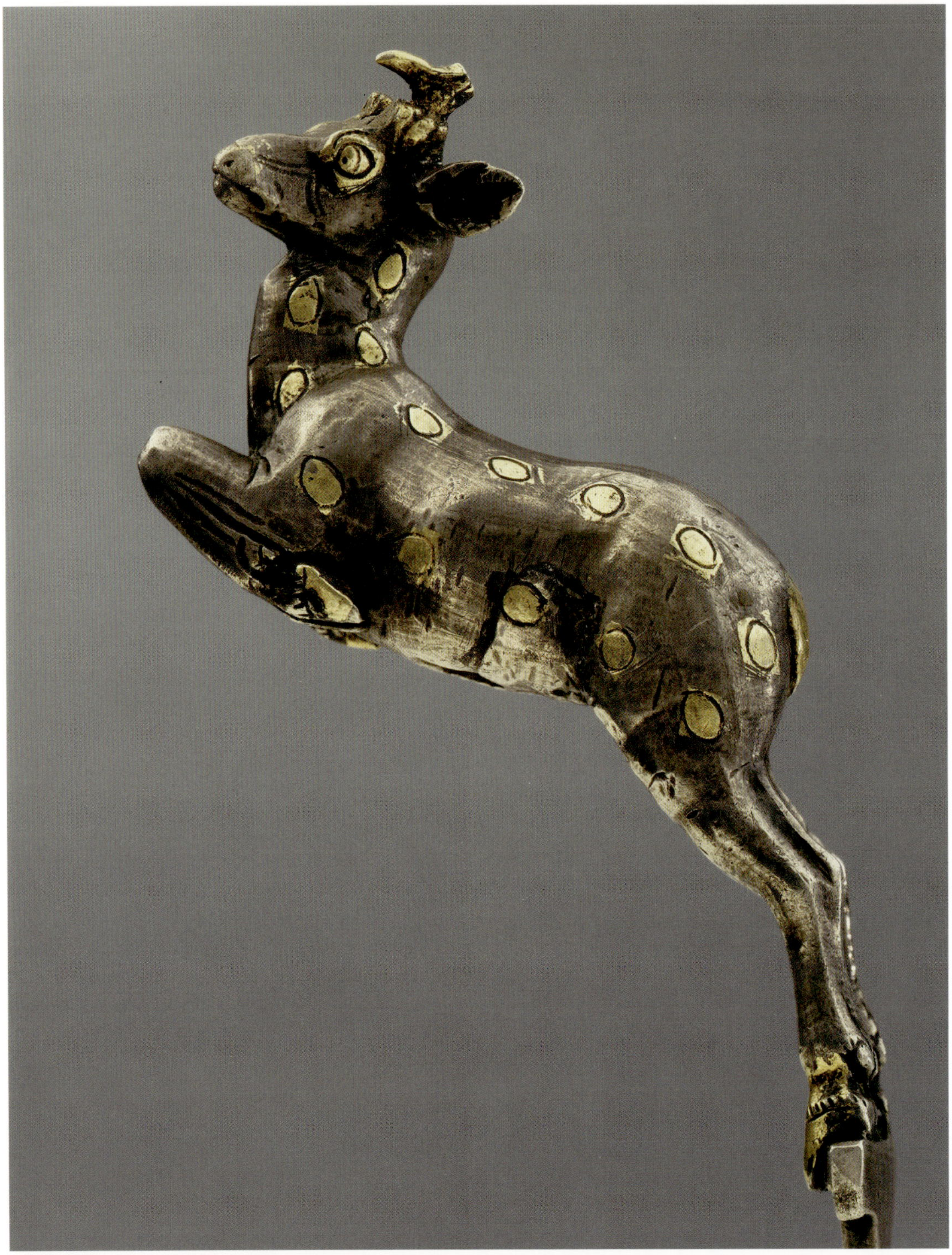

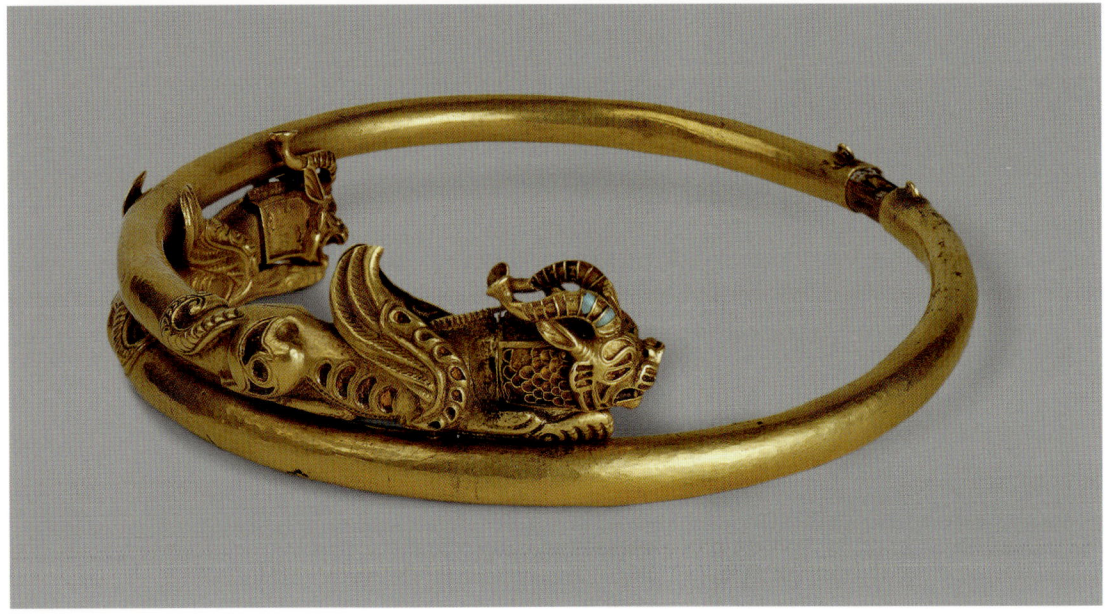

118

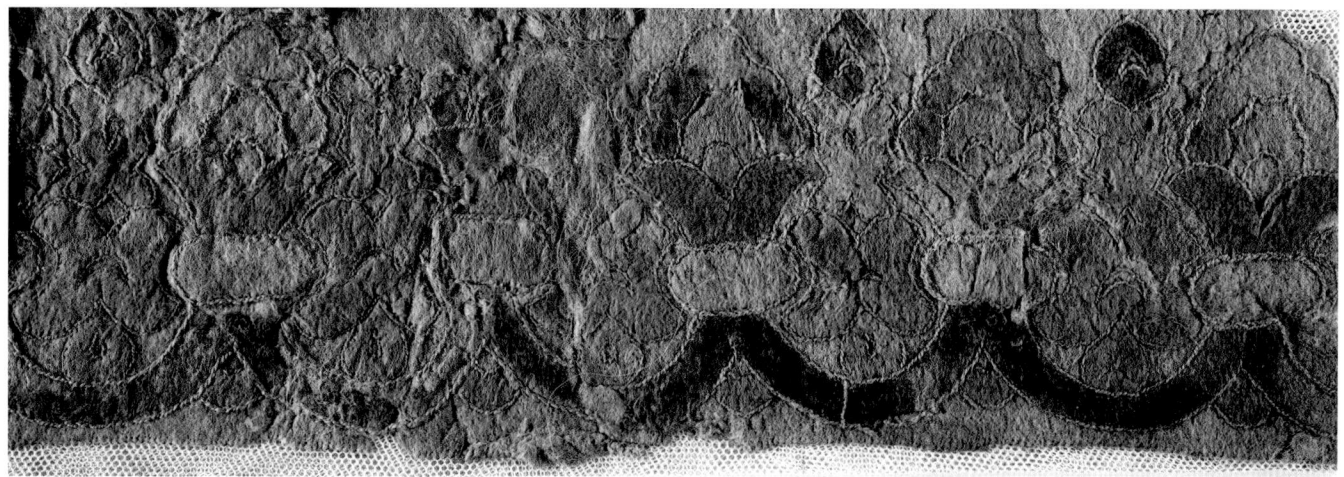

Achaemenid-style bracelets presented to the Persian Great King by the Sakā Tigraxaudā delegation, as depicted in the famous Persepolis relief (see fig. 7-3).

THE IMPACT OF ACHAEMENID IMPORTS ON LOCAL ELITE CULTURE

It has long been noticed that prestige goods from the Achaemenid world had a profound impact on the local artistic vocabulary in the Eurasian steppes.[55] Many motifs are obviously of foreign origin: neither lotus flowers (fig. 7-11) nor lions (fig. 7-12) can be found in the high valleys of the Altai or the Tianshan. Like the palmette ornament (fig. 7-13), they are clearly of Near Eastern origin. In addition, fantastic creatures such as the griffin (see Samashev, this volume fig. 2-19), the sphinx (see page 106),[56] winged felines (fig. 7-14), and winged bulls (fig. 7-15) ultimately have ancient Near Eastern ancestors, even if these motifs frequently adopted indigenous attributes, such as deer or reindeer antlers (see Samashev, page 30).[57] The few examples of human masks ultimately have their sources, again via the filter of Achaemenid art,[58] in the Egyptian Bes mask.[59] Achaemenid "influence" can also be perceived in formal elements, such as dot-and comma-like ornaments, rendering—in a very stylized way— an animal's musculature (figs. 7-16, 7-17).

Sometimes, local creations remain stylistically very close to their Achaemenid prototypes (figs. 7-18, 7-19). But, in the majority of cases, the transfer of motifs and formal elements resulted in numerous adaptations and transformations, reflecting local taste and the nomadic elite's own worldview. In this way many foreign motifs were readily reinterpreted according to local customs, traditions, and beliefs. Thus, the Bes masks from the bridle of a horse, found in Pazyryk kurgan 1, possibly reflect beliefs related to the magical power of heads of slain enemies, which many steppe nomads (including the Scythians) used to fasten on their horse bridles.[60] Another example is the motif of single animal heads in profile, such as those of lions, bulls, and fantastic creatures. This motif was quite popular in Achaemenid jewelry and personal ornaments, especially on precious textiles, as is known from golden bracteates (fig. 7-20). Precious Achaemenid textiles were imported into the steppes, probably in considerable quantities (see the earlier mention of "Median robes" as standard gifts at the Achaemenid royal and satrapial courts). Thus it does not come as a surprise to find the motif again in Berel, but here it was transformed and adapted to local concepts and beliefs (see Hanks, fig. 6-10).

Especially interesting are two motifs derived from religious motifs connected with Achaemenid royal iconography. In one case it might deliberately have retained some of its original religious connotation or at least was still used as a marker of status: a small square element executed in leather and fixed on top of a hood worn by the grave owner of Pazyryk kurgan 3 (fig.7-21). It clearly recalls the crenellated top of the so-called tower altars known from Achaemenid seal designs that are closely

7-9　　Partly gilded vessel handle shaped like a deer. Silver and gold, cast and gilded, H. 16 cm, Siberian collection of Peter I, Iran (said to have come from the Bukhtarma valley), 5th–4th century BCE. The State Hermitage Museum, St. Petersburg: S-273.

7-10　　Torque. Gold, turquoise, and wood, chased, H. 16.5 cm, Siberian collection of Peter I, Eastern Iran, 4th–3rd century BCE. The State Hermitage Museum, St. Petersburg: Z-568.

7-11　　Detail of a carpet with lotus pattern. Felt, 68.5 cm x 10.5 cm, Pazyryk barrow no. 2, 4th century BCE. The State Hermitage Museum, St. Petersburg: 1684/261.

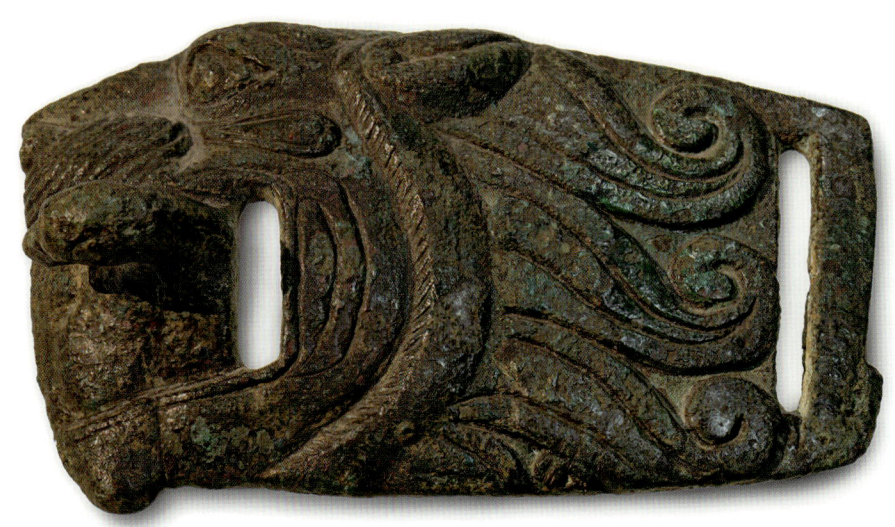

7-12 Buckle depicting a profiled lion head with horse head in its mouth. Bronze, Berkara (Karatau region), 4th–3rd century BCE. Central State Museum, Almaty: KP 11171. Checklist no. 108.

related to royal iconography (fig. 7-22).⁶¹ It is important to note that at least the Sakā-period nomads in Semirechye were familiar with the religious connotation of such "stepped merlons," as they appear on a magnificent "altar" found in 1953 near the kurgan cemetery of Issyk (fig. 7-23).⁶² One wonders whether this element on the headdress in Pazyryk points to some sacerdotal function of the person buried in kurgan 3.

A second element borrowed from the royal iconography of Achaemenid court art is the winged sun disc. This motif might have found its way into the steppe primarily on portable objects such as seals, as demonstrated by a chalcedony cylinder seal from the Achaemenid period found in a rich Sarmatian kurgan in Kosika at the lower Volga (fig. 7-24).⁶³ In Pazyryk, the winged sun-disc appears in a stylized but still discernible form as an ornament on two saddle arches from kurgan 5 (fig. 7-25). The playful way it is alternated, and actually tripled, suggests that in this case the motif had already lost its original religious connotation and was merely used as an exotic ornament.⁶⁴ This same tendency can be observed on some furniture elements found in the Pazyryk barrows: the annulated decor of the legs of little dish-tables is clearly inspired by Near Eastern furniture.⁶⁵

In some details "Achaemenid" iconographic vocabulary remains visible in the Western Central Asian steppes long after the fall of the Persian empire. This is possibly illustrated by a series of golden garment appliqués with the depiction of a horseman from an elite burial in the kurgan cemetery of Tenlik in eastern Semirechye, dating to the third or second century BCE (fig. 7-26). They seem to show a distinctive saddle cloth with a border of stepped half-merlons that is known from depictions from Achaemenid-period Anatolia up to third-century Pazyryk.⁶⁶ In addition, the Tenlik rider possibly wears a somewhat crude interpretation of the Persian *bashlyk*.

It thus can be seen that artistic features and traditions from Achaemenid territories, primarily the Eastern satrapies, had a profound impact on the artistic vocabulary of steppe art but also on aspects of self-representation among the nomadic elites. It seems, however, that this impact becomes fully effective and visible only at the very end of the Achaemenid period and in the following decades, as the Pazyryk kurgans are now dated to the years ca. 300–250 BCE.⁶⁷ This dating corresponds to our hypothesis of a substantial drain, out of the Eastern territories of the former Achaemenid realm and into the steppes, of luxury items and prestige goods during and immediately after the downfall of the Persian Empire.

INDIAN CONNECTIONS

Recently it has become clear that some objects from Pazyryk, formerly held to be of regional origin, in fact ultimately came from India. This has been suggested for two shirts made of cotton from barrow 2, one completely preserved, the other only in nine fragments.⁶⁸ Another object of Indian origin found in Pazyryk, and formerly believed to come from Central Asia, is a plain "silver" mirror with ox-horn handle from the same barrow (fig. 7-27). Recent investigations have not only shown that it is made of tin bronze instead of silver, but also that the chemical "fingerprint" of the metal markedly differs from Altai materials and rather points to an Indian origin for this mirror (corresponding with formal parallels known from pre-Mauryan-period India).⁶⁹ Another example of an Indian import is Indian silk found in kurgan 1 at Ak-Alakha 3, formerly thought to be from China.⁷⁰

At this point it is difficult to know how these objects reached the nomadic elites in Southern Siberia. They might have been traded, via either Western Central Asia or China. Perhaps they came via the oases of the Tarim basin, some of which were inhabited by Sakā groups that entertained close cultural ties to their relatives in the steppes and toward India.⁷¹ A good example

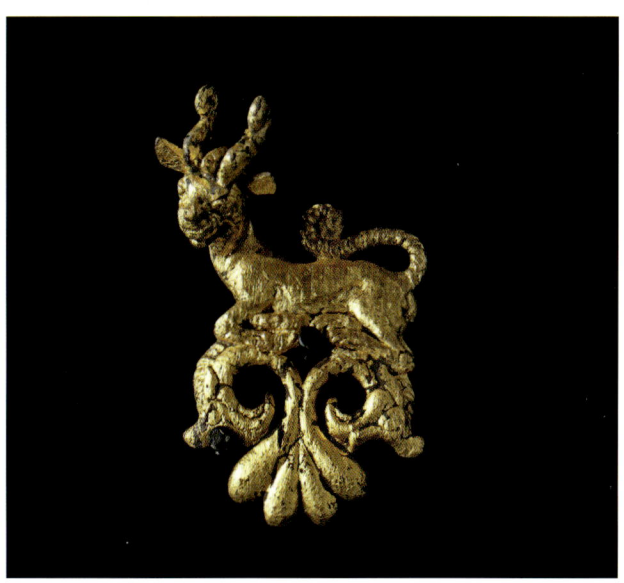

7-13   Horned feline resting between two raptor heads and a palmette. Berel, kurgan 11, late 4th–early 3rd century BCE. Presidential Center of Culture, Astana.

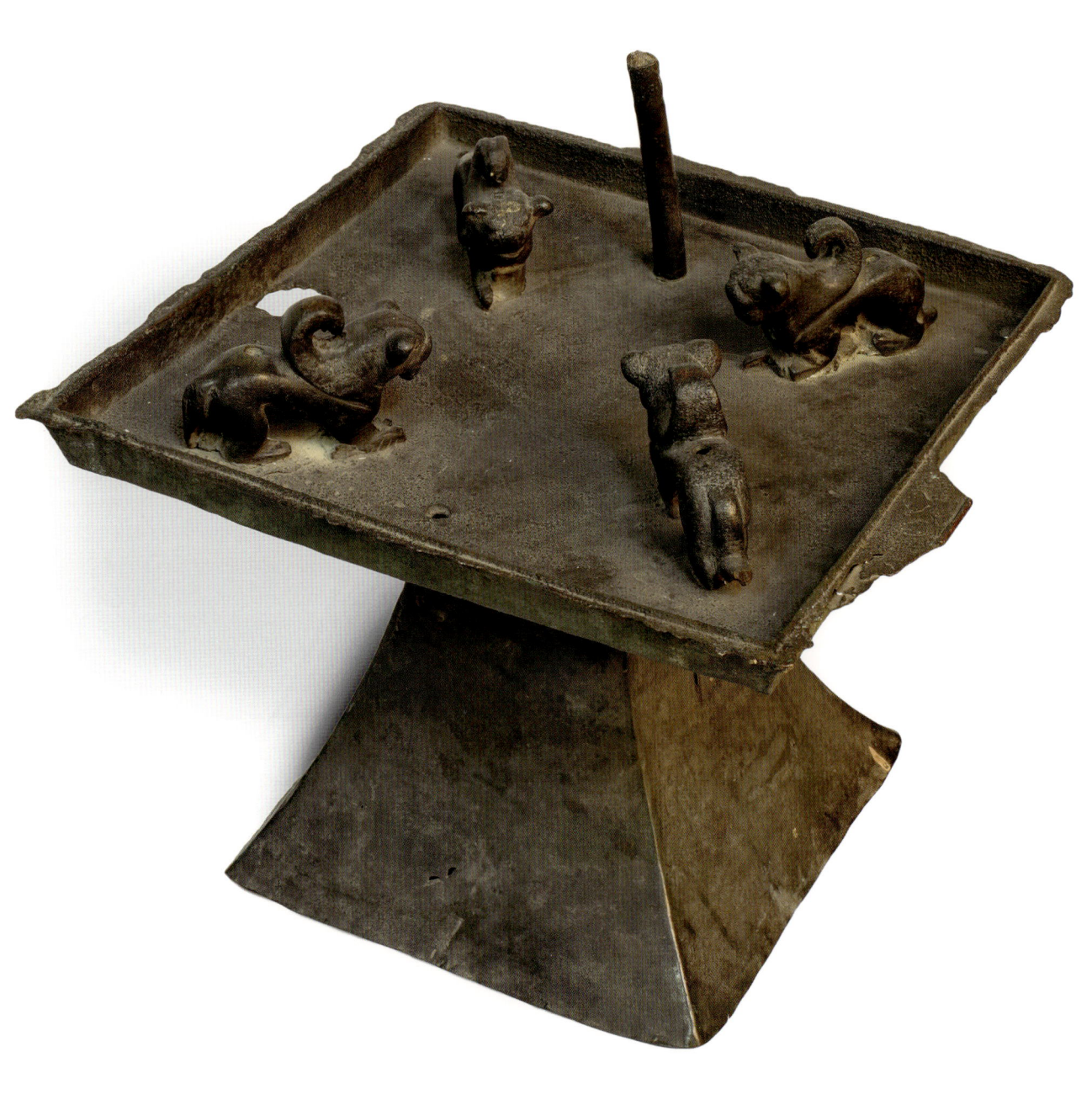

7-14 Square footed tray with figures of winged tigers. Bronze, Almaty, chance find 1912, 5th–3rd century BCE, Central State Museum, Almaty: KP 2281. Checklist no. 144.

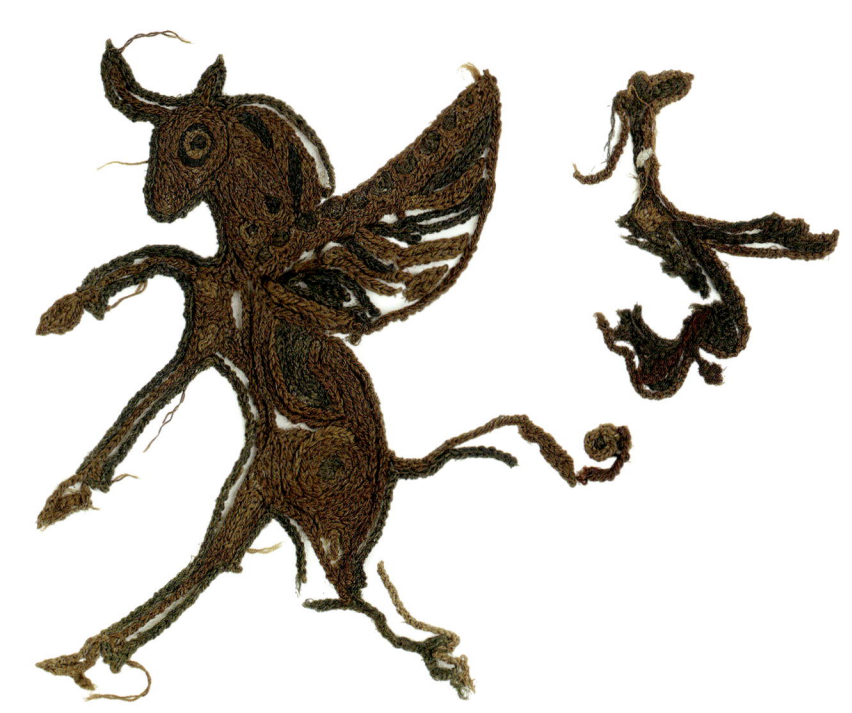

7-15 Embroidery of a winged-bull from saddle cloth. Wool, Berel, kurgan 11, late 4th–early 3rd century BCE. A. Kh. Margulan Institute of Archaeology, Almaty. Checklist no. 80.

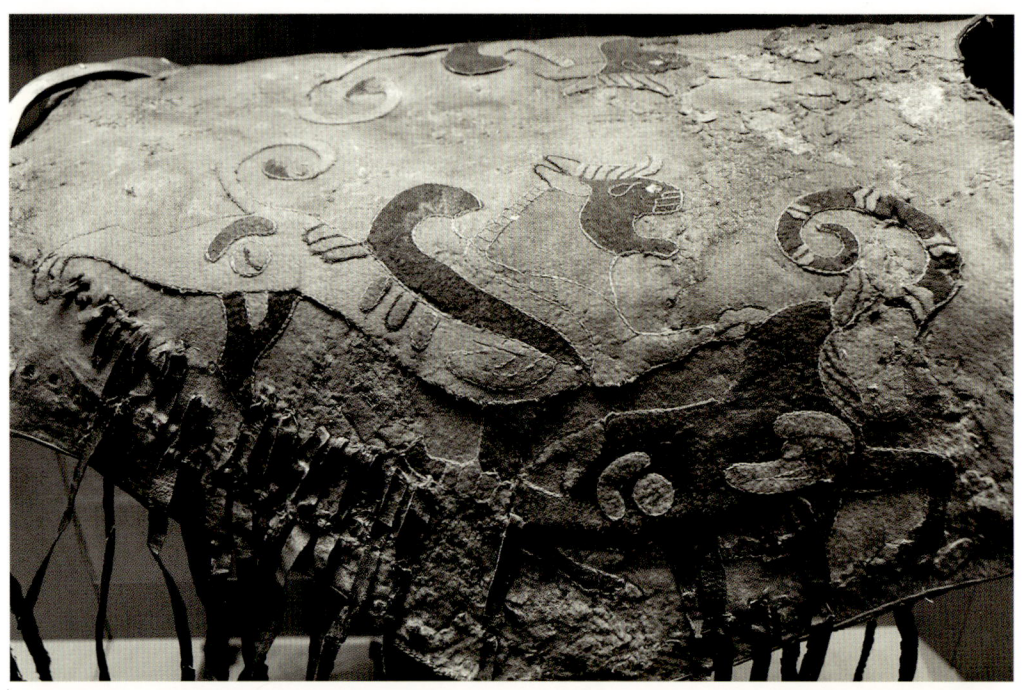

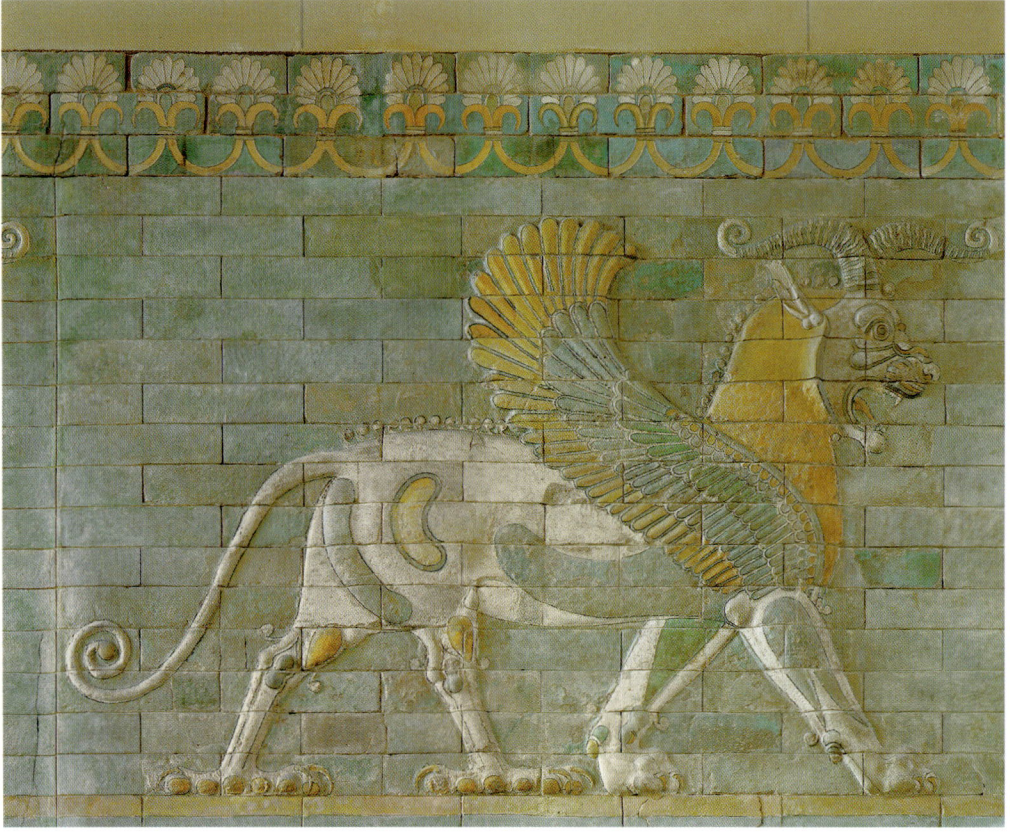

7-16   Saddle cover with felt appliqué of a lion-griffin seizing a mountain goat. 59 cm x 56 cm, Pazyryk barrow no. 1, 4th–3rd century BCE. The State Hermitage Museum, St. Petersburg: 1295/139.

7-17   Winged bull (lion-griffin). Colored glazed tiles, from the palace in Susa, Iran. 6th–4th century BCE, Achaemenid. Musée du Louvre, Paris: Sb3323.

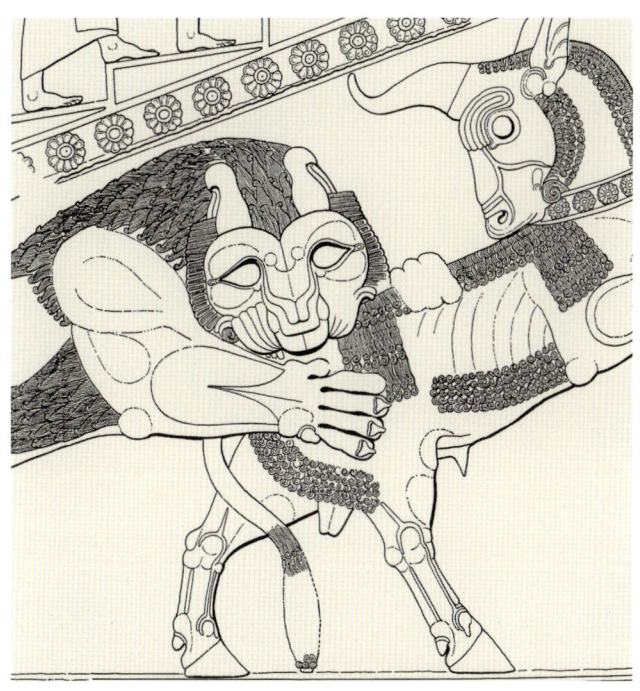

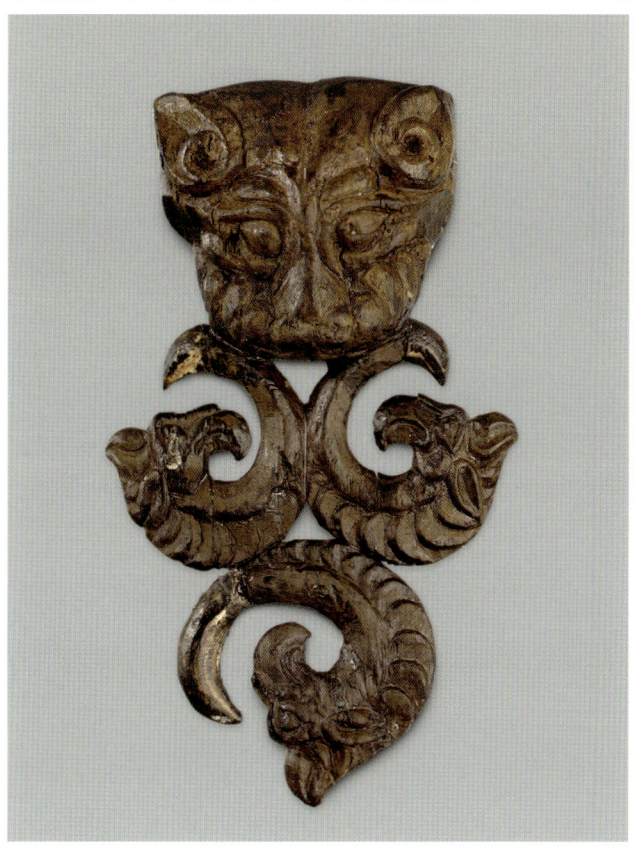

7-18   Drawing of a detail of the Apadāna staircase showing a lion seizing a bull, from the western facade of the west staircase of the palace of Darius I at Persepolis.

7-19   Feline face and three griffin heads from horse tack. Wood, Berel, kurgan 11, late 4th–early 3rd century BCE. Presidential Center of Culture, Astana: 4441/1-2. Checklist no. 45.

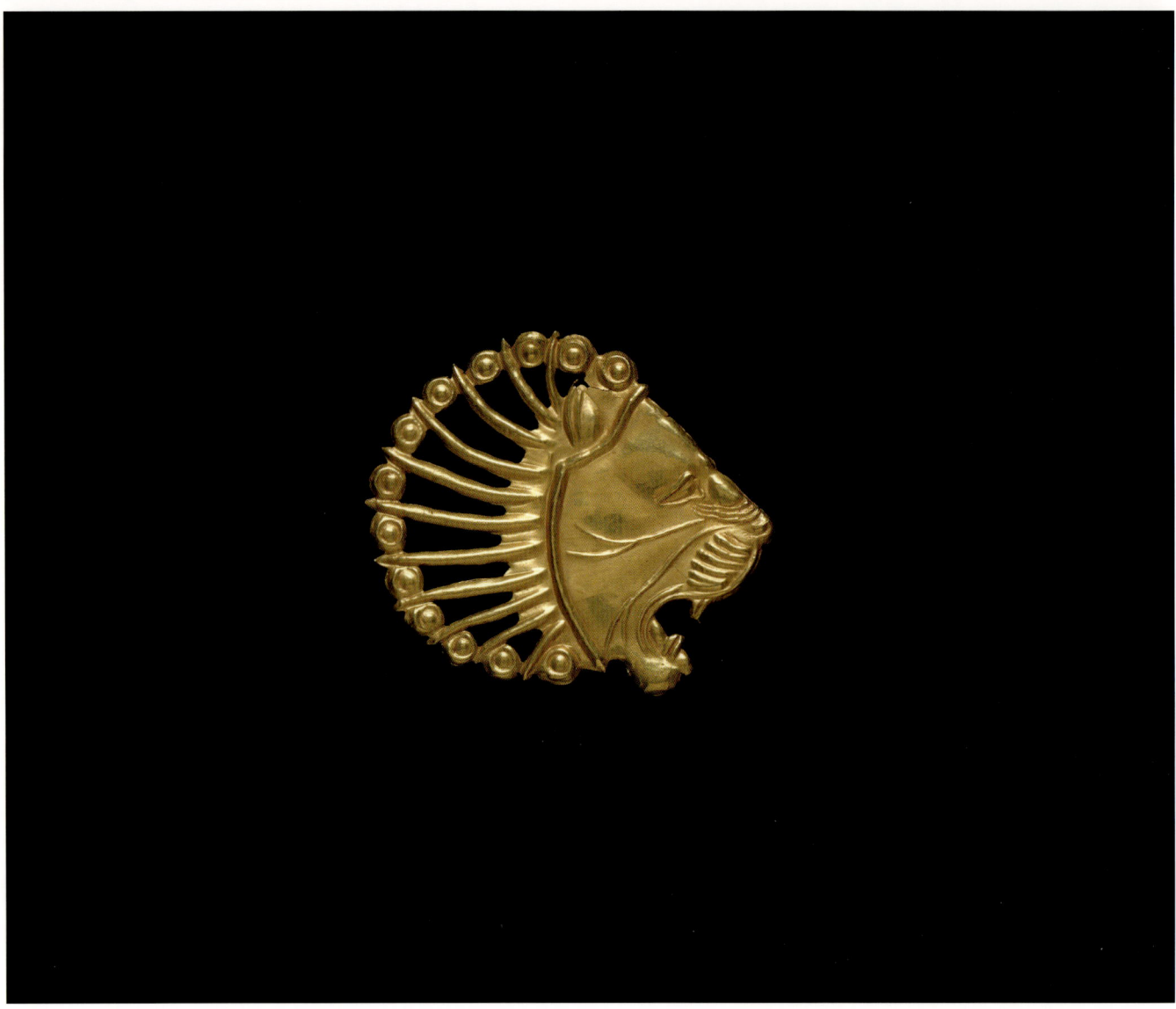

of relationships with Xinjiang is a jar from Semirechye, painted with geometric motifs (resembling a vine-scroll pattern). It finds some parallels in the painted pottery from Early Iron Age cultures in Xinjiang (fig. 7-28). Perhaps even the famous felt wall hangings from Pazyryk kurgan 5 were actually produced in the Tarim basin.

CHINA AND NEW ELITE NETWORKS IN THE POST-ACHAEMENID PERIOD

The inventory of elite barrows at Pazyryk are important for yet another reason: they foreshadow a new trend that becomes important in the following period, namely, the growing impact of Chinese prestige goods on the self-representation of nomadic elites in the Central Asian steppes.[72] This can be seen in Chinese imports such as silk fragments, a bronze mirror fragment, and remains of Chinese lacquer in kurgans 3, 6, and particularly 5 at Pazyryk (which now dates to ca. 250 BCE).[73] Interestingly, the Pazyryk material also reveals some local adaptations to Chinese models, both regarding artistic conventions and self-representation of the elite.[74] The most impressive finding related to this phenomenon is the discovery of a (disjointed) four-wheeled wagon in kurgan 5. It was probably used only for ceremonial purposes, in the context of regionally practiced rituals.[75] But, curiously, the wagon resembles Chinese prototypes.[76]

Obviously, during the late Warring States period (ca. 300–221 BCE), many nomadic groups in Central Asia

7-20   Appliqué in the shape of a lion's head. Gold, 4.75 cm x 5.72 cm, Iran, Achaemenid, 6th–4th century BCE. The Metropolitan Museum of Art, New York, Gift of Khalil Rabenou, 1956: 56.154.1.

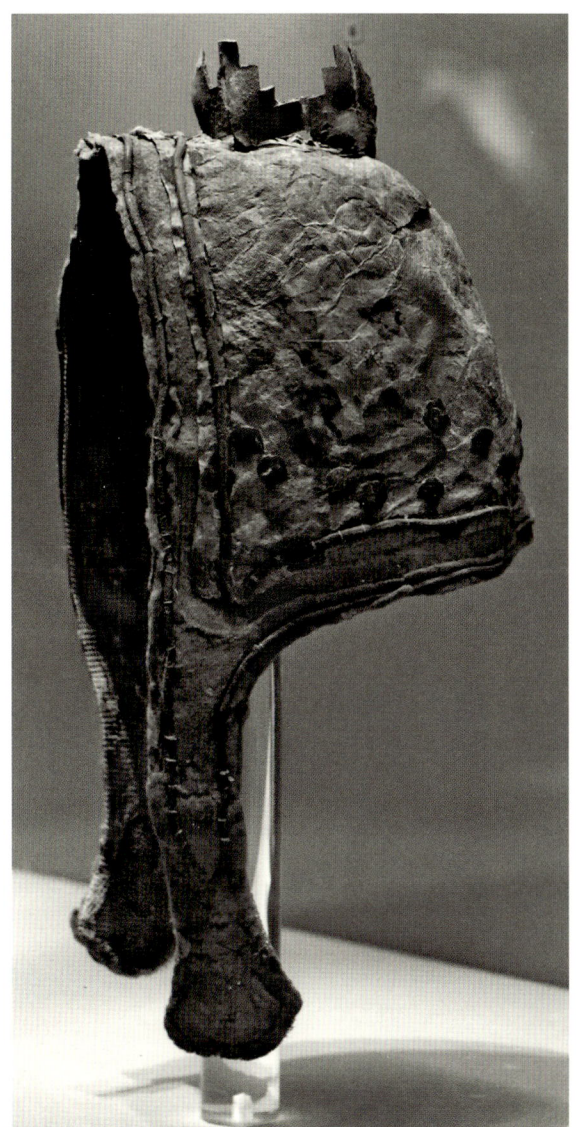
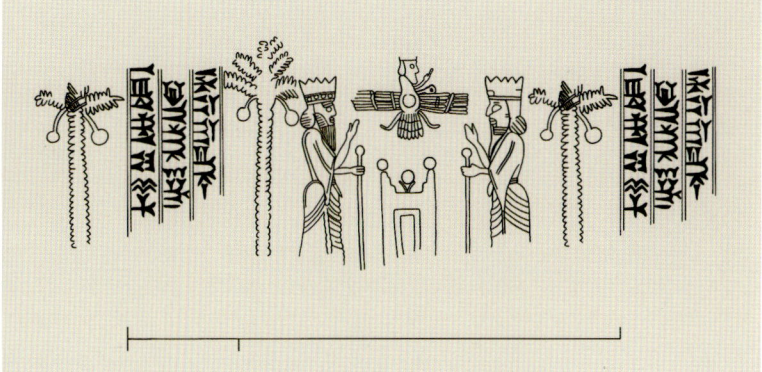
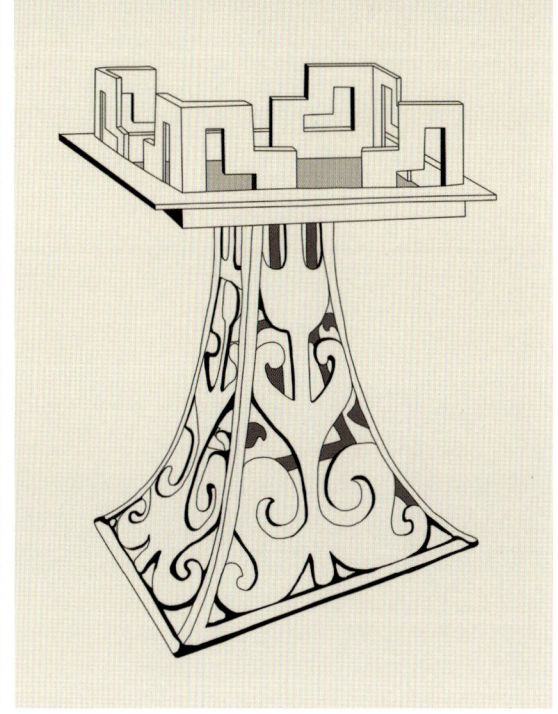

were brought politically and culturally into closer contact with Chinese polities. But why? It seems as if this trend was ultimately incited by a very practical reason: the growing need for horses in China after the military reforms in *Zhao* (趙) in 307 BCE, creating—for the first time in the state of Chinese history—cavalry units on a large scale and resulting in a flourishing horse trade with nomads in the north.[77] Thus, it is only logical to assume that this trade substantially increased the influx of Chinese prestige goods into the Eurasian steppes.

Political and cultural relations between the Eurasian steppes and China became even stronger during the following centuries (fig. 7-29). China was finally united in 221 BCE and flourished during the Han period (206 BCE–220 CE), while during the same period a number of important changes took place in the steppes. In the east the powerful *Xiongnu* (匈奴) established their rule over "all the people who draw the bow."[78] This pushed other groups (Sakā, *Yuezhi* [月支], *Wusun* [烏孫]) westward. While the Sakā and Yuezhi finally turned south, conquered Bactria from the Greeks, and later subdued parts of eastern Iran (Sīstān)[79] and most of northern India, the Wusun established themselves in the northwestern Tianshan, in what is now southern Kazakhstan and northern Kyrgyzstan.

The little that is known about the political history of the Wusun is owed exclusively to Chinese reports. But beyond the usual topoi characteristic for Chinese

7-21 Male headdress. Pazyryk barrow no. 3, 4th–3rd century BCE. The State Hermitage Museum, St. Petersburg: 1685/16.

7-22 Composite drawing of a seal from Persepolis (PFS 11*) with depiction of a "tower altar."

7-23 Drawing of a square-footed tray with stepped merlons on top. Found in 1953 near the cemetery of Issyk.

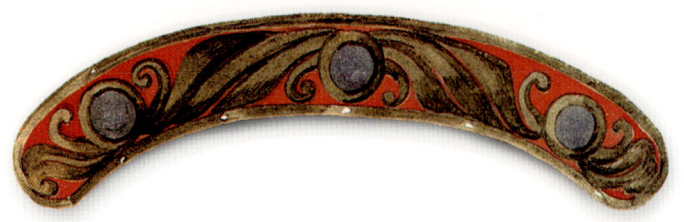

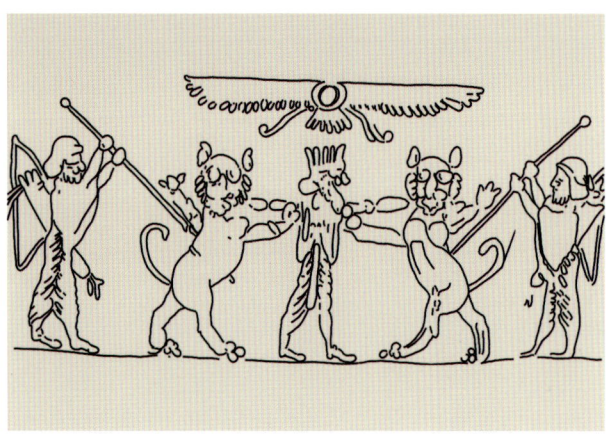

descriptions of their northern neighbors in the steppes,[80] these reports tell us that there was a distinct elite stratum among the Wusun: rich Wusun nomads could own as many as 4,000 to 5,000 horses. At the top of the hierarchy was a ruler called a *kunmo* (昆莫) or *kunmi* (昆彌), while below him ranked a "supreme leader of the left" and a "supreme leader of the right," pointing to an organization of the Wusun army (and state) into two wings, as is typical of many pastoral states in the Eurasian steppes.

The Wusun entered into particularly close relationships with Han China after the famous diplomatic mission of *Zhang Qian* (張騫) into Central Asia between 138 and 125 BCE. As crucial allies of China against the Xiongnu, members of the Wusun elite were especially courted by the Han: between 110 and 105 BCE, the Wusun *kunmo* even received a Han princess for marriage. As noted above, this was a popular method among nomadic elites to extract prestige goods from their sedentary neighbors, and indeed the princess brought "imperial carriages, wearing apparel and equipment for imperial use . . . and a very rich store of gifts."[81] Imported Chinese prestige goods must have circulated widely among the Wusun nobility, because the princess regularly met with the Wusun aristocracy "when a banquet was set out, and she presented the noblemen who attended the king with valuables and silk."[82] The influx

and wide circulation of Chinese imports seem to have had a profound impact on the taste of the nomadic elites and, consequently, on local artistic conventions—just as "Achaemenid" imports did in the previous period. A spectacular example is represented by two fragments from a diadem, found by chance in 1939 in a heavily disturbed burial in a crevice in the Kargaly valley, about 30 kilometers to the east of Almaty (fig. 7-30).[83] The burial contained roughly 300 items—appliqués of costumes and headdresses, as well as body decor—all made of gold and many decorated with turquoise incrustations, as exemplified by an exquisite finger ring and earring (figs. 7-31, 7-32).

Each of the two fragments of the diadem (fig. 7-30) consists of a thin perforated gold band with turquoise, carnelian, garnet, and colored-paste incrustations and features an undulating cloudscape inhabited by birds, wild beasts, and fantastic creatures.[84] They form two converging processions. On the smaller (left) fragment a horned deer can be discerned, preceded by a roe-deer and a winged chimera (composed of a feline's body and a wolf's head?). This composite being is mounted by a winged furry creature with long flowing hair, turning its head backward and holding a flower. In front of this group appears a winged horse, standing on a plinth above a pillar or column evolving from a highly stylized mountain. The opposing procession of the larger (right) fragment is closed by another furry creature holding a flower, this time riding a ram. It is preceded by a little bear and a third winged creature, with a flower, on a mountain goat. In front of this group we see again a winged horse on a plinth above a stand evolving from another mountain. But unlike the procession preserved in the smaller (left) fragment, the winged horse on the right fragment is preceded by another winged creature, apparently with long ears in addition to its long flowing hair. This time a horned dragon serves as a mount. Above both processions fly wild geese.

The winged furry creatures holding flowers depicted in this scene closely resemble little winged *genii*, called

7-24   Drawing of a chalcedony cylinder seal with a scene of heroic encounter between the "Persian royal hero," two lions, and two spearmen. Note the winged sun-disc above the central figure in the lower panel. Found in a Sarmatian-period kurgan in Kosika, Lower Volga.

7-25   Drawing of leather facing from the upper edge of a saddle arch. Pazyryk barrow no. 5, 4th–3rd century BCE. (After Rudenko 1970, pl. 164A.)

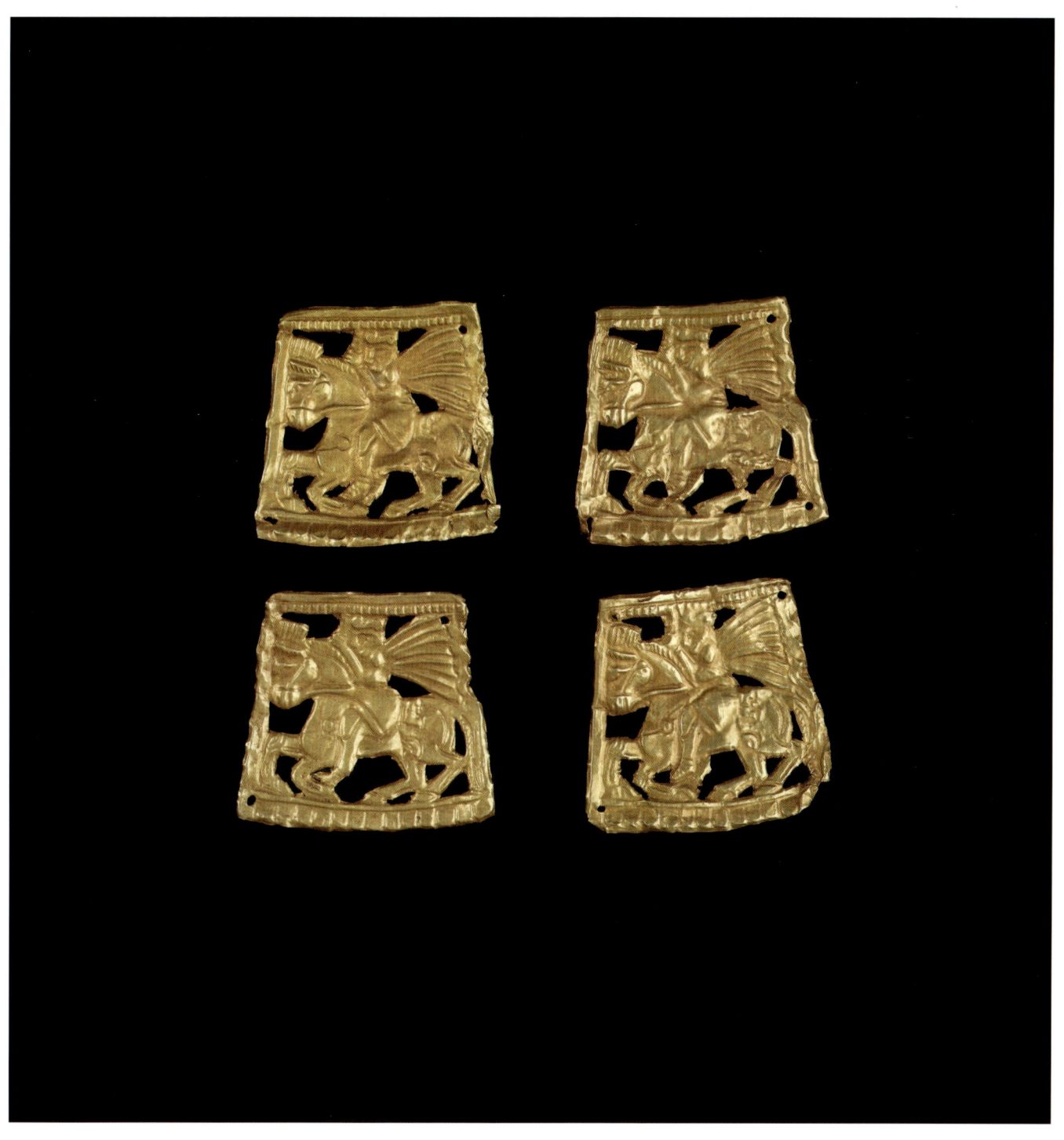

7-26   Plaques with a horse rider (4). Gold, Tenlik Mound
(Taldy-Kurgan, Almaty region), 3rd–2nd century BCE.
Museum of Archaeology, Almaty. MA 135а,б,в,г.
Checklist no. 156.

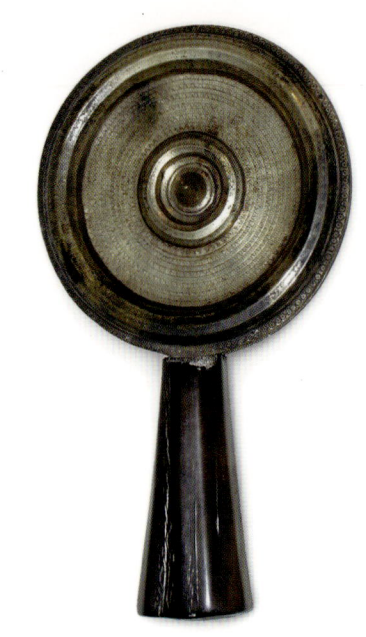

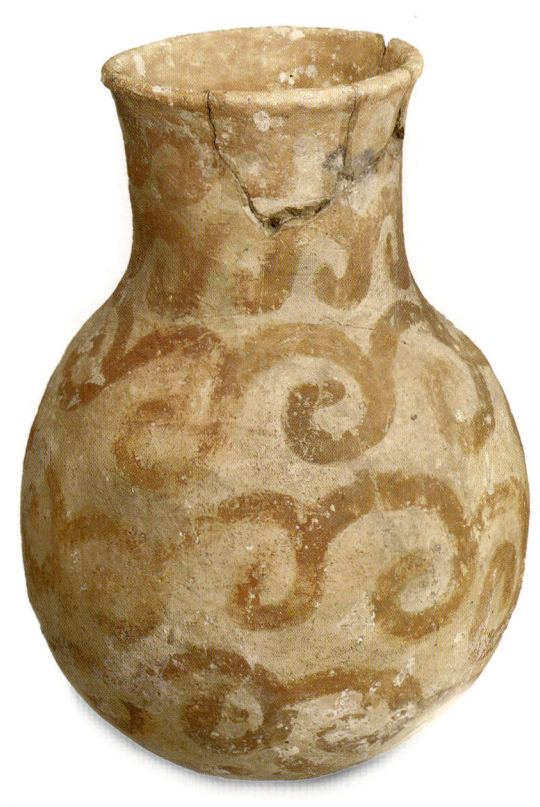

7-27 Indian tin-bronze mirror with ox-horn handle. Diam. 15 cm, handle L. 11.5 cm, Pazyryk barrow no. 2, 4th century BCE. The State Hermitage Museum, St. Petersburg: 1684/89.

7-28 Jar painted with geometric motifs. Fired clay, Semirechye/Zhetisu (Almaty region), 3rd century BCE–3rd century CE. Museum of Archaeology, Almaty: ЦАЭ-85. Checklist no. 159.

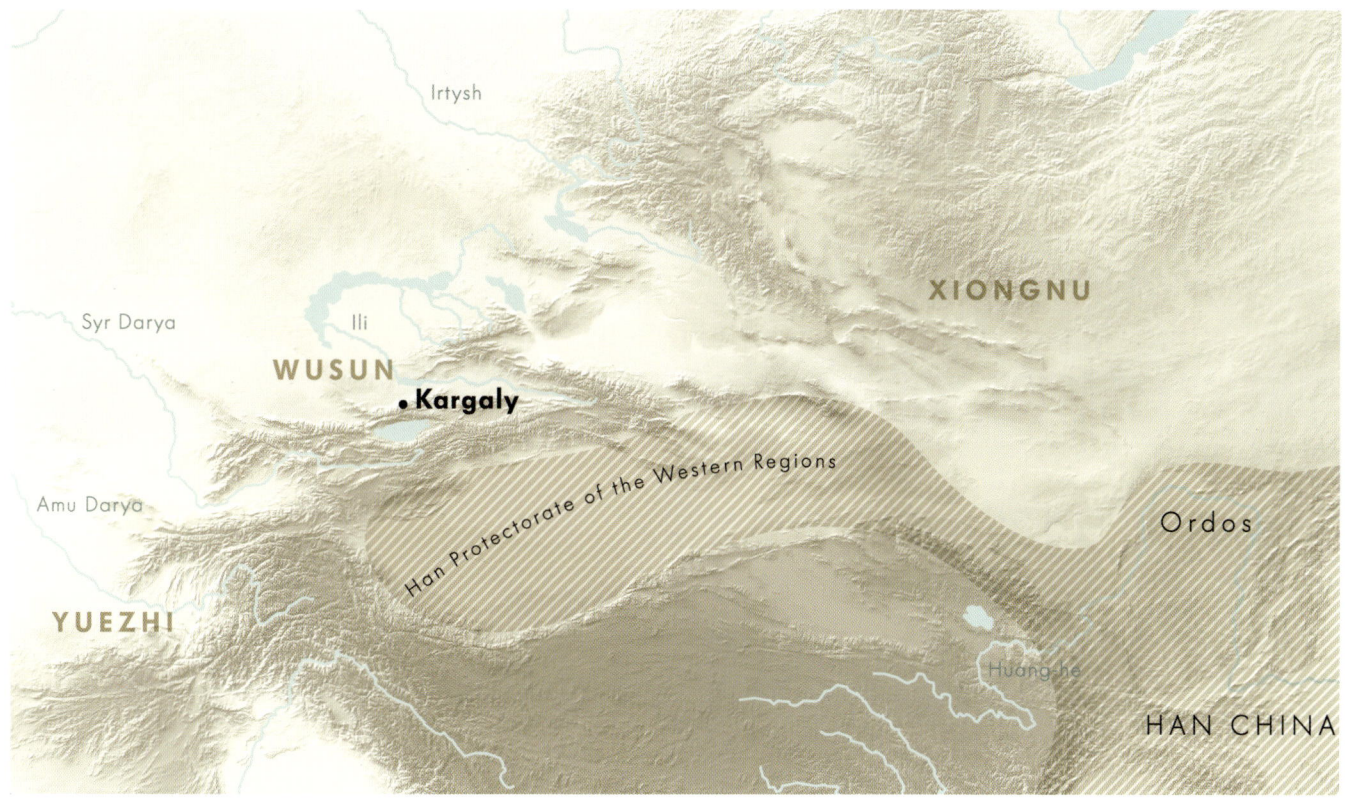

| Han Empire around 50 BCE

"feathered men" (*yuren* 羽人) in Chinese decorative arts. They are known to represent "immortals" (*xian* 仙) and appear in China beginning in the second century BCE on mortuary goods, such as lacquer coffins, funerary banners, bronze mirrors, pottery or jade carvings, as well as in tomb paintings and on tomb reliefs (figs. 7-34, 7-35).[85] They regularly inhabit mountains or swirling clouds and ride animals. One of their riding animals, a dragon, also appears on the Kargaly diadem (fig. 7-30).

Although it is not excluded that the motif of the "feathered man" in Chinese decorative arts actually reflects non-Chinese influences,[86] its combination with the dragon and the cloud-shaped background of the Kargaly diadem suggest that the master who executed this superb piece drew upon Chinese iconographic models from depictions of celestial scenes for his composition. One possible source for him could have been Han-period mirrors, as they are known to have widely circulated in Central Asia and Siberia.[87] But this is not to say that the decoration on the Kargaly diadem indeed depicts "immortals": probably they were reinterpreted according to local mythological or cosmological beliefs now unknown to us.
This is all the more likely as not all the elements of the composition are necessarily of Chinese origin. Deer and mountain goats in a converging procession are known, for example, from the contemporary Sarmatian steppes in the west, as shown by the famous diadem from the Khokhlach kurgan (near Novocherkassk), dating to the first century CE or the first half of the second century CE.[88] Another element that deserves special attention is the unsaddled winged horse, standing on a two-stepped plinth supported by a stand evolving out of a mountain. There are parallels in Chinese celestial scenes for pedestals on stands rising from a mountain, namely, depictions of the "Queen-Mother of the West" (*Xi Wangmu* 西王母).[89] However, here we deal with a winged horse! Of course, the motif of winged horses is well known from Chinese contemporary art (and from many other parts of the Old World). But what is peculiar is that both horses in the Kargaly scene do not join the overall movement of the two converse processions, but stand calmly on a postament-like construction. In fact, the arrangement is reminiscent of the depiction of a statue on a column or another kind of pedestal, something widely known from the Graeco-Roman world (as is the form of the plinth). A similar iconographic transfer can be observed on a much-discussed Sasanian plate in the Metropolitan Museum of Art in New York.[90]

7-29 Map of northwestern Han China and contiguous Central Asia from the 2nd century BCE to the 1st century CE, showing general locations of the Yuezhi, Wusun, and Xiongnu nomadic groups.

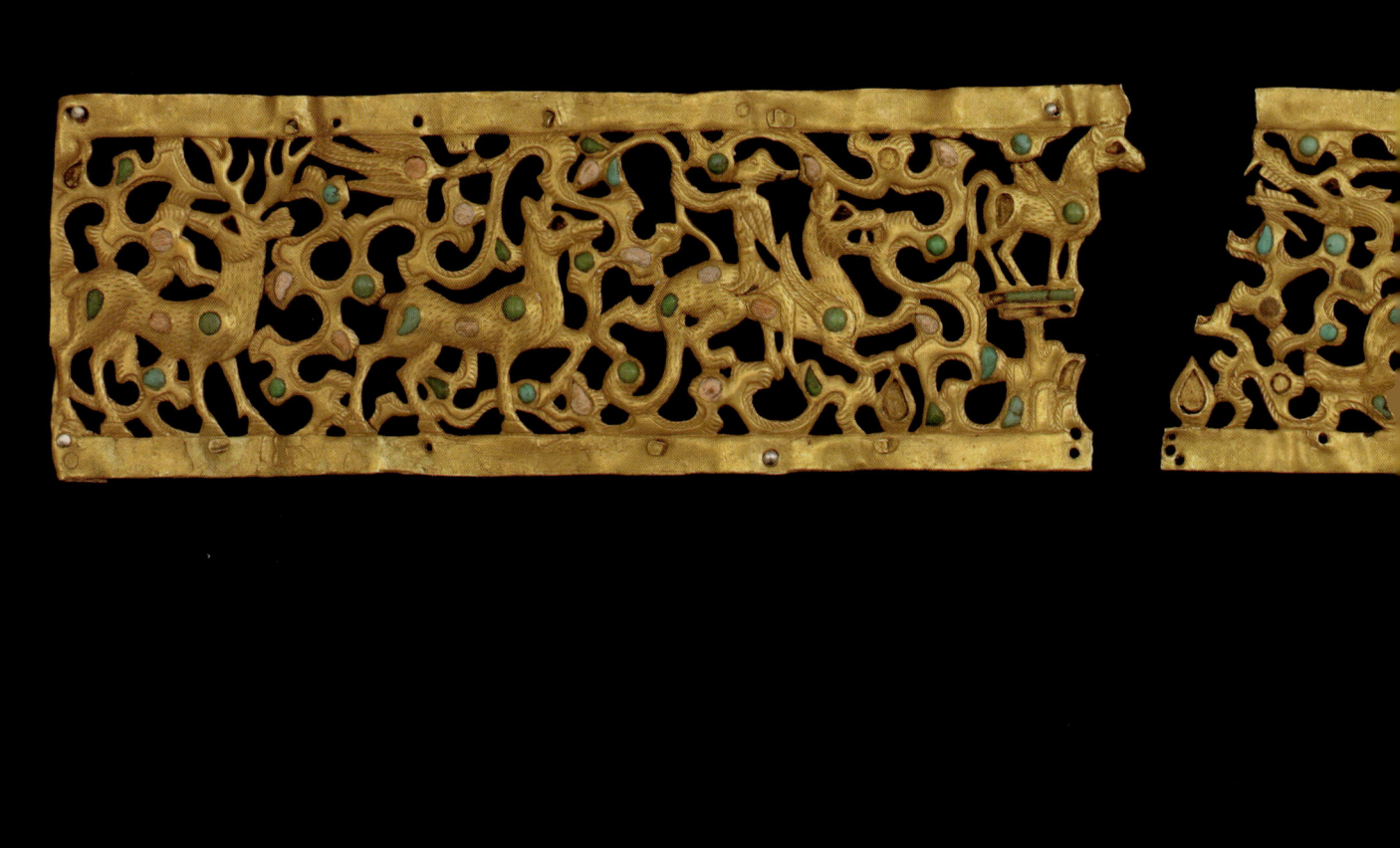

7-30 Diadem. Gold, turquoise, carnelian, and coral, Kargaly (Almaty region), 2nd century BCE–1st century CE (Wusun). Central State Museum, Almaty: KP 3990. Checklist no. 182.

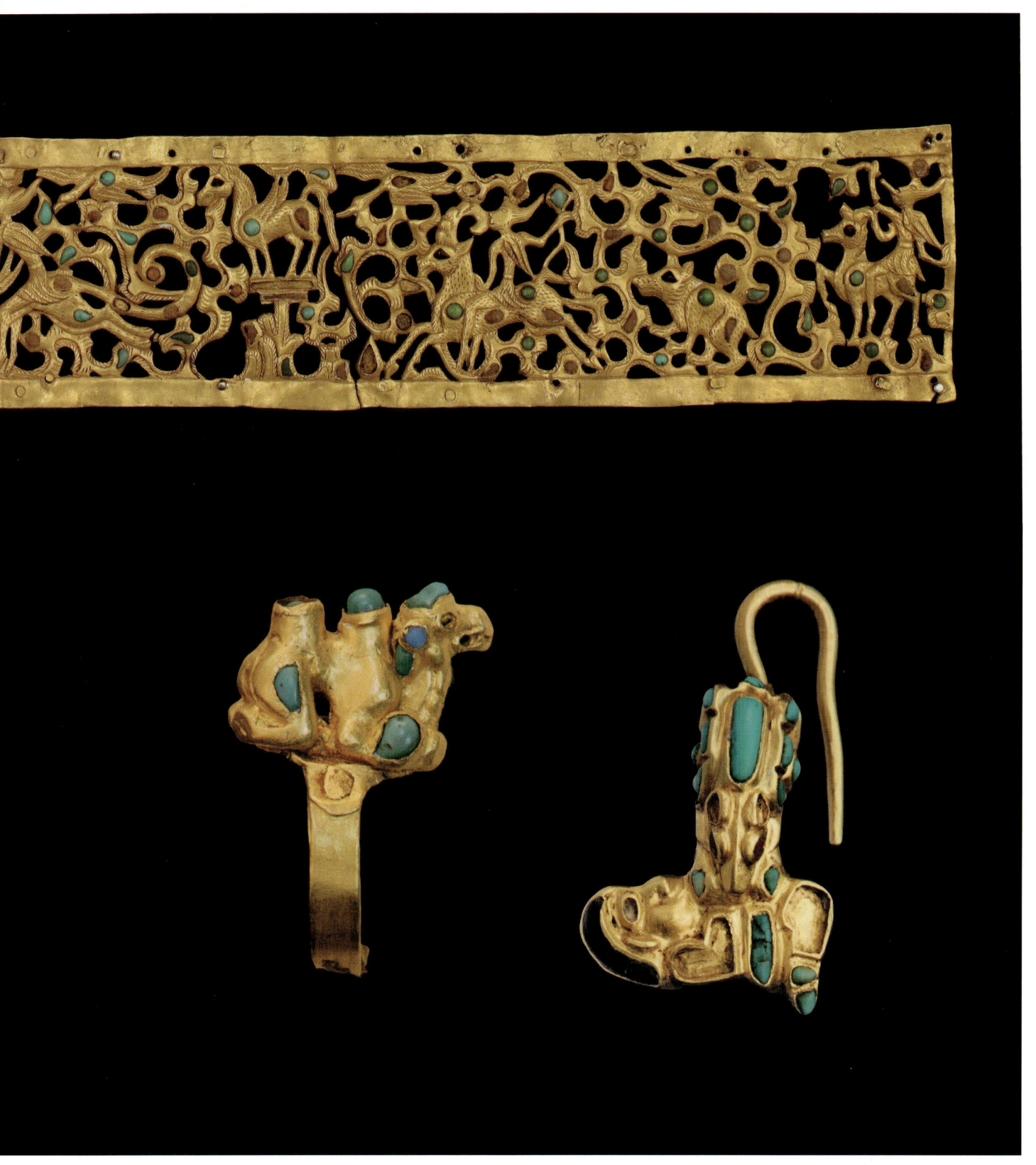

7-31 Ring with Bactrian camel. Gold and turquoise (?), Kargaly (Almaty region), 2nd century BCE–1st century CE (Wusun). Central State Museum, Almaty: KP 3991. Checklist no. 187.

7-32 Earring with an animal attacking a man. Gold, turquoise, carnelian, and jasper, Kargaly (Almaty region), 2nd century BCE–1st century CE (Wusun). Central State Museum, Almaty: KP 3995. Checklist no. 186.

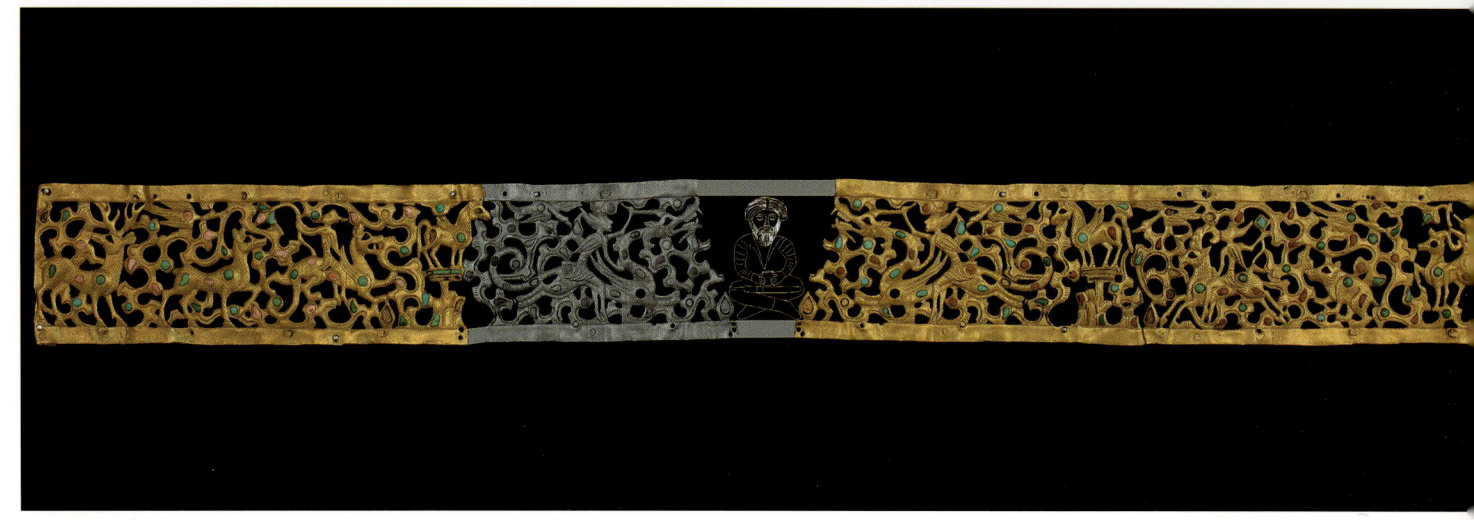

A number of small perforations indicate that the Kargaly diadem was sewn on a textile background—perhaps a felt or woven cloth hat. It seems to have been in use for a prolonged period as it clearly features traces of repair. Apparently a part of the diadem had already been lost in antiquity. But there are some hints that allow for a possible reconstruction (fig. 7-33). First of all, it must be noted that the presently preserved fragments are in conflict with an overall principle of composition, namely, a general (though no absolute) symmetry. This is strongly suggested by, first, the two mirror-inverted winged horses and, second, the same length of each procession behind them (each consisting of three animals, with and without riders). A single "feathered man" riding a dragon to the left clearly disturbs this symmetry and is, from a narrative point of view, somewhat illogical: what would be the ultimate "destination" of both processions? To restore a heraldic notion it is therefore most logical to assume a second dragon-rider in front of the left horse and a central element thus flanked by two dragon-riding "feathered men." But what was depicted in the center of the composition? Admittedly, this is not an easy question to answer and no definite solution can be presented. However, we might advance some suggestions based on parallels in contemporary Sarmatian materials from the Northern Pontic steppes. One possible option is a tree, as on the diadem from Khokhlach mentioned above, or on the headgear from barrow 10 in Kobyakovo.[91] But another solution seems more likely: a frontal figure of a banqueter.[92] This would make perfect sense of the general celestial iconography of the Kargaly diadem as the motif of the banqueter is, throughout Western Central Asia, well-known in the context of paradise scenes.

However that may be, the diadem from Kargaly impressively demonstrates that the decorative art of pastoral nomads continued to flourish in the Wusun period. In particular, the introduction of Chinese iconographic features resulted in a new and highly innovative artistic language in the steppes. Political mobility among the steppe aristocracy, extensive elite networks, and transcontinental trade soon spread this new artistic vocabulary over large parts of the Eurasian steppe and beyond, marking a new chapter in the history and culture of nomadic elites in Central Asia.

7-33 Reconstruction of Diadem from fig. 7-30 proposed by author.

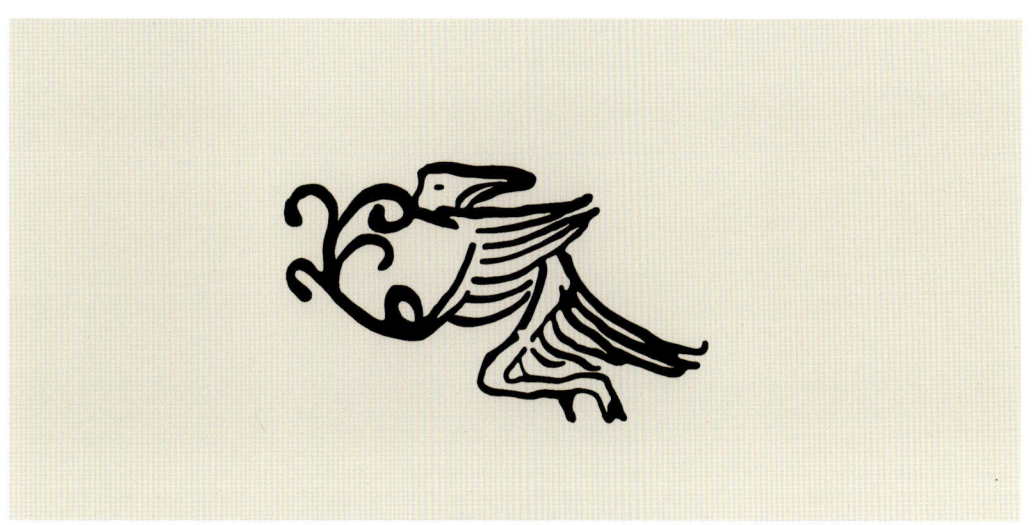

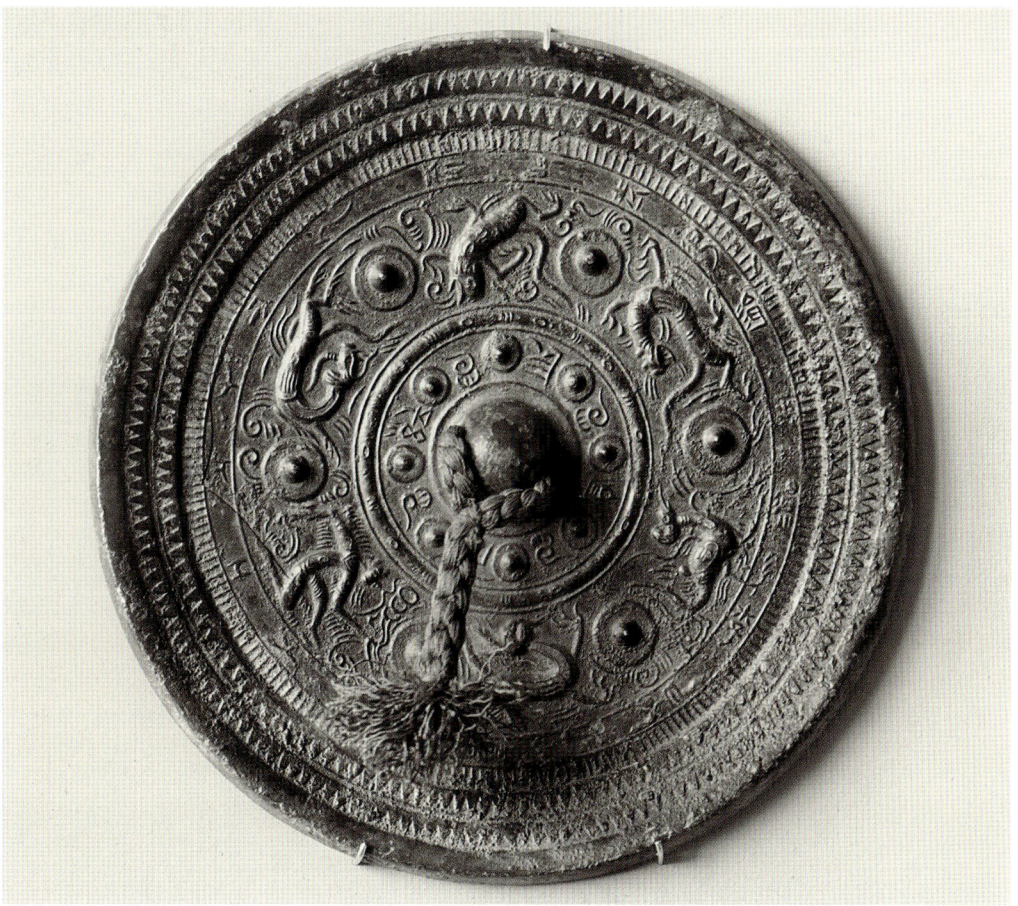

7-34 Drawing of an immortal from a Western Han bronze mirror. Mid- to late 1st century BCE.

7-35 Mirror. Bronze, Diam. 14.3 cm., China, Han dynasty (206 BCE–220 CE). The Metropolitan Museum of Art, Rogers Fund, 1912: 12.134.45.

NOTES

I wish to thank Fiona Kidd, Sarah Laursen, Judith Lerner, Karen Rubinson, and Lillian Tseng for their comments and suggestions. Any errors remain my responsibility alone.

1. Jettmar 1967; Brentjes 1982; Kossack 1987.
2. See Hanks this volume.
3. See the recently excavated burials of mounted nomads at Liushiu in the Kunlunshan, dating to around ca. 1000 BCE (Wagner et al. 2011).
4. See Грязнов 1980 and essays this volume by Samashev and Bokovenko and by Hanks.
5. This "code" is sometimes called the Scythian triad, referring to (1) a typical repertoire of weapons, (2) horse tack, and (3) "animal-style" artwork.
6. Čugunov, Parzinger, and Nagler 2003 and Samashev and Bokovenko, and Hanks this volume.
7. See Toleubaev this volume.
8. Галанина 1997; Ivantchik 2001.
9. Höllmann et al. 1992; Bunker 1997; Di Cosmo 2002, 77–78.
10. Ivantčhik 1993.
11. Bunker 1997.
12. See Chang this volume.
13. Khazanov 1994.
14. Togan 1998, 146–48.
15. Paul 2004, 1070–74, aptly concludes that "pastoral states" seem to have had "pour finalité principale d'organiser les échanges qui, en retour, ont façonné la nature de ces États" (1071). In fact, no example of "spontaneous" state formation in the steppes can be observed (Christian 1998).
16. Fletcher 1986, 23; Di Cosmo 1999; Paul 2004, 1070–74.
17. The term Sakā is used in this essay in a very broad, generic sense for all the various nomadic groupings to the northeast of the Achaemenid territories, not restricted to the Semirechye and not necessarily to groups who called themselves Sakā. On the various ethnonyms relating to Western Central Asian nomads during the Achaemenid period, see Vogelsang 1992, 106–15, 180–200, 221–22, 229–35.
18. Much less is known for this early period about the role of the oases territories in the Tarim basin, south of the Tianshan, as markets for nomads north of the mountains. But their importance is documented for later periods, including the Early Turkic period (Stark 2008, 190–94).
19. Briant 1982.
20. Dalton 1964, 35–40, cat. 23 (fig. 50), cat. 26 (pl. XI), cat. 39 (pl. XII), cat. 111 (fig. 60 on p. 30), cat. 134 (pl. XVIII), cats. 144–45 (pl. XX). On questions of the origin and authenticity of the ensemble, see Curtis 2004.
21. Kuz'mina 1977, 203–4.
22. Галанина 1997, 102, 212.
23. Bunker 1983; Linduff 2009.
24. With the exception, perhaps, of the torques (see discussion below in the text).
25. Briant 2002, 305.
26. This is known from an oracle request to the god Shamash relating to Bartatua's request: "Shamash, great lord, give me a firm, positive answer to what I am asking you! Bartatua, king of the Scythians, who has now sent his messengers to Esarhaddon, king of Assyria, concerning a royal daughter—if Esarhaddon, king of [Assyria], gives him his royal daughter in marriage, will Bartatua, king of the Scythians [Akk. (kur)iškuza], speak to [Esarhaddon, king of Assyria] in good faith, true and serious words of peace? Will he honour the oath of [Esarhaddon, king of Assyria]? Will he do everything that is pleasing to Esarhaddon, king of Assyria?" (trans. Kuhrt 2007, 33).
27. Hdt. 8.85. On the king's "benefactors," see Briant 2002, 303–4.
28. Dandamayev 1979; Dandamayev 1992, 159–62. But, of course, the Sakā mentioned in these documents did not till their plots themselves; instead they leased them for a rent to the business house in Nippur.
29. If Xen. Cyr. 8.3 is to be believed (Kuhrt 2007, 515). See also the oral traditions preserved in Ctesias regarding 20,000 Sakā horsemen (a clearly exaggerated number) under the command of a certain Amorges (Ἀμόργης, a name that clearly reflects the Sakā haumavargā), supporting Cyrus in a battle against "Indians" (Lenfant 2004, 111–12).
30. In Salamis, Sakā bowmen even served as marines (Hdt. 8.96.1, 8.184.2, 8.130.1). Interestingly, Sakā are also mentioned as sailors in Babylonia (Dandamayev 1992, 162). Among the Greeks their exotic attire must have caused some sensation, as the Sakā "had tall, upward pointed caps fixed on their heads, wore trousers, carried their native bow and dagger, and besides this sagaris battle axes" (Hdt. 7.64.2).

31 Clarysse and Thompson 2007.
32 Wu 2010.
33 Briant 2002, 38–40, 49, 127.
34 On the course of this war, which brought Alexander almost to the brink of defeat, see Holt 1988.
35 In this source they are called Massagetes (Μασσαγέται).
36 Stark 2002, 375.
37 Савелева and Смирнов 1972; Treister 2010, 236–49; Игуменшева 2011.
38 Melikian-Chirvani 1993.
39 Treister 2010, 223–36.
40 For a complete catalogue, see ibid. 251–56.
41 Смирновъ 1909, 12, pl. V/17; Руденко 1962; Иванов et al. 1984; Treister 2010, 224.
42 Lerner 1991, 9–12; Баркова 2009, 5–13. The woolen textile of the saddle cloth was imported; it was incorporated into a local product.
43 Марсадолов 2010.
44 Moorey 1998.
45 Harper et al. 1984, 48–49.
46 Смирновъ 1909, 14, pl.V/18; Иванов et al. 1984, 20. The possibility is not excluded that the handle actually stems from one of the plundered Berel kurgans: according to a document issued to confirm receipt of the handle by the Russian Imperial Academy and dated to November 30 1735, it was "found by Corporal Ivan Bundin of the Yenisei Regiment with soldiers near the river Bukhmarta [i.e., Bukhtarma], in [a] Bugrovaya osyp'" (на Бугровой осыпи; Матеріалы для исторіи Императорской академіи наукъ, томь второй (1731–35), Санктпетербургъ 1886, 827. I suppose that *"Bugrovaya osyp,"* which literally translates as "debris of a mound," simply means "kurgan." The pieces of the "Siberian collection" sent by Prince Gagarin to Peter the Great were just called "bugrovye veshchi" (бугровые вещи) at that time (Дьянія Петра Великаго, мудраго Преобразователя Россіи, собранныя по достовѣрнымъ и источникамъ и расположенныя по годамъ. Сочиненія И. И. Голикова, Москва 1789, vol. 9, 443).
47 Lerner 1991, 9–12; Баркова 2009, 5–13
48 The "floppy triangle and circle" ornament (Barnett 1968, 43–44).
49 Vogelsang 1992.
50 On lapis lazuli, see Casanova 2001.
51 On pre-Han silk in Bactria, see Левушкииа 1987 and Good 1995.
52 Rudenko 1970, 76–77. The seeds were probably intended for medical purposes.
53 For example, the famous French goldsmith Guillaume Boucher, who worked in Karakorum for the Mongol Great Khans (Olschki 1946). The craftsmen quarter in Karakorum has been studied recently by a German-Mongol team (Bemmann, Ėrdėnėbat, and Pohl 2010).
54 Галанина 1997, 57–58.
55 Azarpay 1959; Руденко 1961; Jettmar 1967; Rubinson 1990; Lerner 1991.
56 The vertically doubled winged sphinxes on the two silver plaques from Issyk, illustrated here as examples, are particularly close to Near Eastern prototypes—see, for instance, the treatment of the horns, which is very untypical for steppe art and rather resembles Achaemenid depictions (see page 106). Note also the relative rarity of silver in metalwork from the Iron Age steppe. Therefore, the possibility is not excluded that these plaques are actually products from a provincial workshop in the Achaemenid east.
57 Jettmar 1967, 134.
58 Abdi 2002.
59 Lerner 1991, 8.
60 Ibid; Knauer 2001.
61 Garrison 1998. The "stepped merlon" has a millennia-old tradition in Near Eastern monumental architecture; see Porada 1967. "Stepped merlons" also figure on Achaemenid royal crowns, but the Pazyryk headdress appliqué is rectangular and has merlons only in the corners.
62 Мартынов 1955.
63 Klochkov 1997, 38–43.
64 Azarpay 1959, 335.
65 Kyrieleis 1969; Rudenko 1970, 65–68, pl. 51; Jamzadeh 1996.
66 See the Çan Sarcophagus (Sevinç et al. 2001, 400, fig. 3-6), and further examples from Anatolia and northwestern Iran (Borchhardt and Bleibtreu 2008, 189, pls. 3 and 9). The most famous example is, doubtlessly, the celebrated Alexander mosaic from Pompei (Nickel 1989, 20). For Pazyryk, see Rudenko 1970, 169, pl. 160.
67 Hajdas et al. 2004.
68 Полосьмак and Шумакова 2000.
69 Marsadolov and Maršak 2000; Васильков 2002.

70 Полосьмак and Баркова 2005, 30.
71 Wang 1987; Debaine-Francfort 1990; Francfort 1998; Bunker 2001.
72 Лубо-Лесниченко 1994.
73 Лубо-Лесниченко 1987; Bunker 1991.
74 Bunker 1991, 21–22. Earlier exposure of nomadic elites in Western Eurasia to Chinese prestige goods and subsequent adaptations remained isolated and short-lived; see, for example, the finds of cast-bronze helmets (Варёнов 1994; Rubinson 2006).
75 Both its axles were unmovable, and its large multispiked wheels were probably too fragile for the difficult terrain in the Altai highlands. Such a function would also explain why the wagon was made so that it could be easily disassembled (and perhaps carried on horseback over larger distances).
76 Rudenko 1970, 191–92. However, the canopy rests on balusters that show the same annulated decor as the Near Eastern furniture mentioned above.
77 On the horse trade and the creation of cavalry units in late Warring States China, see Di Cosmo 2002, 131–38.
78 Quotation from a letter by the Xiongnu ruler to the Chinese emperor Wendi (179–157 BCE), preserved in Shiji 110, 2896, and other texts (after Di Cosmo 2002, 196).
79 The name of this region, Sīstān, ultimately goes back to the original Sakastān ("land of the Sakā").
80 Hanshu 96b, 3903: "[The people] do not work at cultivating the fields or planting trees, but in company with their stock animals they go in search of water and pasture" (trans. Hulsewé and Loewe 1979, 144).
81 Hanshu 96b, 3903 (trans. ibid., 148).
82 Ibid.
83 Бернштам 1940, 23.
84 On the resemblance to Chinese cloud representations, see Watt 2002, 203.
85 Bulling 1960, 67–68; Watt 2002, 202; Tseng 2011, 192–98, and *passim*; Wallace 2012. A striking parallel is offered by the long ears of a dragon-rider with the depiction of an immortal with similar ears in a mural from a tomb dating to the second half of the first century BCE, discovered in 2004 on the campus of Xi'an University of Technology (Tseng 2011, 349–50, fig. 5.59).
86 Watt 2002, 202–3.
87 Лубо-Лесниченко 1975, 11–12, 38–40; Литвинский 1978, 98–105.
88 Zassetskaia 1995.
89 Zhu 1992, fig. 46. I wish to thank Lillian Tseng for pointing me to this example.
90 Harper 1978, 8. It also shows two winged horses, in this case together with two youths, which stand on low postaments decorated with an acanthus frieze. Although this plate is clearly later than the Kargaly diadem, it also draws from Western iconographic models.
91 Ilioukov 1995.
92 For my reconstruction I used the depiction of a banqueting warrior in the center of the composition on a torque from barrow 10 in Kobyakovo, dated to the beginning of the first century CE and ascribed to a Bactrian workshop (Guguev 1996, 53–59).

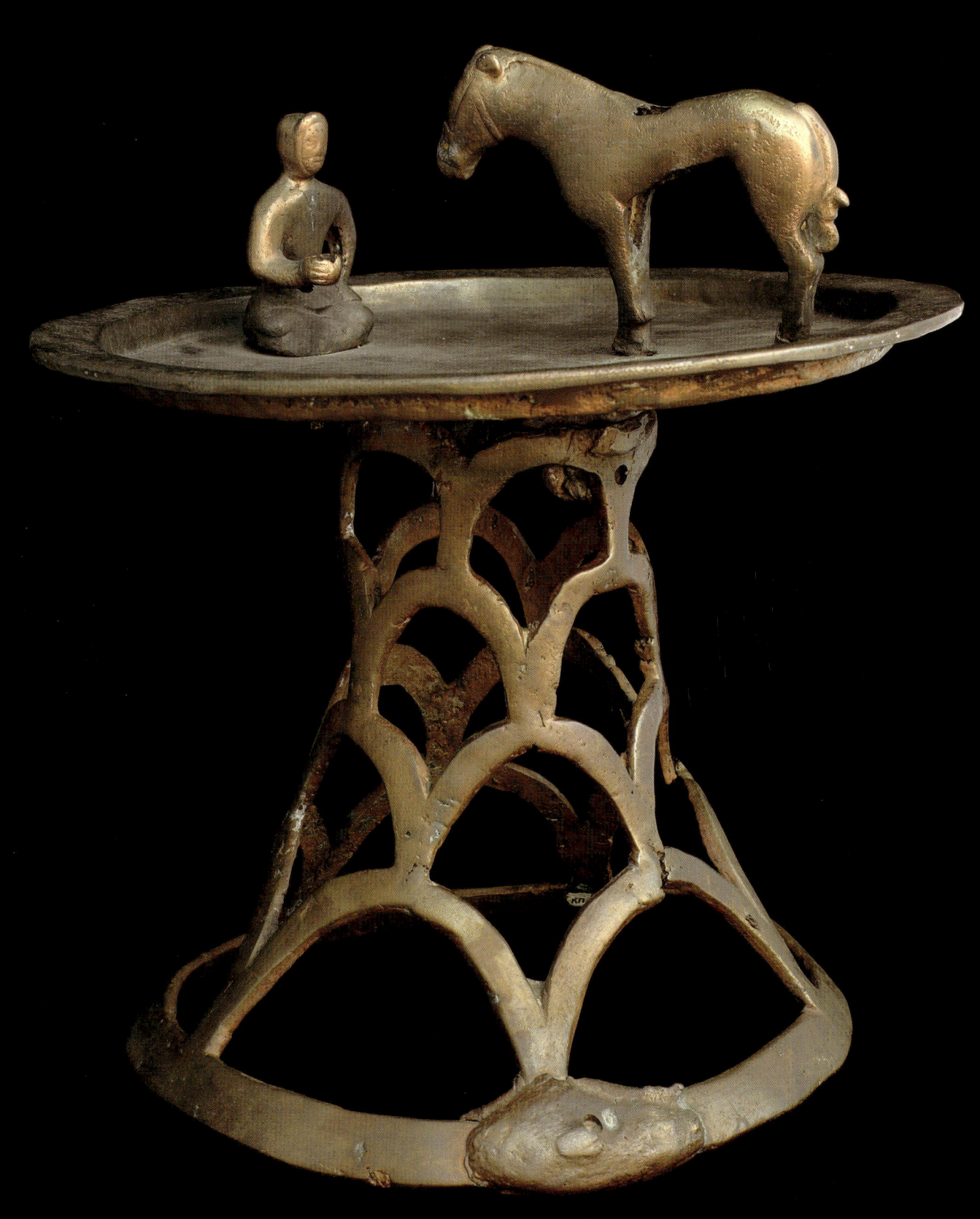

CYCLES OF IRON AGE MOBILITY AND SEDENTISM: CLIMATE, LANDSCAPE, AND MATERIAL CULTURE IN SOUTHEASTERN KAZAKHSTAN

Claudia Chang

This chapter examines how climate, landscape, and environment shaped the Iron Age nomadic world in Semirechye, or the "seven rivers region," of southeastern Kazakhstan. The Tianshan Range serves as a natural geographical border for the vast Eurasian steppe found to the north. Ecological niches include alpine conifer forest, mixed deciduous and conifer forests with shrub meadows, vast grasslands, and shrubs and grasses of the semiarid deserts (fig. 8-1). Elsewhere in the forest-steppes, steppes, deserts, and mountains across the major environmental zones of Eurasia, archaeologists have discovered evidence for the evolution of Iron Age mobile economies based upon pastoral pursuits, alongside fishing, hunting, foraging, and farming. The first millennium BCE was a period of dynamic social and cultural change throughout the nomadic world. Splendid elite kurgans with their rich burial inventories demonstrate the worldly and spiritual sophistication of an aristocratic elite. Yet at the base of society, commoners were the backbone. Who were these commoners and how did they live?

Round tray on conical stand with figures of seated man and standing horse in center. Bronze, Issyk, Semirechye/Zhetisu (Almaty region), chance find 1953, 5th–3rd century BCE. Central State Museum, Almaty: KP 8591. Checklist no. 142.

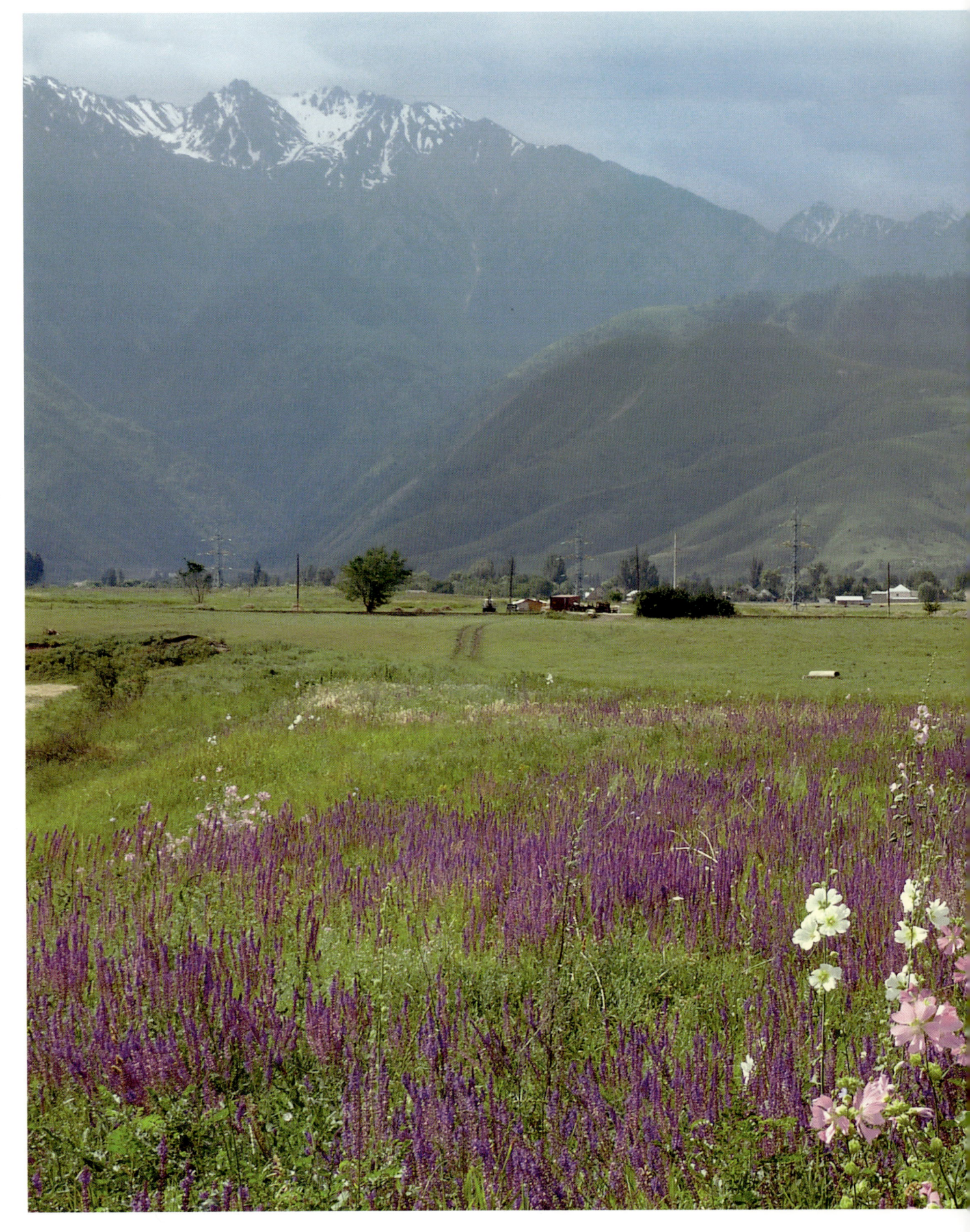

8-1　Talgar region in early summer, view to south with Tianshan Mountains, 2011.

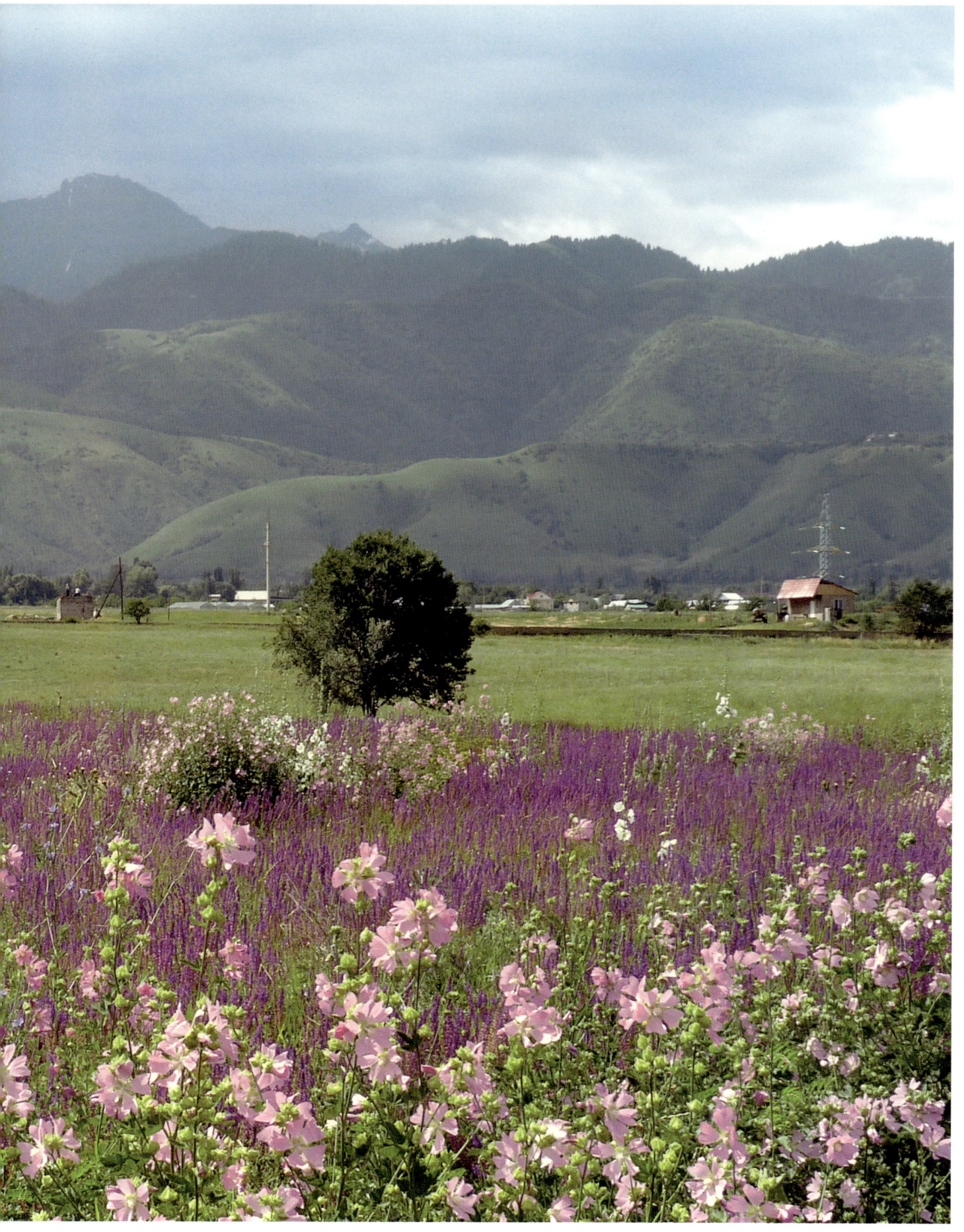

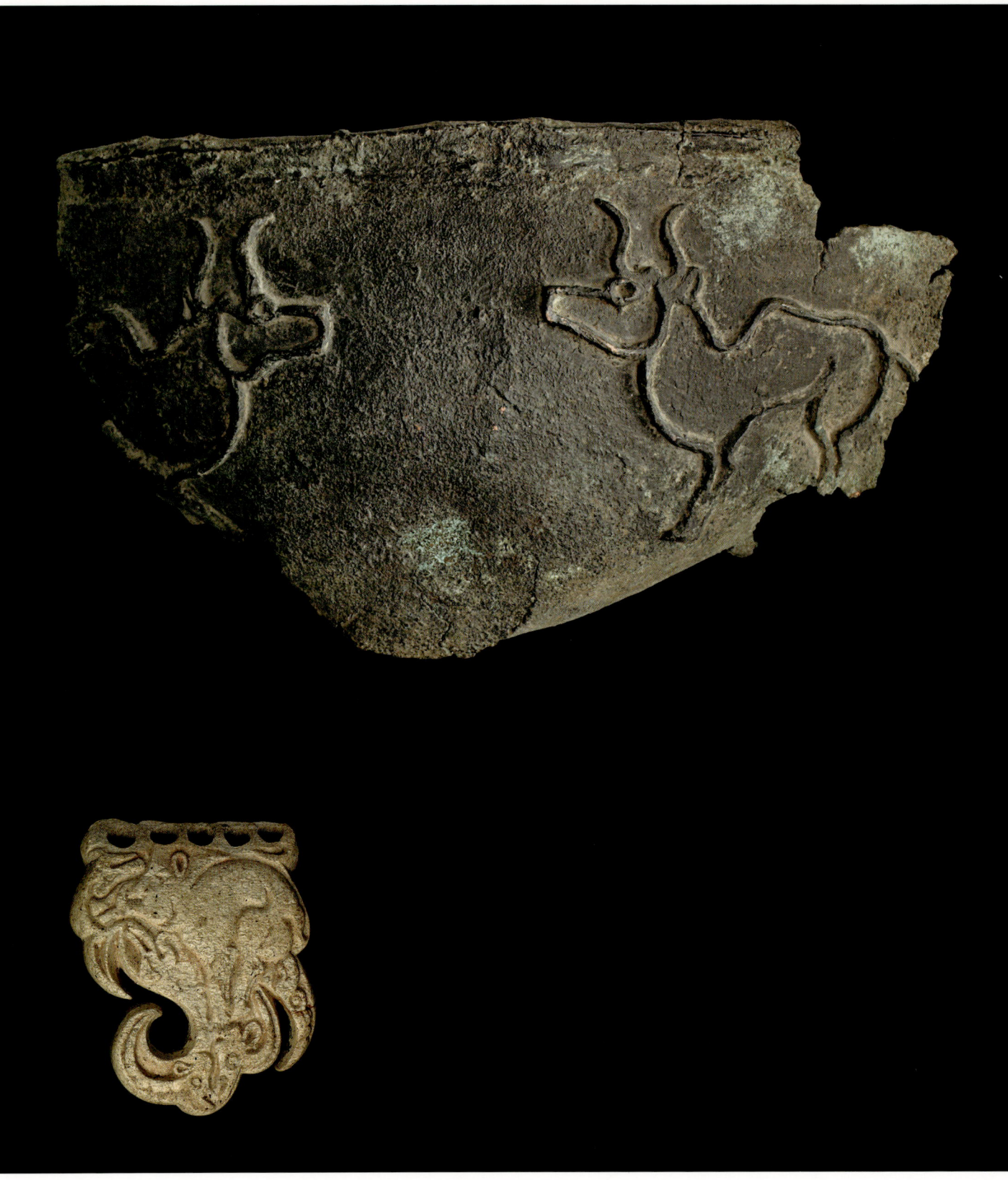

8-2 (top) Cauldron fragment depicting saiga antelope in relief. Copper alloy, Almaty, chance find 1952, 5th–3rd century BCE. Central State Museum, Almaty: KP 26605. Checklist no. 107.

8-3 (bottom) Clasp in the form of a stylized bird of prey with cervid and running-boar decoration. Horn (maral, Siberian red deer), Tasmola 5, kurgan 3 (Karaganda region), 7th–6th century BCE. Museum of Archaeology, Almaty: MA 736. Checklist no. 114. Although this object would have been oriented with the attachment holes to the left, it is illustrated here to feature the image of the boar.

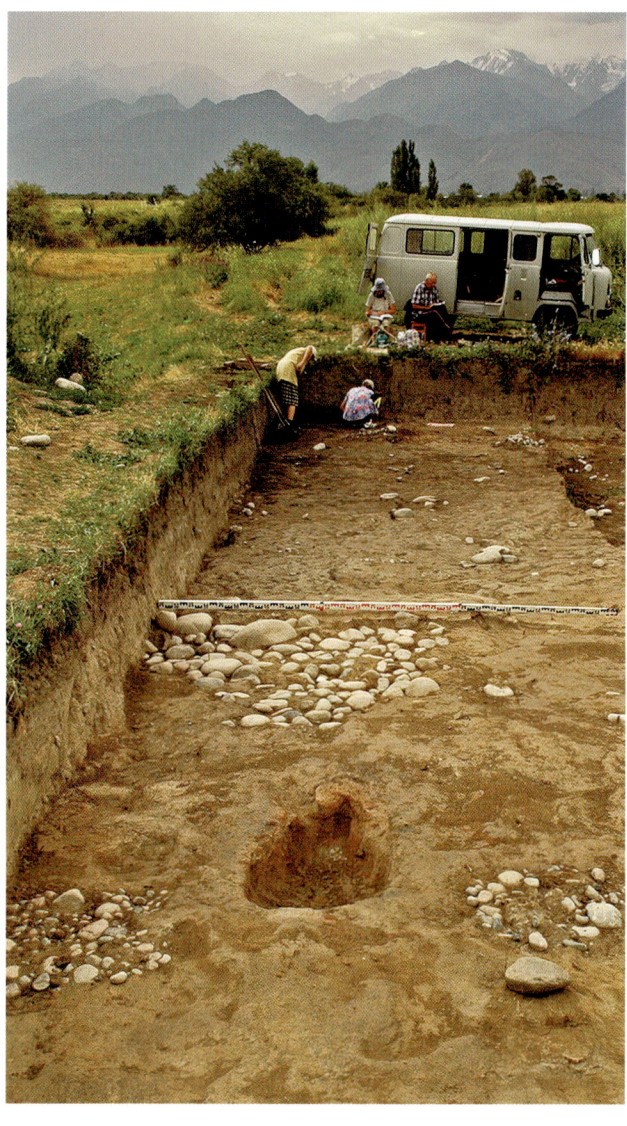

herders living in fixed, year-round communities, much like peasants today, also belonged to that same world. Thus, a new model for the Iron Age nomadic world can be put forth—one that emphasizes the nomadic orientation of the aristocratic elite and the sedentary nature of farmers and herders living in village and hamlet settlements in fertile areas.[2]

Intricately fashioned animal-style artifacts from the elite burial kurgans of the Altai and Semirechye tell an important story about the upper stratum of this society (fig. 8-2).[3]

Like the finds from the Egyptian tombs of pharaohs, these items are far removed from the ordinary lives of common folk, those who make up the economic and social backbone of any society. Yet these beautifully crafted items speak to us in a direct way: they provide hints about the nature of power, ideological representation, and spiritual concerns. But where must one turn to discover how a culture adapted to its natural environment? The "shreds and patches" of archaeological finds—such as the lines of burial mounds found along old stream beds and the fragments of mud-brick walls and platforms, pit dwellings, and plastered floors at an Iron Age settlement—are our clues. The remains of sheep and cattle bones, cracked or shattered for marrow and lying near a fireplace, or the charred seeds of wheat, barley, or millet found in the ashes of that same fireplace, become the most concrete evidence for reconstructing the Iron Age nomadic world (fig. 8-4).

To answer such a general question, recent archaeological research in the Talgar alluvial fan serves as a case study for investigating the more mundane, everyday aspects of the lives of common people. How did the ancient nomadic cultures of the Sakā and Wusun exploit these varied environments of Semirechye? Evidence from three Iron Age settlements has already proved that the Talgar folk practiced both the herding of sheep, goats, cattle, and horses as well as the farming of wheat, millet, and barley.[1] Through the lens of Talgar archaeological research, it is now possible to speculate that the Eurasian steppe world was far more complex than previously thought. The true pastoral nomads who moved their flocks and herds throughout the year on a seasonal round were not the only ones who occupied this landscape. Settled farmers and

The juxtaposition between the elite and the common people may be explained through interpretation of the Iron Age economy and society. The elite kurgans found throughout the Eurasian steppe, notably in the Altai and Semirechye, are the most obvious testimony to the existence of a panregional steppe culture, expressed by a set of shared symbols, such as animal-style art (fig. 8-3). These symbols, like the nomadic "banners" of later historic periods, served as a cultural expression of panregional alliances among groups of loosely organized aristocratic orders or houses, each tied to specific territories and political units.[4] In contrast, at the Iron Age settlements of Talgar, metal artifacts fashioned of iron, bronze, or copper are rare finds, often fragmentary, and almost never exhibiting any of the rich symbols of animal-style art.

8-4 Archaeologists taking soil samples for ancient seed recovery from hearth at Tseganka 8 in 1999.

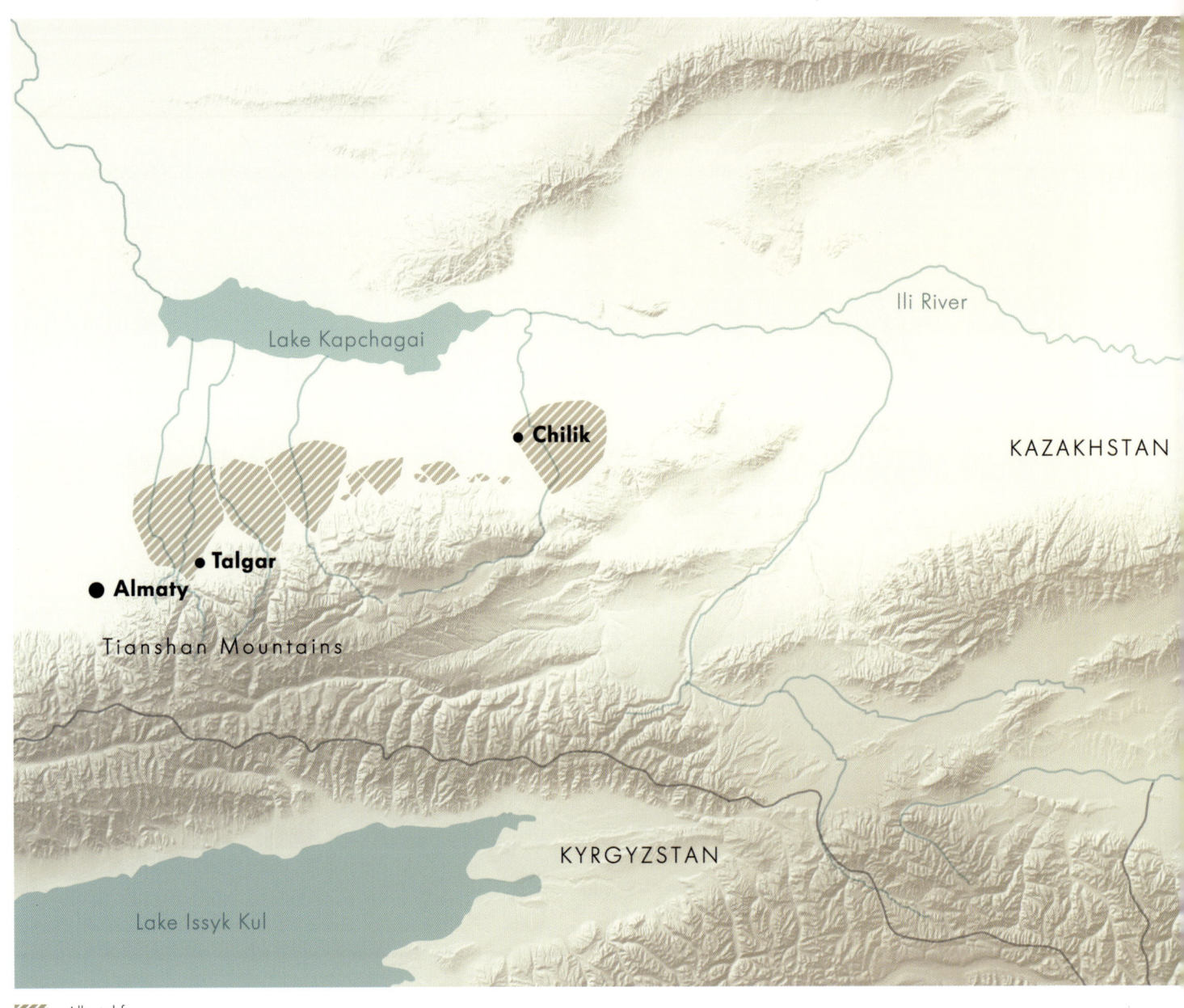

THE SETTING

Semirechye, known as Zhetisu in Kazakh, was named after the seven rivers that flow from south and west into Lake Balkhash. The entire region is bounded to the south by the Tianshan Mountains and to the north and east by the Dzhungar Mountains. The climate of Semirechye is typically continental, with snowfall in the winter, hot and wet or dry summers, and peak rainfall in the spring and fall. The rich mosaic of environments ranges from conifer trees and alpine meadows at high elevations, mixed forests interspersed with meadows in the foothills and upland plateaus, and grass and shrub steppe lands and semiarid deserts. This mountain-steppe zone covers a broad expanse between Kyrgyzstan to the south and west and China to the east. The glacier-fed rivers and streams flow north into the Ili River, forming over forty large alluvial fans. These broad, gently sloping alluvial fans are comprised of chernozems and chestnut soils covering ancient gravels.[5] Today these alluvial fans are used for large-scale cultivation of wheat and other cereals. Fourteen alluvial fans, including some of the largest and most impressive, such as the Talgar fan, are found in the area between the modern cities of Almaty and Chilik (an east–west distance of roughly 125 kilometers) (fig. 8-5).

8-5 Map showing the Ili River and twelve of the fourteen alluvial fans between the modern cities of Almaty and Chilik.

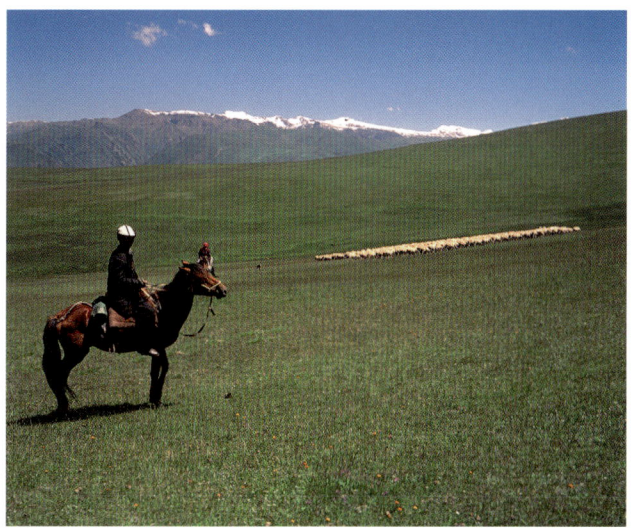

PASTORAL NOMADIC MOBILITY IN THE IRON AGE

Pastoral nomads are defined as any group of people who travel with their herds and flocks between seasonal pastures to exploit water and pasture resources (fig. 8-6). The ancient Iron Age folk who occupied the vast territories of the Eurasian steppe have been labeled pastoral nomads. These herdsmen used their flocks and herds for such important products as meat, milk, wool, hides, and dung (for fuel or fertilizer). Pastoralists and their herd animals were limited by the availability of water, pasture, or fodder (hay that could be stored). However, there were also pastoralists who engaged in fishing, hunting, gathering, and cultivation. In academic parlance, this dependency on other forms of plant or animal exploitation is labeled as multiresource pastoralism.[6] In A. Khazanov's writings about Eurasian steppe nomadism in temperate zones, he specifically indicates that nomads could and did coexist with seminomads and also with agriculturalists.[7]

Ethnographic examples of pastoral nomads suggest at least three generalized patterns of mobility: (1) vertical transhumance, or the seasonal movement of herdsmen and their animals to upland pastures in the summer months and a return to lowland winter pastures; (2) long-distance longitudinal or meridian movement between different seasonal pastures (for example, the long-distance movement from winter pastures in the semiarid regions of the Ili Basin to summer pastures along the foothills of the Tianshan); and (3) a circular round throughout the year among different ecological zones (in desert areas pastoralists might follow a radial pattern).[8]

The long-term fluctuations of climate and vegetation throughout the Eurasian steppe during the Bronze Age (2500–1100 BCE) had an effect on ancient economic adaptations. Pollen records show that Eurasian landscapes gradually expanded to open grasslands after 2300, reaching their fullest extent in about 1200.[9] The shift from a warm and wet climate to a dry and cold climate toward the end of the Bronze Age (1100) also might have resulted in the widespread development of mobile pastoralism at the expense of mixed herding and farming economies.[10] However, most recent research has indicated that sociopolitical factors for the origins of Iron Age mobile pastoralism are as compelling as previous ecological arguments based on climate change.[11] Recent archaeological research in the Talgar region questions the hypothesis that climate change led to the evolution of steppe pastoralism during the Iron Age. Surveys and excavations of Sakā and Wusun-period settlements in the Talgar region demonstrate that their ancient Iron Age occupants participated in both farming and herding economies.[12]

A NEW MODEL FOR NOMADIC MOBILITY AND SEDENTISM DURING THE IRON AGE

This model for nomadic mobility and sedentism builds upon D. Sneath's discussion of the Inner Asian headless state, specifically the evolution of the nomadic state from the Xiongnu through the Mongol periods as headless and decentralized.[13] These circumstances stand in contrast to those of an agrarian state, such as the Chinese Dynasties, in which government was centralized and bureaucratic. The "headless state" model stands in contrast to previous models in which nomadic states or empires are described as developing hierarchy in response to their external relations (often described as parasitic) with centralized agrarian states. The Inner Asian states—such as those of the Scythians, the Xiongnu, and the Mongols—are characterized as decentralized and led by units of aristocratic elites who controlled vast territories and organized armed cavalries through alliances with neighboring or distantly affiliated aristocratic groups.[14] For example, during times of conflict or need, the Xiongnu or Mongol leader relied upon the decimal system (division into tens, hundreds, and thousands, which were also ranked hierarchically from leaders to chiefs to commanders to household administrators) to recruit a military force or to undertake communal tasks.[15]

8-6 Contemporary Kazakh shepherd in Asi Valley, 2003.

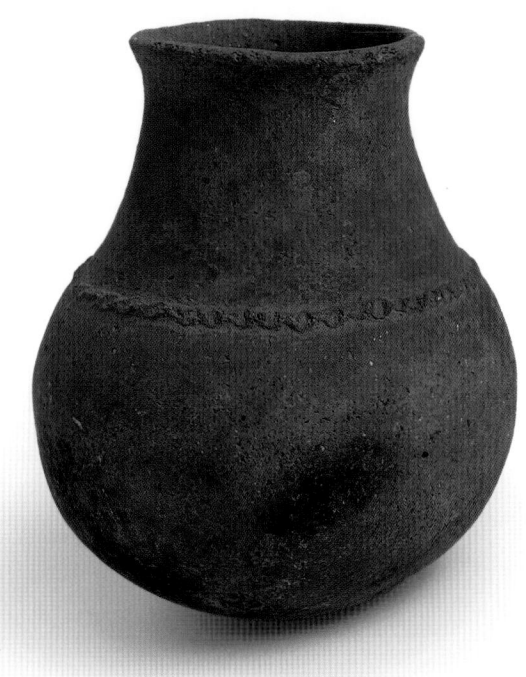

The notion of a headless state can be applied to the political and economic organization of an Iron Age nomadic confederacy such as the Sakā (eighth–third century BCE) or Wusun (third century BCE–fourth century CE) of Semirechye. The Sakā or Wusun nomadic elite might have employed an earlier version of the decimal system and its inherent hierarchical structure to organize communal work forces for raiding, warfare, monument building, funerary and other rituals, feasting, and the construction of irrigation canals. Even if the decimal system was not in operation during the first millennium BCE, the ability of nomadic people to rapidly coalesce as a single force and to disperse across vast territories fits into what is known about the flexibility and plasticity of nomadic mobility. It is thus now possible to discuss decentralized states and confederacies as wielding as much power as a centralized bureaucratic agrarian state. Furthermore, the existence of such flexible strategies for employing authority and power over others is better suited to those who already live in highly diverse environments. Therefore, the cycles of nomadic mobility and sedentism proposed for the northern edge of the Tianshan Mountains, encompassing an area of forty alluvial fans, have the following elements: (1) a multiresource economic base that included herding of sheep, goats, cattle, and horses, cultivation of wheats, barley, and millets, foraging of wild plants, hunting of wild game (deer, hare, fox, wild pig, and birds), and fishing; (2) a flexible social structure that relied upon decentralized aristocratic nomadic elites who maintained control over commoners, including soldiers, craftsmen (see fig. 8-7), herders, and farmers; (3) an ideological and religious commitment to the nomadic world marked by an elite mortuary complex of linear clusters of burial mounds on the landscape and shared animal-style motifs fashioned for the aristocratic elite; and (4) the panregional nomadic identity important for a decentralized state or empire.

ARCHAEOLOGICAL EVIDENCE FOR IRON AGE ADAPTATIONS IN THE TALGAR REGION

From the mountain pasture areas of the Talgar slopes to the semiarid areas of the Ili Valley (a distance of less than 60 kilometers), there are geographical features of the following types: mountain valleys, foothills, alluvial fans, and flat marsh and semiarid areas. The vegetation zones range from high alpine forests to semiarid desert shrubs and grasslands within a relatively short distance. Therefore, Iron Age people could carry out a number of economic activities, such as hunting, fishing, herding, and farming, following a pattern of vertical mobility between the mountains and the steppe. In the Talgar region, Iron Age people practiced vertical pastoral transhumance alongside farming; during the hot sum-

8-7   Jar. Clay, 3rd century BCE–3rd century CE. Museum of Archaeology, Almaty: ЦАЭ-57/33. Checklist no. 122.

mer season at the peak of agricultural production, herd animals were moved to higher mountain pastures, where there was more rainfall and better pasture conditions (fig. 8-8). After cereal harvests, herd animals could be moved back to the alluvial fan, where they could graze off the stubble and fallow fields. During an occupation span from roughly 800 BCE to 100 CE at three Iron Age sites (Tseganka 8, Taldy Bulak 2, and Tuzusai) on the Talgar fan, the majority of animal bones have been identified as domesticated animals—including sheep, goats, cattle, horses, camel, and dog—and a very small percentage of wild animals—birds, roe and red deer, hare, fox, and wild pig.[16] Plant domesticates include millets (foxtail and broomcorn), wheat, barley, and grape. In the early phases of Iron Age occupation before 400 BCE, millets predominated, while for later periods higher percentages of wheats have been discovered.[17] This gradual intensification of cereal cultivation may be an indication that water control or channeling was practiced on the Talgar alluvial fan.

IRON AGE SOCIAL ORGANIZATION

Iron Age social organization in Semirechye has been reconstructed primarily through the interpretation of burial mounds and their inventories. K. Akishev and G. Kushaev[18] used the dimensions of twenty-five kurgans in the Ili Valley site of the Bes Shatyr area to indicate differences in wealth, and thus possible stratification, into three major groupings: (1) the smallest mounds (6–18 meters in diameter, 2–8 meters in height) for enlisted warriors; (2) the medium-size mounds (25–38 meters in diameter, 5–6 meters in height) for the aristocratic class; and (3) the king-size mounds (45–100 meters in diameter, 6–17 meters in height) for chiefs and clan leaders. Evidence for the burials of common people have yet to be discovered in the archaeological record in this region. The social organization of the Talgar area is unknown, although both Tseganka 8 and Taldy Bulak 2 (fig. 8-9) were most likely small hamlets consisting of small circular or subrectangular pit houses, while Tuzusai (over 13 hectares in area)—with its mud-brick platforms and walls and agglomerated pit houses—was most likely a centralized village. There appears to be a ranked hierarchy of settlements on the Talgar fan, which could indicate the presence of social inequality within and among settlements.

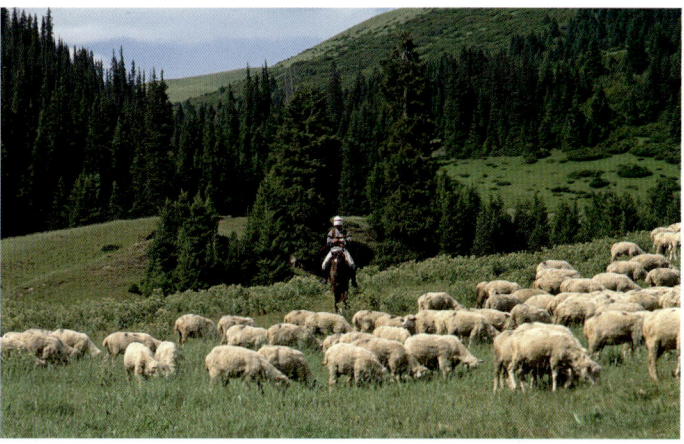

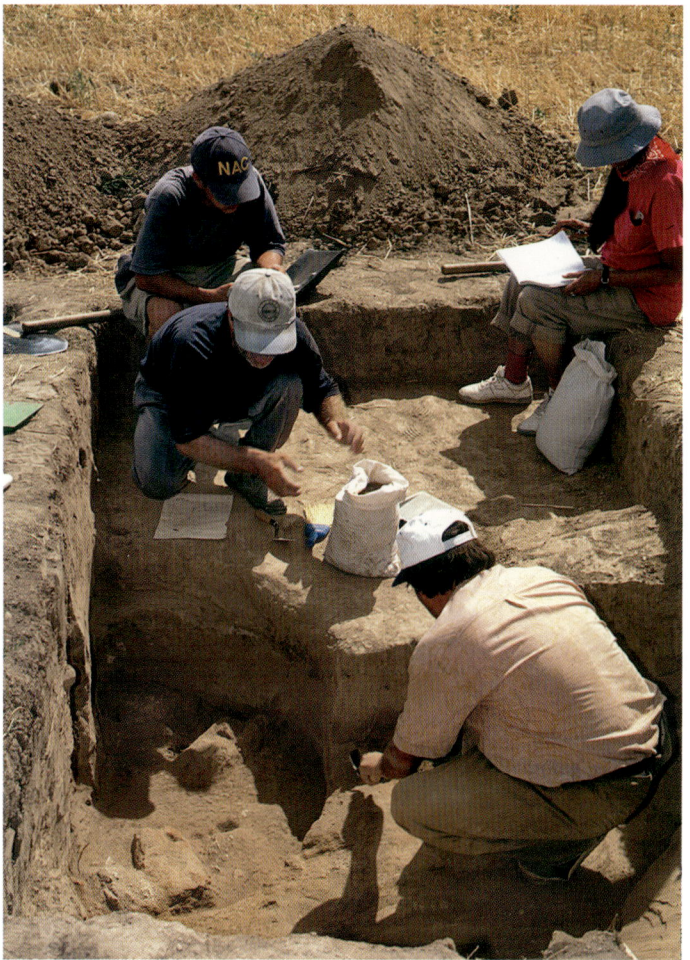

8-8 Summer pasture in upper Turgen Valley, 1997.

8-9 Excavations at Iron Age site of Taldy Bulak 2 in 2007, view to south showing cobblestone pavement and fire pit in foreground.

THE SYMBOLIC AND IDEOLOGICAL LANDSCAPE OF IRON AGE SEMIRECHYE

The distribution of burial kurgans interspersed with Iron Age settlements across the Talgar fan, especially along ancient streambeds, is important. Surveys in the Talgar region in the late 1990s and early 2000s identified about 225 kurgans grouped into sixty-two clusters forming alignments along ancient streambeds. The clusters, ranging from 2 or 3 kurgans up to 9 kurgans and found along ancient streambeds, represented a symbolic landscape. How did Iron Age people conceptualize this landscape in terms of spiritual or material power in a given area? The spatial distribution of Iron Age burial mounds across natural landscape features such as foothills, valleys, and streambeds must have had significance as places of power, collective activity, and ritual.

A PANREGIONAL BURIAL CULT AND STYLE HORIZON

Throughout the Altai and Semirechye, areas separated by vast distances, there was a similar tradition for the building of monumental kurgans and the use of a style horizon found throughout the Eurasian steppe. Historic accounts of Kazakh social organization distinguish between the "white-bone" Kazakhs, those said to be the descendants of sultans, and the "black bone," who had no hereditary power.[19] These "white–bone" Kazakhs are reputedly related to Chinggis Khan; more importantly, their elite status provided immediate membership within larger panregional groups. An analogy can be drawn between historic Kazakh social organization and what may have taken place in Semirechye during the Iron Age: aristocratic elites from a distinct geographical region such as the Altai had the ability to enter into alliances with elites from Semirechye through a system of class affiliation. As long as these elite mound builders could align with other distant leaders as allies—even if kinship or genealogical relationships were unknown—there existed the potential for collective action. The most effective political or military control of vast territories in a decentralized political system was through shared ideology and rapid deployment of a hierarchical structure, such as the decimal system. The localization of each aristocratic order was an essential adaptation within highly variable environments and geographic regions. Thus the countervailing force was an ability to coalesce rapidly across vast distances through a shared tradition. The designation of nomadic society into "white bone" and "black bone" serves as another means of designating class and status differences between the rulers and the common folk. In Semirechye the real nomads were elites, not commoners. In the Altai, where the dominant subsistence pattern was pastoral nomadism, both elites and commoners maintained a nomadic orientation. Here the marked distinction between aristocratic elites and commoners was expressed through the material culture of an elite mortuary tradition. The "nomadic world" was the trope for panregional steppe organization. Shared symbols and allegiance to a nomadic worldview might have united the Sakā of Semirechye with those of the Altai (see page 140).

CONCLUSIONS

The Iron Age people of Semirechye adapted to a variety of environmental zones through their effective exploitation of a multiple set of resources. Those living in the rich alluvial fans could farm and practice animal husbandry. During the summer seasons some members of a household could move to high-elevation pastures while others stayed behind to farm. Those who lived in marshy areas or near lakes might have combined mobile pastoralism with hunting or fishing. In semiarid and desert areas, mobile pastoralism was the main form of subsistence. Whether farmer, herder, or craftsman, the common folk of Talgar lived in dispersed villages or hamlets along the ancient streambeds of the fertile alluvial fan. Their leaders, an aristocratic elite, organized the commoners into effective units for military action, rituals, construction of kurgans, and irrigation projects. These leaders could extract surplus agricultural or herd-animal products from the commoners. The aristocratic elite controlled the lower-ranked groups by demanding labor and tribute, but also because they protected these groups from territorial encroachment and outside conflict. The shared symbol system, only apparent from luxury items found in the burial inventories or the burial kurgans themselves, communicated both to those inside and to those outside the local region the relative strength, power, and influence of the aristocratic elite.

NOTES

1. Chang et al. 2003.
2. Ibid.
3. See Stark this volume.
4. Sneath 2007, 181–85.
5. Chernozems in this area are black soils, more specifically reworked loess soils with a high humic content. Chestnut soils are lighter in color with less humic content. The unsorted gravels are Mid-Pleistocene glacial outwash.
6. Sneath 2007.
7. Khazanov 1984, 50.
8. Ibid., 50–51.
9. Хотинский 1977, 198.
10. Hanks 2002a.
11. Koryakova and Epimakhov 2007.
12. Chang et al. 2003.
13. Sneath 2007.
14. Kradin 2002.
15. Sneath 2007.
16. Chang et al. 2003.
17. Spengler, Chang, and Tourtellotte, n.d.
18. Акишев and Кушаев 1963, 86.
19. Sneath 2007, 215.

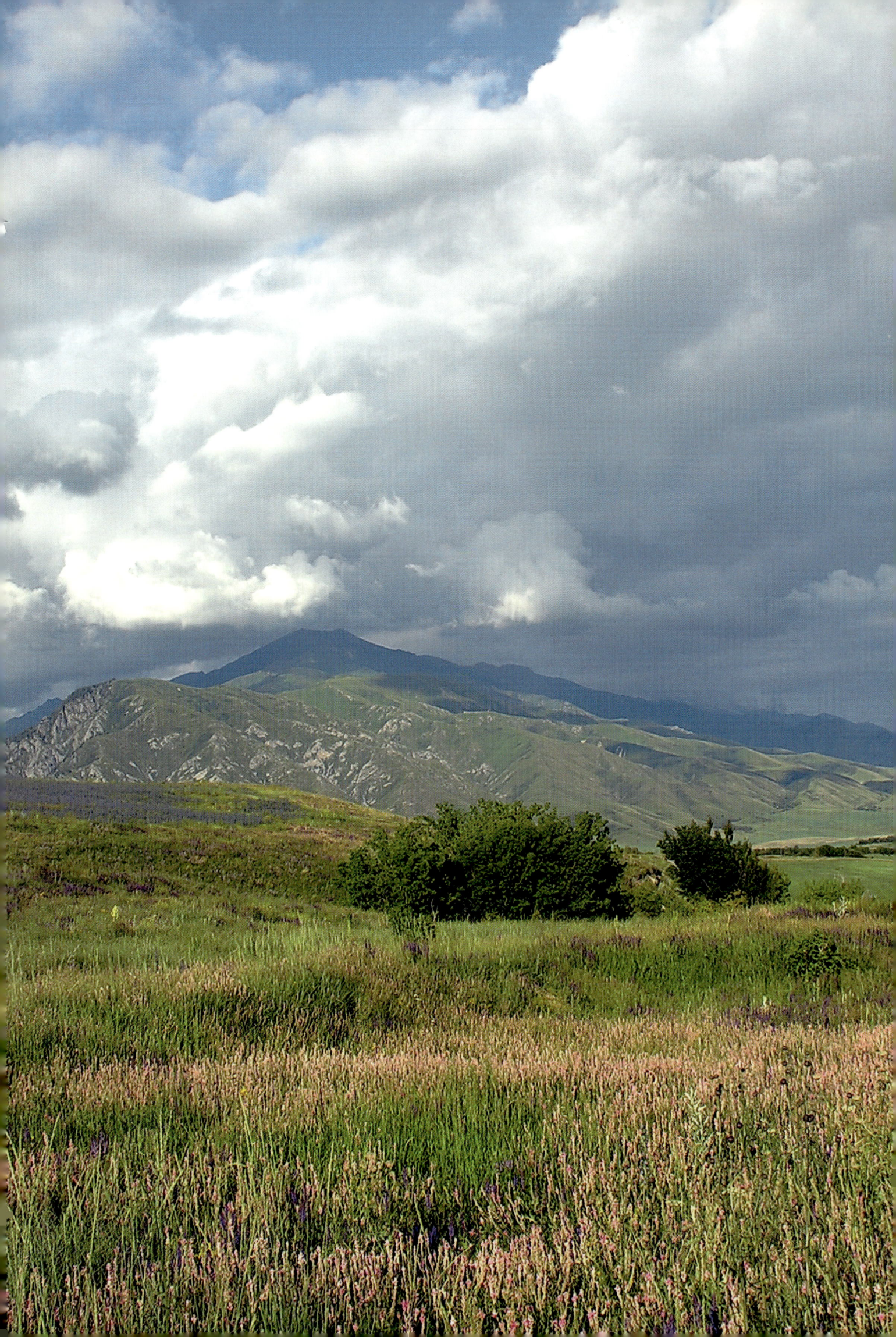

SOCIETY AND CULTURE OF THE NOMADS OF CENTRAL ASIA THROUGH TIME

Nursan Alimbai

ECOLOGICAL CONDITIONS AND THE SOCIAL AND TECHNOLOGICAL ADAPTATIONS OF MOBILE PASTORALISTS

The territory of Kazakhstan encompasses an area of 2,725,000 square kilometers, extending in latitude from north 40° to 50° and in longitude from east 46° to 87°, and occupies one of the innermost regions of the Eurasian continent. Its resources for the organization of agriculture are constrained by a very harsh climate and limited precipitation.

Therefore, practically all the territory of Kazakhstan belongs to the zone of high-risk farming, and only advances made by modern agro-technology have allowed substantial production capabilities. The ecological structure of Kazakhstan is composed principally of steppe, desert, and semi-desert zones; these zones host limited plant cover and water resources with average annual precipitation of less than 350 millimeters per year and a largely continental climate. The dominant landscape and climatic characteristics of the region are determined by the territory's vast distance from the world's oceans and seas. In these climatic conditions, nomadism was the most rational—and, in many parts of Kazakhstan, the only possible—method of exploiting the natural resources necessary to support life in the preindustrial era.[1]

Steppe landscape at the foothills of the Tianshan mountain range.

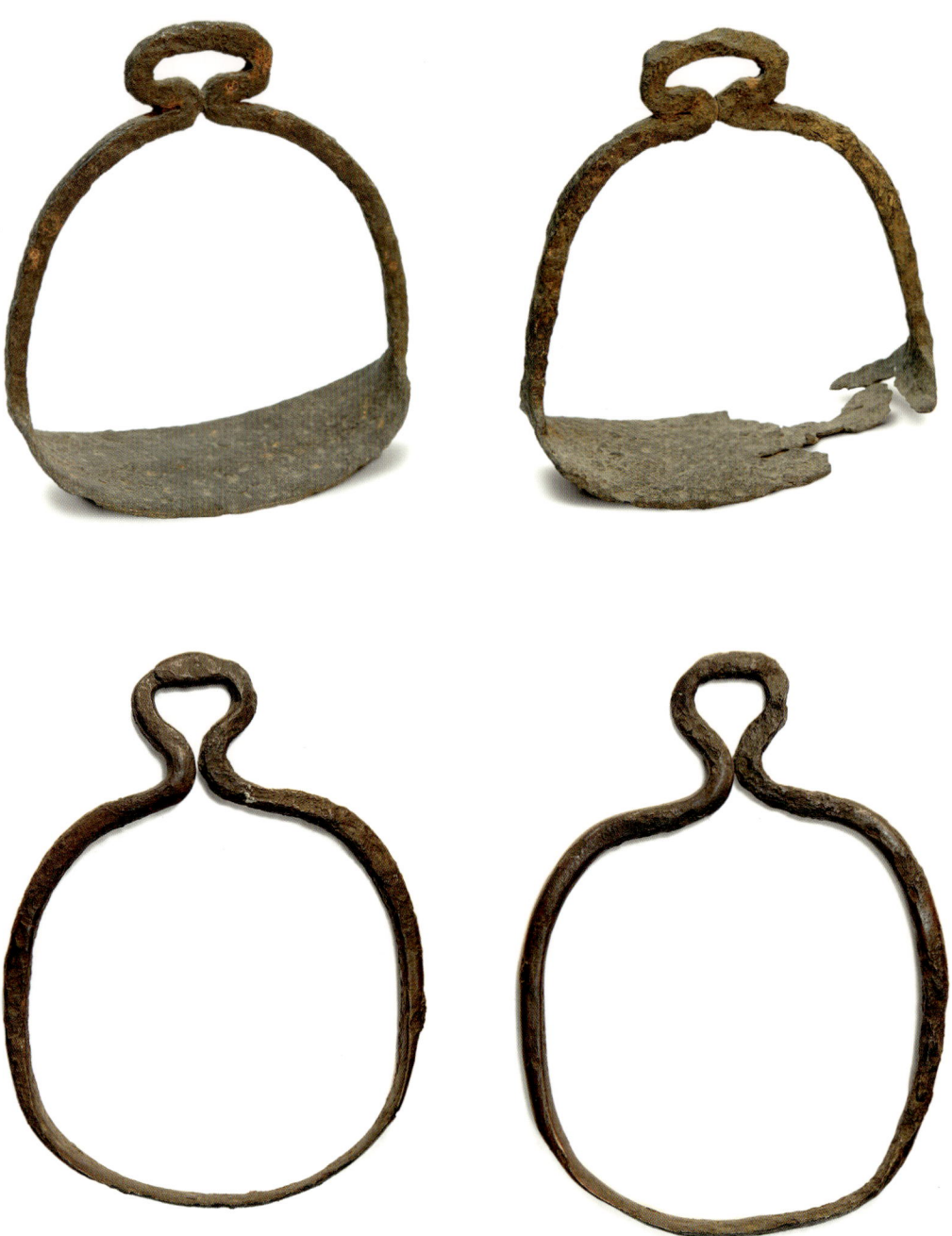

9-1 Old Turkic stirrups. Iron, Western Kazakhstan, chance find 1909, 6th–8th century CE.

9-2 Old Turkic stirrups. Iron, Western Kazakhstan, chance find 1909, 6th–8th century CE.

The beginning of the formation of the nomadic social structure dates to the final phase of the Bronze Age, from roughly the twelfth to the tenth century BCE. The huge territory of Kazakhstan, with its particular geoecological conditions, was an important area in the spread of nomadism in Central Asia. The development of nomadism within its fundamental parameters—sociocultural, economic, political, ideological, institutional—required the emergence of adequate social relations within the nomadic sphere as well as a corresponding life-supporting system. The features of this system developed through time; a crucial period was the Old Turkic Period (sixth–eighth century CE) when many of these features took their "classical" shape.[2] Unfortunately, many questions concerning social relations in nomadic societies during the Old Turkic period are still far from being solved, although these questions are highly relevant for the study of the genesis and evolution of nomadic societies in time and space. Nevertheless, on the basis of historical analogy and comparative ethnographic parallels, it is possible to conclude, with some level of certainty, that precisely during this period nomadism in the large area of the Great Steppe Belt entered its classic phase of development.

Judging from medieval literature and archaeological discoveries of the last century, it was during the Old Turkic Period that a more advanced subsistence system was formed, one that represented optimal sociocultural and technological adaptation to the harsh conditions of the nomadic environment. Many of its features appeared much earlier than mobile pastoralism in the Eurasian steppes, while other features—including specific elements of armament, riding equipment (including functionally important elements of horse tack such as stirrups and the hard saddle), and the collapsible lattice yurt with felt cover—were further perfected throughout the subsequent history of mobile pastoralists in the steppes of present-day Kazakhstan (figs. 9-1–9-7). These and other inventions (for example, multiple methods for the production of cultured milk products) have had universal impact.[3]

In the process of the development of subsistence forms, social relations with specific norms, principles, and institutions also formed within the nomadic sphere. These norms and institutions thoroughly shaped the community of mobile pastoralists.[4]

A clear distinction between social and technological features does not conform with historical reality. Social relations among members of a community have always been vital for the proper function of structural components of subsistence systems, such as settlements, dwellings, furniture, clothing, food, and various kinds of folk knowledge. There is a clear interdependence between a communal type of social relations adapted to the environment and forms of pastoral subsistence, resulting in mobile forms of community. Only a communal form of social relations, developed over centuries as a sociocultural mode of nomadic self-organization under harsh ecological conditions, corresponds to the nomadic type of life-supporting system. In its turn, the communal nature of nomadic society required from the beginning a mobile life-supporting system, highly adapted to specific environmental conditions. Thus, in many ways a balanced view of both social and technological developments explains the effectiveness of nomadic societies in the exploitation of natural resources. To understand processes and key elements of the social history of the Eurasian Great Steppe Belt, in my opinion it is essential to take a closer look at traditional features of social relations in nomadic communities.[5]

Interesting parallels are provided by traditional Kazakh society of the eighteenth to the early twentieth century, a period that I believe should be seen as the final phase of Central Asian nomadism. In traditional Kazakh society all the main components of social and economic life—social organization, the settlement complex, dwelling, clothing, food, various kinds of folk knowledge, and the production cycle—reached a high degree of refinement. They were all highly adapted to the mobile pastoralist way of life and were employed as effective instruments for the optimal use of the environmental resources of the Great Steppe Belt.

COMMUNITY UNITS AND THEIR ROLE IN TRADITIONAL KAZAKH SOCIETY

Social relations within traditional Kazakh society were in many ways similar to those of other Eurasian nomadic societies, even when the ethnic, geographic, or ecological context differed. On a number of levels, these relationships influenced nearly every aspect of nomadic society: material and intellectual culture, including such elements as economic techniques, tools, and strategies; local or communal ethnic self-awareness and self-naming; various types of rituals, customs, rites

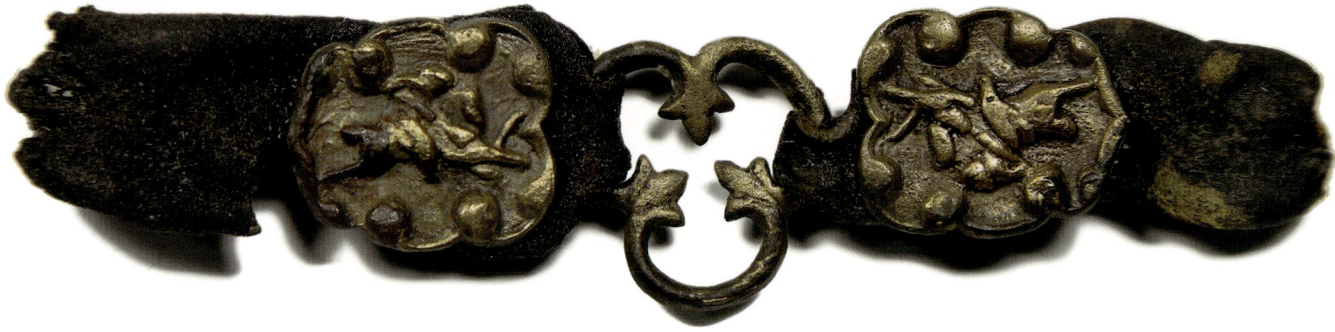

of passage, worldview, kinship structure, genealogy (*shejire*), ethnic stereotypes, moral-ethical and common-law norms of behavior; folkloric traditions; and even migratory routes.

The basic social and economic unit of traditional Kazakh society was the nuclear family, or *birata* (literally, "one ancestor"), which connected the group of blood relatives containing two or three generations in the male line. The *birata* was the main owner of livestock—the most important natural resource, since it was movable. But the *birata* units did not own land, which was indivisible and inalienable within the tribe. Communal territory was a necessary basis for economic production at the individual, family, and community levels. Therefore, the *birata* was not an entirely independent producing unit. It accomplished its function as direct producer only to the extent that it was tightly related to and mutually dependent on other such entities.

Another important and still vital element in Kazakh society is the *jetiata* (literally, "seven forefathers"), or the seven generations of ancestors every Kazakh must be able to know and recite. The *jetiata* forms a genealogically organized group of relatives (whether real or constructed) spanning seven generations in the male line, within which marriages are prohibited. This exogamic barrier to marriage relations was also an effectively institutionalized mechanism of economic and demographic regulation that helped to optimize the resources of the tribal environment.

The main function of community units was to enforce common law and the regulation of land use according to genealogical principles, that is, relationships among patriarchal entities relating to the use of corresponding segments of the tribal (communal) territory. This ensured balanced economic and juridical interactions among the *birata*, or patriarchal groups, in the traditional social system.

Thus, the core units of nomadic Kazakh society were the mutually dependent and mutually supporting core families of the *birata*. But it was the relations among the units that developed the specific social and political potential of the society. Only the framework of the *jetiata* provided institutional, ideological, sociocultural, economic, and even ecological density and intensity critical to the development of various types and levels of social relations within the nomadic sphere, relations that were vital for the entire nomadic community. Segmented access to economic resources was an effective means to guarantee environmental sustainability. But it also created fissions, frictions, and conflicts. Resources were negotiated and assigned along the genealogical principals and norms of *shejire* (literally, "lineage tree"), which therefore constituted an important source of regulation but also a sense of unity within nomadic society.

SHEJIRE: A FOLKLORISTIC GENRE AND ITS INSTITUTIONAL FUNCTIONS

The traditional Kazakh society was mainly founded upon communal principles of social organization. But

9-3 Detail of Old Turkic horse harness. Zevakino barrow, Eastern Kazakhstan, 8th–9th century CE.

these principles are in fact much older and seem to go back at least to the Scythian-Sakā Period. The durability of these principles is probably due to the fact that they provided optimal conditions for the economic subsistence of mobile pastoralists.

Genealogical relations according to the principle of *shejire* were, at various levels, fundamental for the regulation of community relations within the nomadic society.⁶ The main purpose of genealogy, or *shejire*, was to establish relations among the patrilineal units of extended families—that is, among the main subjects of intercommunity relations. This was achieved by the coalescence of "community" and "family" in a seven-generation exogamic structure as the main organizational feature of the traditional Kazakh community. Thus, the genealogical structuring of social relations in the nomadic sphere provided the basis for the institutional organization of society.

Studies in contemporary ethnology have defined a more or less complete series of *shejire* variants, which allow us to follow the genealogy of a certain number of family groups, extending from what is known as the "poetico-mythical" or "cosmological" era to the modern period. About a hundred ethnoregional variants belonging to the same historiographic tradition have come down to us in the form of texts. Based on their ambition and content, they can be classified into six thematic groups:

- The first group of *shejire* has a general ethnic value: the origin of the Kazakhs is chronicled solely through edifying actions by famous historical or mythical figures, whom the tradition presents as the original ancestors of the Kazakh ethnic group.

- A second group relates to the *juz*—independent tribal unions. The Kazakhs were traditionally divided into three *juz*: the Great Juz (*ulu juz*), the Middle Juz (*orta juz*), and the Small Juz (*kichi juz*). This group of *shejire* recounts the origin of these *juz*. We may conclude, based on its function and on an interpretation of its genealogical relationships, that this category of *shejire* reflects the group as a whole.

- A third, the tribal-familial group, is constituted in the same way as the two previous groups of *shejire* but has a more or less concrete relationship to genealogical history. Associated with certain family-communities, it maintains structural ties among these groups. This category is distinct from other groups of *shejire*, particularly the following.

- The fourth, a familial-communal group, is in my view the fundamental systemic and signifying strand in the composition of the *shejire*. More than a narrative about the family-community's roots, it is a description of the structure still in force, that is, of the principles governing generational and sexual differentiation in kinship relations. Thus, the content of this strand of *shejire* is more or less concrete in nature.

- The fifth group, quantitatively insignificant, consists of historical narratives about certain representatives of the steppe aristocracy, for example, the *bi* (chiefs presiding over traditional judicial procedure) and the *rubas* (family and tribal chiefs). These accounts have a close organic link to a precise family-community, which must be viewed as an essential sociocultural context and the condition allowing for the *shejire*'s narrative interpretation of the origin of these privileged categories of nomads, an interpretation intended to defend the primacy of the communal principle over the individual principle. In conventional terms, it is possible to relate this group to the following category of *shejire*, which attests to the family chief's desire to trace his origin to famous, often legendary or even mythical figures. It may be deduced, based on its method and the type of interpretation it gives of the family chief's lineage, that this strand of *shejire* developed later than the others and dates to roughly the second half of the nineteenth century. At this time, under the powerful and growing influence of the Russian colonial system on the Kazakh social milieu, the individual principle began to play a fairly tangible role.

- The sixth group deals with two social categories—the *tore* (the Chinggiskhanids, that is, the descendants of Chinggis Khan) and the *koja* (representatives of the Muslim clergy)—and constitutes a special kind of *shejire*, determined above all by the privileged and exceptional position of these individuals within the traditional system of nomadic institutional relations.

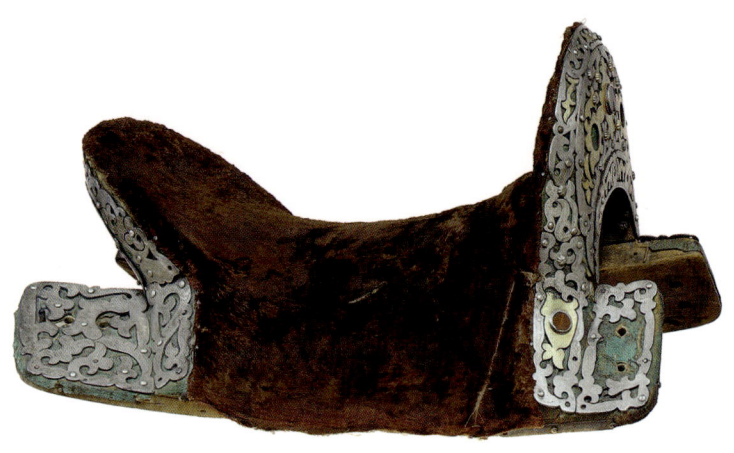

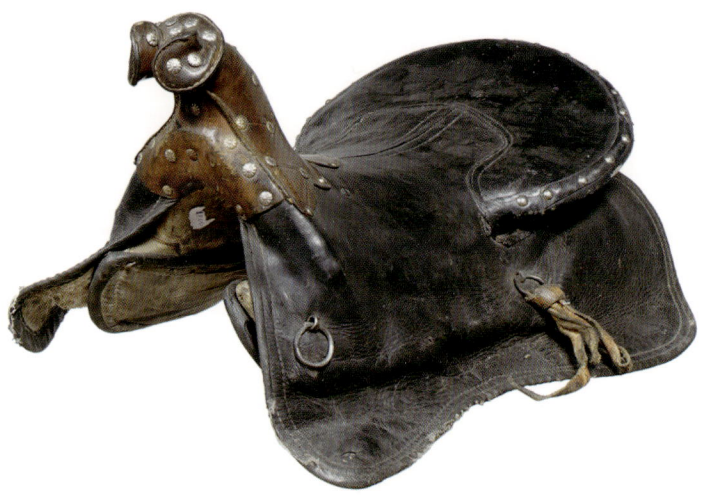

9-4 Kazakh saddle (*Kazaky er*). Wood, leather, and metal, Semipalatinsk region, early 20th century CE.

9-5 Saddle (*Kurandy er*). Wood and leather, Dzhambul region, early 20th century CE.

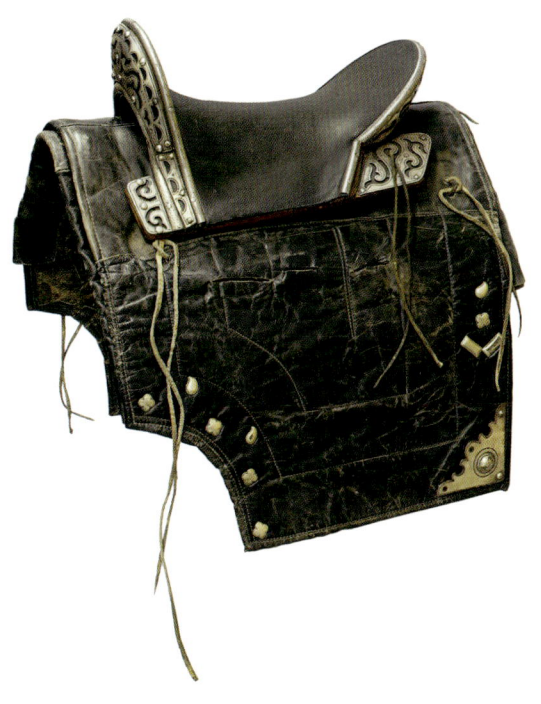

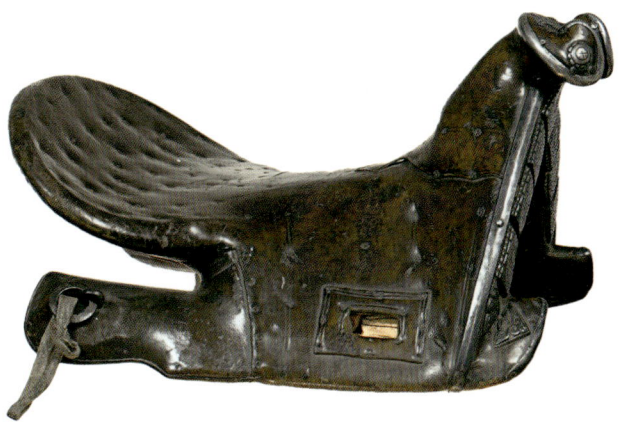

9-6 Kazakh saddle. (*Kazaky er*). Wood, leather, and metal, Almaty region, early 20th century CE.

9-7 Saddle (*Kurandy er*). Wood, leather, and metal, Almaty region, early 20th century CE.

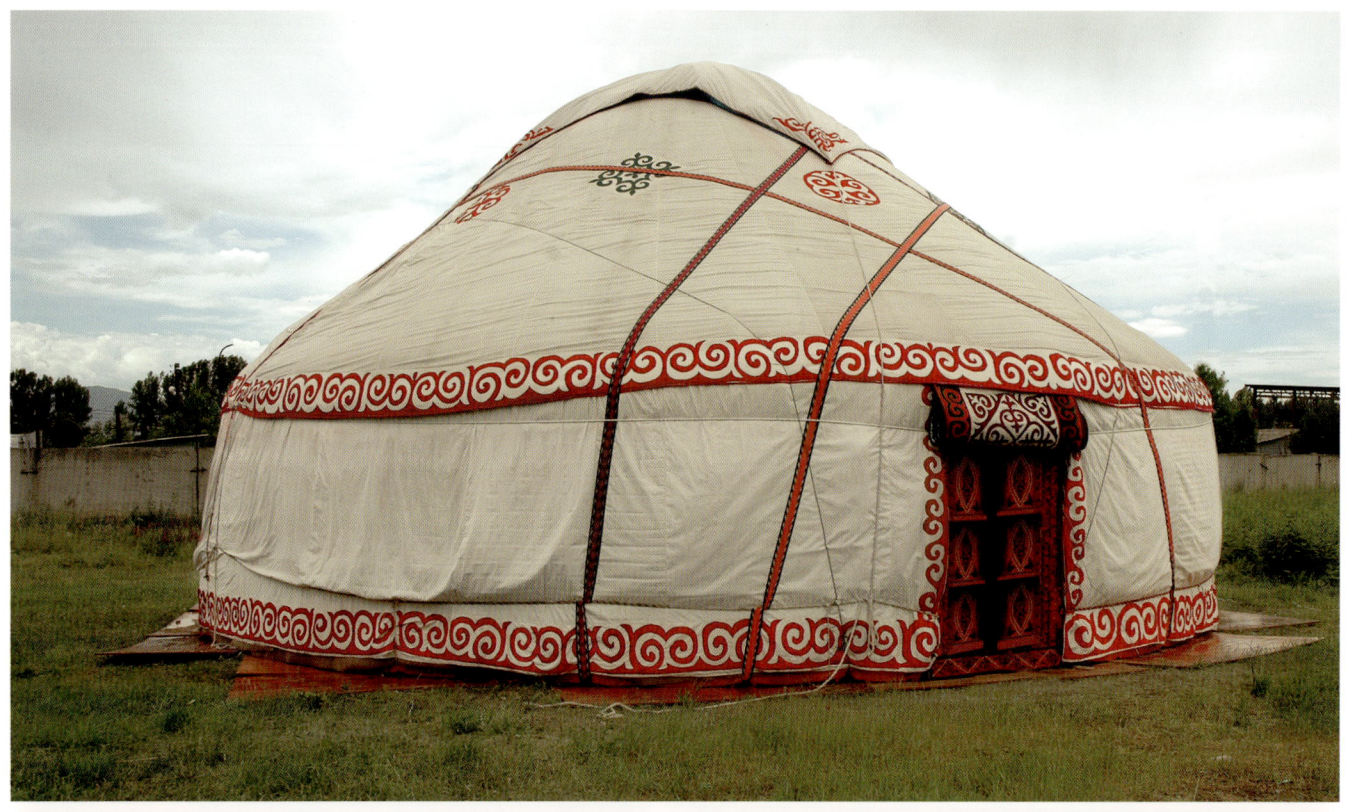

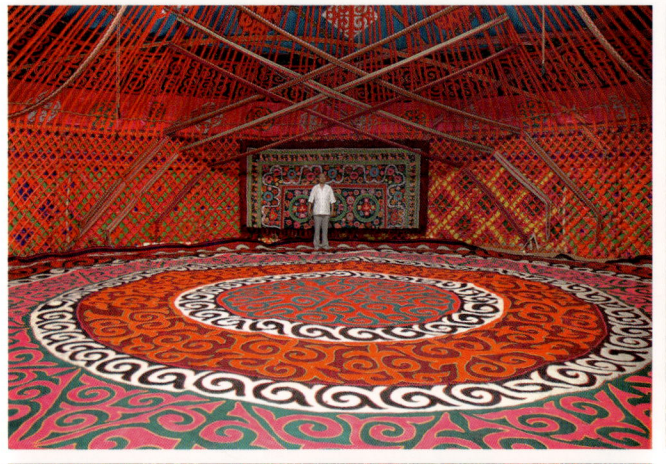

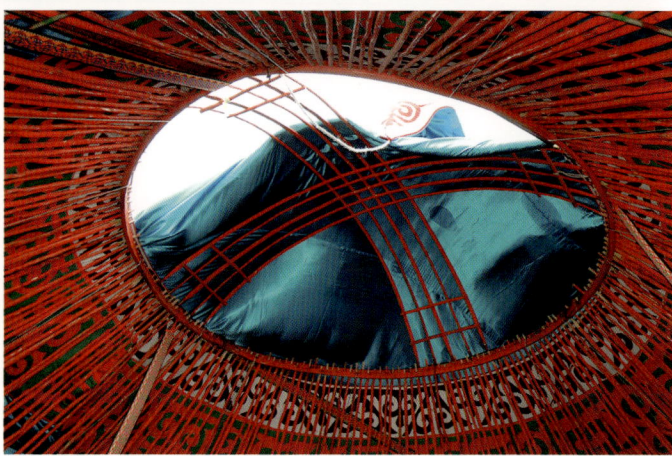

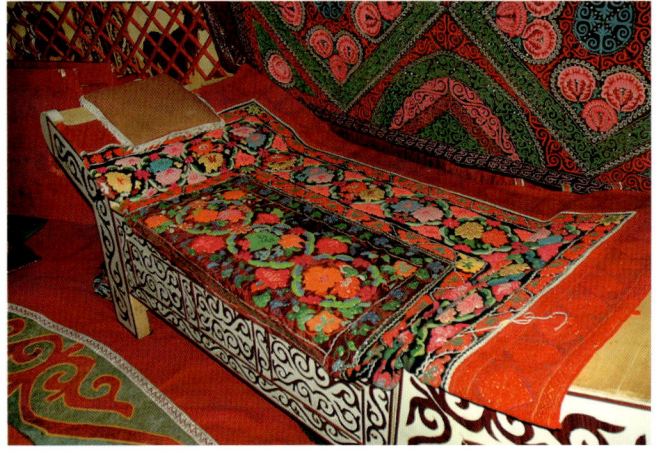

9-8 (top) Kazakh yurt.

9-9 (center left) Interior of yurt.

9-10 (center right) Roof of yurt (*shanyrak*) and dome (*uyk*) of yurt.

9-11 (bottom) Bed in yurt.

A final particularity of the *shejire* is its reference to an "ideal" personified past. To that end, and in complete accord with the poetico-mythical interpretation of history, the names of mythical figures (Alasha Khan, Ouisoun, Argyn, Alchyn, Abak) were introduced into genealogies, but so too were famous and very real historical figures (the prophet Muhammad, Chinggis Khan, Kotan Khan, Koblandy Batyr, Janibek Batyr), who were understood by the *shejire* to be the great founding ancestors of certain tribes or families. Nevertheless, the presence of these figures within the thematic structure of genealogies in no way modifies the definition proposed here of the *shejire* as a given aspect of popular historiography that takes the form of a genre of folklore. Indeed, within the *shejire* the historical role of these individuals was evaluated in the idiom of folklore, which turned historical figures into mythological figures and epic heroes.

Matrilineal kinship ties were known as *jien-nagashy*. They are to be understood within an interfamilial framework and context, in other words, within intercommunity relationships. In terms of the latter, and strictly in accord with the canons and prescriptions of the *shejire*, matrimonial ties had an essential systemic and regulatory function.

All community units were joined in tribes, and finally into *juz* (literally, "country" or "region"), or tribal confederations.[7] As mentioned above, since the course of the fifteenth and sixteenth centuries the Kazakhs were divided into three *juz*—the Great, Middle, and Small *juz*. Their founders were considered to be the sons of the Great Alash, the legendary forefather of all Kazakhs (*Alash balasy*, or "sons of Alash"). Therefore, the ties among *juz*, as also among tribes, bore a linear character and were justified by genealogical reasoning. Strictly speaking, both tribe and *juz* were institutionalized levels of the corresponding intercommunity relations: beyond the *birata*, sociopolitical relationships were expressed, legitimated, and perpetuated in genealogical terms. The basic principle in various spheres of nomadic life remained the core family. Sociospatial and economic organization of family territory took place along seasonal camp sites: the *jailau* (summer pasture), *kuzeu* (fall pasture), *kystau* (winter pasture), and *kokteu* (spring pasture). The unification of these segmented pastures into an extensive system of territories and migration paths among them was an integral part of folk knowledge and indispensable for making practical use of the environment. This knowledge was handed down from generation to generation and further increased the importance of the communal principle of traditional Kazakh society.

THE UNITY OF AESTHETICS AND FUNCTIONALISM IN TRADITIONAL KAZAKH MATERIAL CULTURE

As noted above, community units are tightly bound to specific subsistence forms. Many elements typical of the material culture of mobile pastoralists belong to what are known as "small forms." They are mainly represented by leather, felt, textiles, wood, bone, and partially metal objects and are characterized by their functional mobility. Bulkiness of objects is functionally inconvenient in the mind of the nomads, and is considered aesthetically grotesque, since bulky objects are in opposition not only to the useful nature but also to the dynamic lifestyle of the nomads. At the same time, the organic unity of aesthetics and functionality in the texture of each object, with the primacy of the utilitarian principle, is the most important typological quality of objects in the nomadic sphere. The decoration of items produced by nomads "was subjugated to the purpose and meaning of the objects. . . . The object is fundamental, but the ornament is used to express its buildup and construction. It is called upon to underscore its function."[8] The organic combination of practical everyday-life necessity and aesthetic value in the construction of an object is most beautifully demonstrated by the main portable dwelling—the yurt (figs. 9-8–9-11). The decor of the Kazakh yurt is a kind of symbolic demonstration of the ethnic spirit of the nomadic tradition. It semantically underscores the interrelationship between, on the one hand, the appropriated habitat and, on the other, nature and the cosmos.

THE ROLE OF RELIGION IN TRADITIONAL KAZAKH SOCIETY

It is impossible to imagine the life of the nomads without their religious beliefs, including the ceremonies and rituals of the life cycle. As the spiritual-ideological context of everyday nomadic life, religious beliefs acted as important institutional regulators at practically all levels of social relations.

The absolute majority of modern Kazakhs (approximately 97 percent) call themselves Muslim. The beginning of the spread of this religious system within the territory of Kazakhstan was in the eighth century. However, despite its impressive temporal depth, Islam in its canonical form was never firmly established among nomadic Kazakhs. Therefore, the religious faith of Kazakhs, as well as their ideology and practice of corresponding rituals and ceremonies, can be characterized as a combination of Islamic with shamanistic and "Tengristic" elements, principles, and techniques. In the traditional Kazakh sphere the main institutions, attributes, and precepts of Islam were reworked in accord with the nomadic ideology and worldview. However, one cannot say that shamanistic traditions or Tengri belief had a firm religious position in the nomadic sphere. In any case, in the visible historical past of the eighteenth and nineteenth centuries, the position of Kazakh shamans (*baksy*) was so weak that their main role was reduced to performing the function of healers (*tauyp*).

The main subjects of worship and reverence in the traditional Kazakh sphere were *aruakhs*, spirits of the ancestors that had, according to ancient beliefs, both protective and destructive functions. It was believed that the spirits protected not only people but also animals, as well as the most notable natural and cult objects. For example, a whole system of ritual-ceremonial institutions and rules was called upon to help nomads truly feel the benevolent force of sanctified natural and cultural places or objects (*kiesi bar*, literally, "having spirit-benefactor"), such as sacred mountains, rivers, lakes, groves, natural boundaries, ancient structures, kurgans, and tribal cemeteries. The nomads believed that they had benefactor-masters in the shape of spirits of the ancestors (*aruakhs*) and great animals (for example, the mighty he-camel and the huge maned wolf). The stability and actuality of the multigenerational collective memory of these and other specific natural and cult objects were guaranteed by the whole cycle of legends, stories, and myths—for example, myths describing the creation of the lake Balkhash and the rivers Ili and Karatal, and the formation of the Great Steppe Sary-Arka. Sanctified by tradition, these locations with their spirit-benefactors, together with the corresponding ritual-ceremonial complex, motivated the collective devotion of community members to the tribal territory. In this capacity the locations were very effective institutionalized ideological methods of geographic self-identification for the community.

This essay offers a short characterization of the cultural traditions of the nomads of traditional Kazakh society, who functioned in full accord with the principles and norms of communal relations. These relations were the main mechanism for mobilizing the social energy of community members within the channel of the "precepts of the great ancestors" (*ata-baba joly*), at least some of which may have had their root in the ancient nomadic cultures that are presented in this exhibition.

Translated by Maya Naunton

NOTES

1. *Казахское хозяйство в его естественно-исторических и бытовых условиях: материалы к выработке норм земельного устройства в Каз*АССР 1926; Мацкевич 1929; Вайнштейн 1991; Масанов 1995.
2. Вайнштейн 1991.
3. Ibid.
4. Алимбай 2009a, 317–25.
5. Алимбай 2004, 185–93.
6. Regarding the institutional nature and function of *shejire* among Kazakhs, see Алимбай 2009b, 373–86.
7. The term *juz* refers to a potestarian political federation of tribes. The well-known Orientalist V. P. Yudin, referring to a report by the Russian "servicemen T. Petrov and I. Kunitchin about travel in Kalmyk lands . . . in 1616," and also to materials in the work *Sharaf-nāma-i Shāhī* of the medieval author Hafiz Tanish, speculated that at the beginning of the seventeenth century "the separation of the three *juz* had already occurred." See Ибрагимов и др. 1969, 243.
8. Акишев 1984, 7–9.

APPENDIX A

Technological Analyses of the Horn Artifacts from Berel Kurgan 36

Technological analyses of the artifacts from Berel kurgan 36 have established that most objects were made out of horn from the Siberian red deer, cut into individual strips of various sizes. The longest (25 x 2 cm.) were used for covering the bridle and harness straps (see Samashev this volume, fig. 2-23), and those of medium length (13 x 11 cm.) for the manufacturing of bridle frontlets, cheekpieces (see fig. 2-24), and breast collars. Representations of hybrid elk-griffin creatures (see page 30) were made out of square-shaped sheets of the following sizes: 6.5 x 5 cm., 5.1 x 4.2 cm., and 4 x 4 cm. The smallest strips (4 x 1.4 cm.) were used to make rectangular plaques, which were placed between the griffin-head pendants (see Samashev, fig. 2-25).

The standards according to which these objects were manufactured and their decoration were based on the main shape of each creature. Two stages can be detected in the carving process. After the horn blank was prepared, a set of roundels was carved in relief, and then a hole was cut through the center of the piece. The holes on bridle frontlets, breast collars, and fastenings for the intersection points of bridle straps could also have been cut through after initial decoration of the piece, in which case the relief ornamentation made earlier was partially cut away. These holes were intended for the attachment of complex constructions, which may have included some parts carved in wood (and have not survived), thus creating an overall composition consisting of multiple elements lying in different planes. The representation of mischwesen combines various materials, such as horn, metal foil (gold and tin), and pigment (cinnabar), which resulted in a vivid polychrome appearance.

APPENDIX B

Elemental Analysis of the Gold Decorations from the Baigetobe Kurgan at Shilikty

All figures represent percentages.

EXAMPLE 1: ARGALI

	Cu	Ag	Au	Total
Sample 1	1.77	3.62	94.61	100.00
Sample 2	1.48	4.44	94.08	100.00
Sample 3	1.37	4.67	93.96	100.00
Average	1.54	4.25	94.22	100.00
Standard deviation	0.21	0.55	0.34	
Maximum	1.77	4.67	94.61	
Minimum	1.37	3.62	93.96	

EXAMPLE 2: PLAQUE

	Cu	Ag	Au	Total
Sample 1	0.86	2.19	96.96	100.00
Sample 2	1.21	2.06	96.72	100.00
Sample 3	0.73	1.79	97.48	100.00
Average	0.93	2.01	97.05	100.00
Standard deviation	0.25	0.20	0.39	
Maximum	1.21	2.19	97.48	
Minimum	0.73	1.79	96.72	

EXAMPLE 3: PLAQUE

	Cu	Au	Total
Sample 1	2.18	97.82	100.00
Sample 2	3.34	96.66	100.00
Sample 3	2.90	97.10	100.00
Average	2.81	97.19	100.00
Standard deviation	0.59	0.59	
Maximum	3.34	97.82	
Minimum	2.18	96.66	

EXAMPLE 4: BEAR/WOLF CUB

	Cu	Ag	Au	Total
Sample 1	0.36	3.90	95.75	100.00
Sample 2	0.22	3.66	96.12	100.00
Sample 3	0.17	4.27	95.56	100.00
Average	0.25	3.94	95.81	100.00
Standard deviation	0.09	0.31	0.28	
Maximum	0.36	4.27	96.12	
Minimum	0.17	3.66	95.56	

EXAMPLE 5: BEAR/WOLF CUB

	Cu	Ag	Sn	Au	Total
Sample 1	1.19	6.02	0.77	92.01	100.00
Sample 2	1.09	4.39	0.36	94.16	100.00
Sample 3	2.18	7.34	0.00	90.48	100.00
Average	1.49	5.92	0.38	92.22	100.00
Standard deviation	0.49	1.21	0.31	1.51	
Maximum	2.18	7.34	0.77	94.16	
Minimum	1.09	4.39	0.00	90.40	

EXAMPLE 6: DEER

	Cu	Ag	Au	Total
Sample 1	2.38	5.45	92.18	100.00
Sample 2	1.59	5.81	92.60	100.00
Sample 3	0.95	5.07	93.98	100.00
Average	1.64	5.44	92.92	100.00
Standard deviation	0.71	0.37	0.94	
Maximum	2.38	5.81	93.98	
Minimum	0.95	5.07	92.18	

APPENDIX C

Horse Tack Terminology as Shown on a Reconstruction of the Horse from Kurgan 36 at Berel

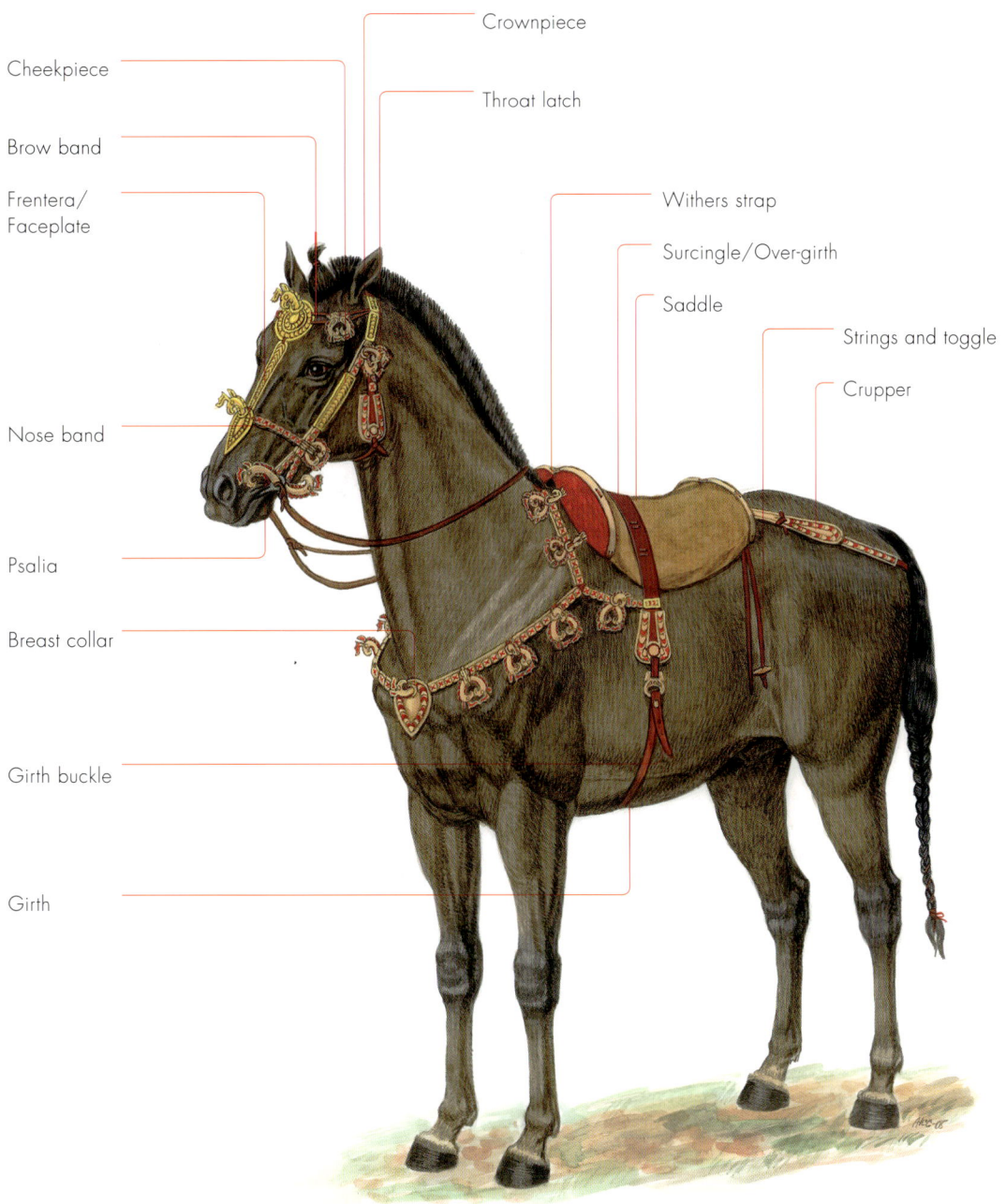

167

CHECKLIST

CSM: Central State Museum, Almaty
MA: Museum of Archaeology, Almaty
MIA: A. Kh. Margulan Institute of Archaeology, Almaty
PCC: Presidential Center of Culture, Astana*

*In January 2012 the Presidential Center of Culture in Astana was replaced by the Multifunctional Scientific-Analytical and Humanitarian-Educational State Enterprise, or the Nazarbayev Center. At the time this catalogue went to press, the final location of individual objects in the Presidential Center collection was unclear. Consequently, where applicable, the checklist retains the Presidential Center of Culture and lists its inventory numbers.

BEREL KURGAN 36

1. Plaque of Facing Elk-Griffin Heads
Horn (Siberian Red Deer)
H. 6.4; W. 5.3; D. 0.6 cm
Berel, Kurgan 36
late 4th–early 3rd century BCE
MIA: B36-21
(Page 30)

2. Plaque of Facing Elk-Griffin Heads
Horn (Siberian Red Deer)
H. 6.5; W. 5.4; D. 0.7 cm
Berel, Kurgan 36
late 4th–early 3rd century BCE
MIA: B36-23

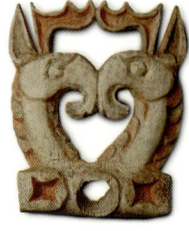

3. Plaque of Facing Elk-Griffin Heads
Horn (Siberian Red Deer)
H. 6.0; W. 5.1; D. 0.8 cm
Berel, Kurgan 36
late 4th–early 3rd century BCE
MIA: B36-26

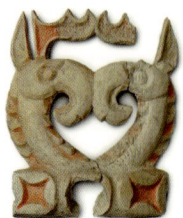

4. Plaque of Facing Elk-Griffin Heads
Horn (Siberian Red Deer)
H. 6.4; W. 5.4; D. 0.7 cm
Berel, Kurgan 36
late 4th–early 3rd century BCE
MIA: B36-28

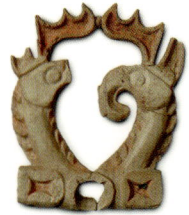

5. Plaque of Facing Elk-Griffin Heads
Horn (Siberian Red Deer)
H. 6.5; W. 5.4; D. 0.9 cm
Berel, Kurgan 36
late 4th–early 3rd century BCE
MIA: B36-30

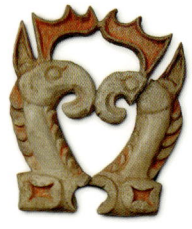

6. Plaque of Facing Elk-Griffin Heads
Horn (Siberian Red Deer)
H. 5.6; W. 4.2; D. 0.7 cm
Berel, Kurgan 36
late 4th–early 3rd century BCE
MIA: B36-31

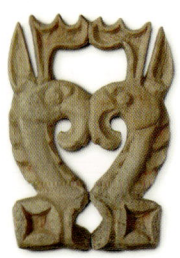

7. Plaque of Facing Elk-Griffin Heads
Horn (Siberian Red Deer)
H. 6.7; W. 5.6; D. 0.8 cm
Berel, Kurgan 36
late 4th–early 3rd century BCE
MIA: B36-40

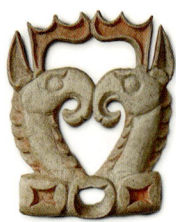

8. Plaque of Facing Elk-Griffin Heads
Horn (Siberian Red Deer)
H. 6.1; W. 5.1; D. 0.7 cm
Berel, Kurgan 36
late 4th–early 3rd century BCE
MIA: B36-47

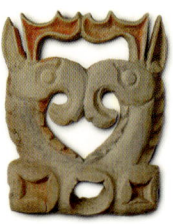

9. Plaque of Facing Elk-Griffin Heads
Horn (Siberian Red Deer)
H. 6.3; W. 5.3; D. 0.7 cm
Berel, Kurgan 36
late 4th–early 3rd century BCE
MIA: B36-48

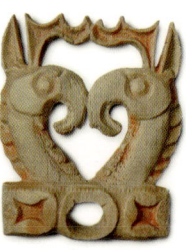

10. Plaque of Facing Elk-Griffin Heads
Horn (Siberian Red Deer)
H. 5.9; W. 4.4; D. 0.7 cm
Berel, Kurgan 36
late 4th–early 3rd century BCE
MIA: B36-61

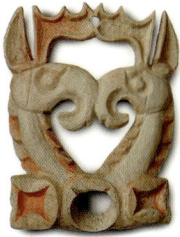

11. Plaque of Facing Elk-Griffin Heads
Horn (Siberian Red Deer)
H. 5.7; W. 5.4; D. 0.8 cm
Berel, Kurgan 36
late 4th–early 3rd century BCE
MIA: B36-62

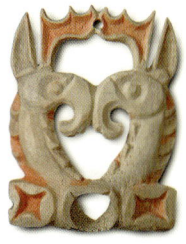

12. Plaque of Facing Elk-Griffin Heads
Horn (Siberian Red Deer)
H. 6.7; W. 4.3; D. 0.7 cm
Berel, Kurgan 36
late 4th–early 3rd century BCE
MIA: B36-67

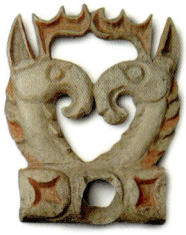

13. Plaque of Facing Griffin Heads from Bridle Brow Band
Horn (Siberian Red Deer)
H. 6.6; W. 5.7; D. 0.7 cm
Berel, Kurgan 36
late 4th–early 3rd century BCE
MIA: B36-51

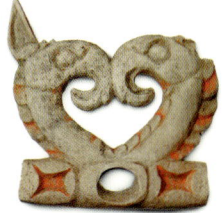

14. Plaque of Facing Griffin Heads from Bridle Brow Band
Horn (Siberian Red Deer)
H. 4.0; W. 3.7; D. 0.6 cm
Berel, Kurgan 36
late 4th–early 3rd century BCE
MIA: B36-34

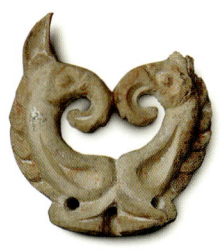

15. Psalia with Elk-Griffin Head Terminals
Horn (Siberian Red Deer)
H. 12.6; W. 4.8; D. 1.3 cm
Berel, Kurgan 36
late 4th–early 3rd century BCE
MIA: B36-54A

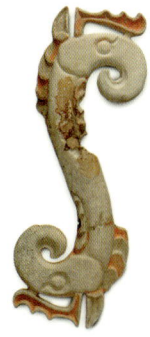

16. Psalia with Elk-Griffin Head Terminals
Horn (Siberian Red Deer), Gold Foil
H. 12.6; W. 4.8; D. 1.3 cm
Berel, Kurgan 36
late 4th–early 3rd century BCE
MIA: B36-56
(Fig. 6-9)

17. Jointed Bit
Iron
L. 18.5; Diam. (rings): 3.8, 3.4 cm
Berel, Kurgan 36
late 4th–early 3rd century BCE
MIA: B36-03a,b
(Fig. 6-9)

18. Round Element with Scale Pattern from Bridle Brow Band
Horn (Siberian Red Deer), Gold Foil
Diam. 8.5; D. 0.3
Berel, Kurgan 36
late 4th–early 3rd century BCE
MIA: B36-33
(Fig. 5-3b)

19. Bar with Chevron Pattern from Bridle Faceplate
Horn (Siberian Red Deer), Gold Foil
L. 16.4; H. 107; D. 0.4 cm
Berel, Kurgan 36
late 4th–early 3rd century BCE
MIA: B36-63
(Fig. 2-23)

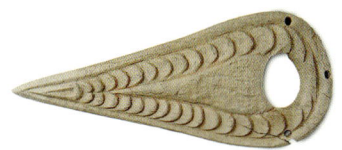

20. Teardrop-Shaped Element with Scale Pattern from Bridle Nose Band
Horn (Siberian Red Deer), Gold Foil
H. 11.7; W. 4.8; D. 0.6 cm
Berel, Kurgan 36
late 4th–early 3rd century BCE
MIA: B36-41

21. U-Shaped Element with Scale Pattern from Bridle Throat Latch
Horn (Siberian Red Deer)
H. 10.4; W. 5.7; D. 0.7 cm
Berel, Kurgan 36
late 4th–early 3rd century BCE
MIA: B36-39

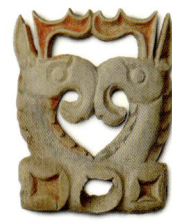

22. U-Shaped Element with Scale Pattern from Bridle Throat Latch
Horn (Siberian Red Deer), Gold Foil
H. 9.9; W. 5.7; D. 0.6 cm
Berel, Kurgan 36
late 4th–early 3rd century BCE
MIA: B36-66
(Fig. 2-24)

23. Bar with Scale Pattern from Bridle Cheekpiece
Horn (Siberian Red Deer)
L. 11.8; H. 1.4; D. 0.3 cm
Berel, Kurgan 36
late 4th–early 3rd century BCE
MIA: B36-43

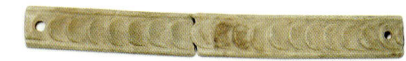

24. Bar with Scale Pattern from Bridle Cheekpiece
Horn (Siberian Red Deer)
L. 11.4; H. 1.4; D. 0.3 cm
Berel, Kurgan 36
late 4th–early 3rd century BCE
MIA: B36-60

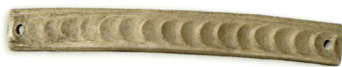

25. Bar with Scale Pattern from Bridle Crownpiece
Horn (Siberian Red Deer)
L. 7.2; H. 1.3; D. 0.4 cm
Berel, Kurgan 36
late 4th–early 3rd century BCE
MIA: B36-52

26. Bar with Scale Pattern from Bridle Crownpiece
Horn (Siberian Red Deer)
L. 7.1; H. 1.3; D. 0.3 cm
Berel, Kurgan 36
late 4th–early 3rd century BCE
MIA: B36-36

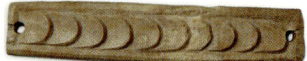

27. Bar with Scale Pattern from Bridle Crownpiece
Horn (Siberian Red Deer)
L. 7.2; H. 1.4; D. 0.4 cm
Berel, Kurgan 36
late 4th–early 3rd century BCE
MIA: B36-59

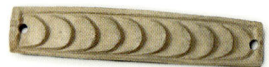

28. Bar with Scale Pattern from Bridle Crownpiece
Horn (Siberian Red Deer)
L. 4.7; H. 1.5; D. 0.6 cm
Berel, Kurgan 36
late 4th–early 3rd century BCE
MIA: B36-16

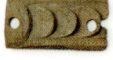

29. Teardrop-Shaped Element with Scale Pattern from Breast Collar
Horn (Siberian Red Deer)
H. 13.2; W. 10.5; D. 0.6 cm
Berel, Kurgan 36
late 4th–early 3rd century BCE
MIA: B36-01

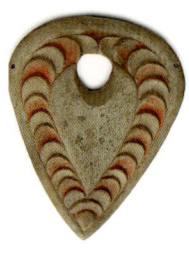

30. U-Shaped Element with Scale Pattern from Saddle Girth
Horn (Siberian Red Deer)
H. 10.1; W. 7.2; D. 0.8 cm
Berel, Kurgan 36
late 4th–early 3rd century BCE
MIA: B36-15

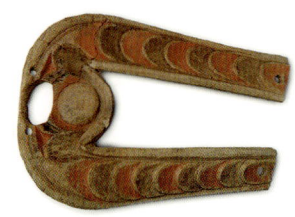

31. U-Shaped Element with Scale Pattern from Saddle Girth
Horn (Siberian Red Deer)
H. 10.2; W. 7.1; D. 0.8 cm
Berel, Kurgan 36
late 4th–early 3rd century BCE
MIA: B36-46

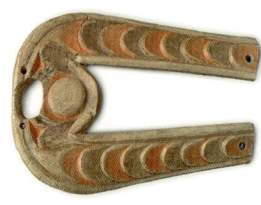

32. Buckle from Saddle Girth
Horn (Siberian Red Deer)
L. 7; W. 4.4; D. 0.8 cm
Berel, Kurgan 36
late 4th–early 3rd century BCE
MIA: B36-08

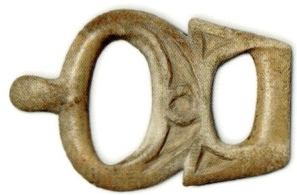

33. Saddle Trim (2)
Horn (Siberian Red Deer)
L. 10.4, 14.9; W. 1.6, 1.6; D. 0.2, 0.2 cm
Berel, Kurgan 36
late 4th–early 3rd century BCE
MIA: B36-3a

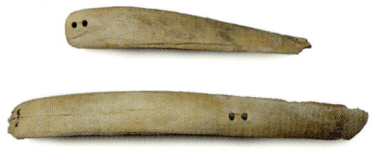

34. Saddle Trim
Horn (Siberian Red Deer)
L. 9.9; W. 1.4; D. 0.3 cm
Berel, Kurgan 36
late 4th–early 3rd century BCE
MIA: B36-12b

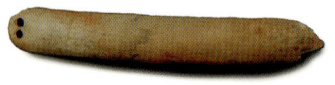

35. Toggle
Horn (Siberian Red Deer)
L. 3.3; H. 1.4; D. 0.8 cm
Berel, Kurgan 36
late 4th–early 3rd century BCE
MIA: B36-05
(no image available)

36. Bar with Scale Pattern and Rounded Terminal from Crupper
Horn (Siberian Red Deer)
L. 26.2; H. 4.0; D. 0.8 cm
Berel, Kurgan 36
late 4th–early 3rd century BCE
MIA: B36-03

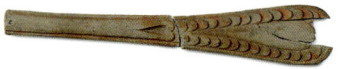

37. Bar with Scale Pattern and Rounded Terminal from Crupper
Horn (Siberian Red Deer)
L. 25.5; H. 4.5; D. 0.5 cm
Berel, Kurgan 36
late 4th–early 3rd century BCE
MIA: B36-04

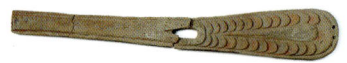

38. Bar with Scale-Pattern Ornament from Crupper
Horn (Siberian Red Deer)
L. 25.1; H. 1.8; D. 0.5 cm
Berel, Kurgan 36
late 4th–early 3rd century BCE
MIA: B36-06/1

39. Bar with Scale-Pattern Ornament from Crupper
Horn (Siberian Red Deer)
L. 21; H. 1.8; D. 0.4 cm
Berel, Kurgan 36
late 4th–early 3rd century BCE
MIA: B36-06/2

40. Bars with Cut-Out and Painted Ornament from Horse Tack (9)
Horn (Siberian Red Deer)
L. 3.9–6.6; H. 1.3–5.2; D. 0.4–0.9 cm
Berel, Kurgan 36
late 4th–early 3rd century BCE
MIA: B36-09, B36-10, B36-22, B36-27, B36-49, B36-50, B36-58, B36-64, B36-65
(see also fig. 2-25)

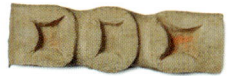

41. Ball with Cut-Out and Painted Ornament from Horse Tack
Horn (Siberian Red Deer)
Diam. 1.5; D. 0.7 cm
Berel, Kurgan 36
late 4th–early 3rd century BCE
MIA: B36-68

42. Square with Cut-Out and Painted Ornament from Horse Tack
Horn (Siberian Red Deer)
H. 1.5; W. 1.4; D. 0.7 cm
Berel, Kurgan 36,
late 4th–early 3rd century BCE
MIA: B36-52

BEREL KURGAN 11

43. Feline Face and Stylized Ornaments from Horse Tack
Wood, and Tin and Gold Foil
H. 9.0; W. 6.0; D. 1.6 cm
Berel, Kurgan 11
late 4th–early 3rd century BCE
PCC: 5581
(cover illustration)

44. Feline Face and Zoomorphic Ornaments from Horse Tack
Wood, Gold Foil
H. 9.7, W. 6.4, D. 1.7 cm
Berel, Kurgan 11
late 4th–early 3rd century BCE
PCC: 4439

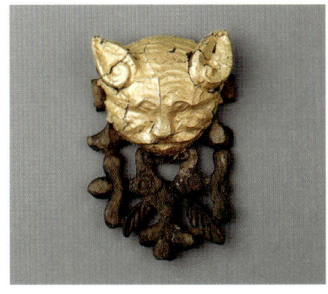

45. Feline Face and Three Griffin Heads from Horse Tack
Wood
H. 14.2; W. 8.2; D. 2.0 cm
Berel, Kurgan 11
late 4th–early 3rd century BCE
PCC: 4441/1-2
(Fig. 7-19)

46. Feline Face from Horse Tack
Wood, Gold
H. 9.4; W. 10.7; D. 1.4 cm
Berel, Kurgan 11
late 4th–early 3rd century BCE
PCC: 4953
(Fig. 2-9)

47. Plaque of Lion-Griffin Head with Ungulate Head in Mouth from Horse Tack
Wood
H. 8 cm
Berel, Kurgan 11
late 4th–early 3rd century BCE
PCC: 6203
(Fig. 6-10)

48. Sculpted Ibex Horns from Ceremonial Horse Headdress
Wood, Gold
L. ca. 60 cm
Berel, Kurgan 11
late 4th–early 3rd century BCE
MIA
(Page 76)

49. Sculpted Ibex Horns from Ceremonial Horse Headdress
Wood, Gold, Leather
L. 70 cm
Berel, Kurgan 11
late 4th–early 3rd century BCE
MIA
(no image available)

50. Plaque of Argali Head Suspended from Ribbed Bar from Horse Tack
Wood, and Tin and Gold Foil
H. 8.8; W. 8.0; D. 1.1 cm
Berel, Kurgan 11
late 4th–early 3rd century BCE
PCC: 4933

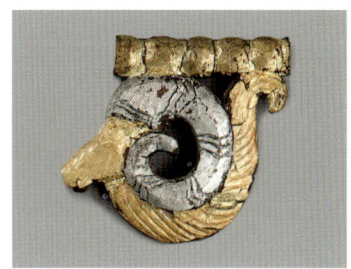

51. Plaque of Argali Head Suspended from Ribbed Bar from Horse Tack
Wood, Gold Foil
H. 12.0; W. 12.3; D. 1.0 cm
Berel, Kurgan 11
late 4th–early 3rd century BCE
PCC: 6182

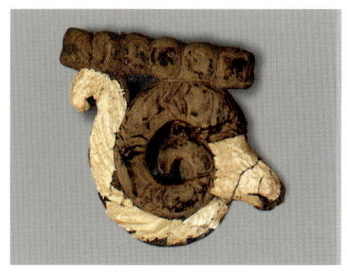

52. Plaque of Argali Head Suspended from Ribbed Bar from Horse Tack
Wood, Gold Foil
H. 7.6; W. 8.7; D. 1.0 cm
Berel, Kurgan 11
late 4th–early 3rd century BCE
PCC: 4954

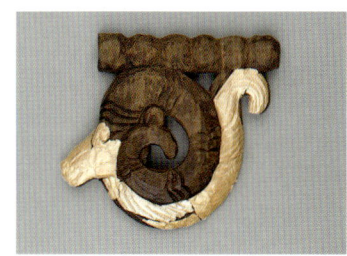

53. Plaque of Argali Head Suspended from Ribbed Bar from Horse Tack
Wood
H. 7.8; W. 8.3; D. 0.9 cm
Berel, Kurgan 11
late 4th–early 3rd century BCE
PCC: 5574

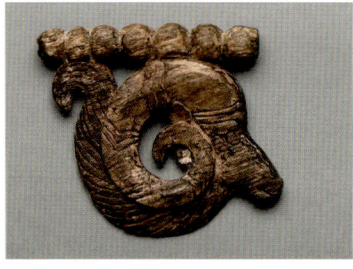

54. Plaques of Feline Attacking a Horned Animal Head from Horse Tack (2)
Wood
H. 5.7, 6.5; W. 6.3, 7.0; D. 1.0, 1.0 cm
Berel, Kurgan 11
late 4th–early 3rd century BCE
PCC: 8707, 8708

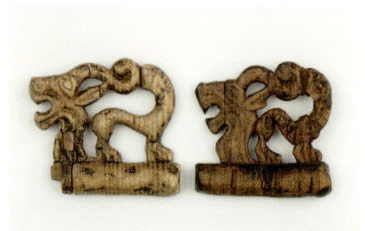

55. Plaque of Feline Attacking Horned Animal Head from Horse Tack
Wood
H. 5.4; W. 6.3; D. 1.0 cm
Berel, Kurgan 11
late 4th–early 3rd century BCE
PCC: 4442

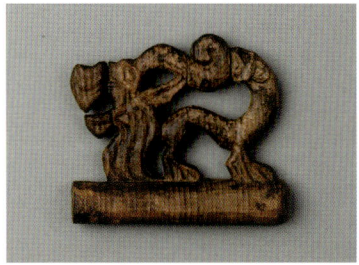

56. Plaque of Feline Attacking Horned Animal Head from Horse Tack
Wood, Gold Foil
H. 5.3; W. 5.6; D. 1.1 cm
Berel, Kurgan 11, late 4th–early 3rd century BCE
PCC: 4932
(Fig. 2-16)

57. Plaque of Addorsed Deer Heads from Horse Tack
Wood
H. 6.2; W. 7.5; D. 1.2 cm
Berel, Kurgan 11
late 4th–early 3rd century BCE
PCC: 8283
(Fig. 2-10)

58. Plaque from Horse Tack of Addorsed Deer Heads
Wood
H. 6.8; W. 6.4; D. 1.0 cm
Berel, Kurgan 11
late 4th–early 3rd century BCE
PCC: 4937

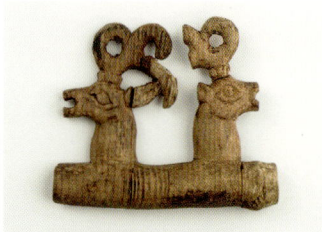

59. Plaque of Griffin Head from Horse Tack, Left Facing
Wood
H. 7.0; W. 4.5; D. 0.9 cm
Berel, Kurgan 11
late 4th–early 3rd century BCE
PCC: 8724

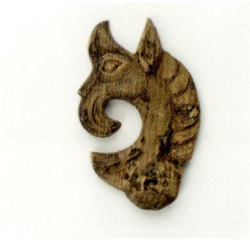

60. Plaques of Griffin Head from Horse Tack, Right Facing (2)
Wood
H. 6.0, 6.6; W. 4.3, 4.3; D. 0.6, 0.6 cm
Berel, Kurgan 11
late 4th–early 3rd century BCE
PCC: 5576, 4961
(Fig. 2-12)

61. Plaque of Griffin Head from Horse Tack, Right Facing
Wood
H. 6.6; W. 4.5; D. 0.9 cm
Berel, Kurgan 11, late 4th–early 3rd century BCE
PCC: 4939
(no image available)

62. Plaque of Griffin with Outstretched Wings from Horse Tack
Wood
H. 5.7; W. 6.5; D. 0.7 cm
Berel, Kurgan 11
late 4th–early 3rd century BCE
PCC: 4443

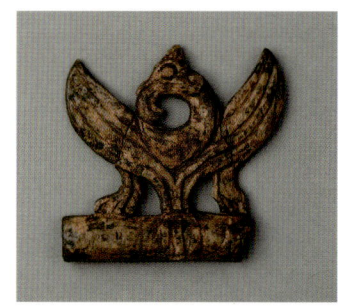

63. Plaque of Griffin with Outstretched Wings from Horse Tack
Wood, Gold Foil
H. 6.0; W. 4.7; D. 0.9 cm
Berel, Kurgan 11
late 4th–early 3rd century BCE
PCC: 8739

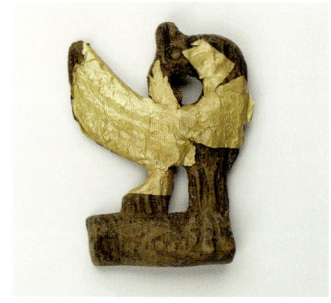

64. Plaque of Griffin with Outstretched Wings from Horse Tack
Wood
H. 6.9; W. 6.8; D. 0.7 cm
Berel, Kurgan 11
late 4th–early 3rd century BCE
PCC: 4956

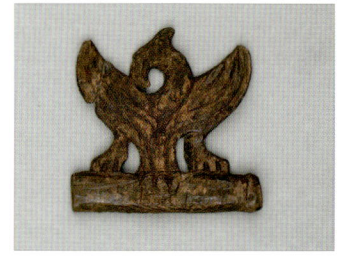

65. Plaque of Griffin with Outstretched Wings from Horse Tack
Wood, Tin Foil
H. 6.6; W. 6.9; D. 1.0 cm
Berel, Kurgan 11
late 4th–early 3rd century BCE
PCC: 5557

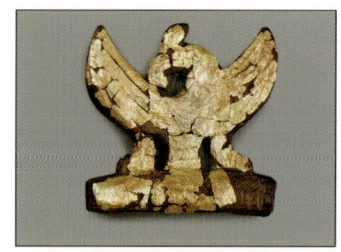

66. Plaque with Vegetal and Zoomorphic Design from Horse Tack
Wood, Tin Foil
H. 7.7; W. 6.6; D. 0.8 cm
Berel, Kurgan 11
late 4th–early 3rd century BCE
PCC: 8802
(Fig. 2-13)

67. Bridle Cheekpiece with Vegetal Ornament
Wood
H. 7.9; W. 12.8; D. 1.3 cm
Berel, Kurgan 11
late 4th–early 3rd century BCE
PCC: 5561

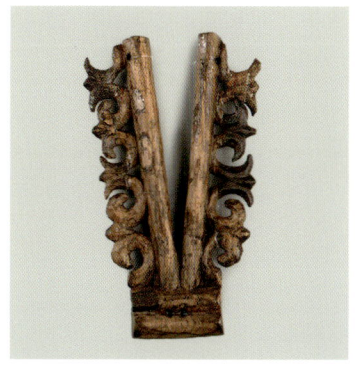

68. Plaque of S-Shaped Ornament from Horse Tack (3 elements)
Wood, Tin(?) Foil
H. 4.4; W. 5.0; D. 0.6 cm
Berel, Kurgan 11
late 4th–early 3rd century BCE
PCC: 4445

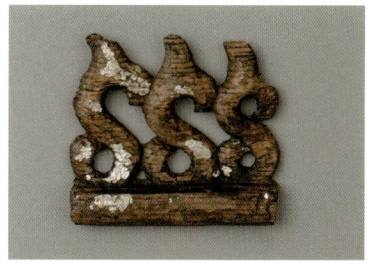

69. Plaque with S-Shaped Ornament from Horse Tack (4 elements)
Wood, Gold Foil
H. 3.8; W. 8.2; D. 0.7 cm
Berel, Kurgan 11
late 4th–early 3rd century BCE
PCC: 4446
(Fig. 2-14)

70. Plaque Depicting Tiger Attacking Elk
Wood
H. 4.0; W. 4.0; D. 0.6 cm
Berel, Kurgan 11
late 4th–early 3rd century BCE
PCC: 4958
(Fig. 2-17)

71. Disk with Central Boss from Horse Tack
Wood, Gold Foil
Diam. 7.0; D. 0.3–0.7 cm
Berel, Kurgan 11
late 4th–early 3rd century BCE
PCC: 4941

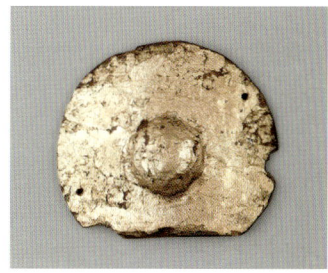

72. Ornaments from Horse Tack (2)
Wood
H. 2.5, 2.3; Diam.1.5, 1.5 cm
Berel, Kurgan 11
late 4th–early 3rd century BCE
PCC: 6222, 6223
(Fig. 2-15)

73. Plaque from Horse Tack
Wood, Gold Foil
H. 4.2; W. 1.5; D. 0.4 cm
Berel, Kurgan 11
late 4th–early 3rd century BCE
PCC: 5589

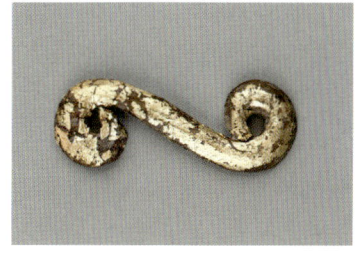

74. Plaque from Horse Tack
Wood
H. 2.6; W. 3.2; D. 0.2 cm
Berel, Kurgan 11
late 4th–early 3rd century BCE
PCC: 5585

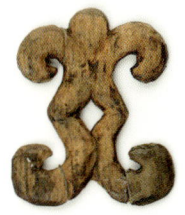

75. Ribbed Bar from Horse Tack
Wood, Tin Foil
H. 1.1; W. 6.6; D. 1.1 cm
Berel, Kurgan 11
late 4th–early 3rd century BCE
PCC: 4936
(no image available)

76. Ribbed Bars from Horse Tack (2)
Wood
H. 2.5, 2.3; W. 6.5, 7.0; D. 1.0, 1.0 cm
Berel, Kurgan 11
late 4th–early 3rd century BCE
PCC: 4949 (illus.), 6211

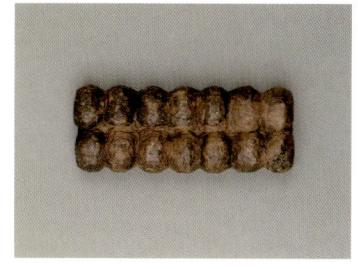

77. Ribbed Bar from Horse Tack
Wood
H. 1.4; W. 6.5; D. 1.0 cm
Berel, Kurgan 11
late 4th–early 3rd century BCE
PCC: 8731

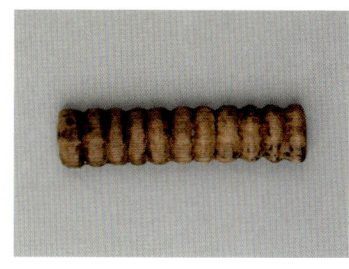

78. Ribbed Bar from Horse Tack
Wood, Tin Foil
H. 1.5; W. 4.9; D. 0.8 cm
Berel, Kurgan 11
late 4th–early 3rd century BCE
PCC: 4962

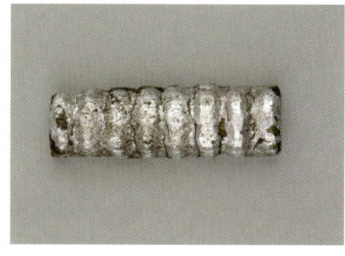

79. Saddle Decorated with Tigers Attacking Elk, with Border of Horned, Winged Sphinxes
Felt, Wood
L. 70.0; W. 41.0
Berel, Kurgan 11
late 4th–early 3rd century BCE
MIA
(Fig. 5-14)

80. Embroidery of Winged Bull from Saddle Cloth
Wool
H. ca. 16 cm
Berel, Kurgan 11
late 4th–early 3rd century BCE
MIA
(Fig. 7-15)

81. Horned Sphinx from Coffin Shroud
Wood
H. 2.8; W. 5.0; D. 1.6 cm
Berel, Kurgan 11
late 4th–early 3rd century BCE
PCC: 6204

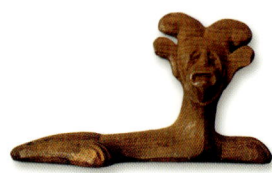

82. Horned Sphinx from Coffin Shroud
Wood, Gold Foil
H. 3.2; W. 5.0; D. 1.6 cm
Berel, Kurgan 11
late 4th–early 3rd century BCE
PCC: 6212
(Fig. 2-21)

83. Horned Sphinx from Coffin Shroud
Wood
H. 2.8; W. 5.0; D. 1.6 cm
Berel, Kurgan 11
late 4th–early 3rd century BCE
PCC: 6209

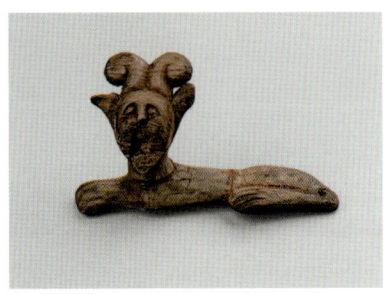

84. Headrest
Wood
L. 45 cm
Berel, Kurgan 11
late 4th–early 3rd century BCE
MIA
(Fig. 5-6)

BEREL KURGAN 10

85. Ornament from Human Headdress Depicting Horse with Ibex and Argali Decoration
Wood
H. 11.5; W. 8.5; D. 5.5 cm
Berel, Kurgan 10
late 4th–early 3rd century BCE
MIA
(Fig. 6-11)

86. Statuette of Argali
Wood
H. 8.6; W. 6.0; D. 1.8 cm
Berel, Kurgan 10
late 4th–early 3rd century BCE
MIA

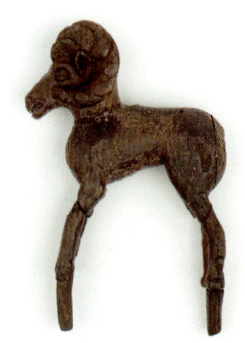

87. Element from Horse Tack with Animal Head and Other Ornament
Wood, Gold
L. 9.0 cm; H. 4.0
Berel, Kurgan 10
late 4th–early 3rd century BCE
MIA

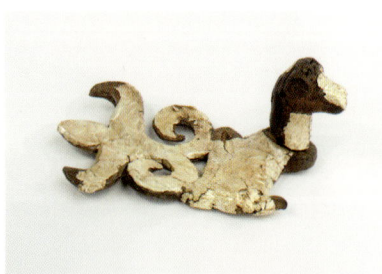

88. Psalia with Griffin-Head Terminals
Wood, Gold Foil
L. 21.0; W. 4.8 cm
Berel, Kurgan 10
late 4th–early 3rd century BCE
MIA

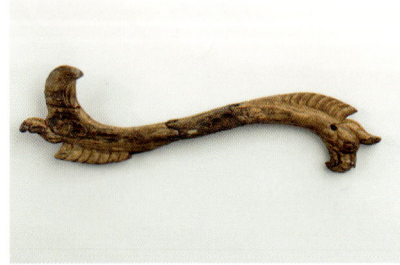

89. Psalia with Griffin-Head Terminals
Wood, Gold Foil
L. 21.0; W. 4.8 cm
Berel, Kurgan 10
late 4th–early 3rd century BCE
MIA
(no image available)

90. Plaques with Fish from Horse Tack (3)
Wood
H. 4.6–5.8; W. 3.6 cm
Berel, Kurgan 10
late 4th–early 3rd century BCE
MIA
(See also fig. 5-11)

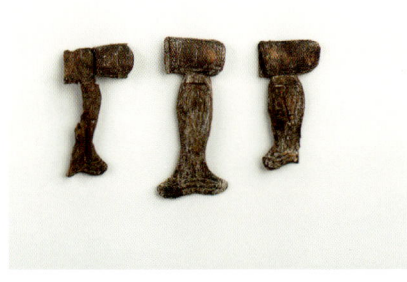

91. Plaques with Ibex Head from Horse Tack (2)
Wood
H. 7.3, 7.5; W. 2.7, 4.8; D. 1.1, 1.1 cm
Berel, Kurgan 10,
late 4th–early 3rd century BCE
MIA

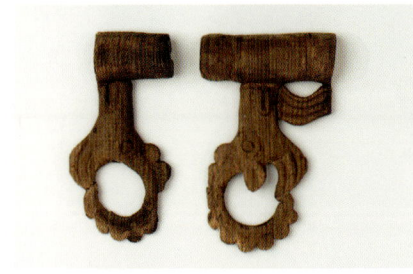

92. Plaque with Vegetal Design from Horse Tack
Wood
H. 6.9; W. 7.1; D. 1.1 cm
Berel, Kurgan 10
late 4th–early 3rd century BCE
MIA

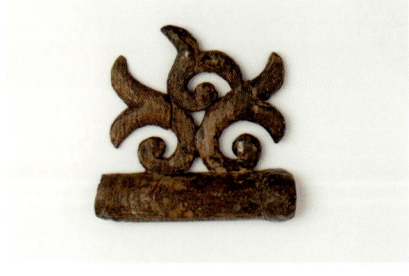

93. Pierced Boar Tusks (1 carved)
Boar Tusk
H. 4 cm
Berel, Kurgan 10(?)
late 4th–early 3rd century BCE
MIA
(Fig. 1-2)

94. Roundels with Horned Animal-Head Decoration (2)
Wood
Diam. ca. 3, ca. 5 cm
Berel, Kurgan 10
late 4th–early 3rd century BCE
MIA: P22-16, P23-25

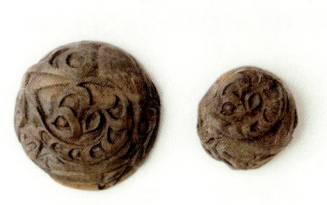

BEREL OTHER KURGANS

95. Jug with Lentoid Body
Clay
H. 52.5. Diam. 28.0
Berel, Kurgan 8
late 4th–early 3rd century BCE
MIA
(Fig. 5-9)

96. Jug with Asymmetrical Neck
Clay
H. 52.5; W. 30.0 cm
Berel, Kurgan 11/18(?)
late 4th–early 3rd century BCE
MIA
(Fig. 5-8)

97. Mirror with Griffin Handle
Bronze
H. 1.2 cm; Diam. 7.0 cm
Berel, Kurgan 8
late 4th–early 3rd century BCE
MIA

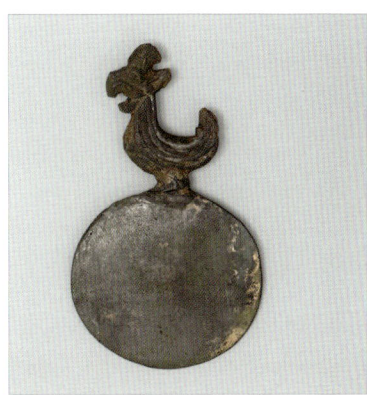

98. Arrowheads (6)
Bone (5), Bronze (1)
L. ca. 4.5 cm
Berel, Kurgan 9
late 4th–early 3rd century BCE
MIA: K9-N13
(Fig. 6-7)

99. Arrowheads (9)
Bone
L. ca. 4.5–5.2 cm
Berel, Kurgan 9
late 4th–early 3rd century BCE
MIA: K9-N13
(no image available)

100. Pipe for Smoking Hemp, with Eight Pebbles
Bronze, Stone
W.12 cm; H. 9 cm
Berel, Kurgan 9
late 4th–early 3rd century BCE
MIA

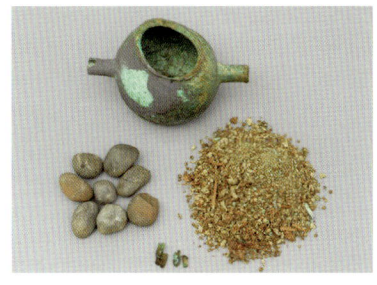

101. Jointed Bit
Cast Bronze
L. 24.5 cm
Berel, Kurgan 72
late 4th–early 3rd century BCE
MIA
(Fig. 6-5)

ENVIRONMENT

102. Petroglyph of Three Horned Animals
Stone
H. 52 cm; W. 50 cm
Semirechye/Zhetisu (Almaty region)
2nd–1st millenium BCE
MA

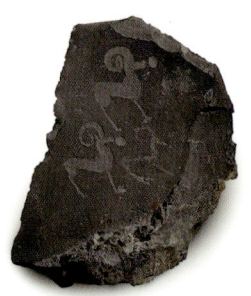

103. Petroglyph of Two Horses Pulling Cart and Two Horsemen and Four Horses
Stone
H. 57; W. 45; D. 23 cm
Eshkiolmes, Semirechye/Zhetisu (Dzhungar Mountains), 1st millennium BCE
CSM: KP 25866/1-2
(Page 92)

104. Petroglyph Depicting Two Human Figures Wearing Animal Masks
Stone
L. 36; W. 42; Thick. 12.5 cm
Tamgaly, Semirechye/Zhetisu (Almaty region), 2nd–1st millenium BCE
MA

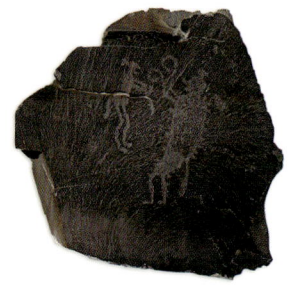

105. Petroglyph of a Spoke-Wheeled Chariot
Stone
L. 58; W. 48; Thick. 13.5 cm
Tamgaly, Semirechye/Zhetisu (Almaty region), 2nd–1st millenium BCE
MA
(Fig. 6-1)

106. Petroglyph of Camel
Stone
L. 30.6; W. 25.5; Thick. 9.5 cm
Semirechye/Zhetisu (Almaty region)
1st millennium BCE
CSM: KP 25866/4

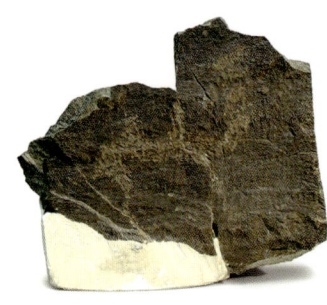

107. Cauldron Fragment Depicting Saiga Antelope in Relief and Protome of Feline Predator
Copper Alloy
Fragment H. 37.4; W. 38.8 cm;
Protome L. 7.2; H. 3.2, cm
Almaty, chance find 1952, 5th–3rd century BCE
CSM: KP 26605; 3733
(See also fig. 8-2)

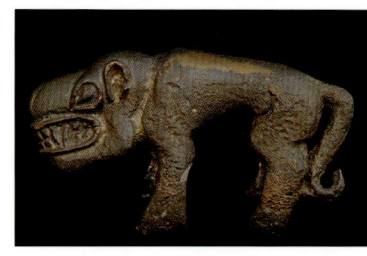

108. Buckle Depicting Profiled Lion Head with Horse Head in Mouth
Bronze
H. 4.9; W. 8.2; D. 2.6 cm
Berkara (Karatau region)
4th–3rd century BCE
CSM: KP 11171
(Fig. 7-12)

109. Finials with Ibex Tops
Bronze
H. 11.2; W. 7 cm
Tasmola 5 (Karaganda region)
7th–6th century BCE
MA: MA 677a/b

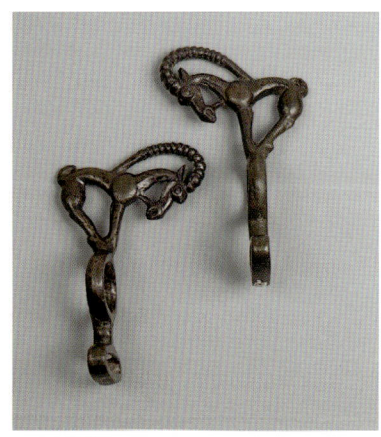

110. Finials with Ibex-Head Tops (2)
Bronze
H. 11.7, 11.5; W. 4.0, 4.0;
D. 1.8, 2.0 cm
Kzyl-Tagan (Taldy-Kurgan, Almaty region)
7th–6th century BCE
MA: RB-23/1, RB-23/2

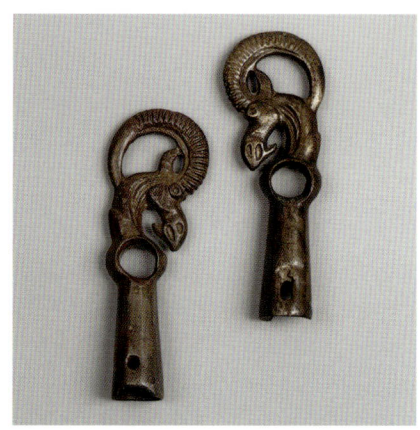

111. Plaque Depicting Fighting Bactrian Camels
Bronze
H. 6.8; W. 7.1 cm
Besoba (Aqtobe region)
6th–4th century BCE
MA: MA 76a
(Fig. 4-6)

112. Plaques of Bactrian Camels (3)
Bronze
L. 5.3; H. 4.6 cm
Besoba (Aqtobe region)
6th–4th century BCE
MA: **MA 761 а, б, в**

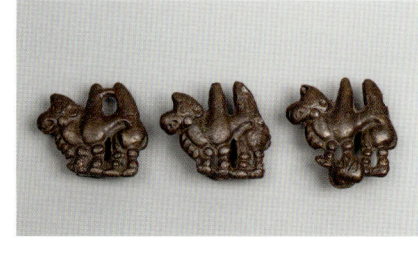

113. Plaques of Bactrian Camels (2)
Bronze
L. 6.9; H. 6.2 cm
Besoba (Aqtobe region)
6th–4th century BCE
MA: MA 76/1, 2

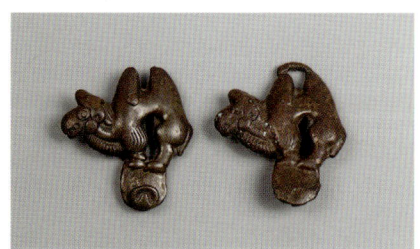

114. Clasp in Form of Stylized Bird of Prey with Cervid and Running-Boar Decoration
Horn (Maral, Siberian Red Deer)
L. 5; W. 4.2 cm
Tasmola 5, Kurgan 3 (Karaganda region)
7th–6th century BCE
MA: MA 736
(Fig. 8-3)

115. Harness Ring in Form of Coiled Boar
Horn (Maral, Siberian Red Deer)
L. 6.5; H. 4.5 cm
Nurmanbet 2, Kurgan 3
7th–6th century BCE
MA: MA 725
(Fig. 1-10)

116. Plaque in Form of Fish
Horn
H. 3.8; W. 5.7 cm
Kazakhstan, unknown location
1st millennium BCE
MA
(Fig. 5-12)

117. Object in Form of Fish
Horn
H. 0.9; W. 6.5 cm
Kazakhstan, unknown location
1st millennium BCE
MA

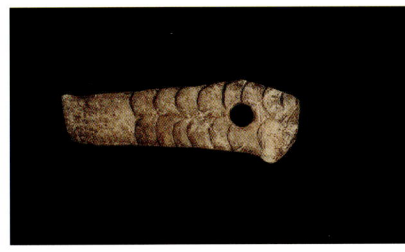

118. Cauldron-Shaped Goblet
Clay
H. 17.7; Diam. 18.9 cm
Kula-Zhurga Kurgan (East Kazakhstan)
7th–6th century BCE
MA: БАЭ-58/2

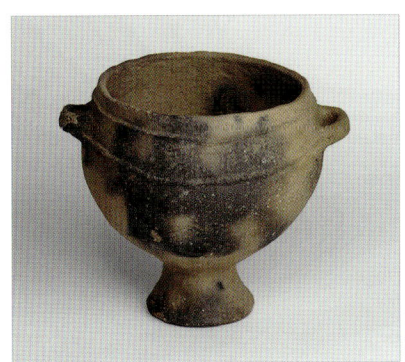

119. Jar
Clay
H. 22; Diam. 11 cm
Issyk, Semirechye/Zhetisu (Almaty region)
5th–4th century BCE
MA: MA 24/3

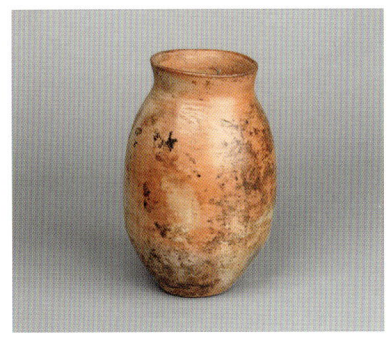

120. Jar
Clay
H. 19.5; Diam. 11 cm
Issyk, Semirechye/Zhetisu (Almaty region)
5th–4th century BCE
MA: MA 37/5

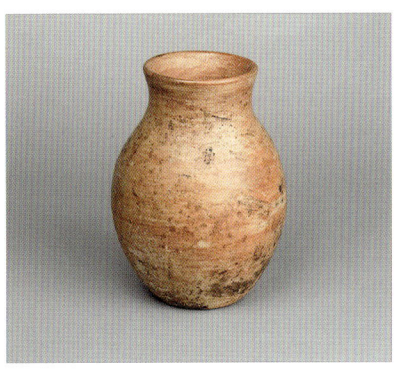

121. Shallow Bowl
Clay
H. 5.5; Diam. 13.5 cm
Issyk, Semirechye/Zhetisu (Almaty region),
5th–4th century BCE
MA: MA 37/3

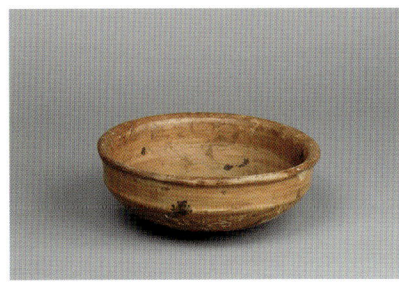

122. Jar
Clay
H. 15.5; Diam. 13 cm
Kazakhstan, unknown location
3rd century BCE–3rd century CE
MA: ЦАЭ-57/33
(Fig. 8-7)

SOCIETY

123. *Akinakes* (Dagger) with Double Griffin-Head Hilt
Bronze
L. 26.5; W. 2.7 cm
6th–4th century BCE
PCC: И-880

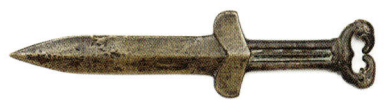

124. *Akinakes* (Dagger) with Double Eagle-Griffin Hilt
Bronze
L. 22.9; W. (blade) 3.0 cm
Kazakhstan, unknown location
6th–4th century BCE
CSM: KP 26806

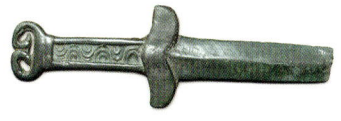

125. *Akinakes* (Dagger) with Double Tiger-Griffin Hilt
Iron
L. 24.1; W. (hilt) 5.55 cm
Kazakhstan, unknown location
6th–4th century BCE
CSM: KP 10646

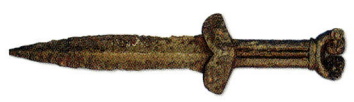

126. Arrowheads (5)
Bone
L. 5.3–8.0cm
Nagorinsk, 6th–5th century BCE
МЛ: ЗКЭ-63

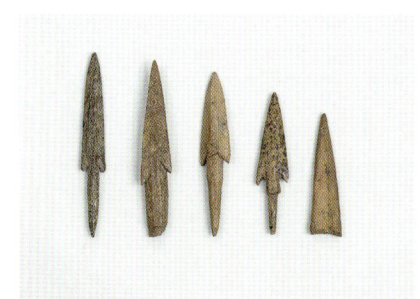

127. Arrowheads (6)
Bronze
L. 3.2–4.2cm
Nagorinsk, 6th–5th century BCE
MA: ЦКАЭ-81

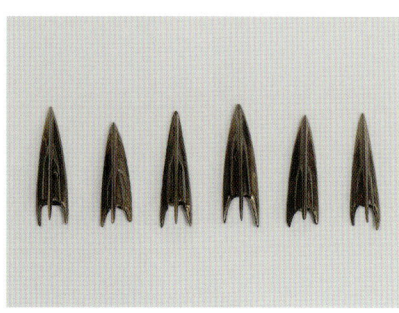

128. Arrowheads (10)
Bronze
L. 2.4–3.3cm
Nagorinsk, 6th–5th century BCE
MA: ЦКАЭ-81

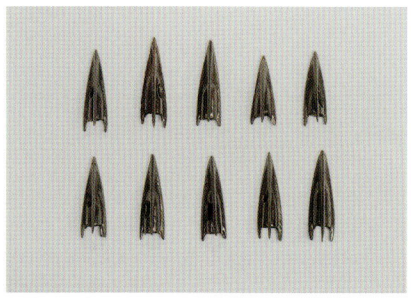

129. Arrowheads (12)
Bronze
L. 2.9–3.5cm
Nagorinsk, 6th–5th century BCE
MA: ЦКАЭ-81

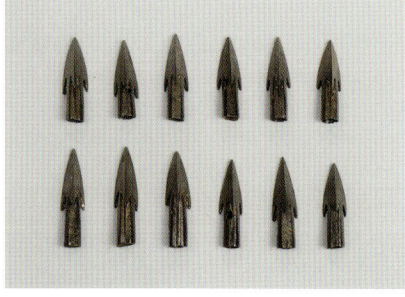

130. Spearhead
Bronze
L. 28 cm
Lebedevka 3, Kurgan 1 (Southern Urals)
2nd–4th century CE
MA: L66/K35

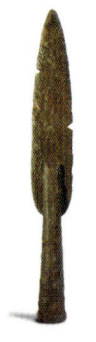

131. Jointed Bit and Psalias
Cast Bronze
L. 16.5; W. 3; L. 18.2 cm
Tasmola (Karaganda region)
7th–6th century BCE
MA: ЦКАЭ-61/62
(Fig. 1-4)

132. Mirror with Handle of Two Horned Mountain-Goat Heads
Bronze
L. 14.5; Diam. 10.2 cm
Tasmola 1 (Karaganda region)
5th–3rd century BCE
MA: ЦКАЭ-62/23

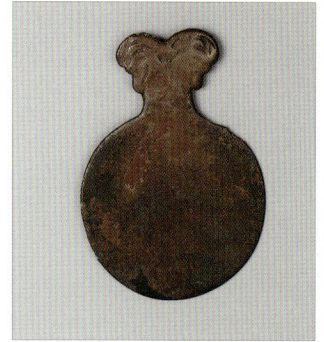

133. Mirror Back with Six-Pointed Star
Bronze
Diam. 15.3 cm
Kazakhstan, unknown location
3rd century BCE–2nd century CE
MA

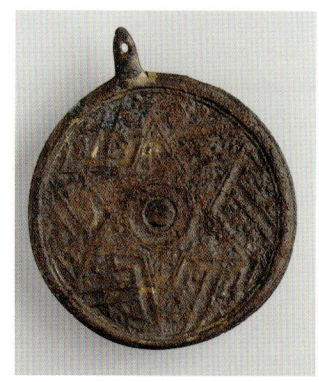

134. Bell
Bronze
H. 8.1; Diam. 6.4 cm
Tasmola (Karaganda region)
7th–6th century BCE
MA: MA 667a

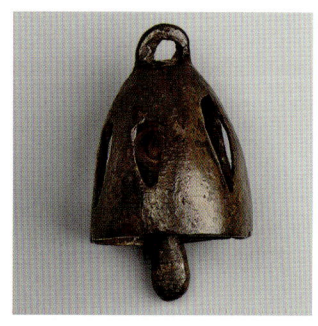

RITUAL VESSELS

135. Tripod Cauldron with Legs in Form of Horned Sheep
Copper Alloy
H. 58.9; Diam. 53 cm
5 km south-west of Almaty, chance find 1912, 5th–3rd century BCE
CSM: KP 2283
(Fig. 1-3)

136. Tripod Cauldron with Legs in Form of Elongated Tigers
Copper Alloy
H. 48.1; Diam. 51.3 cm
Findspot unknown, chance find 1913 5th–3rd century BCE
CSM: KP 2280

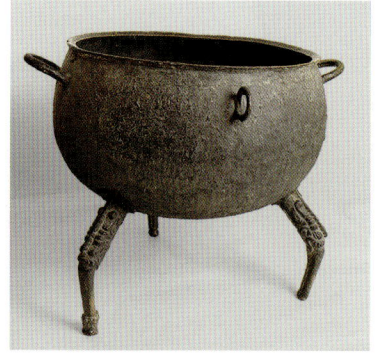

137. Cauldron on Conical Foot with Looped Decoration
Bronze
H. 40; Diam. 39 cm
Almaty Region, 6th–4th century BCE
MA

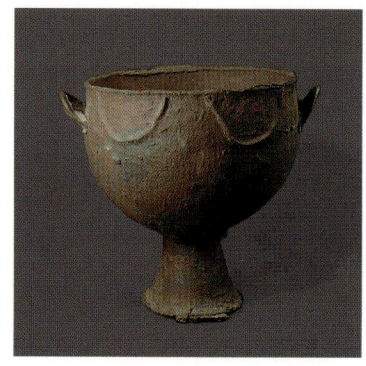

138. Cauldron with Swastika Decoration
Bronze
H. 21 cm; Diam. 33
Semirechye/Zhetisu (Almaty region), chance find, 5th–3rd century BCE
MA

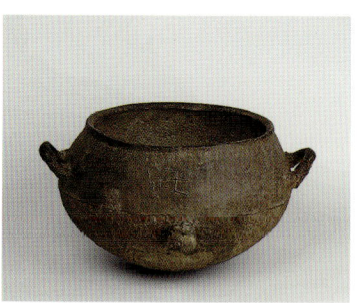

139. Small Cauldron
Bronze
H. 22; Diam. 18 cm
Semirechye/Zhetisu (Almaty region)
8th–3rd century BCE
MA

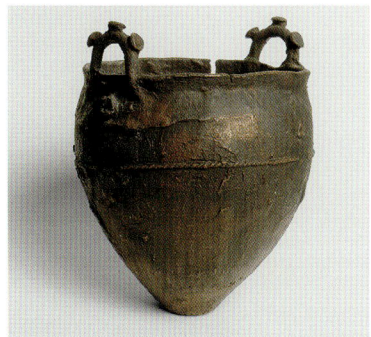

140. Ritual Vessel with Handles and Spout in Form of Wild Boar
Bronze
H. 11.8; Diam. (top) 11.8;
L. (handle) 17.2
Almaty, chance find 1952
5th–3rd century BCE
CSM: KP 8664

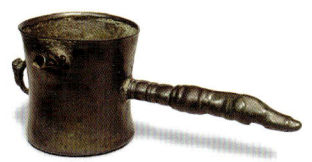

141. Round Tray on Conical Stand with Two Figures of Bactrian Camels in Center and Eight around Rim
Copper Alloy
H. 22; Diam. 24 cm
Semirechye/Zhetisu (Almaty region)
5th–3rd century BCE
PCC: И-881

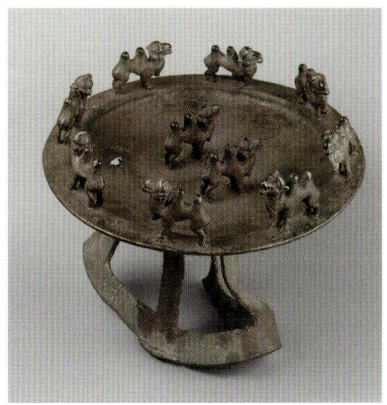

142. Round Tray on Conical Stand with Figures of Seated Man and Standing Horse in Center
Bronze
H. 27.6; Diam. 25.5 cm
Issyk, Semirechye/Zhetisu (Almaty region) chance find 1953, 5th–3rd century BCE
CSM: KP 8591
(Page 140)

143. Round Tray on Conical Stand with Figures of Two Wolves and Two Ravens around Prone Ibex in Center and Sixteen Snow Leopards around Rim
Bronze
H. 24.9; Diam. 34.9 cm
Ermensay gorge, Almaty, chance find 1993, 5th–3rd century BCE
CSM: KP 25195

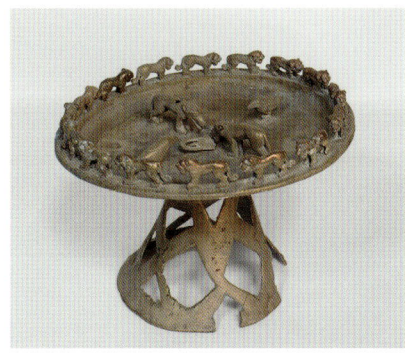

144. Square Footed Tray with Figures of Winged Tigers in Corners
Bronze
H. 37.4; W. 37.2; D. 38.8 cm
Almaty, chance find 1912
5th–3rd century BCE
CSM: KP 2281
(Fig. 7-14)

145. Tray on Conical Stand with Mounted Archer in Center and Fifteen Horned Animals around Rim
Copper Alloy
H. 27.7; Diam. 30 cm
Semirechye/Zhetisu (Almaty region), 4th–2nd century BCE
MA: MA AA-1
(Figs. 6-12a–b)

146. Tray with Three Animal-Head Legs
Stone
H. 15.2; Diam. 29.5 cm
Kuraili, Aqtobe, 6th–5th century BCE
MA: MA 10/3

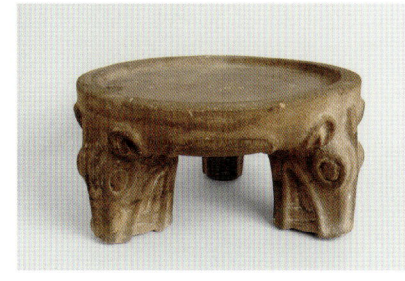

147. Tray with Three Animal-Head Legs
Stone
H. 13.5; Diam. 28 cm
Kazakhstan, unknown location
6th–5th century BCE
MA

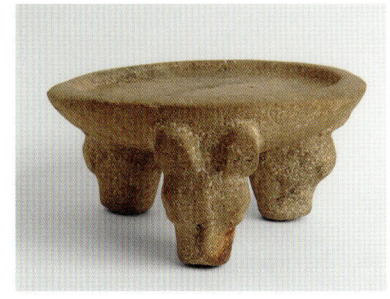

148. Tray with Three Animal-Head Legs
Stone
H. 13; Diam. 29 cm
Nagorinsk, 6th–5th century BCE
MA: 81

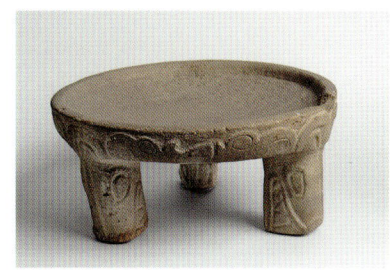

149. Tray with Three Animal-Head Legs
Stone
H. 8.5; Diam. 19 cm
Almaty region, 6th–5th century BCE
PCC: И-883

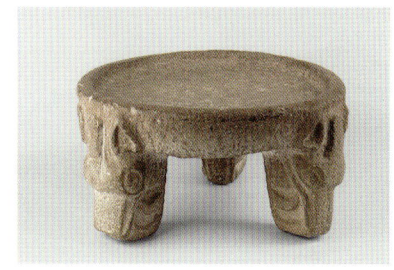

150. Tray with Four Ridged Legs
Stone
H. 12; Diam. 25 cm
Nagorinsk, 6th–5th century BCE
MA

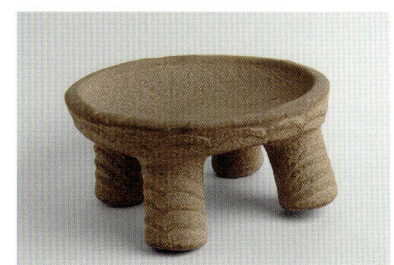

151. Round Stone Relief of Argali Head
Stone
H. 7.1; W. 21.5; Diam. 28.5 cm
Kazakhstan, unknown location
4th–3rd century BCE
CSM: KP 23740

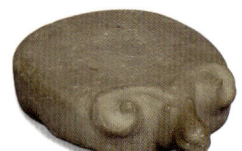

NETWORKS

152. *Akinakes* (Dagger) with Gold Hilt
Iron, Gold
L. 25.5; W. 8 cm
Lebedevka, Southern Urals
6th–4th century BCE
MA: MA 33/1

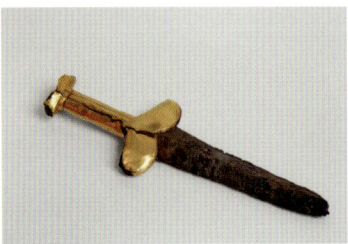

153. *Akinakes* (Dagger) with Decorated Handle
Bronze
L. 29.7; W. 7.5 cm
Nurmanbet, 7th–5th century BCE
MA: ЦКАЭ-62/22

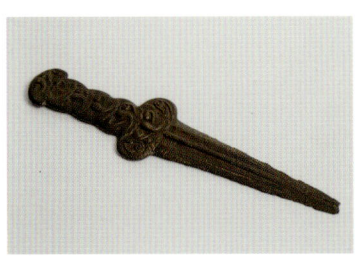

154. Cauldron Protome of Winged Ibexes
Bronze
L. 23; H. 17.5; W. 4.2 cm
Almaty region, chance find n.d.
5th–3rd century BCE
CSM: KP 23732

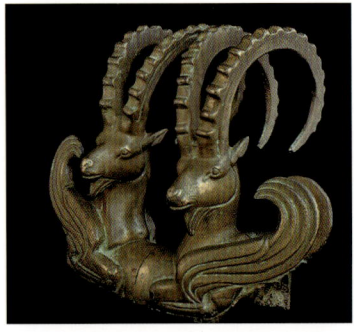

155. Plaques of Double-Horned Winged Sphinxes (2)
Silver H. 6.9, 6.8; W. 3.7, 3.5 cm
Issyk, Semirechye/Zhetisu (Almaty region)
5th–4th century BCE
MA: 35 a,b
(Page 106)

156. Plaques with Horse Rider (4)
Gold
L. 3.6; H. 4.4 cm
Tenlik mound (Taldy-Kurgan, Almaty region)
3rd–2nd century BCE
MA: **MA 135 а, б, в, г**
(Fig. 7-26)

157. Plaque with Reclining Feline
Gold
L. 3.8; H. 3 cm
Tasmola 5, Kurgan 6 (Karaganda region)
6th century BCE
MA: MA 115b

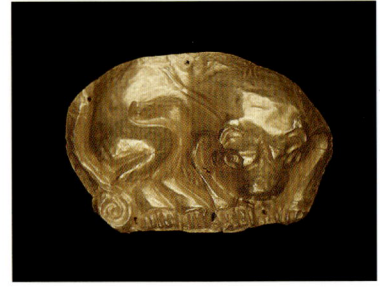

158. Plaques with Felines (3)
Gold
Largest: L. 6.5; H. 4.5 cm
Tasmola 5, Kurgan 6 (Karaganda region)
6th century BCE
MA: **MA 115 а, б, в**

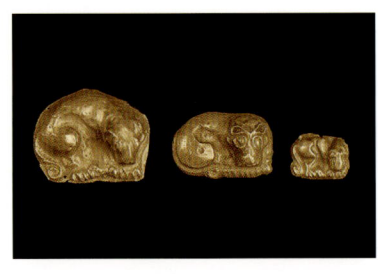

159. Jar Painted with Geometric Motifs
Clay
H. 25; Diam. 17.5 cm
Semirechye/Zhetisu (Almaty region)
3rd century BCE–3rd century CE
MA: CAE-85
(Fig. 7-28)

160. Beads
Glass Beads
L. 9; Diam. 6 cm
Besoba (Aqtobe region)
6th–5th century BCE
MA: MA IIAE-10/15 22, 24

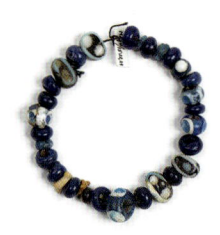

161. Beads
Nacre, Turquoise, Carnelian, Paste
L. 52.5; Diam. 20 cm
Tasmola 5, Kurgan 6 (Karaganda region)
7th–6th century BCE
MA: MA 59

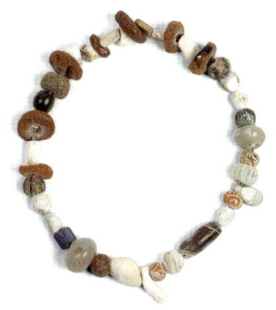

162. Necklace
Amber
L. 68; Diam. 28 cm
Lebedevka 3, Kurgan 2, Southern Urals
2nd–4th century CE
MA

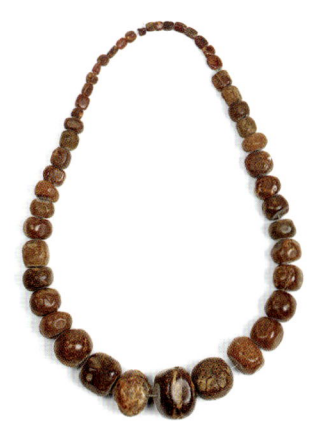

163. Necklace
Rock Crystal
L. 60; Diam. 20 cm
Lebedevka 3, Kurgan 2, Southern Urals
2nd–4th century CE
MA

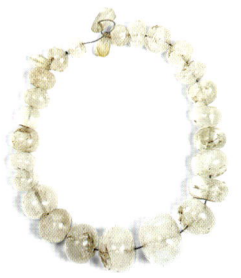

164. Necklace
Turquoise, Carnelian, Paste, Amber
L. 24; D. 9.5 cm
Tasmola 5, Kurgan 6 (Karaganda region)
7th–6th century BCE
MA: MA 2298/1-2

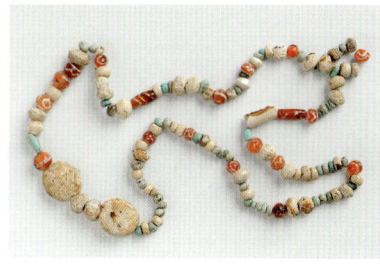

165. Necklace
Turquoise, Carnelian, Paste, Amber
L. 44; Diam. 9.5 cm
Tasmola 5, Kurgan 6 (Karaganda region)
7th–6th century BCE
MA

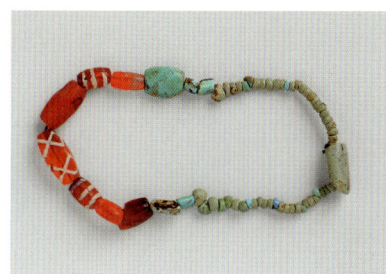

SHILIKTY

166. Plaque of Standing Argali
Gold, Turquoise
H. 4.1; W. 3.97; D. 0.55 cm
Shilikty 3, Kurgan 82, 8th–7th century BCE
CSM: KP 26860
(Page 50)

167. Plaque of "Snow Leopard Mask" Consisting of Two Facing Ibex Heads and Flying Bird
Gold, Turquoise
H. 1.56; W. 2.48; D. 0.2 cm
Shilikty 3, Kurgan 82, 8th–7th century BCE
CSM: KP 26862
(Fig. 3-9)

168. Plaques of "Snow Leopard Mask" Consisting of Two Facing Ibex Heads and Flying Bird (27)
Gold
H. 2.48; W. 1.56; D. 0.2 cm
Shilikty 3, Kurgan 82, 8th–7th century BCE
CSM: KP 26863/1-27

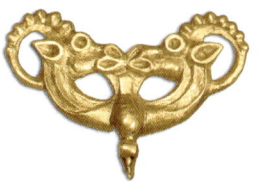

169. Plaque of Perched Raptor (Vulture?)
Gold, Turquoise
H. 2.98; W. 1.6; D. 0.21 cm
Shilikty 3, Kurgan 82, 8th–7th century BCE
CSM: KP 26865/35
(Fig. 3-10)

170. Plaques of Perched Raptor (Vulture?) (17)
Gold
H. 2.98; W. 1.6; D. 0.21 cm
Shilikty 3, Kurgan 82, 8th–7th century BCE
CSM: KP 26865/1-17

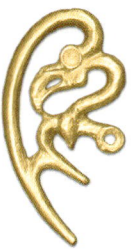

171. Plaque of Standing Wolf or Bear Cub
Gold, Turquoise
L. 1.4; H. 1.0; D. 0.29 cm
Shilikty 3, Kurgan 82, 8th–7th century BCE
CSM: KP 26864
(Fig. 3-11)

172. Plaques of Standing Wolf or Bear Cub (18)
Gold
L. 1.4; H.1.0; D. 0.29 cm
Shilikty 3, Kurgan 82
8th–7th century BCE
CSM: KP 26864/1-18

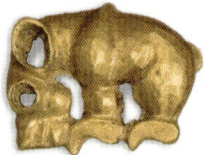

173. Plaque of Two Addorsed Deer Heads
Gold, Turquoise
H. 2.6; W. 2.43; D. 0.2 cm
Shilikty 3, Kurgan 82, 8th–7th century BCE
CSM: KP 26866
(Fig. 3-12)

174. Plaques of Two Addorsed Deer Heads (9)
Gold
H. 2.6; W. 2.43; D. 0.2 cm
Shilikty 3, Kurgan 82, 8th–7th century BCE
CSM: KP 26866/1-9

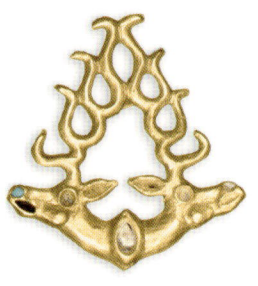

175. Ridged Tubular Beads (5)
Gold
L. 2.03; H. 0.93; D. 0.88 cm
Shilikty 3, Kurgan 82, 8th–7th century BCE
CSM: KP 26868/1,3,4,6,7

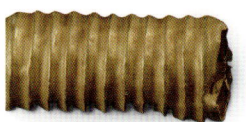

ZHALAULI

176. Teardrop-Shaped Plaques with Granulation and Argali Decoration (8)
Gold
L. 7.4–4.9; H. 3.9–2.67; D. 2.1–1.2 cm
Zhalauli (Kegen district, Almaty region)
7th–6th century BCE
CSM: KP 22030/1-8
(Fig. 1-7)

177. Belt Terminus with Granulation and Argali Decoration
Gold
L. 6.4; H. 2.6; D. 1.1 cm
Zhalauli (Kegen district, Almaty region)
7th–6th century BCE
CSM: KP 22031/1
(Fig. 1-8)

178. Pectoral with Granulation and Argali Decoration
Gold
H. 8; W. 14.5; D. 1.5 cm
Zhalauli (Kegen district, Almaty region)
7th–6th century BCE
CSM: KP 22029

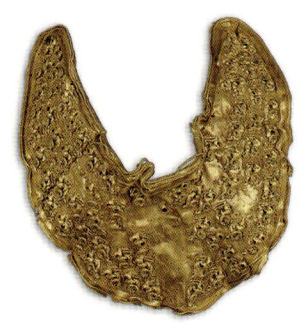

179. Horned Deer with Folded Legs, Two-Sided
Gold
L. 4.9; H. 3.5; D. 1.15 cm
Zhalauli (Kegen district, Almaty region)
7th–6th century BCE
CSM: KP 22030/10
(Fig. 1-9)

180. Plaque with Two Horned Deer and Flying Bird
Gold
H. 4.6; W. 3.8; D. 0.34 cm
Zhalauli (Kegen district, Almaty region)
7th–6th century BCE
CSM: KP 22030/11

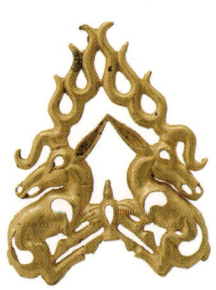

181. Triangular Ornament with Fur ("Needle") Pattern
Gold
H. 18.5; W. 14.6; D. 0.5–0.3 cm
Zhalauli (Kegen district, Almaty region)
7th–6th century BCE
CSM: KP 22038/51

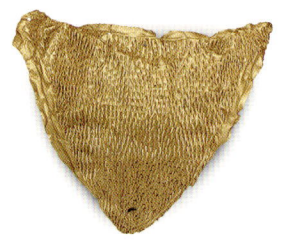

KARGALY (WUSUN)

182. Diadem
Gold, Turquoise, Carnelian, Coral
L. (total) 36.3; H. 5 cm
Kargaly (Myng-Oshakty tract, Almaty region), 2nd century BCE–1st century CE (Wusun)
CSM: KP 3990
(Fig. 7-30)

183. Plaque with Granulation and Inlay
Gold, Turquoise(?)
H. 1.33; W. 1.28 cm
Kargaly (Myng-Oshakty tract, Almaty region), 2nd century BCE–1st century CE (Wusun)
CSM: KP 3997

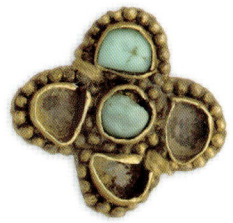

184. Plaque with Granulation and Inlay
Gold, Turquoise(?)
H. 1.45; W. 1.45 cm
Kargaly (Myng-Oshakty tract, Almaty region), 2nd century BCE–1st century CE (Wusun)
CSM: KP 3998

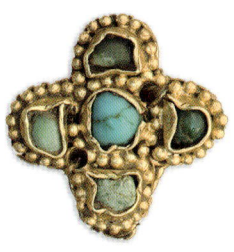

185. Pendant with Granulation and Cells for Inlay
Gold
H. 2.7; W. 2.65 cm
Kargaly (Myng-Oshakty tract, Almaty region), 2nd century BCE–1st century CE (Wusun)
CSM: KP 3996

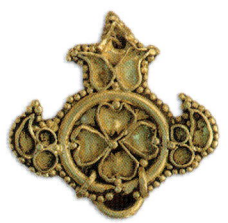

186. Earring with Animal Attacking Man
Gold, Turquoise, Carnelian, Jasper
H. 3.85; W. 2.25 cm
Kargaly (Myng-Oshakty tract, Almaty region), 2nd century BCE–1st century CE (Wusun)
CSM: KP 3995
(Fig. 7-32)

187. Ring with Bactrian Camel
Gold, Turquoise(?)
H. 3.6; W. 2.3 cm
Kargaly (Myng-Oshakty tract, Almaty region), 2nd century BCE–1st century CE (Wusun)
CSM: KP 3991
(Fig. 7-31)

188. Appliqués of Winged Horned Goats (3)
Gold
Largest: H. 2.5; W. 2.08 cm
Kargaly (Myng-Oshakty tract, Almaty region), 2nd century BCE–1st century CE (Wusun)
CSM: KP 4000/6-8

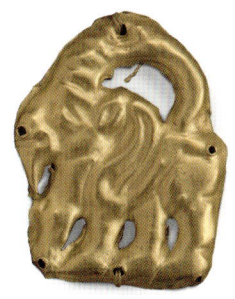

BIBLIOGRAPHY

Abdi 2002
Abdi, K. "Notes on the Iranianization of Bes in the Achaemenid Empire." *Ars Orientalis* 32: 133–62.

Akmetkaliev 2006
Akmetkaliev, R., and Z. Samashev. "New Methods and Techniques for Conserving Wooden Artifacts of Berel." In Chang and Guroff 2006, 45–50.

Allard and Erdenebaatar 2005
Allard, F., and D. Erdenebaatar. "Khirigsuurs, Ritual, and Nomadic Pastoralism in the Bronze Age of Mongolia." *Antiquity* 79(305): 547–63.

Anthony 2007
Anthony, D. *The Horse, the Wheel, and Language: How Bronze-Age Riders from the Eurasian Steppes Shaped the Modern World*. Princeton: Princeton University Press.

Argent 2010
Argent, G. "Do the Clothes Make the Horse? Relationality, Roles and Statuses in Iron Age Inner Asia." *World Archaeology* 42(2): 157–74.

Azarpay 1959
Azarpay, G. "Some Classical and Near Eastern Motifs in the Art of Pazyryk." *Artibus Asiae* 22(4): 313–39.

Barfield 1993
T. Barfield. *The Nomadic Alternative*. Englewood Cliffs, NJ: Prentice Hall.

Barnard and Wendrich 2008a
Barnard, H., and W. Wendrich. "The Archaeology of Mobility: Definitions and Research Approaches." In Barnard and Wendrich 2008b, 1–21.

Barnard and Wendrich 2008b
Barnard, H., and W. Wendrich, eds. *The Archaeology of Mobility: Old World and New World Nomadism*. Cotsen Advanced Seminar Series 4. Los Angeles: Cotsen Institute of Archaeology, University of California.

Barnett 1968
Barnett, R. D. "The Art of Bactria and the Treasure of the Oxus." *Iranica Antiqua* 8: 34–53.

Basilov 1989
Basilov, V. Introduction to *Nomads of Eurasia*, edited by Basilov, 1–8. Los Angeles: National History Museum of Los Angeles County; Seattle: University of Washington Press.

Bemmann, Ėrdėnėbat, and Pohl 2010
Bemmann, J., U. Ėrdėnėbat, and E. Pohl. *Mongolian-German Karakorum Expedition*. Forschungen zur Archäologie aussereuropäischer Kulturen 8. Wiesbaden: Reichert.

Bokovenko 1994
Bokovenko, N. "Tomb of Saka Princes Discovered in the Sayans, Siberia." In *New Archaeological Discoveries in Asiatic Russia and Central Asia*, edited by A. G. Kozintsev and V. M. Masson, 48–53. Archaeological Studies 16. Saint Petersburg: Institute of the History of Material Culture.

Bokovenko 2000
Bokovenko, N. "The Origins of Horse Riding and the Development of Ancient Central Asian Nomadic Riding Harnesses." In Davis-Kimball et al. 2000, 304–10.

Bokovenko 2006
Bokovenko, N. "The Emergence of the Tagar Culture." *Antiquity* 80(310): 860–79.

Borchardt and Bleibtreu 2008
Borchhardt, J., and E. Bleibtreu. "Von der Pferdedecke zum Sattel. Antike Reitkunst zwischen Ost und West." In *Euergetes. Festschrift für Prof. Dr. Haluk Abbasoglu zum 65. Geburtstag*, edited by I. Delemen et al., 167–215. Antalya: Suna & İnan Kıraç Research Institute on Mediterranean Civilizations.

Boyle, Renfrew and Levine 2002
Boyle, K., C. Renfrew, and M. Levine, eds. *Ancient Interactions: East and West in Eurasia*. Cambridge: McDonald Institute for Archaeological Research, University of Cambridge.

Brentjes 1982
Brentjes, B. *Der Tierstil in Eurasien*. Seeman-Beiträge zur Kunstwissenschaft. Leipzig: Seeman-Verlag.

Briant 1982
Briant, P. *Etat et pasteurs au Moyen-Orient ancien*. Collection Production pastorale et société. Cambridge: Cambridge University Press; Paris: Maison des sciences de l'homme.

Briant 2002
Briant, P. *From Cyrus to Alexander: A History of the Persian Empire*. Winona Lake, IN: Eisenbraun.

Bulling 1960
Bulling, A. *The Decoration of Mirrors of the Han Period: A Chronology*. Artibus Asiae, suppl. 20. Ascona, Switzerland: Artibus Asiae.

Bunker 1983
Bunker, E. "Sources of Foreign Elements in the Culture of Eastern Zhou." In *The Great Bronze Age of China: A Symposium*, edited by G. Kuwayama, 84–93. Los Angeles: Los Angeles County Museum of Art.

Bunker 1991
Bunker, E. "The Chinese Artifacts among the Pazyryk Finds." *Source: Notes in the History of Art* 10(4): 20–24.

Bunker 1997
Bunker, E. *Ancient Bronzes of the Eastern Eurasian Steppes from the Arthur M. Sackler Collections*. New York: Arthur M. Sackler Foundation.

Bunker 2001
Bunker, E. "The Cemetery at Shanpula, Xinjiang: Simple Burials, Complex Textiles." In *Fabulous Creatures from the Desert Sands: Central Asian Woolen Textiles from the Second Century BC to the Second Century AD*, edited by D. Keller and R. Schorta, 15–45. Exh. cat. Riggisberger Berichte 10. Riggisberg: Abegg-Stiftung.

Bunker, Chatwin, and Farkas 1970
Bunker, E., B. Chatwin, and A. Farkas. *"Animal Style" Art from East to West*. New York: Asia Society.

Casanova 2001
Casanova, M. "Le lapis-lazuli, la pierre précieuse de l'Orient ancien." *Dialogues d'histoire ancienne* 27(2): 149–70.

Chang 2008
Chang, C. "Mobility and Sedentism of the Iron Age Agropastoralists of Southeast Kazakhstan." In Barnard and Wendrich 2008b, 329–42.

Chang and Guroff 2006
Chang, C., and K. Guroff, eds. *Of Gold and Grass: Nomads of Kazakhstan*. Exh. cat. Bethesda, MD: Foundation for International Arts and Education.

Chang et al. 2003
Chang, C., N. Benecke, F. Grigoriev, A. Rosen, and P. Tourtellotte. "Iron Age Society and Chronology in South-east Kazakhstan." *Antiquity* 77(296): 298–312.

Christian 1998
Christian, D. "State Formation in the Inner Eurasian Steppes." In *Worlds of the Silk Roads: Ancient and Modern*, edited by D. Christian and C. Benjamin, 51–76. Proceedings, Second Conference of the Australasian Society for Inner Asian Studies, Macquarie University, September 21–22, 1996. Silk Road Studies 2. Turnhout: Brepols; NSW Australia: Ancient History Documentary Research Centre, Macauarie University.

Clarysse and Thompson 2007
Clarysse, W., and D. Thompson. "Two Greek Texts on Skin from Hellenistic Bactria." *Zeitschrift für Papyrologie und Epigraphik* 159: 273–79.

Čugunov, Parzinger, and Nagler 2003
Čugunov, K., H. Parzinger, and A. Nagler. "Der skythische Fürstengrabhügel von Aržan 2 in Tuva. Vorbericht der russisch-deutschen Ausgrabungen 2000–2002." *Eurasia Antiqua* 9 (2003): 113–62.

Čugunov, Parzinger, and Nagler 2006
Čugunov, K., H. Parzinger, and A. Nagler. *Der Goldschatz von Aržan. Ein Fürstengrab der Skythenzeit in der südsibirischen Steppe*. Munich: Schirmer/Mosel.

Curtis 2004
Curtis, J. "The Oxus Treasure in the British Museum." *Ancient Civilizations from Scythia to Siberia* 10(3/4): 293–338.

Dalton 1964
Dalton, O. *The Treasure of the Oxus, with Other Examples of Early Oriental Metal-work*. 3rd ed. London: Trustees of the British Museum.

Dandamayev 1979
Dandamayev, M. "Data of the Babylonian Documents from the 6th to the 5th Cent. B.C. on the Sakas." In *Prolegomena to the Sources on the History of Pre-Islamic Central Asia*, edited by J. Harmatta, 95–109. Budapest: Akadémiai Kiadó.

Dandamayev 1992
Dandamayev, M. *Iranians in Achaemenid Babylonia*. Columbia Lectures on Iranian Studies 6. Costa Mesa, CA: Mazda Publishers in association with Bibliotheca Persica.

Davis-Kimball et al. 2000
Davis-Kimball, J., E. Murphy, L. Koryakova, and L. Yablonsky, eds. *Kurgans, Ritual Sites, and Settlements: Eurasian Bronze and Iron Age*. BAR International Series 890. Oxford: Archaeopress.

Debaine-Francfort 1990
Debaine-Francfort, C. "Les Saka du Xinjiang avant les Han (206 av.–220 ap. J.-C.). Critères d'identification." In *Nomades et sédentaires en Asie centrale. Apports de l'archéologie et de l'ethnologie*, edited by H.-P. Francfort, 81–95. Proceedings, Colloque franco-soviétique, Alma Ata, Kazakhstan, October 17–26, 1987. Paris: Éditions du Centre national de la recherche scientifique.

Di Cosmo 1999
Di Cosmo, N. "State Formation and Periodization in Inner Asian History." *Journal of World History* 10(1): 1–40.

Di Cosmo 2002
Di Cosmo, N. *Ancient China and Its Enemies: The Rise of Nomadic Power in East Asian History*. Cambridge: Cambridge University Press.

Drews 2004
Drews, R. *Early Riders: The Beginnings of Mounted Warfare in Asia and Europe*. London: Routledge.

Fitzhugh 2009
Fitzhugh, W. "Pre-Scythian Ceremonialism, Deer Stone Art, and Cultural Intensification in Northern Mongolia." In *Social Complexity in Prehistoric Eurasia: Monuments, Metals and Mobility*, edited by B. Hanks and K. Linduff, 378–411. Cambridge: Cambridge University Press.

Fletcher 1986
Fletcher, J. "The Mongols: Ecological and Social Perspectives." *Harvard Journal of Asiatic Studies* 46(1): 11–50.

Frachetti 2008a
Frachetti M. *Pastoralist Landscapes and Social Interaction in Bronze Age Eurasia*. Berkeley: University of California Press.

Frachetti 2008b
Frachetti, M. "Variability and Dynamic Landscapes of Mobile Pastoralism in Ethnography and Prehistory." In Barnard and Wendrich 2008b, 366–96.

Frachetti et al. 2010
Frachetti, M., N. Benecke, A. Mar'yashev, and P. Doumani. "Eurasian Pastoralists and Their Shifting Regional Interactions at the Steppe Margin: Settlement History at Mukri, Kazakhstan." *World Archaeology* 42(4): 622–46.

Francfort 1998
Francfort, H.-P. "De l'art des steppes au sud du Taklamakan." *Bulletin of the Asia Institute*, n.s. 12: 45–58.

Francfort 1999
Francfort, H-P. "Il mausoleo ghiacciato del principe Scita/The Frozen Mausoleum of the Scythian Prince." *Ligabue Magazine* 18 (35): 24–63.

Francfort and Jacobson 2004
Francfort, H.-P., and E. Jacobson. "Approaches to the Study of Petroglyphs of North and Central Asia." *Archaeology, Ethnology, and Anthropology of Eurasia* 18: 53–78.

Francfort, Ligabue, and Samashev 2006
Francfort, H.-P., G. Ligabue, and Z. Samashev. "The Gold of the Griffins: Recent Excavations of a Frozen Tomb in Kazakhstan." In *The Golden Deer of Eurasia: Perspectives on the Steppe Nomads of the Ancient World*, edited by J. Aruz, A. Farkas, and E. Valtz Fino, 114–27. New York: The Metropolitan Museum of Art; New Haven: Yale University Press.

Garrison 1998
Garrison, M. "The Seals of Ašbazana (Aspathines)." In *Studies in Persian History: Essays in Memory of David M. Lewis*, edited by M. Brosius and A. Kuhrt, 113–39. Achaemenid History 11. Leiden: Nederlands Instituut voor het Nabije Oosten.

Garrison forthcoming
Garrison, M., and M. Root. *Seals on the Persepolis Fortification Tablets*. Vol. 2, *Images of Human Activity*. Chicago: Oriental Institute Publications.

Good 1995
Good, I. "On the Question of Silk in Pre-Han Eurasia." *Antiquity* 69: 959–568.

Gorbunov, Samashev, and Severskii 2005
Gorbunov, A., Z. Samashev, and E. Severskii. *The Treasures of Frozen Burial Mounds of the Kazakh Altai: Materials of the Berel Burial Site*. In English and Russian. Almaty: Ministry of Education and Science of the Republic of Kazakhstan, A. Kh. Margulan Institute of Archaeology.

Grjaznov 1984
Grjaznov, M. *Der Grosskurgan von Aržan in Tuva, Südsibirien*. Materialien zur allgemeinen und vergleichenden Archäologie 23. Munich: C. H. Beck, 1984.

Gryaznov 1969
Gryaznov, M. *The Ancient Civilization of Southern Siberia: An Archaeological Adventure*. Translated by J. Hogarth. New York: Cowles Book Company.

Guguev 1996
Guguev, V. "The Gold Jewelry Complex from the Kobyakov Pit-Burial." In *Ancient Jewelry and Archaeology*, edited by A. Calinescu, 51–61. Bloomington: Indiana University Press.

Hahn 1891
Hahn, E. "Waren die Menschen der Urzeit zwischen der Jägerstufe und der Stufe des Ackerbaus Nomaden?" *Das Ausland* 64: 481–87.

Hajdas et al. 2004
Hajdas, I., G. Bonani, I. Slusarenko, and M. Seifert. "Chronlogy of Pazyryk 2 and Ulandryk 4 Kurgans Based on High Resolution Radiocarbon Dating and Dendrochronology—A Step towards More Precise Dating of Scythian Burials." In *Impact of the Environment on Human Migration in Eurasia*, edited by E. Scott, A. Alekseev, and G. Zaitseva. NATO Science Series 4, Earth and Environmental Sciences 42. Dordrecht: Kluwer Academic.

Hanks 2000
Hanks, B. "Iron Age Nomadic Burials of the Eurasian Steppe: A Discussion Exploring Burial Ritual Complexity." In Davis-Kimball et al. 2000, 19–30.

Hanks 2001
Hanks, B. "Kurgan Mortuary Practices in the Eurasian Iron Age—Ideological Constructs and the Process of Rituality." In *Holy Ground: Theoretical Issues Relating to the Landscape and Material Culture of Ritual Space Objects*, edited by A. Smith and A. Brookes, 39–48. Papers from a session held at the Theoretical Archaeology Group Conference, Cardiff, 1999. BAR International Series 956. Oxford: Archaeopress.

Hanks 2002a
Hanks, B. "'The Eurasian Steppe 'Nomadic World' of the First Millennium BC: Inherent Problems within the Study of Iron Age Nomadic Groups." In Boyle, Renfrew, and Levine 2002, 183–98.

Hanks 2002b
Hanks, B. "Societal Complexity and Mortuary Rituality: Thoughts on the Nature of Archaeological Interpretation." In *Complex Societies of Central Eurasia from the 3rd to the 1st Millennium BC: Regional Specifics in Light of Global Models*, edited by K. Jones-Bley and D. G. Zdanovich. Vol. 2, *The Iron Age: Archaeoecology, Geoarchaeology, and Paleogeography; Beyond Central Eurasia*, 355–73. Journal of Indo-European Studies Monograph Series 45–46. Washington, DC: Institute for the Study of Man.

Hanks and Linduff 2009
Hanks, B., and K. Linduff, eds. *Social Complexity in Prehistoric Eurasia: Monuments, Metals, and Mobility*. Cambridge: Cambridge University Press.

Härke 1997
Härke, H. "The Nature of Burial Data." In *Burial and Society: The Chronological and Social Analysis of Archaeological Burial Data*, edited by C. K. Jensen and K. H. Nielsen, 19–27. Aarhus, Denmark: Aarhus University Press.

Harper 1978
Harper, P. *The Royal Hunter: Art of the Sasanian Empire*. Exh. cat., Asia House Gallery. New York: Asia Society

Harper et al. 1984
Harper, P., O. Muscarella, H. Pittman, and I. Spar. "Ancient Near Eastern Art." *The Bulletin of the Metropolitan Museum of Art* 41(4): 1–56.

Hind 2011
Hind, J. "The Black Sea: Between Asia and Europe (Herodotus' Approach to His Scythian Account)." In *The Black Sea, Greece, Anatolia and Europe in the First Millennium BC*, edited by G. Tsetskhladze, 77–93. Colloquia Antiqua 1. Leuven: Peeters.

Höllmann et al. 1992
Höllmann, T., G. Kossack, G. Tian, and S. Guo. *Maoqinggou. Ein eisenzeitliches Gräberfeld in der Ordos-Region (Innere Mongolei)*. Materialien zur allgemeinen und vergleichenden Archäologie 50. Mainz: Philipp von Zabern.

Holt 1988
Holt, F. *Alexander the Great and Bactria: The Formation of a Greek Frontier in Central Asia*. Mnemosyne, bibliotheca classica Batava, suppl. 104. Leiden: Brill.

Honeychurch and Amartuvshin 2008
Honeychurch, W., and C. Amartuvshin. "States on Horseback: The Rise of Inner Asian Confederations and Empires." In *Archaeology of Asia*, edited by M. Stark, 255–78. Cambridge: Blackwell.

Honeychurch, Wright, and Amartuvshin 2009
Honeychurch, W., J. Wright, and C. Amartuvshin. "Re-writing Monumental Landscapes as Inner Asian Political Process." In Hanks and Linduff 2009, 330–57.

Houle 2009
Houle, J.-L. "Socially Integrative Facilities and the Emergence of Societal Complexity on the Mongolian Steppe." In Hanks and Linduff 2009, 358–77.

Hulsewé and Loewe 1979
Hulsewé, A., and M. Loewe. *China in Central Asia: The Early Stage (125 B.C.–A.D. 23); An Annotated Translation of Chapters 61 and 96 of The History of the Former Han Dynasty*. Sinica Leidensia 14. Leiden: Brill.

Ilioukov 1995
Ilioukov, L. "Kobiakovo, le kourgane d'une princesse sarmate." In Schiltz 1995, 61–66.

Ivančik 1993
Ivančik, A. *Les Cimmériens au Proche-Orient*. Orbis biblicus et orientalis 127. Fribourg, Switzerland: Éditions Universitaires; Göttingen: Vandenhoeck & Ruprecht.

Ivančik 2001
Ivančik, A. *Kimmerier und Skythen. Kulturhistorische und chronologische Probleme der Archäologie der osteuropäischen Steppen und Kaukasiens in vor- und frühskythischer Zeit*. Steppenvölker Eurasiens 2. Moscow: Paleograph Press.

Ivantchik 2011
Ivantchik, A. "The Funeral of Scythian Kings: The Historical Reality and the Description of Herodotus (4.71–72)." In *The Barbarians of Ancient Europe: Realities and Interactions*, edited by L. Bonfante, 71–106. New York: Cambridge University Press.

Jacobson 1987
Jacobson, E. *Burial Ritual, Gender and Status in South Siberia in the Late Bronze– Early Iron Age*. Papers on Inner Asia 7. Bloomington: Indiana University, Research Institute for Inner Asian Studies.

Jacobson 1993
Jacobson, E. *The Deer Goddess of Ancient Siberia: A Study in the Ecology of Belief*. Studies in the History of Religions 55. Leiden: Brill.

Jamzadeh 1996
Jamzadeh, P. "The Achaemenid Throne-Leg Design." *Iranica Antiqua* 31: 101–46.

Jensen and Nielsen 1997
Jensen, C., and K. Nielsen, eds. *Burial and Society: The Chronological and Social Analysis of Archaeological Burial Data*. Aarhus, Denmark: Aarhus University Press.

Jettmar 1967
Jettmar, K. *Art of the Steppes*. Art of the World. New York: Greystone.

Khazanov 1983
Khazanov, A. *Nomads and the Outside World*. Translated by J. Crookenden. Cambridge Studies in Social Anthropology 44. Cambridge: Cambridge University Press.

Khazanov 1994
Khazanov, A. *Nomads and the Outside World*. Translated by J. Crookenden. 2nd ed. Madison: University of Wisconsin Press.

Klochkov 1997
Klochkov, I. "Two Cylinder Seals From a Sarmatian Grave Near Kosika." *Ancient Civilizations from Scythia to Siberia* 3(1): 38–48.

Knauer 2001
Knauer, E. "Observations on the 'Barbarian' Custom of Suspending the Heads of Vanquished Enemies from the Neck of Horses." *Archäologische Mitteilungen aus Iran und Turan* 33: 283–332.

Koryakova and Epimakhov 2007
Koryakova, L., and A. Epimakhov. *The Urals and Western Siberia in the Bronze and Iron Ages*. Cambridge World Archaeology. Cambridge: Cambridge University Press.

Kossack 1987
Kossack, G. "Von den Anfängen des skytho-iranischen Tierstils." In *Skythika. Vorträge zur Entstehung des skytho-iranischen Tierstils und zu Denkmälern des Bosporanischen Reichs*, edited by H. Francke, 24–86. Proceedings, Ausstellung der Leningrader Eremitage, Munich, September 7, 1984. Abhandlungen (Bayerische Akademie der Wissenschaften, Philosophisch-Historische Klasse), n.F. 98. Munich: Verlag der Bayerischen Akademie der Wissenschaften.

Kradin 2002
Kradin, N. "Nomadism, Evolution and World-Systems: Pastoral Societies in Theories of Historical Development." *Journal of World-Systems Research* 8(3): 368–88.

Kuhrt 2007
Kuhrt, A. *The Persian Empire: A Corpus of Sources from the Achaemenid Period*. London: Routledge.

Kuz'mina 1977
Kuz'mina, E. "Les relations entre la Bactriane et l'Iran du VIIIè au IVè siècle av. J.C." In *Le Plateau iranien et l'Asie centrale des origines à la conquête islamique. Leurs relations à la lumière des documents archéologiques*, edited by J. Deshayes, 201–14. Proceedings, March 22–24, 1976. Colloques internationaux du Centre National de la Recherche Scientifique 567. Paris: Éditions du Centre national de la recherche scientifique.

Kyrieleis 1969
Kyrieleis, H. *Throne und Klinen. Studien zur Formgeschichte altorientalischer und griechischer Sitz- und Liegemöbel vorhellenistischer Zeit*. Jahrbuch des Deutschen Archäologischen Instituts (Ergänzungsheft) 24. Berlin: De Gruyter.

Lenfant 2004
Lenfant, D. *Ctésias de Cnide. La Perse. L'Inde. Autres fragments. Texte établis, tradui et commenté*. Collection des Universités de France publiée sous le patronage de l'Association Guillaume Budé. Paris: Les Belles Lettres.

Lerner 1991
Lerner, J. "Some So-Called Achaemenid Objects from Pazyryk." *Source: Notes in the History of Art* 10(4): 8–15.

Linduff 2009
Linduff, K. "Chinese Production of Signature Artifacts for the Nomad Market in Zhou China." In *Metallurgy and Civilisation: Eurasia and Beyond (in association with the University of Science and Technology, Beijing and the Institute for Archaeo-Metallurgical Studies, London)*, edited by J. Mei and T. Rehren, 90–96. Proceedings, 6th International Conference on the Beginnings of the Use of Metals and Alloys, Beijing. London: Archetype in association with the University of Science and Technology, Beijing, and the Institute for Archaeo-Metallurgical Studies, London.

Linduff and Rubinson forthcoming
Linduff, K., and K. Rubinson. "Gender Archaeology in East Asia and Eurasia." In *A Companion to Gender Prehistory*, edited by Diane Bolger. New York: Blackwell, forthcoming.

Marsadolov and Maršak 2000
Marsadolov, L., and B. I. Maršak. "Early Indian Mirrors and the Problem of the Pre-Mauryan Figurative Art." In *South Asian Archaeology, 1997*, edited by M. Taddei and G. de Marco, 1953–63. Proceedings, Fourteenth International Conference of the European Association of South Asian Archaeologists, Rome, July 7–14, 1997. Serie orientale Roma (Istituto italiano per l'Africa e l'Oriente) 90. Roma: Istituto italiano per l'Africa e l'Oriente.

McGahern et al. 2006
McGahern, A., M. Bower, C. Edwards, P. Brophy, G. Sulimova, I. Zakharov., M. Vizuete-Forster, M. Levine, S. Li, D. MacHugh, and E. Hill. "Evidence for Biogeographic Patterning of Mitochrondrial DNA Sequences in Eastern Horse Populations." *Animal Genetics* 37(5): 494–97.

McHugh 1999
McHugh, F. *Theoretical and Quantitative Approaches to the Study of Mortuary Practice*. BAR International Series 785. Oxford: Archaeopress.

Melikian-Chirvani 1993
Melikian-Chirvani, A. "The International Achaemenid Style." *Bulletin of the Asia Institute* 7: 111–30.

Metropolitan Museum of Art 1975
Metropolitan Museum of Art. *From the Lands of the Scythians: Ancient Treasurers from the Museums of the U.S.S.R., 3000 B.C.–100 B.C.* New York: The Metropolitan Museum of Art.

Moorey 1998
Moorey, P. "Material Aspects of Achaemenid Polychrome Decoration and Jewellery." *Iranica Antiqua* 33: 155–72.

Nickel 1989
Nickel, H. "The Emperor's New Saddle Cloth: The Ephippium of the Equestrian Statue of Marcus Aurelius." *Metropolitan Museum Journal* 24: 17–24.

Olschki 1946
Olschki, L. *Guillaume Boucher: A French Artist at the Court of the Khans*. Baltimore: The Johns Hopkins Press.

Olsen 2003
Olsen, S. "The Exploitation of Horses at Botai, Kazakhstan." In *Prehistoric Steppe Adaptation and the Horse*, edited by M. Levine, C. Renfrew, and K. Boyle, 83–103. Cambridge: McDonald Institute Monographs. Cambridge: McDonald Institute for Archaeological Research.

Outram et al. 2009
Outram, A., N. Stear, R. Bendrey, S. Olsen, A. Kasparov, V. Zaibert, N. Thorpe, and R. Evershed. "The Earliest Horse Harnessing and Milking." *Science* 323(5919): 1332–35.

Parker Pearson 1982
Parker Pearson, M. "Mortuary Practices, Society and Ideology: An Ethnoarchaeological Study." In *Symbolic and Structural Archaeology*, edited by I. Hodder, 99–113. New Directions in Archaeology. Cambridge: Cambridge University Press, 1982.

Parker Pearson 2000
Parker Pearson, M. *The Archaeology of Death and Burial*. Texas A&M University Anthropology Series 3. College Station: Texas A&M University Press.

Parzinger 2006
Parzinger, H. *Die frühen Völker Eurasiens. Vom Neolithikum bis zum Mittelalter*. Munich: C. H. Beck.

Parzinger 2008
Parzinger, H. "The Scythians: Nomadic Horsemen of the Eurasian Steppe." In *Preservation of the Frozen Tombs of the Altai Mountains*, edited by J. Han, 19–24. UNESCO Publications. http://whc.unesco.org/uploads/news/documents/news-433-1.pdf.

Paul 2004
Paul, J. "Perspectives nomades. État et structures militaires." *Annales. Histoire, Sciences Sociales* 59(5/6): 1069–93.

Polosmak 1991
Polosmak, N. "Un nouveau kourgane à 'tombe gelée' de l'Altaï (rapport préliminaire)." *Arts Asiatiques* 46: 5–20.

Polosmak 1994
Polosmak, N. "The Ak-Alakh 'Frozen Grave' Barrow." *Ancient Civilizations from Scythia to Siberia* 1(3): 346–54.

Polosmak 1999
Polosmak, N. "The Burial of a Noble Pazyryk Woman." *Ancient Civilizations from Scythia to Siberia* 5(2): 125–63.

Polosmak and Trunova 2004
Polosmak, N., and V. Trunova. "An Analysis of Pazyryk Hair." *Archaeology, Ethnography and Anthropology of Eurasia* 1(17) 2004: 73–80.

Porada 1967
Porada, E. "Battlements in the Military Architecture and in the Symbolism of the Ancient Near East." In *Essays in the History of Architecture Presented to Rudolph Wittkower*, edited by D. Fraser, H. Hibbard, and M. Lewine, 1–12. London: Phaidon.

Renfrew 2002
Renfrew, C. "Pastoralism and Interaction: Some Introductory Questions." In Boyle, Renfrew, and Levine 2002, 1–12.

Rubinson 1990
Rubinson, K. "The Textiles from Pazyryk: A Study in the Transfer and Transformation of Artistic Motifs." *Expedition* 32(1): 49–61.

Rubinson 2006
Rubinson, K. "Helmets and Mirrors: Markers of Social Transformation." In *The Golden Deer of Eurasia: Perspectives on the Steppe Nomads of the Ancient World*, edited by J. Aruz, A. Farkas, and E. Valtz Fino, 32–39. New York: The Metropolitan Museum of Art; New Haven: Yale University Press.

Rudenko 1970
Rudenko, S. *Frozen Tombs of Siberia: The Pazyryk Burials of Iron Age Horsemen.* Translated and with a preface by M. Thompson. Berkeley: University of California Press.

Salzman 2004
Salzman, P. *Pastoralists: Equality, Hierarchy, and the State.* Boulder, CO: Westview.

Samašev 2007
Samašev, Z. "Die Fürstengräber von Berel'." In *Im Zeichen des Goldenen Greifen: Königsgräber der Skythen*, edited by W. Menghin, 132–39. Exh. cat. Martin-Gropius-Bau, Berlin; Kunsthalle der Hypo-Kulturstiftung, Munich; Museum für Kunst und Gewerbe, Hamburg. Munich: Prestel.

Samashev 2006
Samashev, Z. "Culture of the Nomadic Elite of Kazakhstan's Altai Region (Based on Materials from the Berel Necropolis)." In Chang and Guroff 2006, 35–44.

Samashev, Bazarbaeva, and Zhumabekova 2002
Samashev, Z., G. Bazarbaeva, and G. Zhumabekova. "Die 'goldhütenden Greife' des Herodot und die archäologische Kultur der frühen Nomaden im kazachischen Altai: Skythenzeitliche Kurgane von Berel' und Tar Asu." *Eurasia Antiqua* 8: 237–76.

Samashev and Borodovskii 2004
Samashev, Z., and A. Borodovskii. "Decorative Horn Horse Trappings from the Berel Necropolis." In English and Russian. *Archaeology, Ethnology and Anthropology of Eurasia* 3(19): 82–87.

Samashev and Mylnikov 2004
Samashev, Z., and V. Mylnikov. *Woodworking of Ancient Cattle-Breeders of Kazakh Altai: Materials of Complex Analysis of Wooden Objects from Barrow 11 of Berel Burial Ground.* In English and Russian. Almaty: Ministry of Education and Science of the Republic of Kazakhstan, A. Kh. Margulan Institute of Archaeology.

Samashev et al. 2000a
Samashev, Z., G. Bazarbaeva, G. Zhumabekova, and S. Sungatai. *Berel.* In Kazakh, Russian, and English. Almaty: Ministry of Education and Science of the Republic of Kazakhstan, A. Kh. Margulan Institute of Archaeology.

Samashev et al. 2000b
Samashev, Z., G. Bazarbaeva, S. Zhumabekova, and H.-P. Francfort. "Le kourgane de Berel' dans l'Altaï kazakhstanais." *Arts Asiatiques* 55: 5–20.

Schiltz 1995
Schiltz, V., ed. *Entre Asie et Europe. L'or des Sarmates; Nomades des steppes dans l'antiquité.* Exh. cat. Daoulas, France: Centre culturel Abbaye de Daoulas.

Scholz 1995
Scholz, F. *Nomadismus. Theorie und Wandel einer sozio-ökologischen Kulturweise.* Erdkundliches Wissen 118. Stuttgart: F. Steiner.

Scott, Alekseev, and Zaitseva 2004
Scott, E., A. Alekseev, and G. Zaitseva. *Impact of the Environment on Human Migration in Eurasia.* Proceedings, NATO Advanced Research Workshop on Impact of the Environment on Human Migration in Eurasia, St. Petersburg, Russia, November 15–18, 2003. Dordrecht, The Netherlands: Kluwer.

Sevinç et al. 2001
Sevinç, N., R. Körpe, M. Tombul, C. Rose, D. Strahan, H. Kiesewetter, and J. Wallrodt. "A New Painted Graeco-Persian Sarcophagus from Çan." *Studia Troica* 11: 383–420.

Sher 1988
Sher, Y. "On the Sources of the Scythic Animal Style." *Arctic Anthropology* 25(2): 47–60. Seeman-Beiträge zur Kunstwissenschaft Leipzig: Seeman-Verlag.

Sneath 2007
Sneath, D. *The Headless State: Aristocratic Orders, Kinship Society, and Misrepresentations of Nomadic Inner Asia.* New York: Columbia University Press.

Spengler, Chang, and Tourtellotte n.d.
Spengler, R., C. Chang, and P. Tourtellotte. "Agricultural Production in the Central Asian Mountains at the Dawn of the Silk Route: Tuzusai, Kazakhstan (410–150 BC)." Unpublished manuscript, Department of Anthropology, Sweet Briar College, Sweet Briar, VA.

Stark 2002
Stark, S. "Nomaden und Sesshafte in Mittel- und Zentralasien. Nomadische Adaptionsstrategien am Fallbeispiel der Alttürken." In *Grenzüberschreitungen. Formen des Kontakts zwischen Orient und Okzident im Altertum*, edited by M. Schuol, U. Hartmann, and A. Luther, 363–404. Oriens et Occidens 3. Stuttgart: F. Steiner.

Stark 2008
Stark, S. *Die Alttürkenzeit in Mittel- und Zentralasien. Archäologische und historische Studien.* Nomaden und Sesshafte 6. Wiesbaden: L. Reichert.

Taylor 2010
Taylor, T. "Modeling the 'Amazon' Phenomenon: Colonization Events and Gender Performances." In *Eventful Archaeologies: New Approaches to Social Transformation in the Archaeological Record*, edited by Douglas J. Bolender, 132–50. The Institute for European and Mediterranean Archaeology Distinguished Monograph series, IEMA Proceedings, 1. Albany: State University of New York Press.

Togan 1998
Togan, I. *Flexibility and Limitation in Steppe Formations: The Kerait Khanate and Chinggis Khan.* Ottoman Empire and Its Heritage 15. Leiden: Brill.

Toleubaev 2006
Toleubaev, A. "Snow Leopards, Eagle-Felines, and Golden Deer: Treasures from the 'Hill of Horse Races.'" In Chang and Guroff 2006, 51–55.

Treister 2010
Treister, M. "'Achaemenid' and 'Achaemenid-Inspired' Goldware and Silverware, Jewellery and Arms and Their Imitations to the North of the Achaemenid Empire." In *Achaemenid Impact in the Black Sea: Communication of Powers*, edited by J. Nieling and E. Rehm. Black Sea Studies 11. Aarhus, Denmark: Aarhus University Press.

Tseng 2011
Tseng, L. *Picturing Heaven in Early China.* Harvard East Asian Monographs 336. Cambridge, Mass.: Harvard University Asia Center for the Harvard-Yenching Institute.

Vogelsang 1992
Vogelsang, W. *The Rise and Organisation of the Achaemenid Empire: The Eastern Iranian Evidence.* Studies in the History of the Ancient Near East 3. Leiden: Brill.

Wagner et al. 2011
Wagner, M., X. Wu, P. Tarasov, A. Aisha, C. Ramsey, M. Schultz, T. Schmidt-Schultz, and J. Gresky. "Radiocarbon-Dated Archaeological Record of Early First Millenium B.C. Mounted Pastoralists in the Kunlun Mountains, China." *Proceedings of the National Academy of Sciences of the United States of America*, 1–6.

Wallace 2012
Wallace, L. "Betwixt and Between: Depictions of Immortals in Eastern Han Dynasty Tomb Reliefs (25–220 CE)." *Ars Orientalis* 41 (forthcoming).

Walser 1966
Walser, G. *Die Völkerschaften auf den Reliefs von Persepolis.* Teheraner Forschungen 2. Berlin: Mann.

Wang 1987
Wang, B. "Recherches historiques préliminaires sur les Saka du Xinjiang ancien." *Arts Asiatiques* 42: 31–44.

Watt 2002
Watt, J. "The Legacy of Nomadic Art in China and Eastern Central Asia." In *Nomadic Art of the Eastern Eurasian Steppes: The Eugene V. Thaw and Other New York Collections*, edited by E. Bunker, 199–209. Exh. cat. New York: The Metropolitan Museum of Art.

Wu 2010
Wu, X. "Enemies of Empire: A Historical Reconstruction of Political Conflicts between Central Asia and the Persian Empire." In *The World of Achaemenid Persia: History, Art and Society in Iran and the Ancient Near East*, edited by J. Curtis and S. Simpson, 545–63. Proceedings of a conference at the British Museum, London, September 29–October 1, 2005. London: I. B. Tauris.

Yablonsky 2000
Yablonsky, L. "'Scythian Triad' and 'Scythian World' Kurgans." In Davis-Kimball et al. 2000, 3–8.

Zaitseva et al. 2007
Zaitseva, G., K. Ghugnov, A. Alekseev, V. Gergachev, S. Vasiliev, A. Sementsov, G. Cood, E. Scott, J. Plicht, H. Parzinger, A. Nagler, H. Jungner, E. Sonninen, and N. Bourova. "Chronology of Key Barrows Belonging to Different Stages of the Scythian Period in Tuva (Arzhan-1 and Arzhan-2 Barrows). *Radiocarbon* 49(2): 645–58.

Zassetskaia 1995
Zassetskaia, I. "Le kourgane 'Khokhlatch,' ou trésor de Novotcherkassk." In Schiltz, 55–60.

Zhu 1992
Zhu Xilu, ed. *Jiaxiang Han huaxiang shi* [Han carved stones in Jiaxiang]. Jinan, People's Republic of China: Shandong meishu chubanshe.

Акишев 1973
Акишев, К. А. "Саки азиатские и скифы европейские (общее и особенное в культуре)". *Археологические исследования в Казахстане*, 43–58. Алма-Ата: Наука.

Акишев 1978
Акишев, К. А. *Курган Иссык*. Москва: Искусство.

Акишев 1984
Акишев, К. А. *Искусство и мифология саков*. Алма-Ата: Наука.

Акишев и Кушаев 1963
Акишев, К. А., Кушаев, Г. А. *Древняя культура саков и усуней долины реки Или*. Алма-Ата: Наука.

Акишев и Акишев 1997
Акишев, К. А, Акишев, А. К. "Саки Жетысу: социум и культура". *Новости Археологии*, 30–37. Туркестан.

Алексеев и др. 2005
Алексеев, А. Ю., Боковенко, Н. А., Васильев, С. С., Дергачев, В. А., Зайцева, Г. И., Ковалюх, Н. Н., Кук, Г., ван дер Плихт, Й., Посснерт, Г., Семенцов, А. А., Скотт, Е. М., Чугунов, К. В. *Евразия в скифскую эпоху. Радиоуглеродная и археологическая хронология*. Санкт-Петербург: Теза.

Алексеев 1974
Алексеев, В. П. "Новые данные о европеоидной расе в Центральной Азии". *Бронзовый и железный век в Сибири*, 370–90. Новосибирск: Наука.

Алимбай 2004
Алимбай, Н. "Евразийское кочевничество как общинный тип социальности. Введение в проблематику". *Урбанизация и номадизм в Центральной Азии: история и проблемы (материалы международной научной конференции)*, 185–93. Алматы: Дайк Пресс.

Алимбай 2009а
Алимбай, Н. "Кочевая община казахов: проблемы этносоциологической реконструкции". *Известия Российского государственного педагогического университета им. А. И. Герцена* 96: 317–25.

Алимбай 2009b
Алимбай, Н. "Казахское шежире как фольклорный жанр (вопросы изучения шежире как исторического источника)". *Труды Центрального музея* 2: 373–86. Алматы.

Ануфриев 1997
Ануфриев, Д. Е. "Социальное устройство пазырыкского общества Горного Алтая". *Социально-экономические структуры древних обществ западной Сибири (материалы всероссийской научной конференции)*, 108–11. Барнаул.

Арсланова 1974
Арсланова, Ф. Х. "Погребальный комплекс VIII–VII веков до нашей эры из Восточного Казахстана". *В глубь веков*, 46–60. Алма-Ата: Наука.

Артамонов 1966
Артамонов, М. И. *Сокровища скифских курганов в собрании Государственного Эрмитажа*. Прага: Артия; Ленинград: Советский художник.

Баркова 2009
Баркова, Л. Л. "Новые исследования импортных тканей из Больших Алтайских курганов". *Сообщения Государственного Эрмитажа* 67: 5–21.

Бейсенов 2010
Бейсенов, А. З. "К изучению особенностей крупных курганов раннего железного века Центрального Казахстана". *Материалы II Международной научной конференции "Кадырбаевские чтения—2010"*, 77–79. Актобе.

Беленицкий и Распопова 1980
Беленицкий, А. М., Распопова, В. И. "Согдийские «золотые пояса»". *Страны и народы Востока* 22: 213–18.

Бернштам 1940
Бернштам, А. Н. "Золотая диадема из шаманского погребения на р. Каргалинке". *Краткие сообщения института материальной культуры* 5: 23–31.

Боковенко 1986а
Боковенко, Н. А. *Начальный этап культуры ранних кочевников Саяно-Алтая (по материалам конского снаряжения)*. Автореферат диссертации на соискание научной степени кандидата исторических наук. Ленинград.

Боковенко 1986b
Боковенко, Н. А. *Начальный этап культуры ранних кочевников Саяно-Алтая*. Ленинград: Наука.

Боковенко 1992
Боковенко, Н. А. "К проблеме реконструкции конских уборов скифской эпохи Южной Сибири". *Северная Евразия от древности до средневековья (тезисы конференции к 90-летию со дня рождения М.П. Грязнова)*, 123–25. Санкт-Петербург.

Боковенко 2008
Боковенко, Н. А. "Формирование конфедераций номадов Центральной Азии и миграции скифо-сакских племен". *Номады казахской степи: этносоциокультурные процессы и контакты в Евразии скифо-сакской эпохи*, 134–46. Астана.

Боковенко и Красниенко 1987
Боковенко, Н. А., Красниенко, С. В. "Могильник Медведка II на юге Хакасии". *Памятники археологии в зонах мелиорации Южной Сибири*, 23–45. Ленинград: Наука.

Бородовский 1999
Бородовский, А. П. "Центры художественной косторезной обработки скифской эпохи на юге Западной Сибири". *Итоги изучения скифской эпохи Алтая и сопредельных территорий*, 23–26. Барнаул: Издательство Алтайского университета.

Бородовский 2005
Бородовский, А. П. "Упряжь и раскрой рога в Западной Сибири (по материалам археологии и этнографии)". *Западная и Южная Сибирь в древности (сборник научных трудов, посвященных 60-летию со дня рождения Ю. Ф. Кирюшина)*, 58–62. Барнаул: Издательство Алтайского университета.

Вайнберг, Горбунова и Мошкова 1992
Вайнберг, Б. В., Горбунова, Н. И., Мошкова, М. Г. "Основные проблемы в изучении памятников древних скотоводов Средней Азии и Казахстана." *Степная полоса Азиатской части СССР в скифо-сарматское время*, 21–30. Археология СССР. Москва: Наука.

Вайнштейн 1991
Вайнштейн, С. И. *Мир кочевников центра Азии*. Москва: Наука.

Варёнов 1994
Варёнов, А. В. "Бронзовые шлемы на границах чжоуского Китая и их кубанские аналоги". *Древние культуры Южной Сибири и Северо-восточного Китая*, под редакцией В. Е. Ларичева и Л. Юнь, 86–94. Новосибирск: Наука.

Васильков 2004
Васильков, Я. В. "Древние индийские зеркала из скифо-сарматских курганов Алтая и Южного Приуралья". *Степи Евразии в древности и средневековье. Материалы международной научной конференции, посвящённой 100-летию со дня рождения М. П. Грязнова*, под редакцией Ю. Ю. Пиотровского, 28–33. Санкт-Петербург: Издательство Государственного Эрмитажа.

Васютин 2002
Васютин, С. А. "Типология потестарных и политических систем кочевников". *Кочевая альтернатива социальной эволюции. Цивилизационное измерение*, т. 6, 63–71. Москва: Институт Африки РАН.

Васютин 2003
Васютин, С. А. "Моделирование потестарно-политической системы пазырыкского общества". *Исторический опыт хозяйственного и культурного освоения Западной Сибири. Сборник научных трудов*, кн. 1, 19–24. Барнаул: Издательство Алтайского университета.

Виданова 1938
Виданова, Е. С. "Катандинский халат (по материалам реставрационной мастерской Государственного Исторического Музея)". *Труды Государственного Исторического Музея* 8, 169–78. Ленинград.

Волков 1978
Волков, В. В. "Улангомский могильник (по материалам раскопок 1972 г.)". *Археология и этнография Монголии*, 101–7. Новосибирск: Наука.

Волков 1981
Волков, В. В. *Оленные камни Монголии*. Улан-Батор: Научный мир.

Галанина 1997
Галанина, Л. К. *Келермесские курганы. "Царские" погребения раннескифской эпохи*. Москва: Палеограф.

Горбунов, Самашев и Северский 2005
Горбунов, А. П., Самашев, З. С., Северский, Э. В. *Сокровища мерзлых курганов Казахского Алтая*. Алматы: Иль-Тех-Кітап.

Грач 1980
Грач, А. Д. *Древние кочевники в центре Азии*. Москва: Наука.

Грязнов 1950
Грязнов, М. П. *Первый Пазырыкский курган*. Ленинград: Издательство Государственного Эрмитажа.

Грязнов 1961
Грязнов, М. П. "Древнейшие памятники героического эпоса народов Южной Сибири". *Археологический сборник Государственного Эрмитажа* 3: 7–31. Ленинград.

Грязнов 1968
Грязнов, М. П. "Тагарская культура". *История Сибири*, т. 1, 187–96. Ленинград: Наука.

Грязнов 1980
Грязнов, М. П. *Аржан: царский курган раннескифского времени*. Ленинград: Наука.

Грязнов 1992
Грязнов, М. П. "Алтай и Приалтайская степь". *Степная полоса Азиатской части СССР в скифо-сарматское время*, 161–78. Археология СССР. Москва: Наука.

Дженито 1994
Дженито, Б. "Археология и современные концепции социальной организации кочевников". *Статистическая обработка погребальных памятников азиатской Сарматии*, вып. I, Савроматская эпоха, 11–17. Москва: Восточная литература.

Жаутиков 2006
Жаутиков, Т. М. "Геология и золотоносность Шиликтинской долины". *Отчет Шиликтинской археологической экспедиции*. Алматы.

Завитухина 1983
Завитухина, М. П. *Древнее искусство на Енисее. Скифское время*. Ленинград: Издательство Государственного Эрмитажа.

Збруева 1952
Збруева, А. В. *История населения Прикамья в ананьинскую эпоху*. Материалы и исследования по археологии СССР 30. Москва/Ленинград: Издательство Академии Наук СССР.

Ибрагимов и др. 1969
Ибрагимов, С. К., Мингулов, Н. Н., Пищулина, К. А., Юдин, В. П. *Материалы по истории казахских ханств XV–XVIII веков*. Алма-ата: Наука.

Иванов, Луконин и Смесова 1984
Иванов, А. А., Луконин, В. Г., Смесова, Л. С. *Ювелирные изделия Востока. Коллекция особой кладовой отдела Востока Государственного Эрмитажа. Древний, средневековый периоды*. Москва: Искусство.

Игуменшева 2011
Игуменшева, Е. В. "Пути проникновения импортных изделий на территорию Южного Приуралья в «савроматскую» и раннесарматскую эпохи (историография проблемы)". *Российская Археология* 2011(1): 62–67.

Исмагулова 2008
Исмагулова, А. О. *Антропологические исследования остеологических материалов и скульптурная реконструкция шиликтинского «золотого человека»*. Научный отчет. Алматы.

Кадырбаев и Марьяшев 1977
Кадырбаев, М. К., Марьяшев, А. Н. *Наскальные изображения хребта Каратау*. Алма-Ата: Наука.

Казахское хозяйство 1926
Казахское хозяйство в его естественно-исторических и бытовых условиях: материалы к выработке норм земельного устройства в КазАССР. Ленинград.

Кашкинбаев 2008a
Кашкинбаев, К. А. *Макроскопические, микроскопические и физико-химические исследования проб из Шиликтинского погребального комплекса.* Рукопись отчета. Алматы.

Кашкинбаев 2008b
Кашкинбаев, К. А. "Остеопатология берельских лошадей". *Номады казахских степей: этносоциокультурные процессы и контакты в Евразии скифо-сакской эпохи* (сборник материалов международной научной конференции), 340–41. Астана.

Кашкинбаев и Самашев 2005
Кашкинбаев, К. А., Самашев, З. С. *Лошади древних кочевников Казахского Алтая.* Алматы: Археология.

Киселёв 1951
Киселёв, С. В. *Древняя история Южной Сибири.* Москва.

Клочко 1992
Клочко, Л. С. "Скифская обувь". *Советская археология* 1992(1): 26–33.

Кляшторный и Савинов 1998
Кляшторный, С. Г., Савинов, Д. Г. "Пазырыкская узда. К предыстории хунно-юечжийских войн". *Древние культуры Центральной Азии и Санкт-Петербург. Материалы всероссийской научной конференции, посвященной 70-летию со дня рождения А. Д. Грача,* 169–77. Санкт-Петербург: Культ-информ-пресс.

Кореняко 2002
Кореняко, В. А. *Искусство народов Центральной Азии и звериный стиль.* Москва: Восточная литература.

Королькова 2006
Королькова, Е. Ф. *Звериный стиль Евразии.* Санкт-Петербург: Петербургское востоковедение.

Крадин 2002
Крадин, Н. Н. *Империя Хунну.* Москва: Логос.

Кубарев 1987
Кубарев, В. Д. *Курганы Уландрыка.* Новосибирск: Наука.

Кубарев 1991
Кубарев, В. Д. *Курганы Юстыда.* Новосибирск: Наука.

Кузнецов 1960
Кузнецов, А.Т. "Климатические особенности Казахстана". *Вопросы географии Казахстана. Труды отдела географии,* вып. 7, 108–35. Алма-Ата.

Левушкина 1987
Левушкина, С. В. "О возникновении шелководства в античной Бактрии". *Общественные науки в Узбекистане* 9: 44–47.

Лубо-Лесниченко 1987
Лубо-Лесниченко, Е. И. "Пазырык и Западный Меридиональный путь". *Страны и народы Востока* 25: 233–48.

Лубо-Лесниченко 1994
Лубо-Лесниченко, Е. И. *Китай на Шелковом пути. Шелк и внешние связи древнего и раннесредневекового Китая. Культура народов Востока.* Москва: Восточная литература.

Майтдинова 2003
Майтдинова, Г. М. *История костюма таджикского народа,* т. 1: Генезис костюма таджиков (древность и раннее средневековье). Душанбе.

Максимова, Ермолаев и Марьяшев 1985
Максимова, А. Г., Ермолаев, А. С., Марьяшев, А. Н. *Наскальные изображения Тамгалы.* Алма-Ата: Өнер.

Маргулан и др. 1966
Маргулан, А. Х., Акишев, К. А., Кадырбаев, Т. К., Оразбаев, А. Т. *Древняя культура Центрального Казахстана.* Алма-Ата: Наука.

Марсадолов 2000
Марсадолов, Л. С. *Археологические памятники IX–III веков до н.э. горных районов Алтая как культурно-исторический источник (феномен пазырыкской культуры).* Автореферат диссертации на соискание ученой степени доктора культурологии. Санкт-Петербург.

Марсадолов 2010
Марсадолов, Л. С. "Переднеазиатские серебряные поясные накладки из кургана Пазырык-2 на Алтае". *Торевтика в древних и средневековых культурах Евразии,* под редакцией А. А. Тишкина. *Труды Сибирской Ассоциации исследователей первобытного искусства* 6, 71–75. Барнаул.

Мартынов 1955
Мартынов, Г. С. "Иссыкская находка". *Краткие сообщения института материальной культуры* 59: 150–56.

Мартынов 1989
Мартынов, А. И. "О степной скотоводческой цивилизации I тыс. до н.э.". *Взаимодействие кочевых культур и древних цивилизаций,* 184–292. Алма-Ата: Наука.

Масанов 1995
Масанов, Н. Е. *Кочевая цивилизация казахов (основы жизнедеятельности номадного общества).* Алматы: Социнвест; Москва: Горизонт.

Мацкевич 1929
Мацкевич, Н. Н. "Сравнительная длина кочевок казахского населения бывшей Семипалатинской губернии". *Записки Семипалатинского отдела общества изучения Казахстана* 18: 1–30.

Мачинский 1971
Мачинский, Д. А. "О времени первого активного выступления сарматов в Поднепровье по свидетельствам античных письменных источников". *Археологический сборник Государственного Эрмитажа* 13: 30–54.

Мачинский 1997
Мачинский, Д. А. "Сакральные центры Скифии близ Кавказа и Алтая и их взаимосвязи в конце IV—середине I тыс. до н.э.". *Стратум: структуры и катастрофы. Сборник символической индоевропейской истории,* 73–94. Санкт-Петербург.

Миносян 2008
Миносян, Р. С. "Технология и техника изготовления шиликтинских золотых изделий". *Исследование, реконструкция и публикация шиликтинского золотого человека,* 18–32. Научный отчет. Алматы.

Мирошина 1977
Мирошина, Т. В. "Об одном типе скифских головных уборов". *Советская археология* 1977(3): 79–94.

Молодин 2000
Молодин, В. И. "Пазырыкская культура: проблемы этногенеза, этнической истории и исторических судеб". *Археология, этнография и антропология Евразии* 4(4): 131–42.

Молодин и др. 2000
Молодин, В. И., Ромащенко, А. Г., Воевода, М. И., Чикишева, Т. А. "Мультидисциплинарный анализ носителей пазырыкской культуры (археология, антропология, генетика)". *Скифы и сарматы в VII–III веках до н.э.: палеоэкология, антропология и археология (сборник статей),* 59–66. Москва: РАН ИА, ГИМ

Мургабаев 2008
Мургабаев, С. "Үлкен Қаратау петроглифтеріндегі ерте темір кезеңінің бейнелері". *Қазақ даласының көшпенділері: Еуразиядағы скиф-сақ дәуіріндегі этноәлеуметтік-мәдени үрдістер мен қарым-қатынастар,* 258–66. Астана.

Мургабаев 2010
Мургабаев, С. "Үлкен қаратаудың жартас суретіндегі «ойсыл қара» стилі". *Материалы II международной научной конференции "Кадырбаевские чтения—2010"*, 58–63. Актобе.

Новгородова 1989
Новгородова, Э. А. *Древняя Монголия*. Москва: Наука.

Новоженов 2002
Новоженов, В. А. *Петроглифы Сары Арки*. Алматы: Издательство ИА им. А. Х. Маргулана, МОН РК.

Переводчикова 1994
Переводчикова, Е. В. *Язык звериных образов. Очерки искусства евразийских степей скифской эпохи*. Москва: Восточная литература.

Полосьмак 1994
Полосьмак, Н. В. *Стерегущие золото грифы*. Новосибирск: Наука.

Полосьмак 2001
Полосьмак, Н. В. *Всадники Укока*. Новосибирск: Инфолио Пресс.

Полосьмак и Шумакова 2000
Полосьмак, Н. В., Шумакова, Е. В. "Юго-западные связи Пазырыкской культуры (ткани)". *Взаимодействие культур и цивилизаций. В честь юбилея В. М. Массона*, под редакцией Ю. Е. Березкина. Санкт-Петербург: Институт истории материальной культуры РАН.

Полосьмак и Баркова 2005
Полосьмак, Н. В., Баркова Л. Л. *Костюм и текстиль пазырыкцев Алтая (IV–III века до н.э.)*. Новосибирск: Инфолио.

Полосьмак и Кундо 2005
Полосьмак, Н. В., Кундо, Л. П. "Пазырыкцы в поисках красного цвета". *Центральная Азия: источники, история, культура (материалы международной научной конференции, посвящённой 80-летию доктора исторических наук Е.А. Давидович и действительного члена Академии наук Таджикистана, академика РАЕН, доктора исторических наук Б.А. Литвинского; Москва, 3–5 апреля 2003 г.*, 589–99. Москва: Восточная литература.

Пшеничнюк 2001
Пшеничнюк, А. Х. "Филипповские курганы в центре скифского мира: открытия и исследования". *Золотые олени Евразии. Каталог выставки*, 26–37. Санкт-Петербург: Издательство Государственного Эрмитажа.

Пяткин и Миклашевич 1990
Пяткин, Б. Н., Миклашевич, Е. А. "Сеймино-турбинская изобразительная традиция: пластика и петроглифы". *Проблема изучения наскальных изображений в СССР*, 146–53. Москва: Наука.

Раевский 1977
Раевский, Д. С. *Очерки идеологии скифо-сакских племен*. Москва: Наука.

Раевский 2001
Раевский, Д. С. "Скифский звериный стиль. Поэтика и прагматика". *Древние цивилизации Евразии. История культуры*, 364–382. Москва: Восточная литература.

Райс 2004
Райс, Т. Т. *Скифы. Строители степных пирамид*. Москва: Центрполиграф.

Руденко 1948
Руденко, С. И. *Второй пазырыкский курган: результаты работ экспедиции Института истории материальной культуры Академии наук СССР в 1947 г. (предварительное сообщение)*. Ленинград: Издательсво Государственного Эрмитажа.

Руденко 1951
Руденко, С. И. "Сокровища Пазырыкских курганов". *По следам древних культур*, 113–42. Москва: Государственное издательство культурно-просветительной литературы.

Руденко 1952
Руденко, С. И. "Одежда саков". *Горноалтайские находки и скифы*. Москва/Ленинград: Издательство Академии Наук СССР.

Руденко 1953
Руденко, С. И. *Культура населения горного Алтая в скифское время*. Москва/Ленинград: Издательство Академии наук СССР.

Руденко 1958
Руденко, С. И. *Древнее искусство Алтая*. Ленинград: Издательсво Государственного Эрмитажа.

Руденко 1960
Руденко, С. И. *Культура населения Центрального Алтая в скифское время*. Москва/Ленинград: Издательство Академии Наук СССР.

Руденко 1961
Руденко, С. И. *Искусство Алтая и Передней Азии (середина I тыс. до н.э.)*. Москва: Наука.

Руденко 1962
Руденко, С .И. *Сибирская коллекция Петра I. Археология СССР. Свод археологических источников Д, 3–9*. Москва/Ленинград: Издательство Академии Наук СССР.

Савелева и Смирнов 1972
Савелева, Т. В., Смирнов, К. Ф. "Ближневосточные древности на Южном Урале". *Вестник древней истории* 1972(3): 106–23.

Савинов 1994
Савинов, Д. Г. *Оленные камни в культуре кочевников Евразии*. Санкт-Петербург: Издательство Санкт-Петербургского университета.

Савинов 2000
Савинов, Д. Г. "Реалистические изображения лошадей скифского времени и сейминская изобразительная традиция". *Исторический ежегодник*, 179–87. Омск.

Сала и Деом 2005
Сала, Р., Деом, Ж. М. *Наскальные изображения Южного Казахстана*. Алматы: Лаборатория геоархеология.

Самашев 1992
Самашев, З. С. *Наскальные изображения Верхнего Прииртышья*. Алма-Ата: Ғылым.

Самашев 2004
Самашев, З. С. *Древние всадники Западной Азии*. Труды Центрального музея, т. 1, 230–66. Алматы.

Самашев 2006
Самашев, З. С. *Петроглифы Казахстана*. Алматы: Өнер.

Самашев 2008
Самашев, З. С. "Древние номады Казахских степей". *Номады Казахских степей: этносоциокультурные процессы и контакты в Евразии скифо-сакской эпохи (сборник материалов международной научной конференции)*, 169–80. Астана.

Самашев 2010
Самашев, З. С. "Изобразительные памятники бронзового века". *Материалы II Международной научной конференции "Кадырбаевские чтения—2010"*, 4–33. Актобе.

Самашев, Фаизов и Базарбаева 2001
Самашев, З. С., Фаизов, К. Ш., Базарбаева, Г. А. *Археологические памятники и палеопочвы Казахского Алтая*. Алматы: ОФ "Берел".

Самашев, Скрипникова и Верба 2001
Самашев, З. С., Скрипникова, М. И., Верба, М. П. "Эволюция почв как показатель климатических изменений в межгорных долинах западной части Казахского Алтая (на примере Берельского некрополя)". *Природные условия, история и культура Западной Монголии и сопредельных регионов. Труды V Международной научной конференции (20–24 сентября 2001 года, г. Ховд, Монголия)*, 157–58. Томск.

Самашев и Мыльников 2004
Самашев, З. С., Мыльников, В. *Деревообработка у древних скотоводов Казахского Алтая (материалы комплексного анализа деревянных предметов из кургана 11, могильника Берел)*. Алматы: ОФ "Берел"

Самашев и Бородовский 2004
Самашев, З. С., Бородовский, А. П. "Роговые украшения конской узды и упряжи из Берельского Некрополя". *Археология, этнография и антропология Евразии* 3(19): 82–87.

Самашев, Толеубаев и Джумабекова 2004
Самашев, З. С., Толеубаев, А., Джумабекова, Г. *Сокровища степных вождей*. Алматы: ОФ "Берел"

Самашев и Косинцев 2004
Самашев, З. С., Косинцев, П. А. "Погребальный обряд лошадей в могильнике Берел". *Комплексные исследования древних и традиционных обществ Евразии (сборник научных трудов)*, 274–76. Барнаул.

Самашев и др. 2007
Самашев, З. С., Джумабекова, Г., Базарбаева, Г., Онгар, А. *Древнее золото Казахстана*. Алматы: Өнер.

Самашев и др. 2010
Самашев, З. С., Сапашев, О., Оралбай, Е., Толегенов, Е., Исин, А., Сайлаубай, Е. *Памятники монументального искусства Восточного Казахстана (древность и средневековье)*. Алматы: Археология.

Самашев и др. 2011
Самашев, З. С., Онгар, А., Оралбай, Е., Киясбек, Г. *Храм-святилище Кызылуийк*. Астана: Археология.

Смирновъ 1909
Смирновъ, Я. И. *Восточное серебро. Атласъ древней серебряной и золотой посуды восточнаго происхожденія, найденной преимущественно въ предѣлахъ Россійской имперіи*. Санкт-Петербургъ.

Суразаков 1983
Суразаков, О. "О социальной стратификации пазырыкцев". *Вопросы археологии и этнографии Горного Алтая*, 72–87. Горно-Алтайск: Горно-Алтайский научно-исследовательский институт истории, языка и литературы.

Тишкин 2005
Тишкин, А. А. "Проблема происхождения бийкенской культуры Алтая раннескифского времени и выделение основных этапов ее развития". *Социогенез в Северной Азии*, часть 1, 322–27. Иркутск: Издательство Иркутского государственного технического Университета.

Тишкин и Дашковский 2007
Тишкин, А. А., Дашковский, П. К. "Результаты радиоуглеродного датирования памятников пазырыкской культуры Ханкаринский дол и Яломан-III". *Радиоуглерод в археологических и палеоэкологических исследованиях (материалы конференции, посвящённой 50-летию радиоуглеродной лаборатории ИИМК РАН, 9-12 апреля 2007 г., Санкт-Петербург)*, 291–99. Санкт-Петербург: ИИМК РАН,

Толеубаев (Төлеубаев) 2001
Төлеубаев, Ә.Т. "Ғұндар мемлекеті—түркі мемлекеттерінің бастауы". *Байырғы түркі өркениеті. Жазба ескерткіштер. Халықаралық конференция материалы*, 262–67. Алматы: Ғылым.

Толеубаев (Төлеубаев) 2004
Төлеубаев, Ә.Т. "Шілікті жазығы—сақтардың алғашқы мемлекетінің ту тіккен ордасы". *Қазақ тарихынан*, 326–36. Алматы: Жалын баспасы.

Толеубаев (Төлеубаев) 2006
Төлеубаев, Ә.Т. "Сақ қауымындағы қоғамдық құрылыс және мемлекеттілік мәселесі". *Мемлекеттілік және ұлы дала. Халықаралық ғылыми конференцияның материалы*, 214–17. Астана.

Толеубаев 2011
Толеубаев, А.Т. "Итоги исследований памятников раннего железного века Тарбагатая и Жетысуского Алатау". *Свидетели тысячелетий: археологическая наука Казахстана за 20 лет (1991–2011)*, 156–74. Алматы.

Хазанов 2000
Хазанов, А. М. *Кочевники и внешний мир*. Издание третье, дополненное. Алматы: Дайк Пресс.

Хотинский 1977
Хотинский, Н. А. *Голоцен Северной Евразии*. Москва: Наука.

Черемисин 2008
Черемисин, Д. В. "К семантике образа клювовидного оленя в пазырыкском Искусстве". *Тропою тысячелетий (сборник научных трудов, посвященный М. А. Дэвлет)*, 99–105. Кемерово: Кузбассвузиздат

Черников 1949
Черников, С. С. *Древняя металлургия и горное дело Западного Алтая*. Алма-Ата: Издательство АН КазССР

Черников 1960
Черников, С. С. *Восточный Казахстан в эпоху бронзы*. Материалы и исследования по археологии СССР 88. Москва/Ленинград: Издательство Академии Наук СССР.

Черников 1965
Черников, С. С. *Загадка золотого кургана*. Москва: Наука.

Чикишева 2003
Чикишева, Т. А. "Население Горного Алтая в эпоху раннего железа по данным антропологии". *Население Горного Алтая в эпоху раннего железного века как этнокультурный феномен: происхождение, генезис, исторические судьбы (по данным археологии, антропологии, генетики)*, вып. 1, 63–120. Новосибирск: Издательство СО РАН

Чугунов 2001
Чугунов, К. В. "Локально-хронологические особенности культуры Тувы в середине I тыс. до н.э." *Евразия сквозь века*, 173–78. Санкт-Петербург: Филологический факультет Санкт-Петербургского государственного университета

Шер 1980
Шер, Я. А. *Петроглифы Средней и Центральной Азии*. Москва: Наука.

Шер 1998
Шер, Я. А. "О возможных истоках скифо-сибирского звериного стиля". *Вопросы археологии Казахстана*, вып. 2, 218–30. Алматы/Москва: Ғылым.

Шилов и Очир-Горяева 1997
Шилов, В. П., Очир-Горяева, М. А. "Курганы скифской эпохи из могильников Аксеновский–I–II". *Памятники предскифского и скифского времени на юге Восточной Европы. Материалы Института Археологии России*, вып. 1, 127–52. Москва.

Яблонский 2001
Яблонский, Л. Т. "Скифы, сарматы и другие в контексте достижений отечественной археологии XX века". *Российская археология* 2001(1): 56–65.

Яценко 2006
Яценко, С. Я. *Костюм древней Евразии: ираноязычные народы*. Москва: Восточная литература.

PHOTOGRAPHY AND DRAWING CREDITS

Unless noted otherwise below, object photography from the Central State Museum is © The Central State Museum of the Republic of Kazakhstan, Almaty, and was photographed by A. Kisabaev, D. Suhov, A. Akishev, and R. Sherbaev; object photography from the Presidential Center of Culture is © The Presidential Center of Culture of the Republic of Kazakhstan, Astana, and was photographed by Viktor Kharchenko; object photography from the A. Kh. Margulan Institute of Archaeology is © A. Kh. Margulan Institute of Archaeology of the Republic of Kazakhstan, Almaty, and was photographed by Viktor Kharchenko; and object photography from the Museum of Archaeology is © Museum of Archaeology of the Republic of Kazakhstan, Almaty, and was photographed by Viktor Kharchenko.

Inside cover, pages 12–13: Base map based on the NASA SRTM-Data, compiled and designed by Matthias Gütte. Additional design by CoDe. Communications and Design, New York © 2012 ISAW

Chapter 1:
Page 20: The State Hermitage Museum, St. Petersburg
Fig. 1-1: M. P. Gryaznov © Institute of Material Culture, Russian Academy of Science, St. Petersburg
Fig. 1-5: Photograph © The State Hermitage Museum, St. Petersburg/photo by Vladimir Terebenin
Fig. 1-6: N. Bokovenko, The State Hermitage Museum, St. Petersburg

Chapter 2:
Page 30, figs. 2-3c, 2-23—2-25: Y. Cherkashin © A. Kh. Margulan Institute of Archaeology, Almaty
Figs. 2-1, 2-2, 2-4a–b, 2-5, 2-6, 2-22b: Z. Samashev © A. Kh. Margulan Institute of Archaeology, Almaty
Fig. 2-3a: V. Efimov, after reconstruction by Z. Samashev © Z. Samashev
Fig. 2-3b: A. Ongar © A. Kh. Margulan Institute of Archaeology, Almaty
Fig. 2-4c: K. Ahmetzhan © Z. Samashev
Figs. 2-7, 2-8, 2-11, 2-14, 2-18–2-21: Y. Cherkashin © Presidential Center of Culture, Astana
Fig. 2-22a: V. Efimov © A. Kh. Margulan Institute of Archaeology, Almaty

Chapter 3:
Figs. 3-1, 3-2, 3-4–3-7, 3-13: © A. Toleubaev
Figs. 3-3a–b: Completed by students of the Semi Palatinsk College of Geodesics and Cartography, D. Zh. Kabdiev/A. N. Lukovenko © A. Toleubaev

Chapter 4:
Page 62, figs. 4-10, 4-13a, 4-15a–d, 4-18: © Y. Cherkashin
Figs. 4-1, 4-4, 4-5, 4-21, 4-22: © Z. Samashev
Figs. 4-2, 4-7–4-9, 4-11, 4-12, 4-13b, 4-14, 4-16, 4-17, 4-19, 4-20: © S. Myrgabayev
Fig. 4-3: © Sören Stark

Chapter 5:
Figs. 5-1, 5-2, 5-3a, 5-4, 5-5, 5-7, 5-11: © Z. Samashev
Figs. 5-3b, 5-13: © A. Kh. Margulan Institute of Archaeology, Almaty

Chapter 6:
Figs. 6-2a–b: © Jean-Luc Houle
Fig. 6-3: © Bryan K. Hanks
Fig. 6-4: Photograph © The State Hermitage Museum, St. Petersburg/photo by Vladimir Terebenin
Fig. 6-6: © Museum of Archaeology, Almaty
Fig. 6-9: Y. Cherkashin © A. Kh. Margulan Institute of Archaeology
Fig. 6-10: Y. Cherkashin © Presidential Center of Culture, Astana

Chapter 7:
Figs. 7-1, 7-29: Base map based on the NASA SRTM-Data, compiled and designed by Matthias Gütte. Additional design by Sören Stark and CoDe. Communications and Design, New York © 2012 ISAW
Figs. 7-2, 7-4: © Trustees of the British Museum
Fig. 7-3: After Walser 1966, pl. 18
Figs. 7-5a–b, 7-6a–b, 7-7, 7-9–7-11, 7-27: Photographs © The State Hermitage Museum, St. Petersburg/photos by Vladimir Terebenin, Leonard Kheifets, Yuri Molodkovets, and Sergeev Tikhomirova
Figs. 7-8a–b, 7-20, 7-35: © The Metropolitan Museum of Art, New York. Image source: Art Resource, NY
Fig. 7-13: © Presidential Center of Culture, Astana
Figs. 7-16, 7-21: Sören Stark © The State Hermitage Museum, St. Petersburg
Fig. 7-17: Erich Lessing/Art Resource, NY
Fig. 7-18: Ann Searight © Trustees of the British Museum
Fig. 7-22: Composite drawing of PFS 11* courtesy of M. B. Garrison, M. C. Root, and the Persepolis Seal Project
Figs. 7-23, 7-24, 7-34: Drawings by Sören Stark
Fig. 7-25: After Rudenko 1970, pl. 164A
Fig. 7-33: Reconstruction drawing by Sören Stark

Chapter 8:
Figs. 8-1, 8-4, 8-6, 8-8, 8-9: © Perry A. Tourtellotte
Fig. 8-5: Base map based on the NASA SRTM-Data, compiled and designed by Matthias Gütte. Additional design by Matthias Gütte, Perry A. Tourtellotte, Claudia Chang, and CoDe. Communications and Design, New York © 2012 ISAW
Fig. 8-7: © Museum of Archaeology, Almaty

Chapter 9:
Page 152, figs. 9-1–9-11: © Nursan Alimbai

Appendix C:
© Z. Samashev

Checklist:
Nos. 2–15, 18, 20, 21, 23–34, 36–42: Y. Cherkashin © A. Kh. Margulan Institute of Archaeology, Almaty
Nos. 43, 44, 47, 81: Y. Cherkashin © Presidential Center of Culture, Astana
No. 100: © A. Kh. Margulan Institute of Archaeology, Almaty
Nos. 122, 139, 146–153 © Museum of Archaeology, Almaty

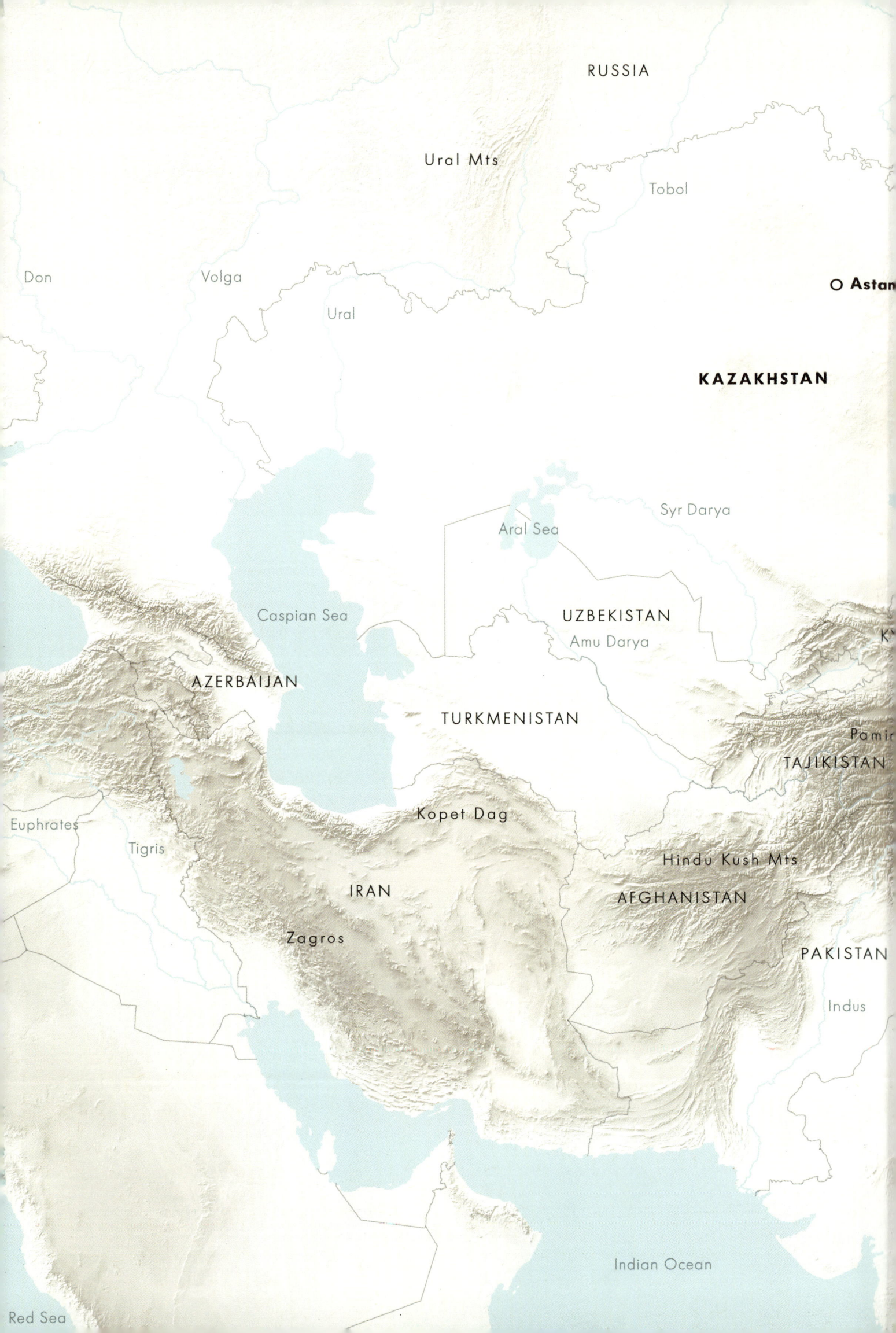